D1756061

Petroleum, Industry and Governments

Energy and Environmental Law & Policy Series Supranational and Comparative Aspects

VOLUME 24

Editor

Kurt Deketelaere

Professor of Law, University of Leuven, Belgium,
Honorary Chief of Staff, Flemish Government
Honorary Professor of Law, University of Dundee, UK
Secretary – General, League of European Research Universities (LERU), Belgium

Editorial Board

The aim of the Editor and the Editorial Board of this series is to publish works of excellent quality that focus on the study of energy and environmental law and policy.

Through this series the Editor and Editorial Board hope:

- to contribute to the improvement of the quality of energy/environmental law and policy in general and environmental quality and energy efficiency in particular;
- to increase the access to environmental and energy information for students, academics, non-governmental organizations, government institutions, and business;
- to facilitate cooperation between academic and non-academic communities in the field of energy and environmental law and policy throughout the world.

Petroleum, Industry and Governments

A Study of the Involvement of Industry and Governments in Exploring for and Producing Petroleum

Third Edition

Bernard Taverne

Wolters Kluwer
Law & Business

Published by:
Kluwer Law International
PO Box 316
2400 AH Alphen aan den Rijn
The Netherlands
Website: www.kluwerlaw.com

Sold and distributed in North, Central and South America by:
Aspen Publishers, Inc.
7201 McKinney Circle
Frederick, MD 21704
United States of America
Email: customer.service@aspenpublishers.com

Sold and distributed in all other countries by:
Turpin Distribution Services Ltd
Stratton Business Park
Pegasus Drive, Biggleswade
Bedfordshire SG18 8TQ
United Kingdom
Email: kluwerlaw@turpin-distribution.com

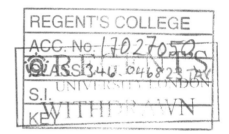

Printed on acid-free paper.

ISBN 978-90-411-4563-5

© 2013 Kluwer Law International BV, The Netherlands

Printed and Bound by CPI Group (UK) Ltd, Croydon, CR0 4YY.

Table of Contents

Sources

The following sources have been used:

(a) Original legal documents belonging to the public sector, such as Conventions, Treaties, Protocols, Laws, Acts, Regulations, model contracts, model clauses for licenses and Petroleum Agreements, in the form as found in official publications of national governments or international organizations (State Gazette, Official Gazette, Official Journal, etc.); or as placed in original language or after translation into English, on websites of the internet by national government Ministries or Departments, the European Union, the United Nations, or by private sector entities;

(b) In respect of statistical information presented in the Tables and throughout the text:
- (i) BP Statistical Review of World Energy 2007 / 2009 / 2012
- (ii) World Energy Outlook 2012, a publication of the International Energy Agency, Paris, France;
- (iii) Statistical Pocketbooks, publications of the European Commission;
- (iv) Middle East Economic Survey (MEES);
- (v) US Department of Energy's Energy Information Administration (EIA);
- (vi) OPEC Brief; and home page (internet) of the Organization of Petroleum Exporting Countries (OPEC).

(c) In respect of information on scientific, technical, historical and government policy facts and matters:
- (i) IPCC WG I Assessment Reports 1990-2007;
- (ii) Energy Technology Perspectives 2010 / 2012, publications of the International Energy Agency, Paris, France;
- (iii) Information placed by institutions, government organizations, interested parties, etc. on the website of Wikipedia, the free encyclopedia;

(iv) Policy Papers and Annual Reports of the European Commission;
(v) Robert Peele's Mining Engineers' Handbook, volume I;
(vi) Petroleum Resources Assessment Reports of the US Geological Survey (USGS);
(vii) Journals and Newspapers of internationally recognized reputation;
(viii) Science publications, such as *Nature* and *Science*.

Preface to the First Edition

Petroleum, Industry and Governments describes and discusses the main aspects of the involvement of industry and governments with the production and use of petroleum. Within this setting this book gives an account of the technical and environmental aspects of the production of oil and natural gas, and the latter's position and function in the economy. It reviews government policies and attitudes towards petroleum and national and international regulation of onshore or offshore petroleum operations, including petroleum taxation. The book describes the development and working of the oil and natural gas markets, the cost of supply and the establishment of producer prices. Attention is paid to the internationalization of the extractive industry, the way this industry is organized and the old and new forms and manifestations of political risk, with which this industry has to cope. In addition this book contains a special chapter on production economics and the final chapter is devoted to the main forms of inter-company production agreements (joint ventures and unitization agreements). This book elaborates on the subjects described and discussed in the author's 'Introduction to the Regulation of the Petroleum Industry (Laws, Contracts and Conventions)' (first published 1994) and 'Cooperative Agreements in the Extractive Petroleum Industry' (first published 1996). However, this book is not merely an updated version of the earlier publications. Here, the occasion has been utilized to expand the scope of the discussion by paying attention to the value of petroleum for the economy and to its other economic aspects. As a result of this extension into the field of economy and economics, it is believed that this book is of special importance and interest to petroleum venture managers, as well as for independent consultants and other professionals with a commercial business background who are required to give advice with respect to the economic, regulatory and cooperative aspects of petroleum operations. In writing this book, the author has drawn on a total thirty-seven years' experience with the technical, economic and legal aspects of the international petroleum industry acquired during employment with the Royal Dutch/Shell Group, as well as his appointment as part-time professor at the Delft University of Technology.

The book is based and relies on original material consisting of the officially or otherwise published texts of laws, contracts, etc., official statements and policy documents and further on statistical data as made available to the public by international organizations and institutes, by international oil companies and trade journals.

Leidschendam, The Netherlands
April 1999

Preface to the Second Edition

In the year 2000, just one year after the publication of the first edition (1999), the global oil market reached a turning point. Against all expectations, predictions and growing concerns about climate change, the demand for oil started to rise quite steadily in response to an expanding world economy. From the years 2000 to 2006, world consumption increased from 76.3 million b/d to 84 million b/d. Over this period, China's oil consumption rose from 4.8 million b/d to 7.4 million b/d, even overtaking Japan thereby. International prices reacted more sharply, in particular after 2005 the price reached spectacular levels: in November 2007 Brent Dated was nearing the USD 100/b mark. To put the matter in its proper perspective, exactly the same crude had in 1998 been priced at USD 12.72. Even when correcting for the current weakness of the US dollar, this is an astonishing development. Nonetheless in the first quarter of 2008, these trends continued. In the last part of said quarter, the Brent price regularly exceeded USD 100/b in line with a further weakening of the US dollar. The world's annual consumption of natural gas also increased over the period: from 2,428 billion cubic metres in 2000 to 2,851 billion cubic metres in 2006. In light of these trends, the second edition undertook a new attempt, using the latest available information about future consumption, available reserves etc., to try to estimate the time that is left to the world economy before the oil and natural gas reserves are exhausted and practicable and acceptable alternatives must have been found to replace them. It is further investigated whether such alternatives exist.

Next to worrying about the prices of petroleum and the lifetime of the reserves, governments had to focus their attention on CO_2-emissions caused by the use of oil and natural gas and to make a start with taking measures and formulating policies which should help or which were thought to be necessary to reduce said emissions and so to fulfil the commitments accepted by them in this regard under the Kyoto Protocol (effective 16 February 2005). The often conflicting policy options open to governments and the consequences, if any, for both oil and natural gas and the petroleum industry are reviewed and discussed.

In the intervening years, governments have been active in further developing petroleum legislation although the changes introduced have not led to any significant difference with the systems and provisions described in the first edition. Nonetheless, legislation or contracts referred to and presented in the first edition as examples of 'current' legislation or contracts have been kept still 'current' by including in the second edition any changes and additions that were found to have been made thereto over the last years.

Finally, the text of the second edition has been restructured, subjects have been rearranged in different chapters, the chapter 'on Government Policies' has completely been rewritten and the chapter 'on Production Economics' has been deleted and replaced by a new chapter 'on Charters and Interstate Agreements'. To the latter, a description and discussion of the 1959 Treaty on Antarctica and its Protocol of 1991 have been added.

Leidschendam, The Netherlands
April 2008

Preface to the Third Edition

In sharp contrast to the globally expressed concern about the emission of CO2 stemming from the burning and combustion of the fossil fuels and the drive to establish by 2020 an universal Climate Agreement with binding commitments for all participants to reduce or even eliminate all such emissions, the demand for petroleum, next to coal an important constituent of the fossil fuels, is robust and is projected even to increase in the coming decades.

It is clearly expected by all parties concerned that future Government policies and measures taken within the framework of the intended Climate Agreement will not lead to a serious curbing of such demand. Apparently it is left to the markets to put a brake on excessive consumption.

For this surprising situation there are very good reasons. In the first place, there are no realistic, practical or cost-effective alternatives for petroleum in all those sectors of the economy which currently depend on petroleum as source of supply of either energy or feedstock. Trying to curb such supply (apart from taking measures to prevent wasteful behaviour or splillage) will have a very negative effect on all those sectors and on the economy at large as well.

In the second place, natural gas itself will serve as an alternative, namely as an alternative for coal in the power sector, not only on account of the fact that natural gas much better scores on the CO2-emission table than coal but also because there are, in the absence of nuclear energy, not enough other reliable non-fossil alternatives available. Under these circumstances the consumption of natural gas may even be stimulated by Governments.

Given a continuing robust or even steadily increasing demand for oil as well as for natural gas, the question arises whether the petroleum industry is able to satisfy this demand and for how long.

As shown in this third edition, the projected total of remaining recoverable reserves (including proved reserves) amount for oil to 5,871 billion barrels. Whereas proved reserves at the end of 2011 are estimated to amount to 1,653 billion barrels, it follows that an impressive 4,218 billion barrels are waiting to materialise, as a result of making new discoveries and extending existing reserves.

The same applies to natural gas for which the reserves figures are respectively 790 tcm, 208 tcm and 582 tcm.

For both oil and natural gas these are staggering figures and it shows that in order to make these figures real, intensive exploration and application of sophisticated production techniques are called for, many times in extreme areas (deep water, Arctic) and/or under extreme conditions.

Given that current yearly rate of oil production amounts to about 31 billion barrels and the yearly rate of gas production to 3,3 tcm, it shows that there is enough scope for much bigger yearly rates of production and for an extended period of time. But then, all this oil and gas might not be needed in the end.

For the moment however any new discovery of oil or natural gas in any country, whether already producing oil or natural gas or not, may count on a warm welcome by the Government concerned and the general public.

This brings into focus the importance of modern petroleum legislation in which the interests of Government and petroleum industry are neatly balanced and the importance of workable agreements of co-operation which allow the industry to combine forces to undertake the aforesaid exploration and production efforts.

As before in the second edition, petroleum legislation is divided into western style, licence-based petroleum legislation on the one hand and non-western style, contract-based petroleum legislation on the other. But within this framework new legislation has been added. Since Governments of non-western countries tend to favour the production sharing contract almost all attention has been focused on this type of contract.

But petroleum legislation, Treaties, Conventions, Declaration, etc. that have slowly lost their relevance for petroleum (operations) and are now mainly of historic interest have been deleted. No longer are described: the 1959 Treaty on Antarctica and 1991 Protocol; the New International Economic Order, and the 1974 Charter of Economic Rights and Duties of States belonging thereto, although it should never be forgotten that the latter must be seen as the legal fundament of the contract-based petroleum legislation. Other changes in this context: the European Energy Charter and Charter Treaty are just referred to in passing, "International Regulation of Offshore Petroleum Operations" has been restricted to a description and discussion of the Convention on the Law of the Sea and of OSPARCON; Dumping Conventions have been deleted.

All statistics and projections regarding reserves, production and consumption of oil and natural gas have been updated.

Leidschendam, The Netherlands
September 2013

Chapter 1

Introduction to Petroleum

1.1   PHYSICAL ASPECTS

1.1.1   DESCRIPTION

Petroleum (literally meaning 'rock oil') consists of, naturally occurring and through geological processes, generated hydrocarbons and associated non-hydrocarbon substances. These hydrocarbons are hereinafter referred to as 'natural' hydrocarbons in contrast to hydrocarbons manufactured by the refineries.

Said natural hydrocarbons consist of molecules almost exclusively made up of carbon (C) and hydrogen (H) atoms in ratios ranging from four (methane, CH_4) to less than one (asphaltic bitumen). The end member of this range is carbon (C) itself, the main constituent of coals. The number of carbon atoms per molecule determines molecular size and structural complexity. Natural hydrocarbons, including natural carbon, may contain, as an integral part of their molecular structure, small amounts of other elements such as sulphur (S), nitrogen (N) and various metals.

Depending on molecular composition, prevailing reservoir temperature and pressure, natural hydrocarbons may occur in a solid, liquid or gaseous phase, respectively referred to as asphaltic bitumen (including tar and natural asphalt), extra-heavy oil, heavy oil, light oil and natural gas. The hydrocarbon component of natural gas consists mainly of methane (CH_4), but in varying degrees it may be accompanied by slightly larger or heavier (in the sense of containing more carbon atoms per molecule) but still gaseous hydrocarbons, such as ethane (C_2H_6), propane (C_3H_8), butane (C_4H_{10}) and pentane (C_5H_{12}), in liquid form (to be made in a gas plant) the latter are referred to as Natural Gas Liquids (NGL's).

Extra-heavy oil, heavy oil and light oil are referred to as 'crude oil' or 'oil'. In production statistics NGL's are counted as 'oil'.

1.1.2   PHYSICOCHEMICAL PROPERTIES OF THE HYDROCARBON
               MOLECULE

The physicochemical properties of the hydrocarbon molecule depend on the H/C ratio, the structural complexity and the number of carbon atoms comprised in the molecule. The H/C ratio ranges from 4/1 (e.g., gaseous hydrocarbons, starting with methane) to 2/1 (e.g., the diesel oil to gasoline range) to 1/1 (e.g., fuel oils to asphaltic bitumen).

The size of the hydrocarbon molecule is determined by the number of carbon atoms per molecule. This number is related to the H/C ratio as this ratio becomes smaller in the larger molecules (with a corresponding increase of the specific gravity). Methane (CH_4) is the structurally simplest, smallest and lightest hydrocarbon molecule, possessing only a single carbon atom accompanied by four hydrogen atoms. This gives the molecule an H/C ratio of 4, which is the highest H/C ratio possible. At room temperature and atmospheric pressure methane is a gas. By contrast, heavy hydrocarbons with H/C ratios around 1, known as asphaltenes, may have forty or more carbon atoms per molecule. The H/C ratio, the number of carbon atoms per molecule and the structural complexity of the hydrocarbon molecule determine the latter's physicochemical properties, such as specific gravity, viscosity, volatility, heat content and energy density.

Note. The density of oil is expressed in degrees of API gravity, a standard of the American Petroleum Institute which is computed as (141.5/spec. grav.) – 131.5. This means that the lower the specific gravity the higher the API number and vice versa. A specific gravity of 0.92 corresponds with 22 degrees API gravity. The latter number is used for distinguishing light oil from heavy oil, including extra-heavy oil and asphaltic bitumen. The lightest of light oil has a specific gravity of 0.80 which corresponds with 45 degrees API gravity. In stark contrast, extra-heavy oil and asphaltic bitumen have a specific gravity of 1.00 or more which corresponds with an API gravity of 10 degrees or less. Viscosity of oils is measured in centipoise (cP) and ranges at prevailing reservoir temperature from less than 100 cP for light oil to more than 10,000 cP for asphaltic bitumen. It follows that asphaltic bitumen is not only very dense but also very viscous.

From the economic point of view, the most important property of hydrocarbons is their heat content (or calorific value) per standard unit of volume (cubic metres at standard conditions) or per unit of mass (metric ton). One metric ton of the average light oil has a heat content of 42 GJ, which compares with 38 GJ as delivered by 1,000 cubic metres of natural gas under standard conditions of temperature and pressure. Stating it differently, 1,000 cubic metres of natural gas is equivalent in heat content to 0.9 metric tons of crude oil (0.9 toe). It follows that the transportation of natural gas on the basis of energy units delivered is much more expensive than that of crude oil, because the gas if it cannot be used on the spot has to be transported in a pipeline under high pressure or by ocean-going tanker after liquefaction (LNG).

Note. Due to their different volatility the respective hydrocarbon components of oil can be separated from one another in the refinery by the process of distillation. By this process heavy to light distillates are produced, in the range heavy residue/fuel oil/gas oil/kerosene/gasoline/naphta, with corresponding specific gravities of 1.00 to 0.70. Each of those distillates has its own specific use and application in the respective sectors of the economy. In this context, hydrocarbons with a H/C ratio of 2:1, which occupy the range of diesel oil to gasoline, are more suitable for use in internal combustion engines and, therefore, very valuable as transport fuel; so valuable in fact that in the refinery, this range of hydrocarbons is manufactured by catalytic conversion processes from hydrocarbons with a lower H/C ratio, i.e., from the heavier distillates. Finally, from methane, the least complex member of the hydrocarbon family, the same range of hydrocarbon products can be manufactured albeit at considerable cost and with the loss of half of the heat content of the original methane.

1.1.3   GENERATION

Natural hydrocarbons are generated by the chemical conversion of organic matter of marine origin such as plankton and algae that had been deposited in sediments. Said chemical conversion of this organic material is set in motion by geological processes, whereby sediments and the organic matter contained therein become deeply buried and in this process exposed to high temperatures and pressures. In the end the sediments are transformed into sedimentary rocks such as shale (i.e., compressed clays) and limestone (i.e., calcium carbonate ($CaCO_3$) deposited as the calcareous remains of marine animals or precipitated directly from the sea) and their organic contents into hydrocarbons.

Coal is classified as a strictly organic sedimentary rock resulting from the deep burial of organic matter of terrestial origin such as land plants and trees. It consists for a large part (seventy per cent or more) of carbon (C) and for the remainder of volatile and mineral matter, among which are methane, carbon dioxide (CO_2), hydrogen and hydrocarbons, sulphur compounds and other minerals. Depending on their composition, coals are classified as either bituminous coal, including anthracite (referred to as hard coal) or sub-bituminous coal, including lignite and brown coal. The right type of coal may function as source rock for the production of methane jointly with carbon dioxide.

1.1.4   POST-GENERATION: OCCURRENCE, MIGRATION AND
             ACCUMULATION

After their generation, natural hydrocarbons including methane generated within the coal layers are squeezed out of their respective source rocks and start their migration upwards through permeable rock formations with their faults and fissures in the direction of the surface. The migration through the rock strata is slow, at least as far as the liquid hydrocarbons are concerned. But the migration for all hydrocarbons will come to an end when they either emerge at the surface or become trapped and accumulate at a place where the rock strata, through which they are migrating, are either cut off or covered by an impervious type of rock, e.g., a salt dome or salt layer.

But not all natural hydrocarbons will leave the sedimentary rock (amongst which coals) in which they were generated or about to be generated.

Part of the methane that is co-generated with coals together with carbon dioxide will remain behind in the coal seams concerned. This methane is partly chemically and partly physically bound to the carbon atoms and is referred to as 'coal bed methane'. By drilling holes into the coal seams it is produced from the coal itself. In this way, it can be said that the coal beds function as source rock, as well as reservoir rock. It may be expected that coal bed methane will be extracted from the coal in the same manner as gas from shales (see below).

Of much greater importance today is the natural gas that is trapped in shales, which gas is known as shale gas. The existence of this natural gas source has long been known to geologists but till very recently largely ignored due to the combination of a low gas price and the absence of a technically feasible extraction method. Nowadays extraction techniques referred to as 'fracking' have been developed which make the production of shale gas a huge success, in particular in the US but soon also in many other countries.

Equally of importance is so-called tight oil which is light oil that has partly remained behind in mature source rock (organic-rich marine shales) in which it was generated. By applying the fracking techniques developed for the extraction of shale gas it proved possible in particular in the U.S. North Dakota to free and extract the oil from the its source rock.

Tight oil containing shales should not be confused with (immature) oil shales. The latter type of shale is a shale that contains kerogen (to be considered a proto-hydrocarbon) in a finely dispersed form. Through geological processes the oil shale has been uplifted and become exposed at the surface. The geological uplifting has interrupted the natural hydrocarbon generation processes as these are dependent on high temperatures and intensive pressures. After mechanically crushing the shale, kerogen is extracted therefrom and converted into regular hydrocarbons

The rock formation, in which the migrating natural hydrocarbons and associated non-hydrocarbons are eventually entrapped and accumulated, is referred to as the reservoir rock or reservoir. Reservoirs are sedimentary rocks with sufficient pore volume, fissures and permeability allowing the accumulation of natural hydrocarbons as described. Fissured limestone (i.e., rocks mostly consisting of calcium carbonate and relatively clean well-sorted sandstone are examples of suitable reservoirs, i.e., reservoirs from which the natural hydrocarbons can be produced by conventional means as described hereinafter (these hydrocarbons are referred to as conventional oil or conventional gas). In such a suitable reservoir, the natural hydrocarbons will replace formation water and may separate into a liquid (oil) and a gaseous phase (natural gas) with the latter on top (gas-cap gas). As a result, a gas/oil contact and an oil/water contact may be encountered in a reservoir.

There are, however, hydrocarbons containing reservoirs having a very low permeability, so-called tight reservoirs, which prevents extraction of the hydrocarbons contained therein by conventional means. These hydrocarbons are referred to as tight oil or tight gas. By applying fracking techniques to tight reservoirs, a substantial production of oil and gas has become possible. The case of extracting light oil from mature shales by these techniques is discussed above.

As geological time passes, to be measured in millions of years, movements in the earth crust create new faults and/or fissures or re-activate old ones, thereby opening up new channels of communication between the rock layers. A new process of migration may start and the natural hydrocarbons may move to and accumulate in another reservoir or resume their migration to the surface. In some instances, only the gaseous phase plus the lighter components of the liquid phase will escape and move onwards to another reservoir or to the surface. What remains behind in the reservoir after such secondary migration is heavy oil including extra-heavy oil or asphaltic bitumen with a low H/C ratio (1:1 or even less), very viscous and very dense as described above. If the primary or secondary migration is not interrupted by any geological barrier or stopped by the earlier transformation of the liquid hydrocarbons into non-moving heavy oil or bitumen, natural hydrocarbons will eventually emerge at the surface. In this context, 'surface' could be the surface of the dry land or of the bottom of the sea.

When surfacing on dry land, natural gas, whether appearing as free gas or as gas dissolved in the crude oil, will escape into the atmosphere or start burning (if ignited by lightning or by other ways). When surfacing at the bottom in the deep ocean, a chemical reaction with the ocean water may ensue, resulting in the formation of gas hydrates. The latter are crystals of a methane/water compound.

Any liquid hydrocarbons emerging at the surface will first lose their volatile components and over time turn into tar sands, also called oil sands. In the end, all semi-solid hydrocarbons occurring at the surface, and for as long as remaining in contact with the atmosphere, will be oxidized and converted into CO_2 and water and by this process the natural carbon cycle will be closed.

Where reservoir rock is exposed at the surface, any oil contained therein will slowly flow, ooze or drip out of the rock (oil seepages, oil springs). In this way, tar pits or asphalt lakes are formed.

Natural hydrocarbons are found mixed with or accompanied by various non-hydrocarbon substances. This association is a matter of physical bonding as opposed to the chemical bonding of the elements described below. The association or bonding process takes place during the subsoil generation processes or during the hydrocarbons' migration through the rock formations. The chemically-bound elements most commonly encountered in heavy oils are sulphur and various metallic compounds. Sulphur has to be removed to prevent the substance from being released into the atmosphere as a by-product of the combustion process. The metallic compounds frequently give problems in chemical conversion processes in which catalysts are used.

Natural gas, whether generated in association with oil or with coals, also contains varying proportions of non-hydrocarbon gases. To a large extent, these non-hydrocarbon gases consist of nitrogen (N_2) and carbon dioxide (CO_2). To a lesser extent, natural gas may contain inert gases, such as argon and helium, or sulphur compounds and also hydrogen sulphide (H_2S). Sulphur compounds have to be removed from the natural gas at the first opportunity, in any case before the gas enters the main transportation facilities to protect the latter from the occurrence of corrosion damage.

1.2 THE EARTH'S CARBON CYCLE

The generation of coal (C) and hydrocarbons (CxHy) from organic matter, as described above, and their ultimate conversion into CO_2 and water either by natural processes or by human intervention form part of the Earth's carbon cycle. In this context, this cycle can best be described as an interaction between atmospheric CO_2 and the Earth's biosphere and lithosphere that take place according to physical, chemical and biological processes.

Natural biological/chemical processes in which CO_2 is involved are: (1) photosynthesis that takes place within terrestrial plants and marine phytoplankton, (2) respiration by organic organism and the latter's decomposition and oxidation, and (3) the forming of calcium carbonate ($CaCO_3$) by marine organism for the purpose of building their skeletons and shells.

Note 1. Photosynthesis is the most important natural biological/chemical process occurring in the biosphere. It is the process in which photons energize the reaction whereby, in the presence of water, CO_2 is converted into oxygen and carbohydrates, the building blocks of plants and phytoplankton (the latter being the microscopic plants that are the basis of the food chain in the ocean).

Note 2. The forming of calcium carbonate by marine organism is thought to become more difficult if by absorbing more and more CO_2 the oceans get more acidic. The calcareous remains of these marine organism form chalk.

Physical and chemical processes are at work when atmospheric CO_2 is absorbed by the oceans; when coal and hydrocarbons are generated in the deep underground in the way as described before; when rain water washes out CO_2 from the atmosphere and chemically binds the latter to the rocks in the form of carbonates (chemical weathering); or when CO_2 is returned to the atmosphere through volcanic eruptions, or by the natural oxidation of hydrocarbons, or coal deposits occurring at the surface or by the oxidation of biomass (plant material).

Note. The CO_2 that is released into the atmosphere through volcanic eruptions originates from calcium carbonate sediments such as chalk and limestone that take part in the geological process of the movement of plates (plate tectonics). Despite the time lag between CO_2-locking up and CO_2-release, volcanic eruptions appear the most important non-anthropogenic source of atmospheric CO_2. In the geological record, evidence has been found of a direct relationship between the intensity of volcanic activity and the average global surface temperature.

Plants, soils and the oceans are referred to as carbon sinks. About half of the CO_2 taken up by plants and soils is returned to the atmosphere through respiration. The same amount is eventually returned through decomposition (natural oxidation). In contrast to carbon sinks, respiration and decomposition form with respect to the atmosphere carbon sources. If the remains of organism, among which most prominently plant material, usually referred to as biomass, rather than being decomposed in contact with the atmosphere become deeply buried they will under the right geological conditions and on a geological timescale, be turned into hydrocarbons or coal respectively as described before.

Unless trapped in a reservoir, transformed into a dense, very viscous residual oil or transformed into gas hydrates, natural hydrocarbons will on a geological timescale find their way to the surface. Gaseous hydrocarbons (mainly methane) will escape into the atmosphere, liquid hydrocarbons will first lose their volatile components, turn into bitumen and thereafter, in a time-consuming process, be oxidized and turned into CO_2 and water.

Coal stays in the underground layer in which it was generated and in this way carbon is permanently removed from the carbon cycle. Should however through geological processes coal layers come into contact with the surface and the atmosphere, the methane contained in the layers will be released and the coal itself (like the surface deposits of semi-solid hydrocarbons) will be oxidized. This time-consuming process is speeded up if, after ignition through natural causes, the coal layers start burning; the subsurface coal fires in China form an important example of this phenomenon. In both instances, CO_2 is generated that subsequently is returned to the atmosphere.

CO_2 is also locked up in limestone and chalk. This CO_2 will only through the geological process of plate tectonics and accompanying volcanic eruptions eventually, on a geological timescale, return to the atmosphere. Despite the time lag between CO_2-lock up and release, volcanic eruptions appear to be the prime natural carbon source in the carbon cycle.

The presence of CO_2 in the atmosphere is of fundamental importance for regulating the average global temperature on the surface of the planet. This is due to the physical molecular property of CO_2 (a property that it shares with water vapour and methane) to absorb infrared light, that is radiated back from the Earth's surface, and of re-emitting the same kind of radiation. That part of the re-emitted radiation that travels back to the Earth's surface will cause an increase of the temperature at that surface. From the study of ice cores, some covering the past 650,000 years, a close parallel connection between atmospheric CO_2 concentrations and surface temperatures was found; in periods of low temperatures, the corresponding atmospheric CO_2 concentrations were equally low and vice versa.

Note 1 This relationship has been confirmed by geological evidence although there has been a geological period (the Eemian interglacial, 130,000 to 115,000 years ago) in which higher surface temperatures then prevailing were ascribed to other factors than to an increased CO_2 concentration.

Note 2. In the extreme case of a zero CO_2 concentration, i.e., in case no CO_2 (or water vapour) would be present in the atmosphere, the average global temperature would be around -20 degrees Celsius compared to the currently prevailing average temperature of +15 degrees, a difference of 35 degrees. The so-called greenhouse effect was first recognized by Joseph Fourier in 1824. By the turn of the century, Svante Arrhenius in Sweden and Thomas C. Chamberlin in the US made the connection between the burning of fossil fuels and this greenhouse effect, predicting that the use of fossil fuels would lead to global warming.

The industrial production of hydrocarbons, coal and biomass (hereinafter carbon fuels), and using the latter as fuel to generate heat, electricity and mechanical power has introduced a completely new source of CO_2 in the Earth's carbon cycle. This anthropogenic source can indeed be described as completely new because firstly the anthropogenic oxidation by way of burning carbon fuels proceeds much faster even in an explosive manner when compared to the slowly developing natural oxidation; and secondly, the carbon fuels that are being burned have been specially mined or extracted or grown as part of an industrial or agricultural process. Without this anthropogenic activity, the natural hydrocarbons and coal would have remained in situ and part of the biomass would have been buried and none of them would, on a human timescale at least, have been oxidized and thus generated CO_2.

The new and anthropogenic source of CO_2 has revealed itself by the fact that since the time of the industrial revolution (1750) and in the absence of significant natural CO_2-emissions such as volcanic eruptions in that period, the value of the global atmospheric concentration of CO_2 has markedly increased from a pre-industrial value of about 280 ppm (0.028 per cent by volume) to 393 ppm (0.0393 per cent by volume) as calculated for 2012. The consequences of this phenomenon for global warming and climate change and government policies in response thereto are discussed in Chapter 4.

1.3   EXTRACTION AND PRODUCTION
            TECHNIQUES

In the pre-drilling days, oil was collected at the places where it spontane-
ously emerged at the surface. Where oil leaked or seeped into pools or
creeks it was skimmed from the surface of the water with cloths and rags
and subsequently bottled and sold. Tar was collected from tar pits or, where
the tar was mixed with sand (tar sands); it was extracted from the sand by
washing the same. In some places, e.g., in Pechelbronn, France, shafts and
galleries were dug to get better access to the oil or tar and to increase its
recovery. These methods to produce oil proved inadequate when more oil
was needed to meet a rising demand for kerosene. This new demand for
kerosene was triggered by the invention of a more suitable kerosene-
burning lamp (around 1850) in which kerosene could burn without smoke
or smell, something that had not been possible in the earlier types of lamp.
More efficient production methods were called for in order to meet the
increased demand. In the US at the time, salt water was produced by boring
holes into the salt water reservoir. In these salt water wells oil was regularly
pumped up together with the salt water. Entrepreneurs got the idea that oil
should be bored for in a similar manner. This idea was put to the test, and
following indications of oil at the surface, by an oil well which was bored
by Drake in 1859 near Titusville, a small town in Pennsylvania. On 27
August 1859 at a depth of only 69.5 feet, oil was struck. This well is
traditionally considered to be the first oil well in history, and as such its
boring (or drilling, as boring later was called, after the invention of the
rotary drill pipe technique) marked the founding of the extractive petroleum industry.

Note 1. In 1860, already hundreds of 100-foot wells had been drilled in
southwestern Ontario, Canada, and the well drilled by Williams three years earlier
(in 1857) might really have been the well that would have been entitled to lay
claim on being the first oil well in history. Outside North America, the first oil
wells were drilled around Baku in the Caucasus in 1871. In Pechelbronn, which
may be considered the West European counterpart of Titusville, the first well was
drilled in 1879, twenty years after the Drake well.

Note 2. The rotary drill pipe technique had its inception in 1882, when the Baker
brothers, drilling contractors of Yankton, Dak, tried a crude bit on a rotating string
of pipe, pumping water down the pipe to raise the cuttings in the annular space
between pipe and walls of hole. About 1895, they teamed up with three Texas
water-well drillers and built the first rotary outfit in Spindletop oil field, Texas, in
1901. Since about 1933 the technique has greatly been improved upon. Drilling to

3,000 metres became possible. (*Source*: R. Peele, *Mining Engineers' Handbook*, 3rd edition, volume I, John Wiley & Sons, Inc., New York, 1956).

Where previously only vertical or slightly deviated holes were drilled, in recent times holes are drilled that end up in a horizontal trajectory that can more or less trace a rock layer, making in this way a much greater part of the borehole accessible to the petroleum contained in the rock.

Note. After the well has been drilled, tubulars are installed in the borehole. The lower part of the space between the outer casing and the borehole is sealed off by the injection of cement in order to prevent, behind the casing, petroleum leaking or escaping from the reservoir. Thereafter the casing at the level of the reservoir earmarked for production is perforated, unless it is decided to leave the bottom of the hole open.

As from the moment the drilling fluid is removed from the well and the counter-pressure is lifted, petroleum in the vicinity of the well and accompanied by formation water and rock particles, starts moving towards and into the well. Whether or not this initial movement will be followed by a natural flow of petroleum through the pores and fissures of the reservoir in the direction of the well bore and how efficient the extraction of the petroleum is depend on:

   (i) reservoir rock characteristics, foremost among which is the perme-
        ability;
  (ii) drive mechanisms (e.g., water-drive or gas-cap drive), by the
        working of which the movable part of the petroleum is displaced
        from the pores and fissures of the reservoir;
 (iii) well spacing and orientation (vertical to horizontal); and
  (iv) the characteristics of the oil to be extracted, foremost among which
        is its viscosity.

After having entered the well, petroleum will flow upwards to the wellhead at the surface through the production tubing installed in the borehole.

If the liquid phase contains a large amount of solution gas, this gas is gradually set free and gas bubbles appear as the borehole pressure decreases in the direction of the wellhead. At the same time, the emerging gas bubbles will expand with decreasing pressure, giving a tremendous boost to the flow of the oil.

If the petroleum concerned consists of an undersaturated oil, i.e., oil that contains hardly any natural gas in solution, and in absence of any abnormal reservoir pressure, stimulating, flow-assisting measures, mechanical or otherwise may have to be applied in order to let the oil flow upwards through the production tubing. Such measures involve the installation in the production tubing of the appropriate equipment, such as gaslift valves, pumps and pump rods.

If petroleum emerging at the wellhead consists of a mixture of oil and (associated) natural gas in different proportions, the field concerned is referred to as an oil field. If petroleum emerging at the wellhead consists of either free gas or coal-generated gas, the field concerned is referred to as a gas field and the natural gas is referred to as non-associated gas.

As said before, natural gas may contain in varying degrees heavier but still gaseous hydrocarbons. In a gas plant these hydrocarbons can be converted into NGL's. The remaining gas stream consists of pure methane which in its turn can, if need be, also be liquified (LNG). But for this process a much more complex liquifaction plant has to be built.

In an oil field, the recovery of light oil (i.e., oil having an API gravity of at least 22 degrees and a viscosity less than 100 cP) including condensate does not need any stimulation, is so to speak self-supporting, provided the reservoir has a satisfactory permeability. By contrast, oil lacking the lighter components usually has a high viscosity or may even have become a semi-solid bitumen, resisting any displacement in the reservoir. If in such a situation the naturally available drive mechanism is too weak, reservoir-stimulating measures have to be taken, costs permitting. Reservoir-stimulating measures, also named Enhanced Oil Recovery (EOR) techniques, range from the injection of natural gas or water (to repressurize the reservoir or to strengthen a failing water-drive mechanism), to injection of CO_2, to injection of steam or special chemical products (to mobilize very viscous oil). All these injection methods have this in common; they require the drilling of wells at the appropriate spots. Application of EOR techniques is therefore expensive, but may result in an impressive increase of the oil extraction efficiency. In some instances, recovery factors of up to eighty per cent may be achievable, compared to recovery factors between fifteen per cent and thirty per cent achieved by conventional, non-stimulated production. It should be added that in some oil fields, due to excellent reservoir characteristics and the presence of strong, long-enduring natural drive mechanisms, very high extraction efficiencies are attained without applying any non-conventional techniques.

The extraction of non-associated gas is generally much more efficient than that of the average crude oil. A recovery factor of eighty per cent to ninety per cent may be expected, but minimum permeability requirements should be satisfied. This means that, where natural gas is concerned, enhanced recovery methods can be dispensed with, making the production costs of gas that much less expensive.

Petroleum emerging at the wellhead is accompanied by rock particles and formation water. After passing the wellhead, the first treatment (in any field) consists in removing these particles and water. In an oil field, water has to be separated from oil; this separation is critical because the production water cannot be discarded if it contains more oil than allowed by the applicable regulations. The next treatment (in an oil field) is the separation of oil from (associated) gas. As a matter of fact, this oil/gas separation treatment can be described as the first stage of the refining process. After their separation, the oil and gas are each conditioned for transportation by pipeline and/or ocean-going tanker to their own, separate markets, except that associated gas, for which there is no commercial destination, even not in the vicinity of the oil field, will be flared or recycled, but not before NGLs will be recovered from the gas if the latter happens to be a wet or rich gas.

Most difficult to extract from their reservoirs and requiring non-conventional methods are: shale gas, shale oil, extra-heavy oil (including natural bitumen), tight oil, tight gas (gas contained in tight sandstones), coal bed methane and gas hydrates.

Currently, most attention is focused on the extraction of gas and oil from mature shales rich in organic material (shale gas and tight oil) and on the extraction of natural bitumen from oil sands.

The shales in question are in the first place source rock, the hydrocarbons generated therein have been expelled and have migrated to their place of accumulation. But as was known for some time there are mature shales in which a considerable amount of gas or oil was left behind. The problem was that shales generally have a low permeabilty which would prevent the extraction of hydrocarbons still present within the shale by conventional means. However, by combining horizontal drilling with the application of the already for a long time known 'hydraulic fracturing or fracking' techniques (but till recently only used in vertical wells) it proved possible to create fissures in the shale along which the hydrocarbons involved could escape and enter the well pipe.

Note. A typical process starts with drilling a vertical hole to a depth of 2,300–2,600 metres, then the drill bit is turned to the horizontal and the hole is continued for about 2 km. After perforating the well casing section by section water, fine sand and fracking fluid are injected under high pressure. The shale around the well casing is fractured and the sand is pressed into the cracks and fissures so made. The composition of the fracking fluid whose purpose it is to deliver the sand in the fractures, is the secret of the fracking operation.

The extraction of natural bitumen from oil sands is also only possible by applying unconventional techniques.

Note. Taking the Athabasca oil sands (Alberta, Canada) as example the natural bitumen in question has an API gravity of less than 10 degrees and a viscosity at prevailing reservoir temperatures greater than 10,000 cP. Its extraction requires special heat treatment provided by hot water and steam. Where these oil sands can be mined in open pits, the bitumen is separated from the sand in an extraction/separation plant near the mining site and further processed in the next plant into petroleum coke and hydrocarbon vapours. These vapours condense into naphta, kerosene and gasoil. The larger part of the oil sand deposits however are too deep below the surface for open pit mining. In this situation the bitumen has to be separated from the sand in situ. The extraction process that is applied in this case is known as steam-assisted gravity drainage (SAGD). The process requires the use of stacked pairs of horizontal wells. By injecting steam through the upper wells the bitumen becomes mobilized whereupon gravity causes the mobilized fluid to move to the lower wells. From there the bitumen is pumped to the surface and further processed into the end-products mentioned above. (Source: US Geological Survey Fact Sheet FS-070-03, August 2003.)

That part of coal-generated natural gas, that remains behind in the coal layer concerned (and is referred to as coal bed methane), is partly physically and partly chemically bound to the carbon atoms. Coal bed methane is produced by drilling holes into the coal layers. It may be expected that the same extraction techniques will be applied as happens in the case of shale gas (see discussion above). When a coal layer is fractured, the pressure is lowered and at least the physical bounds between methane and coal will be broken and the methane will start flowing through the natural pores and artificial fractures.

Coal bed methane is also set free in a coal mine, when coal layers are getting exposed to lower pressures in the course of the mining operations. When this happens in an underground coal mine, methane becomes mixed with the air circulating in the mine. Air/methane mixtures containing between four-and-a-half per cent and fourteen per cent methane will, when ignited, cause an explosion.

Interestingly, experiments are undertaken to produce methane from coal layers by means of injecting CO_2 in the same. CO_2 should break the in the coal layer existing bonds between methane and the carbon atoms and thereby take the place of the methane. Such substitution results in an enhanced recovery of the latter.

Finally there are the gas hydrates. This represents another source of natural gas that can only be exploited by non-convential means. As mentioned earlier, gas hydrates are crystals of a methane/water compound which are formed when natural gas surfaces at the bottom of the deep ocean and then reacts with the ocean water. The gas hydrates deposits are at present not seriously investigated by the industry. This will certainly not change in the future given the fact that shale gas can satisfy the demand for gas for many years to come. Moreover there exists considerable concern about the possibility that as a result of any large scale exploitation the stability of the deposits will be endangered and cause the release of huge amounts of methane in the ocean and from there into the atmosphere. Such release is very unwelcome because methane is a potent greenhouse gas and its presence in the atmosphere would have a very negative effect on global warming.

1.4   SAFETY, HEALTH AND ENVIRONMENTAL ASPECTS

1.4.1   SAFETY, HEALTH AND ENVIRONMENTAL RISKS ASSOCIATED WITH PETROLEUM OPERATIONS

From the beginning of the production of petroleum as an industrial undertaking, it was recognized that persons carrying out or involved in petroleum operations as well as the environment (the latter in this context to be understood as the whole physical and biological world in which humans live and in which the petroleum operations are carried out) were put at risk by:

(i) an oil well eruption (blow-out) at the drilling or production site, a grounding or collision of an oil tanker at sea, or the rupture of a pipeline and the subsequent massive release of oil into the environment (oil spillage); or

(ii) the temporary or permanent occupation of a portion of the land or sea surface or the sea bottom (spatial occupation) required for drilling locations, for the installation and building of (offshore) petroleum facilities and installations, or for construction and laying of (submarine) pipelines.

More recent concerns, in which human health and safety are not directly involved, are environmental risk caused by:

(iii) subsidence and earth tremors. The extraction of petroleum causes compaction in varying degrees of the reservoir rock from which the petroleum is extracted, depending on the characteristics of that rock.

This compaction may in turn lead to subsidence at the surface and may even cause earth tremors;

(iv) the disposal of waste products generated in the course of the petroleum operations; or

(v) abandonment, removal and disposal of production installations, in particular of those placed at sea.

With reference to (i). An oil blow-out, i.e., the uncontrolled, explosive outflow of oil from a well, that may have been caused by a faulty drilling operation or by an accident at the drilling or production site, and the grounding or collision of an oil tanker at sea are serious safety risks. A massive release of oil may follow. When such oil spills occur on land they have generally a limited areal impact and as such never cause permanent damage to the environment: oil escaping from a well usually catches fire and is burned off hence causing little environmental damage.

Note. This has convincingly been demonstrated in the aftermath of the Gulf War in 1991. Iraqi troops retreating from Kuwait set most oil wells on fire. It took more than a year before all fires were extinguished. All the while, the smoke of the burning wells was spread over a large area. The sky over Kuwait was darkened for a long time. Smoke particles have even been found in the Himalaya Mountains. Nevertheless any trace of this man-made calamity has since disappeared from the environment. No lasting damage could ever be found.

By contrast, oil escaping at sea from a damaged or broken up tanker, floats on the water, forming a slick that is moved around by current and wind. If such oil slick stays at sea, it will soon break up by wave action and further disappear through evaporation and oxidation or it will be decomposed through biological processes. Any heavy residue will eventually sink to the sea bottom, and do no further environmental damage. However, if an oil slick is driven up a beach or into an estuary, a viscous layer of oil will spread out over the shore line, with disastrous effects on various forms of marine coastal life, such as seabirds, seals and crustaceans.

Note. Fortunately, due to improved navigational instruments, massive oil spills at sea are actually a rare occurrence. It appears that major, spectacular events are separated by years and together account for only a small fraction of the yearly amount of oil that is released into the sea originating from different sources, such as ports and deliberate or accidental discharges from tankers and other ships. In 1967, the 'Torrey Canyon' wrecked off the coast of Cornwall, spilling more than 30,000 tons of oil into the sea. This particular disaster prompted the International Maritime Organization (IMO) to convene in 1973 a conference of all maritime nations, in order to mutually agree on measures to be taken to prevent pollution from ships. At this conference the International Convention for the Prevention of Pollution from Ships (MARPOL) was adopted. This very important convention was modified in 1978, and finally entered into force on 1 October 1983. A much bigger disaster occurred on 16 March 1978, when the 'Amoco Cadiz', after its steering gear failed in rough seas, ran aground off the coast of Brest, France, spilling its entire cargo of 226,000 tons of oil. Global concern about the environmental risks associated with petroleum and its products rose to a pitch when on 24 March 1989 the oil tanker 'Exxon Valdez' grounded in Prince William Sound, Alaska, releasing thereby about 36,000 tons of oil into the sea. The spillage turned into a disaster when the greater part of the spilled oil ended up at the shore and fouled more than 1,200 miles of Alaskan coastline. In December 1992, the tanker world was again faced with an accident. This time it concerned the 'Aegean Sea', which tanker carried 80,000 tons of oil. On 5 January 1993, the oil tanker 'Braer' carrying 80,000 tons ran aground on its way from Norway to Canada on the coast of one of the Shetland Islands and three years later, in January 1996 a similar sized oil tanker, the 'Sea Empress', was grounded in Milford Haven. In the same year, another IMO Convention was adopted providing for construction standards for oil (product) tankers. The new construction standards were aimed to make such ships safer in the sense of less likely to lose oil in case of a collision or grounding at sea.

To put oil spillage at sea in a proper perspective, it should be noted that oil spillage, whether accidental or deliberate, account only for a small fraction of the total pollution of the sea, the major contributor being polluting substances released from land-based sources, i.e., sewage installations, chemical industry and agriculture, and carried to the sea through the river system.

Finally the disaster that struck the drilling rig Deepwater Horizon in 2011 showed that oil spillage at sea is not solely restricted to that caused by damaged or broken up tankers: oil can also escape from a damaged underwater production site. In such case much more harm to marine life is done, partly by the use of oil dispersants.

Not only oil but also natural gas may be spilled at sea. Such spillage may occur in the event of an accident involving a LNG tanker. Such an accident may result in a massive release of LNG into the atmosphere. When (accidentally) exposed to the atmosphere, the LNG cargo will evaporate quickly and form a low-lying cloud around the tanker. Such a cloud of methane forms with the air, within a range of concentrations, an explosive mixture (as in underground coal mines). Moreover, as long as the cloud lingers around the tanker it will suffocate any person aboard the ship. If a wind is blowing, the cloud will drift away and become diluted. After that, the danger of explosion and suffocation will disappear. In the end, any visible trace of methane will have disappeared. It follows that the environmental risk of operating a LNG tanker is, strictly speaking, negligible. The real, far more important risk is that human health and life will be endangered if a massive release of LNG occurs.

The environmental damage caused by oil escaping from a ruptured or otherwise damaged pipeline shall not extend beyond the place where the breach occurred. This is only true if the damage is an industrial accident and not an act of sabotage. In the latter case, the pipeline concerned will most likely repeatedly targeted resulting in grave environmental damage.

Where natural gas is escaping from a damaged pipeline, there exists the risk of an explosion, depending on the composition of the ensuing air/methane mixture. Therefore, a sudden natural gas release from a pipeline is not likely to cause much environmental damage but is more a matter of a human health and safety.

With reference to (ii). Petroleum equipment, facilities and installations, including pipelines need a place (a site of operation) at the surface or even on the bottom of the sea, where they can be installed and be used and operated. Obviously, every effort will be made to minimize the number and areal extent of the sites required. But there is little room for manoeuvre when it comes to selecting the geographical location of suitable drilling and/or production sites or the routing of pipelines. If the selected site of operation is located within a controlled area, which means an area where the occupation of the desired site requires planning permission, under applicable zoning legislation or an area declared to be an environmentally sensitive area (fragile ecosystem, e.g., all types of wetlands and tropical rain forests), permission under the applicable regulations will be required before the site can be acquired or occupied. If the desired site is located in a non-controlled area, an authorized person is free to try to rent or to buy (from the public or private owner of the land) or simply occupy the selected site, subject only to the applicable conditions of the petroleum authorization concerned. Offshore, the competent authorities have to take into account the interests of shipping and fishing, the laying of submarine pipelines and cables, and the establishment of underwater national parks in coastal waters.

Note. The laying and operating of long-distance pipelines may have a negative impact on the environment by the mere fact of requiring extended strips of land for their routing and by their physical presence (compressor stations along the route), in particular when the pipeline is not buried in the ground. When running above the ground, for instance where soil conditions (e.g., permafrost) do not permit it to be buried, the pipeline forms a physical and visible obstacle in the landscape. If such a pipeline has to run through a wildlife refuge, measures have to be taken to prevent that its presence above the ground has a negative effect on the movements of wildlife, in addition to measures that should prevent any leakage. Such an extraordinary construction is exemplified by the 800-mile long Trans-Alaskan pipeline, running from Prudhoe Bay to Valdez. This pipeline was opened in June 1977 and has a daily capacity of 1.45 million barrels of crude oil. The pipeline had to be raised five feet off the ground in order not to disturb the yearly migrations of the caribou herds. More recently, a controversy has arisen between Canada and the US in connection with the intended routing of a long-distance oil pipeline, named the Keystone XL pipeline, which is meant to carry Canada's heavy crude to the US Gulf Coast. Environmental groups protested against the plans on the ground that the pipeline would traverse sensitive areas where leakage could do much harm, and because they objected to the exploitation of the Canadian oil sands.

Offshore there is less risk of sabotage but on the other hand the additional risk that an incorrectly buried segment of a submarine pipeline will become buoyant and rise from the sea bottom. When this happens, there is the risk that fishing gear will become entangled therein. Then of course there is ever present risk like on land that a pipeline starts leaking and needs repair. Such situation is much better to handle than the outflow of oil that happened on the Deep Horizon underwater production site However this be, the laying and construction of the 1,224 km twin Nord Stream gas pipeline carrying Russian gas from Vyborg to Lubmin in Germany went smoothly and without mishaps.

With reference to (iii). Subsidence is a physical phenomenon that manifests itself over a relatively large surface area. It affects the water system of the land surface and the water table. In a minor manner, it may change the course of rivers and create lakes. The most famous and spectacular example is the subsidence that for many years takes place in and around Lake Maracaibo in Venezuela. Around the lake, dikes had to be built and regularly be increased in height in order to prevent the flooding of the surrounding area. In low-lying coastal or inland areas, i.e., surface areas below sea-level, subsidence causes a relative rise of the water table, necessitating the installation of extra pump capacity to keep the water levels in such areas down and/or measures to strengthen and heighten the sea dikes. Compaction of the reservoir rock may also activate faults and in this manner be the cause of earth tremors. Subsidence and earth tremors do not constitute a human health risk and generally do not cause direct damage to railways, houses and other buildings.

With reference to (iv). In the course of the operations, waste products are produced which could be harmful to the environment (and, depending on the circumstances, also to human health) if not properly disposed of. Distinction may be made between two types of waste products. On the one hand, there are waste products directly related to and connected with the objective of searching for petroleum and producing oil and natural gas, such as spent drilling fluids, drill cuttings, production water and reservoir rock particles, but there is also associated natural gas that cannot be used commercially or re-injected into the reservoir and has to be flared. On the other hand, there are waste products generated as a result of making use of petroleum facilities, such as spent or obsolete material (used drilling bits, spent lubricating oil, all kinds of synthetic material).

With reference to (v). At the end of the production life of an oil or gas field, the petroleum facilities that had been used in such a field have to be abandoned. Depending on the petroleum facility, concerned abandonment may consist in:

(i) the plugging of production wells, removal of wellheads; and
(ii) the removal and dismantling of any other production facility present in the field, from production equipment to field pipelines to field storage tanks.

On the continental shelf, the removal and disposal of abandoned or disused production installations is regulated by international conventions, in particular by the 1982 Convention on the Law of the Sea; the 1992 Convention for the Protection of the Marine Environment of the North-East Atlantic (OSPARCON) and by the 1989 IMO Guidelines and Standards on Removal (see Chapter 9).

1.4.2   PETROLEUM FACILITIES, SITES AND AUTHORIZATIONS

As far as petroleum facilities are concerned, it appears that the use and operation of these facilities may have an adverse effect on health, safety and the environment generally:

– only in exceptional or unavoidable physical circumstances beyond the control of the operator;
– by the deliberate contravention of rules and instructions;
– in cases of irresponsible human behaviour; or
– when a deliberate attempt is made to cause damage (sabotage).

Under normal circumstances however, the environmental risks involved can, in a technical sense, be reduced to any desired level. It all boils down to finding an answer to the question as to what are acceptable levels of safety, health and environmental disturbance, e.g.:

- how stringent safety rules should be;
- how much noise is acceptable;
- how much oil can be allowed to escape from containers, storage tanks and pipelines;
- to what degree may wildlife be disturbed by the presence and operation of a petroleum facility, etc.

In the past, the possession of a petroleum authorization more or less guaranteed that the licensee or the contractor would always have a site at its disposal to install and build the necessary facilities and that the operation of these facilities would be permitted, provided adequate measures were taken to ensure that their operation would be safe and not endanger human health. In modern petroleum legislation, an attempt is made to ensure that the desired protection of the environment should form an integral part of the conditions imposed on the execution of petroleum operations. To this end any authorization, be it a license or a contract of work, will incorporate a reference to planning and environmental legislation that are relevant in respect to petroleum operations and require that the conditions imposed upon the holder of the authorization by the other legislation are adhered to.

Note. Depending on how the authorized area is situated, it is in theory and practice possible that the holder of the authorization does not succeed in obtaining the necessary planning and environmental permits with respect to the site of a drilling operation or field installation that was found by him to be the most suitable one. In such a case, the said holder will be unable to exercise in an optimal manner his rights under his authorization. It is submitted that in such a situation modern petroleum legislation should provide for financial compensation for the loss of opportunity or for the extra costs the authorized person incurs in having to divert or cancel his operations. Obviously, it suits all parties better if the competent authority abstains from granting authorizations in respect of areas which appear to contain so many environmentally sensitive or excluded parts that it is clear from the outset that there will be no room for undertaking petroleum operations in the sense as authorized.

1.4.3   HEALTH AND ENVIRONMENTAL RISKS ASSOCIATED WITH USING OIL PRODUCTS AND NATURAL GAS AS FUEL

When oil products manufactured in the refinery or natural gas are used as transport fuel or as fuel for generating heat and power, the carbon (C) content of these hydrocarbons (CxHy) is transformed into CO_2, or depending on the completeness of the combustion into carbon monoxide (CO), whereas the hydrogen (H_2) content is transformed into water (H_2O).

Note. The transformation of oil products into simple oxides marks an enormous loss in chemical complexity. Only when the former are used as feedstock for the petrochemical industry, advantage can be taken of their complex structure.

Besides CO_2 and CO, the combustion process gives rise to various molecular combinations of nitrogen and oxide (NOx), such as nitric oxide (NO) and nitrogen dioxide (NO_2). If the hydrocarbons contain sulphur (S), sulphur dioxide (SO_2) will be formed. Unless special measures are taken for their sequestration, the gases will after the combustion process be released into the atmosphere and as long as the gases remain in the atmosphere they may take part in chemical reactions or alter the latter's physical properties or conditions. The changes brought about in this environment could either be beneficial, negative or neutral. In any case, each gas acts and reacts in its own distinct manner, the intensity thereof depending on its atmospheric concentration and on the time the gas concerned resides in the atmosphere.

More specifically, the emissions of CO_2 are reinforcing the heat trapping properties of the atmosphere, which result in an increase of the average temperature at the surface (referred to as the greenhouse effect or global warming) with adverse consequences for the world climate and the sea-level (more fully discussed in Chapter 4), whereas NOx gases contribute to smog and acid rain, similarly as SO_2 will do. Finally, combustion of petroleum products, in particular that of diesel oil in diesel engines, causes minute solid particles, also referred to as aerosols, to be emitted into the atmosphere. The aerosol's residence time is short, but during their stay in the atmosphere, aerosols reflect the incoming sun light and have therefore a cooling effect. Furthermore the presence in the atmosphere at ground level of all these exhaust gases and particles constitute a constant human health risk.

Chapter 2

The Petroleum Industry

2.1 ORGANIZATION AND DEVELOPMENT

2.1.1 EARLY ACTIVITIES, EARLY ORGANIZATION

The boring of the first hole for the express purpose of finding and producing oil has marked the start of the production of oil as an industrial undertaking. This historic operation celebrated as the birth day of the extractive petroleum industry took place in the year 1859 near the village of Titusville in northwestern Pennsylvania. On 27 August 1859, oil was struck in this first borehole at a depth of 69.5 feet. On this occasion, the 'boring' operation was performed by a steam-powered cable-tool drilling rig under supervision by L.E. Drake. The latter's example was soon followed and by November 1960 already about seventy-five wells were producing oil, and about fifteen small distillation plants (refineries) were refining this production into kerosene, for which there was a market as illuminating oil for oil lamps. After the technology of the oil lamp was improved, the demand for kerosene dramatically increased, which brought in existence a new but still rather primitive industry that had as its sole purpose the search for and production of oil in order to satisfy this demand.

The early oil producers were independent, non-organized individuals who worked on small-sized plots of land, on which they tried to install as many drilling derricks as space allowed in order to be able to produce oil at the highest rates possible. They sold their production individually to the buyers from the distillation plants. In this manner, a market for oil developed in which many small volume producers traded with many small volume kerosene refiners. The price offered to the individual producer depended on the competitive situation prevailing among the buyers. On the side of the producers, situations of over-supply alternated with periods of shortage due to the wasteful way in which the oil was being produced. This instability on the supply side caused hefty price fluctuations.

Note. Actually, the producers operating on a small piece of land were in most cases producing oil from the same reservoir from which their neighbours were producing. Producers were aware of this, but instead of becoming motivated to pool their interests and jointly develop the common reservoir, they were only intent to drill as many wells as could be accommodated within the boundaries of their land. In this manner, they hoped to maximize production, and to secure for themselves, in competition with the neighbours, a maximum share of the common pool (reservoir). The result was that too many wells were drilled, wells that were not necessary for the ultimate recovery of oil from the common reservoir, thus causing a waste of capital. Apart therefrom, by producing each well at maximum capacity, the well started to produce water much earlier than would be the case under careful reservoir management working with lower production rates. As a result, a well's life expectancy was shortened and ultimate recovery was much lower than otherwise could have been achieved.

In contrast, the owners of a refinery (known as the oil companies) aimed at organization and concentration of commercial power. Rockefeller's Standard Oil Company, which company had been established in 1870 and was restructured as the Standard Oil Trust in 1885, took the lead. Seeking and organizing a concentration of refining capacity was accompanied by expanding activities into the transport and distribution functions. The oil needed to feed the refineries was bought from the producer at the wellhead and the buyer in question took the responsibility for transporting the oil (by pipeline or railroad) to his refinery and for the distribution of the refined products, which in those early days mainly consisted of kerosene. When most refineries came under the control of Standard Oil, the producer price was from then on dictated by the buyer. When around 1885 oil was discovered outside Pennsylvania and oil production had started to spread over the US continent, Standard Oil, later followed by the other oil companies, changed its policy of restricting itself to monopolizing the refinery sector. Instead the oil companies aimed for control over production, not so much for getting control over prices which they already had, but for ensuring an orderly development of the production operations, something the producers themselves, operating as they did within the boundaries of their small plots, were not able or willing to achieve. To this end, oil companies started to acquire production leases for their own risk and account. The pattern that now established itself on the US continent was that of an oil company following and watching the oil prospector waiting for him to make a discovery. The oil company would then try and buy or lease any land on which the discovery was made, together with any land in the surrounding area. By doing so, the oil company sought to forestall that any prospective acreage would fall into the hands of speculators. By cutting out the speculators and collecting large-sized leases, oil companies took the place of the independent producers. As a result of this strategy, the chance was reduced that an oil field would be shared and produced by a multitude of persons, which would only result in a waste of capital, over-production and inflicting damage to the reservoir.

Note. At a later stage, when the science behind reservoir behaviour and drive mechanism became better understood, and the benefits of water injection in the margins of the oil accumulation were recognized, the producers, in the meantime replaced by the oil companies, finally accepted the need for cooperation in the matter of producing from a shared reservoir (see Chapter 11).

2.1.2   INTEGRATION AND INTERNATIONALIZATION (WESTERN PRIVATE SECTOR)

After having gradually replaced the individual small-scale producer, oil companies were no longer satisfied with watching and following prospectors and buying up land where the latter had made discoveries, but decided to undertake the business of prospecting and exploration themselves. To follow up on this new policy, the organization of an oil company had to be expanded and to include the prospecting and exploration function. This so-called vertical integration gradually extended into all activities connected with petroleum: from the search for and producing petroleum, to the refining of oil, to the distribution and sale of the refined products. All these activities became comprised and combined within a single commercial enterprise under a centralized direction.

Meanwhile the oil industry got an international dimension due to the activities of European oil companies which, prompted by the need to satisfy the demand for kerosene, were forced to a global search for oil albeit they had to stay outside the US which was the acknowledged domain of the US oil companies. The European-led outward expansion started already in the last decades of the nineteenth century when oil was discovered in Baku on the Apsheron Peninsula in 1871 and in Atjeh, Sumatra in 1885. The kerosene that was manufactured from this oil was exported to Europe and China and shaped thereby the beginning of an international market outside the US, albeit a market for an oil product and not yet for oil itself.

This market for kerosene started to decline at the turn of the century due to the rapid introduction of electricity and electric light. Nonetheless due to new applications and uses for oil products new markets were opened up in the industrialized countries. In response to this new demand and in search for new supplies, the petroleum industry ventured out of its nineteenth century producing areas and moved further on: first into Persia and that part of the Ottoman Empire that would later become Iraq, later Mexico, Venezuela and then the Arabian Peninsula but also, and in fact initially of greater importance, into new areas inside the US itself, e.g., Texas.

Note. In the process of this expansion many important discoveries were made in the aforesaid countries or regions: to name the most famous ones: 'Spindletop' in Texas in 1901; 'Masjid-i-Sulaiman' field in Persia in 1908; 'Golden Lane' fields in Mexico in 1910; first oil in Venezuela in 1914; 'Kirkuk' field in Iraq in 1927; 'Seria' field in Brunei in 1929, which field, it should be noted, produced in 1940 17,000 barrels per day and thus became a strategic target in the Pacific War; 'Black Giant' field, East Texas, 1930; first oil in Bahrain in 1932; first oil in Kuwait and Saudi Arabia in 1938.

The move into Persia began when William Knox D'Arcy, more of an investor than an oil prospector, acquired (28 May 1901) a concession for oil. The concession he got consisted of an area that covered the whole country with (deliberate) deletion of the five northern provinces, the ones bordering on Tsarist Russia. About seven years later, on 25 May 1908 to be precise, oil was struck in the concession area at Masjid-I-Suleiman. In 1909 D'Arcy's concession was taken over by the Anglo-Persian Oil Company a newly-incorporated company that for raising the necessary finance organized a public offering of its shares in that year. For strategic reasons the UK government acquired in August 1914, a few days after the outbreak of the First World War, a controlling interest of 51.7 per cent in the company. In 1933 the concession was unilaterally cancelled by Reza Shah. A new concession was negotiated, whereby the concession area was reduced to 100,000 square miles located in southwestern Iran, still an extremely large area compared with the leases obtainable at the time in the US. In 1935 Anglo-Persian was renamed Anglo-Iranian.

  Shortly before the outbreak of the First World War, British and German interests turned their attention to the Ottoman Empire, to the region that later would become Iraq, encouraged as they were by the success of Anglo-Persian's venture in neighbouring Persia and by the numerous oil seepages and early discoveries in and around that region. Through the intermediary of the Armenian oil investor Gulbenkian, they established a company in London by the name of the Turkish Petroleum Company (TPC). But before starting their drive to acquire exploration acreage in Iraq, a restructuring of TPC was agreed allowing for the participation of Anglo-Persian in the venture. On 19 March 1914, such agreement was reached whereby the distribution of the shareholding in TPC was fixed as follows: Anglo-Persian Oil Company: fifty per cent; Anglo-Saxon Oil Company (Royal Dutch/Shell): twenty-five per cent; Deutsche Bank: twenty-five per cent; Anglo-Persian and Anglo-Saxon each transferred a 2.5 per cent beneficiary shareholding to Gulbenkian, since then known as Mr Five Percent. On 28 June 1914, the Ottoman Empire granted a concession to TPC, but this concession became invalid after the dissolution of the Empire. In 1920 the shareholding of the Deutsche Bank was transferred to the Compagnie Francaise des Petroles (CFP). On 24 March 1925, TPC received a concession from the post-war Iraqi government.

For some time, US oil groups had expressed their interest to become involved in the exploitation of oil in Iraq and objected to being excluded therefrom by the British and French governments. When on 15 October 1927 oil was discovered in the concession area at Baba Gurgur near Kirkuk, the need for a quick solution grew. After lengthy negotiations involving the said governments, as well as the shareholding companies, an agreement was signed in London on 31 July 1928. Under the terms of this agreement, a group of US companies was permitted to participate in TPC, at the expense of the shareholding owned by Anglo-Persian. The latter shareholder agreed to transfer to the US group one half of its original shareholding, i.e., 23.75 per cent. The US group reduced itself to only two companies, namely Standard Oil Company of New Jersey and Socony-Vacuum Oil Company (Mobil), each with a shareholding of 11.875 per cent and represented by their joint company named the Near East Development Corporation. After the shareholding had been rearranged as agreed, the name of TPC was changed to Iraq Petroleum Company (IPC), to which company the Iraqi government granted a new concession (24 March 1931). The area of this new concession covered the Iraqi territory east of the Tigris River. The territory west of the Tigris River was later given in concession (in two separate concessions) to affiliates of IPC (the Mosul Petroleum Company and the Basrah Petroleum Company respectively). As part of the agreement, the US companies agreed not to seek concessions independently in the territory that before the First World War belonged to the Ottoman Empire, with exception of Kuwait and the Khanaqin district of Iraq. The so-reserved area, which was outlined in red on a map of the Middle East, comprised the whole Arabian Peninsula, with exception of Kuwait. Hence it included the countries which later proved to possess the largest oil reserves in the world. The Red Line Agreement, as the agreement became known, did not stop other major US companies from seeking concessions in the reserved area. For instance, in 1930 Standard Oil Company of California took over in Bahrain a concession from the Eastern and General Syndicate of Major Holmes and on 25 May 1933 the company was granted a concession by the Saudi government, which was further extended in 1939. In both concessions Standard of California was later joined by the Texas Company (later renamed Texaco). After the Second World War, the two concessionaires, realizing the enormous potential of their Saudi concession and the marketing effort and capital investment that the development thereof would require, looked for other US companies for joining them in this venture. The two US shareholders in IPC, Standard Oil of New Jersey and Socony-Vacuum (Mobil) were interested, but were restrained by the terms of the Red Line Agreement. After protracted negotiations with the other IPC shareholders, it was finally agreed in 1948 to terminate this Agreement, which opened the way for the participation of the US shareholders in the Arabian American Oil Company (Aramco). In order to forestall further penetration of US oil companies in the area reserved under the Red Line Agreement, IPC secured through affiliates concessions in Qatar (1934), Oman (1937) and Abu Dhabi (1939). In Kuwait, not included in the reserved area, a concession was granted on 23 December 1934 to Kuwait Oil Company, equally owned by Gulf Oil and Anglo-Persian.

Much later, one more joint venture between the major European and US oil companies was founded in the Middle East. It concerned Anglo-Persian's 1933 concession. On 20 March 1951, this concession was nationalized and taken over by the newly founded National Iranian Oil Company (NIOC). After three-and-a-half years of negotiations, a contract of work, covering the area of the former concession, was made between NIOC and Iranian Oil Participants Ltd, a UK company better known as the Consortium. Shareholders and their shareholding in the Consortium were as follows: forty per cent for Anglo-Iranian Oil Company, the former concessionaire and on this occasion renamed British Petroleum Company (BP) (representing a loss of sixty per cent economic interest); fourteen per cent for Royal Dutch/Shell; six per cent for CFP; forty per cent for a group of US oil companies, distributed among them as follows: seven per cent for each of Standard of New Jersey, Standard of California, Socony Mobil, Texaco and Gulf Oil, and five per cent for Iricon Agency, Ltd., the latter owned by nine US oil companies, among which Standard of Ohio, Atlantic Refining and Getty Oil, the latter each with 0.417 per cent (see Chapter 11).

After the Second World War, the geographical expansion of the exploration and production activities of the petroleum industry continued, partly in response to a heightened demand for oil products, partly motivated by the wish of the Western States to lessen their dependence on oil from the Middle East. In the process, major oil discoveries were made in Alberta, Canada ('Leduc' field, 1947); Nigeria and Algeria (1956) and in

Libya 'Zelten' field, 1959). About a decade later major oil was discovered in 'Prudhoe Bay', on the North Slope, Alaska (1967/1968), with oil flowing in 1977 after the completion of the 800-hundred mile Trans-Alaska pipeline to Valdez, and on the Norwegian North Sea continental shelf ('Ekofisk' field, 1969). One year thereafter, oil was found on the UK North Sea continental shelf ('Forties' field, 1970). In 1972 an important oil discovery was made in Mexico (the 'Reforma' field). All these discoveries demonstrated the existence of oil provinces. Throughout these years, the oil (and natural gas) potential of the Soviet Union, later the Russian Federation, Azerbaijan and Kazakhstan became established.

Note. New oil (and natural gas) discoveries are still continuously being made albeit mostly in technically more challenging, deepwater areas. In the future, the Arctic offshore promises to yield new production of oil and gas. But as far as oil is concerned there are grave concerns about the risk of spillages in that ice covered sea area where any oil spillage may be difficult to contain and may cause lasting environmental damage. In contrast, the current spectacular production of shale gas and tight oil (from shales) is not the outcome of making new discoveries. The existence of the shales from which the gas or oil is extracted was known for a long time, production however had to await the development of the technique of horizontal drilling in combination with the hydraulic fracturing of the shales concerned.

Due to the global spread and at the same time integration of their activities, the US and European oil companies became gradually, and depending on their size, structured as an international oil group (IOG), consisting of a series of companies referred to as affiliates or affiliated companies located in different countries (host countries) and active in different functions. Directly or indirectly these affiliates are controlled and owned through shareholding by a parent company positioned at the top of the corporate structure. In anyone host country, an IOG may be represented by several affiliates each of them bound to and performing a different function (e.g., exploration / production, refining, marketing). Moreover, within any IOG, certain activities are undertaken which are solely meant for the benefit of the IOG itself, e.g., research, finance and internal services. These activities are also organized on the basis of separate corporate identities.

The parent company itself is a public company which is incorporated and has its head office in one of the OECD countries and whose shares are traded at any recognized Stock Exchange. For providing financial and other for its shareholders relevant information as required by the rules of the Stock Exchange where the parent company is listed, the latter is considered and treated as a single commercial entity. The OECD Member State, in which the parent company is incorporated and has established its head office, is referred to as the IOG's home country. In contrast, any affiliate is by preference incorporated in the host country concerned; but if a proper legal infrastructure is absent in such country, the affiliate is of necessity incorporated in the home country of the IOG. Specialized service companies, with exception of finance companies, or operating companies exercising a centralized function, such as trading on the international oil market, are usually established in the home country. Finance companies are by preference established in countries with a favourable fiscal regime, which could be the home country itself.

2.1.3   JOINT VENTURES FOR EXPLORATION AND PRODUCTION

Following the example set by the Middle East joint ventures described above, it has become standard practice among IOGs to form exploration and production joint ventures between their respective operating companies/affiliates and by preference never to seek a large majority in any one single venture. Furthermore, where possible, an operating affiliate will try to enter into a joint venture with the National Oil Company (NOC) or with the state-controlled commercial company of the host country concerned. To this end, operating affiliates (with or without the state company, if any) enter into agreements of cooperation providing rules for jointly applying for a petroleum authorization and, if successful, for jointly conducting exploration and production operations within the limits of the applied for petroleum authorization (see Chapter 11).

2.1.4   STATE-OWNED COMMERCIAL OIL ENTERPRISES

In the past governments of European countries established state-owned commercial oil enterprises which were supposed to compete in the oil market with the private sector and to search for and produce petroleum in foreign territory. One of the reasons behind such policy was to safequard and secure the supply of petroleum to the domestic market. A very early, but incomplete example of a state-owned commercial oil enterprise was the Anglo-Persian Oil Company (later British Petroleum) in which the UK government for strategic reasons acquired in August 1914, a few days after the outbreak of the First World War, a controlling interest of 51.7 per cent. Examples of 100 per cent state-owned commercial companies are the companies that were established in 1953 in respectively France and Italy, viz. Entreprise de Recherches et d'Áctivites Pétrolières (ERAP) and its subsidiary Société Nationale Elf Acquitaine and Ente Nazionale Idrocarburi

(ENI) and its subsidiary Agip Mineraria, and the company that was established in 1975 in the UK, viz. the British National Oil Corporation (BNOC). In Norway the government established a state-owned commercial petroleum company named Statoil in 1972. Later on all of the aforesaid companies were privatized. Nowadays, state-owned or state-controlled commercial oil enterprises are no longer present in free-market economies but only found in the Russian Federation (Gazprom, Rosneft) and China (CNOOC). These companies are primarily involved in domestic petroleum operations but when opportunities are seen are also active abroad.

2.1.5   NATIONAL OIL COMPANIES (NOC'S)

Governments of non-western countries aiming to search for and, if so feasible, exploit petroleum resources in their domain are as a rule making use of a state entity referred to as the National Oil Company (NOC). The first duty of such NOC is to supervise and control the ongoing petroleum operations in the country. Depending on the terms of the prevailing petroleum regime (licenses with state participation or contracts of work) the NOC will also be the vehicle for entering with foreign oil companies into the prescribed agreements. The statutes of such a NOC describing its purpose, mandate, responsibilities and authority will be covered in the petroleum legislation concerned. In some cases, the NOC is authorized to undertake alone or with foreign companies petroleum activities outside its home country. In such case there will not be much difference in scope with the state-owned or state-controlled commercial oil enterprises discussed above. In case of the nationalization or expropriation of the assets of a privately-owned oil company or of the company itself a NOC may be established for the occasion to take over and manage the nationalized assets or company. In this way a number of important NOC's came into existence as a result of the OPEC-inspired take-over's in the 1970s of the concessions and other assets then held by Western IOG's.

Note. As a matter of fact, today's proved reserves of oil and gas are overwelmingly controlled and managed by NOC's or state-owned or state-controlled enterprises. Ranked in order of size of reserves held it concerns companies such as: NIOC (*Iran*), Saudi Aramco, PDVSA (*Venezuela*), Kuwait Petroleum, Gazprom, Qatar Petroleum, the NOC's of Iraq, ADNOC (*UAE*), Turkmengaz, Libya NOC, Petrochina, NNPC (*Nigeria*), Rosneft, Lukoil, Sonatrach (*Algeria*), Pemex (*Mexico*), Petrobras (*Brazil*). The reserves held by the biggest IOG's, such as Exxon Mobil, Royal Dutch Shell and BP are much more modest.

2.1.6   GOVERNMENTS AND IOG'S

The privately owned (western) IOGs are represented by their affiliates in many countries and as such have to deal with many jurisdictions. Only the government of the IOG's home country, through its jurisdiction, fiscal as well as administrative, over the parent company and the latter's head office, is in a position simply by threatening to withdraw fiscal and/or other privileges to exert influence over the global activities of the IOG. For instance, a home government may compel a parent company to cause the suspension or even termination of the IOG's activities (as carried out by the local affiliate) in any host country in cases where such host country for one legitimate reason or another was subjected to the home government's trade sanctions.

Meanwhile, in an attempt to get more control over IOG's, the US and the EU have made or are considering rules and regulations which compel any stock exchange listed parent company to disclose all payments made by its affiliate in connection with the latter's operations in anyone host country. The required transparency should prevent such affiliate to make illegal payments and bribes to officials and other authorities of such country.

But not only will the transparency of money transfers made by an affliate within a host country be scrutinized by home governments, but also the possibility that human rights of citizens of the host country may not have been respected or upheld by an affiliate may lead to action against the parent company. Support for such action can be found in the UN Guidelines regarding the duties of countries and enterprises in the matter of human rights, summarized as: Protection, Respect and Remedies.

In contrast, the government of a host country has only jurisdiction over the locally established IOG-affiliate or rather over that company's assets in the country. Said local assets comprise petroleum exploration and production assets and the underlying petroleum authorization (i.e., licenses, contracts of work). The local affiliate is of course subject to all national rules and regulations and responsible to carry out all its authorized operations in accordance with such legislation.

Very recently it appears to be possible for citizens of a host country to start legal proceedings against a parent company in the courts of its home country in case an affiliate operating in their country is held responsible (and thus liable for paying compensation or penalties) for alleged misdeeds (in environmental matters) or misbehaviour in political matters (e.g., not respecting human rights).

2.2   GLOBAL EXPANSION OF PETROLEUM
             PRODUCTION OPERATIONS

2.2.1   OIL PRODUCTION

Table 2.1   Geographical Distribution and Volume of Oil Production
            (Thousand Barrels Per Day) 1885–1975

	1885	1905	1939	1965	1970	1975
US	60	370	3,460	9,014	11,297	10,008
Canada	-	-	-	920	1,473	1,735
Mexico	-	-	114	362	487	806
Venezuela	-	-	570	3,503	3,754	2,422
Tsarist Russia/FSU	38	151	577	4,858	7,127	9,916
Rumania	-	-	145	266	284	311
Netherlands Indies/Indonesia	-	21	183	486	854	1,306
Persia/Iran	-	-	211	1,908	3,848	5,387
Saudi Arabia	-	-	12	2,219	3,851	7,216
Iraq	-	-	81	1,313	1,549	2,271
Kuwait	-	-	-	2,371	3,036	2,132
Libya	-	-	-	1,220	3,357	1,514
Nigeria	-	-	-	274	1,084	1,785
UK	-	-	-	2	4	34
Norway			-	-	-	189
China	-	-	-	227	615	1,545
OECD	-	-	-	10,779	13,920	13,670
OPEC*	-	-	-	14,386	23,509	27,168
World	101	590	5,669	31,803	48,061	55,825

* OPEC was established on 1 September 1960.

Sources: American Petroleum Institute, L.U. De Sitter, 1950; Petroleum Economist; as from 1965: BP Statistical Review of World Energy 2007; Oil & Gas Journal.

The years shown in Table 2.1 have not arbitrarily been chosen. In the selected years new oil provinces were discovered, new inventions using or needing oil products for their operation came to the market and/or political events took place which made a lasting impact on the demand for oil and oil products.

In respect of the year 1885. This year saw the first appearance of a motor car (a Daimler/Benz) on the road in Germany. The year 1885 was the year, in which for the first time oil was discovered outside Pennsylvania, namely in Northwestern Ohio, and also the year, in which the first well was drilled in Atjeh, Sumatra. Finally, 1885 was the year in which Thomas Edison demonstrated in Manhattan, New York a large-scale application of electric light invented by him a few years earlier. This demonstration foretold the demise of the until then very successful oil lamp and the declining demand for kerosene as a result thereof.

In respect of the year 1905. This year marked the start of the planning of the first mass-produced motor car, namely Ford's T-model, which in 1908 came on the market. It is of importance to note that this type of car was powered by a gasoline engine. The choice for the gasoline engine (rather than for the diesel engine which some years before (around 1893) had been invented by Rudolf Diesel) secured a demand and market for the lighter distillates at the expense of the middle distillates of the refining process. The gasoline market would in the coming decades grow rapidly in line with the growing number of motor cars on the road in as much as these cars, in contrast with heavy duty vehicles, would continue to run on gasoline.

Note. To put the matter in its proper perspective, the real growth in the number of cars started only after the Second World War. Between 1945 and 1990, the number of registered cars grew tenfold, from 40 million to about 400 million. Today an estimated 850 million passenger cars and 50 million trucks are on the road.

The year 1905 is also the year in which the airplane established itself as a means of transport to be taken seriously, after the brothers Orville and Wilbur Wright on 17 December 1903 in Kitty Hawk (North Carolina) had made the first demonstration flight. The use and further development of the airplane opened a new market, initially for aviation gasoline, much later for kerosene (for the jet engine).

In respect of the year 1939. In this year the Second World War began. The volume and geographic distribution of global oil production would prove to be a decisive strategic factor in the outcome of this war. The year 21939 was also the last year of the period in which the US oil industry and the US oil market dominated the world of oil. Soon after the Second World War (in 1948) the US would become a net-importer of oil and the export/import of low-cost oil from the Middle East would since then dominate the international market.

In respect of the post-war years leading up to the year 1975. In those years, world oil production rapidly expanded. US oil production stabilized around 10 million barrels per day. Production from the fields in the Middle East Gulf area increased spectacularly, from 8.387 million barrels per day in 1965 to 19.733 million barrels per day in 1975.

In respect of the year 1975. The year 1975 was the year in which the global oil market started to function.

Between 1975 and 2001, the first year of the next Table, the world oil production increased rather steadily from 55.8 million barrels per day to 74.8 million barrels per day. As from 2001 world production continued to grow, reaching a level of 84.0 million barrels per day in 2011. New producers entered the market, making the latter more global than ever. Most remarkable is the progress made by the Russian Federation, Kazakhstan, Brazil and Angola and the decline showed in the UK.

Table 2.2   Geographical Distribution and Volume of Oil Production (Million Barrels Per Day) 2001–2011

	2001	2003	2005	2007	2009	2011
US	7.7	7.4	6.9	6.8	7.2	7.8
Canada	2.7	3.0	3.0	3.3	3.2	3.5
Mexico	3.6	3.8	3.8	3.5	3.0	2.9
Brazil	1.3	1.5	1.7	1.8	2.0	2.2
Venezuela	3.1	2.6	3.0	3.0	2.9	2.7
Azerbaijan	0.3	0.3	0.5	0.9	1.0	0.9
Kazakhstan	0.9	1.2	1.4	1.5	1.7	1.8
Russian Federation	7.0	8.5	9.4	9.9	9.9	10.3
Iran	3.8	4.0	4.2	4.3	4.3	4.3
Saudi Arabia	9.2	10.1	11.0	10.4	9.8	11.2
Iraq	2.5	1.3	1.8	2.1	2.4	2.8
Kuwait	2.2	2.4	2.7	2.6	2.5	2.9
UAE	2.6	2.7	3.0	3.0	2.8	3.3
Qatar	0.8	0.9	1.0	1.2	1.3	1.7
Algeria	1.6	1.9	2.0	2.0	1.8	1.7
Libya	1.4	1.5	1.7	1.8	1.7	0.5
Nigeria	2.2	2.3	2.6	2.4	2.1	2.5

	2001	*2003*	*2005*	*2007*	*2009*	*2011*
Angola	0.7	0.9	1.4	1.7	1.8	1.7
UK	2.5	2.3	1.8	1.6	1.4	1.1
Norway	3.4	3.3	3.0	2.6	2.4	2.0
China	3.3	3.4	3.6	3.7	3.8	4.1
Indonesia	1.4	1.2	1.1	1.0	1.0	0.9
OECD	21.3	21.2	19.9	19.1	18.5	18.5
EU	3.3	3.1	2.7	2.4	2.1	1.7
OPEC	31.0	31.0	35.0	35.1	34.0	36.0
World	75.0	77.0	81.4	82.0	81.0	84.0

Source: BP Statistical Review of World Energy June 2012.

2.2.2   NATURAL GAS PRODUCTION

*Table 2.3   Geographical Distribution and Volume of Natural Gas Production
(Billion Cubic Metres) 2001–2011*

	2001	*2003*	*2005*	*2007*	*2009*	*2011*
US	555	541	511	546	584	650
Canada	186	185	187	183	164	160
Mexico	38	41	47	54	55	52
Total North America	780	767	745	782	803	864
Total South & Central America	104	119	139	152	152	168
Netherlands	62	58	62	60	63	64
Norway	54	73	85	90	104	101
Russian Federation	526	561	580	592	528	607
Turkmenistan	46	53	57	65	36	59
United Kingdom	106	103	88	72	60	45
Uzbekistan	52	52	54	59	60	57
Iran	66	81	103	112	131	152
Qatar	27	31	46	63	89	147

	2001	2003	2005	2007	2009	2011
Saudi Arabia	54	60	71	74	78	99
UAE	45	45	48	50	49	52
Total Middle East	233	263	320	358	407	526
Algeria	78	83	88	85	80	78
Egypt	25	30	42	56	63	61
Total Africa	131	145	174	203	199	203
Australia	32	33	37	40	42	45
China	30	35	49	69	85	102
Indonesia	63	73	71	68	72	76
Malaysia	47	52	61	65	64	62
Total Asia Pacific	282	322	363	400	440	479
EU	233	224	212	187	171	155
OECD	1097	1093	1079	1101	1122	1168
World	2477	2617	2770	2939	2956	3276

Source: BP Statistical Review of World Energy June 2012.

In the period preceding the discovery in 1959 of the important Slochteren gas field (2500 bcm) in the province of Groningen in the Netherlands natural gas production and consumption were concentrated in the US and Canada, except that soon after the Second World War large-scale natural gas production was developed in the former Soviet Union In all these countries, gas producing fields happened to be located in the vicinity of the places of consumption ensuring that the costs of transportation were manageable, which in turn allowed to keep the cost of supply within the range of those of competing coal and oil products. Under these circumstances, non-associated gas fields could commercially be developed and produced at an early stage. Nonetheless, the consumption and production of natural gas even in the US and Canada really became significant only after the Second World War. This development owed much to improved pipeline technology that then became available and which made it technically possible to build long-distance gas pipelines capable of withstanding the relatively high pressures under which natural gas has to be moved through the pipeline. The construction of the so improved pipelines opened up new local and regional markets and consumption could grow as is illustrated by the following figures: in 1935 US natural gas production sold amounted to 54 bcm; in 1950 and in 1960 this quantity had risen respectively to 178 bcm and 360 bcm. In 2011, US gas production stood at 651 bcm (about twelve times the level reached in 1935), while the country's gas consumption in that year (690 bcm) only marginally exceeded that figure. It is expected that the spectacular development of shale gas production will soon enable the US to export any surplus gas unless of course domestic consumption will be stimulated: e.g., by gas replacing coal as fuel for the powerstations.

In the aftermath of the Slochteren-field discovery mentioned above, many more gas deposits were found on the North Sea continental shelf in the 1960s. These deposits were sufficiently large to support the development of a gas market in that region. On a global scale, however, the commercial prospects of natural gas definitively improved only after and as the (unexpected) result of the first oil price shock (1973/1974), which raised the prices of the competing oil products (e.g., low-sulphur fuel oil and heating oil) dramatically. Export/import of natural gas on a commercial scale became now possible, allowing to absorb the cost of long-distance gas transportation whether by pipeline or by ocean-going LNG-tanker. It became also commercially possible to produce natural gas in high cost areas (e.g., the deeper waters). Since 2000, in response to and as a direct result of the spectacular increase of the international oil price this development has gained further strength. The overall effect becomes apparent when comparing the 1975 world natural gas production (1203 bcm or 1.083 million toe) with the level reached in 2011 (3276 bcm or 2955 million toe). World oil production increased also over this period, namely from 2779 million tonnes in 1975 to 3996 million tonnes in 2012, but not at same rate. Due to the sudden and spectacular availability of shale gas it may be expected that in the coming decades government petroleum policies will favour the use of natural gas as fuel in powerstation above that of coal and oil. If this happens the gap between oil and natural gas production in terms of million toe / year will continue to narrow, in particular if gas will become cheaper when no longer linked to oil prices at the latter's current high levels.

2.3 PROVED RESERVES AND REMAINING RECOVERY

2.3.1 OIL

Table 2.4 *Geographical Distribution and Size of Proved Oil Reserves (Billion Barrels) at End 2010 and End 2011 and Reserves/Production (R/P) Ratios (years)*

	Proved Reserves at end 2010	Proved Reserves at end 2011	R/P Ratio
US	31	31	11
Canada	175	175	*
Mexico	12	11	11
Venezuela	296	296	*
Brazil	14	15	19
Azerbaijan	7	7	21
Kazakhstan	30	30	45
Russian Federation	87	88	23
Iran	151	151	96
Iraq	115	143	*
Kuwait	101	101	97
Saudi Arabia	264	265	65
United Arab Emirates	98	98	81
Qatar	25	25	39
Algeria	12	12	19
Libya	47	47	*
Angola	13	13	21
Nigeria	37	37	41
United Kingdom	3	3	7
Norway	7	7	9
China	15	15	10
Malaysia	6	6	28
Indonesia	4	4	12
World	1622	1653	54

	Proved Reserves at end 2010	*Proved Reserves at end 2011*	*R/P Ratio*
EU	7	7	11
OPEC	1167	1196	91
OECD	235	235	35

* More than 100 years.

Source: BP Statistical Review of World Energy June 2012.

World Energy Outlook 2012 estimates that the total of remaining recoverable reserves (including proved reserves) amounts to 5871 billion barrels, which translates into no less than 190 years of production at the present rate of 84 million barrels per day. It follows that an impressive 4218 billion barrels has to be added to the currently proved reserves by way of making new discoveries and extending existing reserves.

The said 5871 billion barrels are assumed to be made up of conventional oil (2678 billion barrels) and unconventional oil (3193 billion barrels). Conventional oil is for a large part (1124 billion barrels) expected to be produced in the Middle East; in contrast unconventional oil is predominantly expected to come from respectively the Americas (1878 billion barrels), E.Europe/Eurasia (586 billion barrels) and Latin America (538 billion barrels).

2.3.2   NATURAL GAS

Table 2.5   Geographical Distribution and Size of Proved Natural Gas Reserves (Trillion Cubic Metres) at End 2010 and End 2011 and Reserves/Production (R/P) Ratios (years)

	Proved Reserves at End 2010	*Proved Reserves at End 2011*	*R/P Ratios*
US	8.2	8.5	13
Canada	1.8	2.0	12
Mexico	0.3	0.4	7
Venezuela	5.5	5.5	*
Azerbaijan	1.3	1.3	86
Kazakhstan	1.9	1.9	98
Netherlands	1.1	1.1	17

	Proved Reserves at End 2010	*Proved Reserves at End 2011*	*R/P Ratios*
Russian Federation	44.4	44.6	73
Turkmenistan	13.4	24.3	46
United Kingdom	0.2	0.2	4
Iran	33.1	33.1	*
Iraq	3.2	3.6	*
Qatar	25.0	25.0	*
Saudi Arabia	8.0	8.2	82
United Arab Emirates	6.1	6.1	*
Kuwait	1.8	1.8	*
Algeria	4.5	4.5	58
Nigeria	5.1	5.1	*
Libya	1.5	1.5	*
Australia	3.7	3.8	84
China	2.9	3.1	30
Indonesia	3.0	3.0	39
Malaysia	2.4	2.4	39
India	1.1	1.2	27
EU	2.3	1.8	12
Total World	196.1	208.4	64

* More than 100 years

Source: BP Statistical Review of World Energy June 2012

World Energy Outlook 2012 estimates that the total of remaining recoverable natural gas reserves (including proved reserves) amounts to 790 tcm, which translates into no less than 240 years of production at the present yearly rate of 3276 bcm. It follows that it is expected that a volume of 582 tcm will be added to the currently proved reserves by way of making new discoveries and extending existing reserves.

The said 790 tcm are assumed to be made up of conventional gas (462 tcm) and unconventional gas (328 tcm). Conventional gas is for a large part expected to be produced in the Middle East (125 tcm) and in E.Europe/Eurasia (144 tcm); in contrast unconventional gas – i.e., tight gas (81 tcm), shale gas (200 tcm) and coalbed methane (47 tcm) – is globally more evenly distributed, albeit outside the Middle East.

2.3.3   COAL

For comparison purposes (see Chapters 3 and 4), the status of the proved coal reserves is shown in the following Table 2.6.

Table 2.6   Geographical Distribution and Size of Proved Coal Reserves at End 2011 (Billion Tonnes) and Reserves/Production (R/P) Ratios (Years)

	Proved Reserves Hard Coal	*Proved Reserves* Lignite and Brown Coal	*Proved Reserves* Total Coal	*R/P ratio*
US	108.5	128.8	237.3	239
Columbia	6.2	0.4	6.7	79
Kazakhstan	21.5	12.1	33.6	290
Germany	0.1	40.6	40.7	216
Poland	4.3	1.4	5.7	41
Russian Federation	49.1	107.9	157.0	471
Ukraine	15.3	18.5	33.9	390
South Africa	30.2	-	30.2	118
Australia	37.1	39.3	76.4	184
China	62.2	52.3	114.5	33
India	56.1	4.5	60.6	103
OECD	155.9	222.6	378.6	182
World	404.8	456.2	860.9	112

[*] One tonne hard coal equals 0.66 toe; one tonne sub-bituminous coal equals 0.33 toe.

Source: BP Statistical Review of World Energy June 2012.

As shown above, total proved coal reserves (hard coal plus sub-bituminous coal) amount to 573 billion toe. The countries with the largest proved reserves of the economically more important hard coal are in order of magnitude: US, China, India, the Russian Federation, Australia and South Africa. For sub-bituminous coal is the ranking: US, the Russian Federation, China, Germany and Australia.

The total proved coal reserves at the end of 2011 (573 billion toe) compares with the world proved oil reserves of 234 billion tonnes and the world proved natural gas reserves of 187 billion toe.

2.4 POLITICAL RISK (WESTERN PRIVATE SECTOR)

From the perspective of an IOG-affiliate operating in a host country, political risk means the risk that for purely political reasons, not sanctioned by or envisaged under applicable law or the petroleum authorization concerned, said affiliate will lose its petroleum authorization and its other assets in the country or is forced to stop its operations and to abandon its venture.

The most common political reasons underlying political risk are:

(i) a partly politically, partly economically motivated change in attitude of the host government towards IOGs, leading to nationalization or expropriation of its affiliate's rights and assets;

(ii) a breakdown of the internal political stability of the host country, causing civil unrest, civil war or even a de facto break-up of the country and the disappearance of a central government (in such a situation, the country is referred to as a failed State). Such breakdown of internal political stability may make it for an IOG-affiliate physically or for safety reasons impossible to continue its (authorized) petroleum operations in the country; or

(iii) a breakdown of the host country's foreign relations, either with respect to the international community, with respect to the home country of the IOG or with respect to a group of Western States amongst which the home country.

With reference to (i). In case of politically or economically motivated nationalization, the IOG's main concern is to receive adequate and prompt compensation for the losses sustained by its affiliate. Under customary international law, any oil company whose petroleum authorization is cancelled and whose physical assets are nationalized or expropriated by the host government for other reasons than those based on applicable law or on the petroleum authorization that had been granted has the right to receive such compensation. This principle has been confirmed in many bilateral treaties for the promotion and protection of foreign investments.

The issue of nationalization and expropriation of the assets of foreign multinational corporations and of paying compensation if such measures were taken by a developing country had been raised by those countries in the context of formulating and declaring a NIEO and adopting a Charter of Economic Rights and Duties of States (GA Resolution 3281 (XXIX) of 12 December 1974 (see Chapter 10).

More recently, the issue of nationalization and the compensation that has to be paid in such event has been addressed in the 1994 European Energy Charter Treaty (Article 13). In the said article, it is stated that nationalization, where allowed under the terms of the Charter Treaty, should be accompanied by the payment of prompt, adequate and effective compensation. Moreover according to the Charter Treaty (Article 12), a foreign investor has a right to be treated on the same footing as a national investor or any other investor in respect of receiving compensation for losses due to political instability affecting the host country. The compensation has to be paid by the affected host country (see Chapter 10).

With reference to (ii). A breakdown of the internal political stability of a host country may make it, for any IOG-affiliate operating in that country physically or for safety reasons, impossible to continue its operations. In extreme cases the affiliate involved may be forced to abandon its operations altogether and to withdraw from the country.

With reference to (iii). Any IOG-affiliate could find itself operating in a host country that has a dispute with the UN or with a group of concerned Western States on account of not fulfilling its international obligations and, that as a consequence thereof, is subjected to the imposition of trade sanctions. Any IOG-affiliate operating in such a country will suffer heavy losses as long as the sanctions are maintained and may be forced to abandon its petroleum venture. It is also possible that the government of a home country on its own decides to take action against a offending host country and orders the parent company of the IOG to stop investments, to shelve further development or to abandon the venture altogether. A new twist in the matter of human rights can be noted. Apart from taking such an extreme measure of urging the parent company of an IOG to cause its affiliate to spend its operations and/or postpone any new investments, a home government may make use of the presence of the affiliate in the country and ask that this affiliate is directed to take action against such violation, e.g., by registering a protest, by refusing to cooperate, etc. This would be in line with the UN Guidelines regarding the duties of countries and enterprises in the matter of human rights (see subsection 2.1.6), but taking such action could easily have disastrous consequences for those individuals among its personnel, who are citizens of the host country. Moreover the existence of the affiliate itself (and thereby the future of its personnel) would be put at risk since a host government could decide to retaliate by nationalizing such politically active affiliate on account of it having meddled in the internal affairs of the country.

Note. Any IOG whose affiliate is operating in a host country with no stable international relationships may expect sooner or later to be manoeuvred in a situation as described above. While, as mentioned above, a IOG should not be compelled by its home government to direct its local affiliate to undertake political action in as much by such action investments made before the violation took place would be put at risk and/or the safety of its national personnel would be endangered it will be clear that when trade sanctions are imposed on the offending host country the local affiliate will surely be sacrificed and the IOG involved may not count to receive any compensation for the losses sustained by its affiliate.

Chapter 3
Petroleum and the Economy

3.1 GENERAL REVIEW

3.1.1 OIL AND NATURAL GAS

When emerging at the wellhead, petroleum is not suitable for use in the economy, and as such, it is not a marketable product. Before it can be moved to the market, it has to be treated in the field as described in Chapter 1. After this treatment, crude oil, natural gas and possibly NGL's coming from a gasplant are each transported by pipeline and/or by ocean-going tanker to their respective destinations. Associated natural gas for which there is no local market or which cannot be utilized in the oil field concerned for one purpose or another will be flared, but not so before NGLs are recovered from the gas in a gasplant if it proves to be a rich or wet gas.

Note. Before natural gas can be transported by an ocean-going tanker, it is necessary first to recover any NGL's from the gas. The remaining gas is then liquefied (LNG) at the port of export. At its destination, the LNG is gasified and the gas is delivered to a gas company for further conditioning and delivery to the end-user.

Crude oil's destination is the refinery. It is the base material from which a range of products is manufactured such as lubricants, all kind of fuels for generating heat, electricity or mechanical power, and feedstock for the petrochemical industry. The sectors using the oil products as fuel comprise industrial plants, power stations, households and the transport sector (road transport, aviation, shipping).

In contrast to crude oil, most natural gas needs only conditioning, which includes the recovery of NGLs in a gasplant, and can thereafter, directly or through a distribution entity, be sold to the end-user mainly for heating purposes (industrial plant, power stations, households), less for further processing in refineries or in Gas-to-Liquids (GTL) processing plants.

Crude oil and natural gas as such have partly differing, partly overlapping applications and markets; albeit in theory, products made from crude oil in all applications and uses can be replaced by natural gas itself or by products made from natural gas through catalytic conversion. These catalytic conversions are costly in themselves. Moreover, due to the relatively low efficiency of the available conversion techniques, a loss of more than fifty per cent of the heat content of the natural gas being converted should be reckoned with.

3.1.2   OIL

The economic use of oil has a long history. As of the days that liquid or semi-solid natural hydrocarbons such as tar and asphalt were found at the surface, they were recognized to be useful in all sorts of applications. Oil found dripping or oozing from rocks was used as a lubricant, or as medicine for curing all sorts of illnesses, while at the surface burning natural gas played a role in religious rituals. In the pre-drilling days, oil that leaked or seeped into pools or creeks was skimmed from the surface of the water with cloths and rags and subsequently bottled and sold. In some places, e.g., in Pechelbronn, France, shafts and galleries were dug in order to obtain better access to the oil or tar and increase its recovery. Tar found in pits or mixed with sand was utilized in the ancient world as a stone binding material in buildings and in walls. Tar or products distilled from tar (pitch) were widely used as a sealing material, more specifically for caulking seams of ships and boats. The native people of Alberta, Canada, used the tar sands found in outcroppings along the Athabasca River to waterproof their canoes. Much later, tar (coal-tar) was also obtained as a by-product of the manufacturing of town gas, and this coal-tar was applied in a similar fashion (in addition to its use in the chemical industry for the production of aniline, an organic base material).

Note. As could be expected, products made from oil found its use also in warfare. Naphtha, presumably distilled from tar, was, in combination with sulphur and saltpetre, the main ingredient of Greek fire. The latter mixture had been invented by the Greek Kallinikos and was brought by him to Constantinople at the time this city was besieged by the Saracen fleet (673–678). By pouring this mixture out of tubes into the Saracen ships it set them alight and drove them off, saving the city. Since the slightest shock caused the mixture to explode, it could not safely be transported over land and its use was eventually restricted to naval battles, where it proved, as it did on the first occasion in 678, to be very successful and decisive. In fact, this flame-throwing weapon gave the Byzantine fleet for a long time control over the Mediterranean.

About 100 years after the start of the Industrial Revolution (1750), the distillation process was invented which made it possible to split the oil in several fractions (distillates). The fraction that mattered was kerosene (a middle distillate). Unfortunately, there was no use for the lighter distillates (gasoline) and heavier distillates (fuel oil and residue) which therefore had to be discarded.

Kerosene was in demand for burning in lamps. Around 1850, the oil lamp was technically improved (an innovation made in Europe) which led to an increased demand for kerosene and thus in turn for oil. As more fully described in Chapter 1, entrepreneurs took notice and sought to increase production capacity by boring holes for reaching and extracting oil from the subsoil, trying in fact to copy the way in which in those days salt water was bored for and produced.

Note. Before the technically improved kerosene-burning lamp was introduced, light on the streets and in houses and offices was provided by gas lamps, in which inflammable gas (town gas) was burned. Town gas was manufactured from coals which are rich in volatile matter. Apart from gas lamps, there were lamps burning sperm oil or suitable fats, and candles. In this competition, the kerosene lamp had several advantages: kerosene was easy to transport (compared to town gas which had to be piped), it was not expensive (it was cheaper than town gas as well as sperm oil) and the brightness of the light produced was satisfactory, anyway much better than that of candles, although not as good as that of gas light. Under these circumstances, the kerosene lamps succeeded in becoming the most important source of light till this lamp was gradually displaced due to the arrival of electric light, a large scale application of which was in 1885 demonstrated by its inventor, Thomas Edison, in Manhattan, New York. The dominant position of the kerosene lamp and of kerosene came gradually to an end (first in the cities, later in the rural areas). However for oil new markets opened up, in particular for the lighter distillates, such as gasoline, for which previously there had been not much use. This changed dramatically when the first mass-produced car, viz. Ford's T-model introduced in 1908, was equipped with a gasoline engine. Meanwhile crude oils were discovered that yielded less kerosene but more of the heavier fractions than the crudes produced so far (e.g., the light heavy crude oil that was discovered in 1901 at Spindletop, near Beaumont in Texas). The US industry, railways and shipping became interested in these heavier fractions (fuel oil) and recognized their potential for the generation of electricity and steam, a market that hitherto was the exclusive domain of coal.

Finally, some of the heavier refined products proved suitable as a basis for making lubricating oil, whereas the ultra-light refined products, in particular naphtha, became the most important feedstock for the petrochemical industry.

There are many types of crude oil, each type having its own specific value. The specific value depends on its quality and specific gravity. The quality depends on the relative concentration of the different types of hydrocarbon molecules as well as on the presence and concentrations of associated substances. The specific gravity is expressed in degrees API (API stands for American Petroleum Institute). The range 25 to 42 degrees API corresponds with specific gravities from 0.904 to 0.816. Generally, the lower the specific gravity and the higher the API-number, the higher the economic value of the oil. The aforementioned associated substances consist of sulphur and metallic compounds and are mainly found in the heavier oils, whereas the lighter oils, viz. condensates and NGLs, are relatively clean oils. Any sulphur present in the oil must be removed therefrom in order to prevent its release into the atmosphere after refining or after combustion in the car engine. Furthermore, sulphur has a damaging effect on catalysts used in car exhaust systems for the purpose of reducing nitrogen oxide emissions. The metallic compounds may cause problems in the refinery processes as they may hinder or interfere with the catalysts that are being used in such processes. Crude oils containing sulphur or interfering metallic impurities are less valuable because of the costs that have to be made to remove these substances. These costs are mitigated in case the products that have to be removed possess a commercial value of their own.

Note. Sulphur offers a good example. The removal of sulphur takes place in a direct chemical process whereby gypsum ($CaSO_4$) is formed; or by treating the oil or oil fraction with hydrogen (H_2), whereby H_2S is formed; or by concentrating the sulphur in a small residue fraction from which sulphur in its elementary form can be extracted. Elementary sulphur has commercial value; hence the costs of the removal process can partly be recovered. Gypsum may sometimes also have a commercial value depending on whether it can be obtained without too many impurities.

3.1.3   NATURAL GAS

The economic use of and drilling for natural gas lagged far behind that of oil, at least in the world outside the US and Canada. Natural gas' relatively low energy density makes its transportation expensive relative to that of oil. Initially therefore natural gas had to find a market close to the field where it was produced. In the first half of the twentieth century, those geographical conditions were only satisfied in the US and Canada. Outside the US and Canada, the search for hydrocarbons was focused on oil and not on natural gas. Only after the Second World War, large scale natural gas production was developed in the former Soviet Union. In Western Europe started the production and consumption of natural gas only after the discovery of the Slochteren gas field in the Netherlands in 1959 and after finding more commercial discoveries in the North Sea area thereafter.

As a fuel, natural gas is used in power stations, industrial plants and households. In these sectors it is used respectively for generating electricity, heat, space heating and cooking. Its use in North America started in the last decade of the nineteenth century as a substitute for town gas. As town gas was manufactured from coal, natural gas started right from the beginning the competition with coal. Now that town gas is a thing of the past, the real gas-to-coal competition takes place in the market of thermal power generation. In this market natural gas has also competition from fuel oil and from alternative energy products (i.e., nuclear fission energy and renewables, as will hereinafter be further discussed).

Currently, a small part of the natural gas production is used as feedstock for conversion into more valuable chemicals or, alternatively, for conversion into hydrogen (H_2) or into transport fuels, in particular diesel.

Note. The abovementioned conversion processes start with the conversion of methane into synthesis gas or syngas. The latter is a mixture of carbon monoxide (CO) and hydrogen. It is obtained by a process in which methane is mixed with steam and oxygen, with oxygen alone or with air. Further processing of said syngas in accordance with the Fischer/Tropsch principle leads to the synthesis of larger hydrocarbon molecules. In a third stage these hydrocarbons are refined into transport fuels in the diesel range. This process is known as GTL processing which yields in a very clean diesel product, however more costly than diesel manufactured from oil. It is also possible to convert syngas into methanol (CH_3OH). Methanol as such is suitable for use as a transport fuel, but it is also used as feedstock for manufacturing a range of chemicals as well as the standard transport fuels, in particular gasoline. It should be added that research is going on into methods to convert methane directly into methanol. Furthermore, as a low cost source for making hydrogen, methane may in the future become still more important if there will be a demand for hydrogen as transport fuel (see hereinafter).

There are many types of natural gas, each having its own specific value. When used directly as fuel, the specific value of the natural gas depends on its calorific value or heat content. When used as feedstock in catalytic conversion processes, its value derives from the value of the products into which the natural gas is converted, e.g., transport fuels, methanol, hydrogen and chemicals. If natural gas contains non-hydrocarbon gases, whose presence in the gas is a human health risk and/or will cause corrosion damage to pipelines and associated equipment, these gases need to be removed from the natural gas before the latter can be transported to its market, but its value is correspondingly lowered by the amount of the cost of removing these harmful gases. However, the presence of inert gases, such as argon and helium, may be a commercial advantage provided the concentrations are large enough to warrant their sequestration and recovery.

Note 1. Best example of a gas that is harmful in all respects is hydrogen sulphide (H_2S). H_2S is not only toxic (a human health concern) but also extremely corrosive with the potential of causing great damage to pipelines and valves through which the natural gas has to be conducted. Therefore, H_2S has to be removed from the natural gas in the field of production at the earliest stage of treatment possible. The presence of non-inflammable gases, mainly nitrogen (N_2) and carbon dioxide (CO_2), reduces the calorific value (heat content) per cubic metre of the natural gas and hence its commercial value (as a fuel). If natural gas contains a significantly high percentage CO_2, say more than ten per cent, it may be considered worthwhile to separate the CO_2 from the natural gas and return it into the subsoil before the natural gas is transported and sold.

Note 2. As an option to dispose of associated CO_2, the underground storage of CO_2 has received considerable attention. Underground storage of such associated CO_2 is accomplished either by:

-   injecting the CO_2 into the natural gas reservoir from which it was produced, by piping the CO_2 to a oil reservoir, into which it will be injected for the purpose of stimulating and improving the oil recovery; or
-   piping the CO_2 to the location of a depleted gas field, for subsequent injection into such field.

Finally, the location of an oil or gas field has a decisive effect on the value of the natural gas that is or can be produced from that field, since (as explained in the beginning) the cost of transportation of gas to its markets is an important component of the cost of its supply. If the area of operation is located at a long-distance from any gas market, the gas transportation possibilities will weigh heavily in taking a decision whether or not to develop a non-associated natural gas discovery, or how to dispose of any associated natural gas that is unavoidably produced in an oil field.

3.2 FACTORS DETERMINING ECONOMIC USE AND VALUE

3.2.1 THE STATE AND REQUIREMENTS OF PREVAILING TECHNOLOGY

There are two kinds of technology at work here: demand-side technology and supply-side technology.

Demand-side technology is technology that requires for its application or operation the utilization of oil products and/or natural gas, and thus stimulates the demand for these products. The first example of technology that required an oil product for its application was the kerosene-burning lamp. The next example was the invention in 1893 Rudolf Diesel of the internal combustion engine and the use of this type of engine in cars. This created a new market for oil products, for the lighter distillates to be precise, which fraction had hitherto been considered as a nuisance. Present day examples are gas turbines, all kind of combustion engines, oil or gas-fired heating installations, etc. Only wide-spread introduction of the electric car either powered by a battery or by a hydrogen fuel cell could make inroads on the demand for transport fuels. Also more use of nuclear energy in the power stations could have its consequences for the market of natural gas, although in first instance nuclear energy will compete with coal.

Supply-side technology is technology that aims to improve the efficiency of finding and producing petroleum and of transporting the same to its first destination (for oil this means the refineries).

Note. Drilling operations became much more efficient as a result of the invention of rotary drill pipe technique, which allowed drilling much deeper holes as had previously been possible by means of cable-tool drilling (see Chapter 1). Long-distance pipeline transportation of natural gas became possible when pipelines could be made that were capable to withstand the high pressures under which the natural gas had to be transported over such distances. The latter achievement opened a very important gas market in North America. A more recent technological achievement in the field of long-distance transportation of natural gas concerned the technology involved in the liquefaction of natural gas. Such liquefaction makes it possible to transport the gas by ocean-going tanker. In this way gas can be delivered to areas which are beyond the reach of pipelines.

3.2.2   THE COST OF SUPPLY

3.2.2.1   The Components

The cost of supply of oil and natural gas comprises all and any cost incurred by the producer from finding petroleum up to and including the cost of production and transport to the market place. This cost must be recovered from the price (the producer price), which the producer receives in the (global) market place. Hence the cost of supply consists of:

(i) the cost of exploration work preceding discovery including an allocation of the cost of any failed search for new reserves;

(ii) the cost of extraction of petroleum from the discovered reservoirs and the cost of treating and storing the extracted petroleum in the field;

(iii) any production taxes (royalties), export and other duties, fees, area rentals and cash bonuses payable to the host State; and

(iv) the cost of transporting the oil and natural gas production from the field storage facilities and export terminals to the market.

With reference to (i). As far as the individual producer is concerned, the costs that have been spent on discovering the reservoirs from which the oil or natural gas are produced are part of the cost of supply and have to be recovered from the producer price. Usually the total expenditure spent on exploration work is written off over part of the lifetime of the field which has been discovered as a result of the exploration work. Furthermore, any producer is constantly searching worldwide for petroleum reserves, which are needed for replacement of the reserves that are being produced, but not all exploration work wherever undertaken leads to the discovery of new reserves. The costs of any such failed search have to be distributed over the producer's producing ventures.

With reference to (ii). The technical cost of extraction, treatment and storage in the field consists of capital expenditure and operating costs. Capital expenditure represents the cost of acquisition of a capital asset (e.g., a producing well, a production ship, any field treatment and storage facility) and is written off in accordance with a depreciation schedule based on the lifetime of the capital asset in question. Operating costs include the cost of leasing or hiring capital assets. The latter may be substituted for capital expenditure.

The level of the cost of extraction depends on (a combination of):

(i) the characteristics of the geographical location of the oil/gas field (offshore: Arctic waters, deep water or by contrast shallow water;

onshore: desert area or other empty areas or by contrast environmentally sensitive areas such as densely populated areas in general
or tropical rain forests in particular);

(ii) the depth and characteristics of the reservoir; and

(iii) the efficiency of the extraction process and the well productivity
(production rate per well).

With reference to (iii). If production taxes (royalty), export and other duties,
fees, area rentals and cash bonuses have to be paid to the host State the cost
of production are correspondingly increased (see Chapter 8).

With reference to (iv). The cost of transportation consists of capital
expenditure, operating costs and tariffs. Tariffs are payments made for the
use of storage and transportation facilities, including such facilities used at
export terminals. Capital expenditure represents the cost of acquisition of
a capital asset (e.g., a pipeline) and is written off over the lifetime of the
capital asset bought. The level of the cost of transportation from the field
of production to the market place depends on distance and on whether oil
or natural gas is being transported. Only the costs of long-distance
transportation matter. Due to its low energy density, long-distance transportation of natural gas is expensive. It takes place by means of ocean-
going tanker (after the natural gas is liquefied in a special plant) or
high-pressure pipeline. Long-distance transportation of oil is not expensive, provided the oil can be moved by ship (oil tankers). Long-distance
transportation of oil by pipeline is much more expensive, albeit always less
so, than such transport of natural gas. It follows that when an oil field is
situated near port facilities allowing the oil to be carried by tanker, the cost
of supply is not much higher than the cost of its production. Natural gas
however is always at a great disadvantage if its markets are far removed
from the place of production and long-distance transportation by ship or
pipeline is required.

3.2.2.2   High, Medium and Low Cost Unit-Production

When the costs of production (capital and operating costs of extraction and
treatment in the field facilities plus the payments that have to be made to
the State (production taxes, export duties, etc.) are compared with the price
that the producer can obtain in the market (the producer price), distinction
can be made between high cost unit-production (leaving a small margin),
medium costs and low cost unit-production (the latter leaving a large
margin per unit of production).

Conventional oil and gas fall within the category of medium to low cost production. Conventional oil produced in the Middle East Gulf area are the cheapest crudes available. This gives producers in that area (all Member States of OPEC) an enormous economic power (see further Chapter 4).

Non-conventional oil and gas fall within the category of high cost production. High costs result from the fact that the oil or gas:

(i)   must be extracted from reservoirs with low to extreme low productivity characteristics, i.e., reservoirs with a low porosity and/or permeability, requiring the application of advanced drilling and extraction techniques, for example shale gas, coalbed methane and tight oil;

(ii) must be extracted from reservoirs containing heavy oil, including very heavy oil, or natural bitumen, for example Canadian oil sands;

(iii) must be produced in technically challenging areas, such as the deep offshore generally, and some extreme offshore areas, such as the ice covered Arctic waters.

Note. In respect of production cost per unit of volume, no region or country in the world has ever been able and is still not able to compete with the oil producing regions in the Middle East Gulf area. The deciding factor was and still is the impressively high well productivity (production rate per well), a result of large, extensive reservoirs with excellent reservoir characteristics making oil technically very easy and cheap to produce. Moreover the major producing fields are all situated in the vicinity of port facilities (Ras Tanura, etc.) and can be moved over sea at reasonably low cost (causing [but only in a situation of over-supply] problems for the high cost domestic producer).

3.3   MARKETS, PRICES AND PRICING SYSTEMS: OIL

3.3.1   THE EARLY KEROSENE MARKET (1860–1900)

In the nineteenth century, oil yielded after distillation only a single product of commercial interest, viz. kerosene, a middle distillate. Because there was no use for the other fractions such as gasoline oil was refined near the place of production so as to avoid having to transport partly useless material. In those early days, it was the kerosene, and not the crude oil itself, which was shipped around and traded on the international market. In this manner, US kerosene was exported to Western Europe and the Far East (in 1880, fifty per cent of US kerosene production was exported); kerosene refined in Sumatra went to China and Japan; and Russian kerosene, refined in Baku, Caucasus, was similarly exported to Western Europe and the Far East. As a matter of fact, in 1892 a tanker shipped for the first time Russian kerosene from Batum on the Black Sea coast through the Suez Canal to Singapore and Bangkok.

3.3.2   THE PRE-GLOBAL MARKET (1900–1975)

As a result of technical innovations, crude oil was sought not only for its middle distillate, i.e., kerosene, but also and more so for its lighter and heavier distillates. The market for kerosene turned into a market for crude oil and, over the period 1900–1975, this market gradually developed into a global market. As described in Chapter 2, the petroleum industry became gradually dominated by a few major oil companies (also referred to as the seven sisters) operating on a global scale. The majors' global activities began with supplying the markets in Europe and Asia, but, already from the start, the companies had to cope with an over-supply of oil. In the 1920s the situation got worse; too much oil was being exported to the said regions, in particular by the producers in the US and the former Soviet Union. The resulting price cutting competition prompted the majors to negotiate and conclude among themselves (on 28 October 1928) an agreement (subsequently known as the Achnacarry or 'As-Is' Agreement) that provided for mutual cooperation in markets outside the US in order to put an end to the then prevailing unbridled competition. The agreement however was never signed in view of US antitrust regulations. The principal participating companies were:

(i) Anglo-Persian Oil Company, a company formed in 1909 in connection with the famous discovery at Masjid-i-Suleiman, Persia, and which at the time of the 'As-Is' Agreement (as a matter of fact since August 1914) was owned for 51.7 per cent by the UK. Anglo-Persian changed its name in 1935 to Anglo-Iranian Oil Company after its original concession in Persia now Iran in 1933 had been renegotiated, and again changed its name, to British Petroleum (BP), on the occasion of the restructuring of this renegotiated concession in 1954.
(ii) Royal Dutch/Shell, a 60/40 British/Dutch partnership formed in 1907, currently a unified UK company under the name of Royal Dutch Shell plc.

(iii) Standard Oil of New Jersey (later named Exxon, currently merged with Mobil, both companies originating from the dissolution of the Standard Oil Trust in 1911).

Note. Also participating were a number of smaller US oil companies, such as Standard Oil of Indiana (one of the companies emerging from the dissolution of the Standard Oil Trust, later Amoco and finally merged with BP), Standard Oil of New York (another company emerging from the dissolution of the Standard Oil Trust, later merging with Vacuum Oil Company to form Socony-Vacuum, known as Mobil. The latter finally merged with Exxon); The Texas Company (Texaco), a US company founded in 1902, and Gulf Oil, a US company established in 1907 (this company was in 1985 bought by Chevron, the former Standard of California, the latter also one of the companies that emerged from the dissolution of the Standard Oil Trust.

Under the terms of the (informal) 'As-Is' Agreement, the participating companies shared among and between themselves the markets in Europe and Asia based on the situation prevailing in 1928. In addition, the companies agreed to a pricing system for crude oils traded in the global market, where US crudes competed with crudes produced from outside the US. Under the agreed system, the price to be charged to the consumer was based on the oil prices posted by the US producers in the ports in the Gulf of Mexico area. Transportation costs were charged to the consumer as if the crude oil had been shipped from these ports to the actual place of delivery, irrespective of the real place of shipment. This pricing system reflected the fact that, before the Second World War, the US was not only the biggest oil producer in the world but also the biggest exporter of oil. Production was controlled to the extent that each company's production was only allowed to exceed the demands of its allocated market share if any such surplus would be sold to the other companies. The 'As-Is' Agreement was imperfect in the sense that it did not include independent US producers capable of exporting any surplus production to the markets covered by the Agreement. After production in the US was brought under control by the authorities, the effectiveness and relevance of the Agreement and its amendments improved. Of even greater importance for the control of markets and prices was the struggle for obtaining exclusive petroleum rights in the Middle East Gulf area. In this struggle, the same major oil companies were involved as those participating in the 'As-Is' Agreement. By the end of the 1930s, these companies (since then sometimes referred to as the seven sisters i.e., five US and two European companies) operating within the framework of four different incorporated joint ventures, had succeeded in securing exclusive petroleum agreements in the Middle East Gulf countries. As much later became clear, these petroleum agreements dealt with the world's largest reserves of crude oil and very important reserves of natural gas.

Meanwhile in 1922, oil was discovered in Venezuela, a country that after the Second World War would develop into a major exporter of oil and in this context would play a leading role in the establishment of the Organization of Petroleum Exporting Countries (OPEC) (see Chapter 4). By the middle of the 1930s, three of the seven sisters, viz. Royal Dutch/Shell, Gulf Oil and Standard of New Jersey (Exxon), had become the main concession holders in that new oil exporting country, which put these companies in control of exports that in the 1950s and 1960s were competing on the West-European market with their own exports from the Middle East Gulf area.

After the Second World War two important trends became visible. First, the US very soon became (as from 1948) a net-importer of oil; and secondly, the pre-war oil discoveries in the Middle East Gulf area were rapidly developed, yielding fast growing quantities of low cost oil for which a market had to be found. In fact throughout the 1950s and the 1960s, the Middle East Gulf governments were always urging their concessionaires to increase production and exports, a policy which would bring these governments into conflict with Venezuela, because of competing with its exports on the same West-European market. For the companies, it became necessary to adapt the pricing system to the new realities. A second price basing point was established at Ras Tanura, the Saudi Arabian port of export. The FOB (free on board) price posted by the companies Ex Ras Tanura was so related to the US FOB posted price in the Gulf of Mexico area that at a certain selected port of destination, known as the equalization point, the delivered price (FOB posted price plus freight charges to the equalization point) would be equal. Initially, the port of Genoa was selected as the equalization point, and later, in 1949, this point was shifted to New York. As from the introduction of this pricing system the international price of oil was set and controlled by the aforementioned majors. It was clear that the pricing system adopted tended to protect the US producers against competition from the low cost oil that was exported in increasing volumes from the Middle East Gulf area. Due to US government intervention (this government imposed on 11 March 1958 the Mandatory Oil Import Control Program), the US market became a market partly closed off to imports of Middle Eastern oils. The struggle for outlets between the exporting oil producers then concentrated on Western Europe. In that region the majors, as holders of the major oil producing concessions in the Middle East, were confronted with each other's exports, with oil exported from Venezuela and, as from 1955, with oil exported from the former Soviet Union. To counter the competition, the concessionaires were forced to sell their crude oils below the then applicable posted prices.

Note. In 1955, the Middle East petroleum agreements of the 1930s were amended to the effect that the concessionaires were obliged to publish the price at which they were ready to sell their production FOB port of export to all comers, and this price was referred to as the posted price. As a result of this amendment, government revenues (derived from the then prevailing 50/50 profit-sharing arrangement) were henceforward calculated on the basis of the official posted price. In turn, the now adopted fiscal method caused concessionaires, if and when selling their exports below the applicable posted price, to lose the corresponding fiscal relief. Unable to continue with this practice, the concessionaires decided in February 1959 to adjust their posted prices to market realities and to reduce these prices by USD 0.18 per barrel. As a result thereof, Arabian Light ex Ras Tanura was posted at USD 1.90 per barrel. About one year later, in August 1960, the concessionaires again decided to lower their posted prices, initially by USD 0.14 per barrel, later brought back to USD 0.10 per barrel. Arabian Light was correspondingly posted first at USD 1.76 per barrel, and later at USD 1.80 per barrel. The following Table 3.1 illustrates the progression of the posted price during the 1950s up to and including 1960.

Table 3.1   Posted Prices (USD Per Barrel)

	1953	*1954*	*1955*	*1956*	*1957*	*1958*	*1959*	*1960*
Arabian Light ex Ras Tanura (34°)	1.82	1.93	1.93	1.93	2.00	2.08	1.90	1.80
Irani crude ex Bandar Mashur (34°)		1.91	1.91	1.91	1.98	2.04	1.86	1.77
Iraqi crude ex Fao (34°)	1.79	1.90	1.90	1.85	1.92	1.97	1.80	1.72
Kuwaiti crude ex Mina-al-Ahmadi (34°)	1.96	1.72	1.72	1.72	1.78	1.85	1.67	1.59

3.3.3   OPEC AND ITS EARLY PRICING POLICIES

Since any reduction of the posted prices meant to the governments concerned a corresponding loss of fiscal revenues, the posted price reduction that was effectuated in August 1960, was a matter of great concern to the governments of five major oil exporting countries, viz. Saudi

Arabia, Iran, Iraq, Kuwait and Venezuela. Within one month after the latest posting, they met in Baghdad and succeeded at that meeting in reaching agreement on the establishment of an organization of mutual cooperation and assistance named OPEC.

Note. OPEC is more fully discussed in Chapter 4.

At the time, the concessionaires, being the exporting oil producers, were themselves not directly involved with the organization. The governments of the OPEC Member States could therefore only act (in marketing and pricing matters) through and by means of giving or withholding approval to the prices posted by their concessionaires. In fact, the concessionaires kept control over prices throughout the 1960s. The posted prices were maintained at the level fixed in 1960, although the concessionaires had to continue their practice of selling below the posted price, in the light of the competition experienced in the West-European market from Libyan and Middle Eastern crudes produced by other companies (referred to as the independents), which had replaced the exports from the former Soviet Union.

On 16 October 1973, ten days after the outbreak of the Yom Kippur War (also known as the Ramadan War), OPEC finally succeeded to take away control over the international price from their concessionaires. On the aforesaid date, the posted price of Arabian Light ex Ras Tanura was unilaterally raised by no less than seventy per cent, from USD 2.898, the price which in June 1973 had been agreed with the concessionaires, to USD 5.119. Soon thereafter, with effect from 1 January 1974, OPEC raised the posted price again, this time by almost 130 per cent to USD 11.651. These price movements have since been referred to as the first oil price shock or as the first oil crisis, although there was absolutely no physical lack of oil.

Until the end of 1974, posted prices were maintained at their level as fixed on 1 January 1974. As of 1 January 1975, the posted price as such disappeared but continued as the non-published fiscal or export price. Meanwhile a new published price was introduced under the name of 'official government selling price'. This price was fixed at a level of ninety-three per cent of the fiscal price and indicated the price at which concessionaires, which meanwhile had lost a sixty per cent share in their respective concessions, could buy back that so lost share of production. As of 1 January 1975, the official government selling price became the only price that was published, this time by the governments themselves.

Note. To remain in control of prices and pricing, it was necessary for the OPEC governments to bring their state participation policies to a conclusion. The wish to acquire a stake in the petroleum agreements of the 1930s was, for the first time, brought to the foreground at an extra-ordinary meeting of the OPEC Conference in September 1971. Soon afterwards, negotiations with the concessionaires began. After initially having agreed to some intermediate stages of state participation, in the course of 1975 the governments involved finally acquired 100 per cent – and in some instances fifty-five to sixty per cent – of the long-term concessions (Gulf area) and other concessions/long-term leases (Nigeria, Libya, Venezuela) held by the majors in their respective countries. The majors lost thereby control over a large part of their production capacity and oil reserves outside the US, forfeiting forever their capability to dominate the international market and to control the prices. This dramatic turnabout was illustrated by the fact that in 1970, immediately before the governments started the negotiations on participation, the majors possessed about seventy per cent of the then proven world oil reserves outside the US and about the same percentage of the world oil production outside the US.

3.3.4   THE GLOBAL OIL MARKET (AS OF 1975)

In the aftermath of the political turmoil that took place in the Middle East in the first half of the 1970s and as a result of OPEC acquiring during that period the major world oil reserves and oil production capacity, an open, freely accessible global market for internationally traded oil came into operation.

On this market, oil can be freely bought and sold by producers and refineries through the intermediary of oil traders and in accordance with the terms of a sales contract. Such contracts comprise type of oil, price, quantity, quality and delivery date. If the sale does not concern a spot sale but a short, medium or long-term sale, the price is determined in accordance with a formula including references to the spot price or short-term price of one or more comparable benchmark crudes. The two most used benchmark crudes are West Texas Intermediate (WTI), delivery point Cushing, Oklahoma, and Brent Blend (North Sea area). Other bench mark crudes are Dubai and Nigerian Forcados. In accordance with these contracts, oil of the chosen type, quality and quantity is shipped to and delivered at the refinery concerned. In the refinery, the oil in question is converted into specific products which will then be delivered to the end-user in the market for that particular product.

But during the first decades that the market was working it was not a perfect market. Producers prices were not arrived at as a result of freely conducted negotiations between independent selling and buying parties. In reality, prices were determined and established by the actions and measures taken by the Member States of OPEC, regulating and controlling the supply of crude oil to the market within the limits of their prevailing production capacity (see further Chapter 4).

A real turning point in the global oil market becomes apparent in the year 2000. Compared to the foregoing years, OPEC no longer had to contemplate production cut backs in order to support a chosen price level. In fact, prices moved without its intervention at a comfortable level of around 25 USD per barrel, as a matter of fact within a price band (22–28 USD per barrel) that OPEC in March 2000 had set for the price of the OPEC Reference Basket in pursuit of a pricing policy based on production adjustments. As from 2003/2004, the international price started to climb reaching spectacular levels: in November 2007 the spot price of Brent was nearing the 100 USD per barrel mark whereas the yearly average of the same spot price in 1998 had been as low as 12.72 USD per barrel. Even when correcting for the relative weakness of the US dollar, this was an astonishing development. Nonetheless, these trends continued in 2008, but a fallback occurred in 2009, followed again by a period of rising prices easily exceeding 110 USD per barrel for the Brent bench mark in 2011/2012. As from the beginning of 2011 there opened a gap between Brent and WTI while up to then WTI usually fetched a premium on account of its slightly better qualities compared to Brent. One of the reasons for this price reversal must be sought in the unexpected supply of light oil produced from the Bakken formation (Canada and North Dakota).

Table 3.2   A Review of Spot Crude Oil Prices, USD Per Barrel (2000–2011)

Year	Brent Dated	West Texas Intermediate (Cushing)
2000	28.50	30.37
2001	24.44	25.93
2002	25.02	26.16
2003	28.83	31.07
2004	38.27	41.49
2005	54.52	56.59
2006	65.14	66.02
2007	72.39	72.20
2008	97.26	100.06

Year	Brent Dated	West Texas Intermediate (Cushing)
2009	61.67	61.92
2010	79.50	79.45
2011	111.26	95.04

Source: BP Statistical Review of World Energy June 2012.

Table 3.3   Geographical Distribution and Volume of Oil Consumption* (Million Barrels Per Day) 2001–2011

	2001	2003	2005	2007	2009	2011
US	19.6	20.0	20.8	20.7	18.8	18.8
Japan	5.4	5.4	5.3	5.0	4.4	4.4
China	4.9	5.8	6.9	7.8	8.2	9.8
India	2.3	2.4	2.6	2.8	3.3	3.5
Russian Fed.	2.5	2.6	2.6	2.6	2.7	3.0
EU	14.8	14.8	15.0	14.8	14.0	13.5
OECD	48.2	48.7	50.0	49.6	46.0	46.0
World	77.2	79.7	83.9	86.3	84.6	88.0

* Inland consumption plus international aviation, marine bunkers and refinery fuel

Source: BP Statistical Review of World Energy June 2012.

Table 3.3 shows that the consumption of oil is concentrated in the OECD Member States. In 2011 these States accounted for fifty-two per cent of the world oil consumption. Some refineries however wholly or partly export their products, so statistically the country's registered consumption of oil may exceed its domestic or inland consumption. Since 2003, China has joined the ranks of the big consumers, thereby surpassing Japan.

Table 3.4   Comparison of Geographical Distribution of Oil Production and Consumption in 2011(Million Barrels Per Day)

Country/Region	Oil Production	Oil Consumption
US	7.8	18.8
Canada	3.5	2.3
Venezuela	2.7	0.8

Country/Region	Oil Production	Oil Consumption
Brazil	2.2	2.7
Norway	2.0	0.3
The Russian Federation	10.3	3.0
Saudi Arabia	11.2	2.9
Iran	4.3	1.8
Nigeria	2.5	n.a.
Algeria	1.7	0.3
Japan	-	4.4
China	4.1	9.8
India	0.9	3.5
South Korea	-	2.4
OECD	18.5	45.9
OPEC	35.8	n.a.
EU	1.7	13.5
World	83.6	88.0

While accounting for fifty-two per cent of the world oil consumption, the OECD countries' share of world oil production is only twenty-two per cent. To put it differently, seventy-eight per cent of the world oil is at the moment produced outside the OECD area. Of this share, fifty-five per cent is being produced by the Member States of OPEC and forty-five per cent by others (non-OPEC, non-OECD).

Note. The geographical discrepancy between areas of production and consumption requires that oil must be transported over considerable distances. Fortunately, distance is not a problem in a commercial or technical sense since the oil can be transported over sea and the costs of such transport is relatively low compared to the cost of production. Where OPEC-production must be qualified as low cost to very low cost production, it could (if OPEC or one of its Members would be inclined to do so) be supplied to the major consuming areas at very competitive prices. In the past such marketing strategy had once been followed by Saudi Arabia in 1986 causing then a collapse of the international producer's price (see further Chapter 4).

3.4   MARKETS, PRICES AND PRICING SYSTEMS:
           NATURAL GAS

3.4.1   GENERAL

Due to its inherent physical constraints, natural gas cannot at low cost be transported around the world and brought to the places where a demand for gas exists. This lack of low cost mobility has prevented the forming of a global gas market. Instead natural gas is sold to dedicated markets connected with the producing fields by a (long-distance) pipeline or by ocean-going LNG tanker. Against this background, a gas producer sells its gas (that can be either associated natural gas collected from an oil field or non-associated natural gas produced from a gas field) either:

(i) directly to the end-users located in the market concerned; or
(ii) to a gas transport and trading enterprise (a gas company), whose business it is to condition the gas bought from the producer and to transport and deliver the conditioned gas to the final consumer.

In situation (i), it is the gas producer who is responsible for the transportation of its production all the way from the field of production, wherever located, to the intake point of the end-user. In situation (ii), it is the gas company who operates a pipeline system, treatment plant and even one or more underground storage facilities. Such a company may have sales contracts with several customers and several producers and therefore be better able to balance supply and demand and to cope with seasonal fluctuations. In particular, such a balancing act between seasons will be possible if the gas company is in possession of and operates underground storage facilities.

   Except in markets where there truly exists gas to gas competition, the price to be paid by the end-user, which comprise general industry, power stations and the gas companies supplying households, is a formula price derived from and tied to the price actually paid or assumed to have to be paid by said end-users in the local or regional market on a calorific basis for competing or potentially competing fossil fuels, such as low-sulphur coal, low-sulphur fuel oil and heating oil. The prices of these fossil fuels are incorporated in the price formula used in the usually long-term sales contract. In addition the end-users may have to pay eco-taxes. In long-term gas sales contracts, it is stipulated that the sales price is reviewed every six months.

Note 1. Fuel prices incorporated in any gas price formula should exclude any eco-tax levied on those fuels. Even if no eco-tax is applicable but only a simple energy tax, imposing a levy on the heat content of the fuel (or electricity) consumed, the formula prices should exclude such energy tax, provided the same energy tax will be levied on the gas.

Note 2. The maximum price, that a power plant is prepared to pay to a gas producer, is a price that allows this power plant to produce electricity at the same cost as when the plant had to use low-sulphur coal or low-sulphur fuel oil. In comparing gas prices with the prices of competing fuels, due account should be taken of differences in efficiency of converting heat into electricity and the capital and operating costs of the conversion facilities. If for instance by using natural gas instead of coal, a greater heat conversion efficiency can be achieved, say forty-five per cent instead of thirty-five per cent (which means that compared to coal a greater part of the heat content of the gas is converted into electricity), correspondingly more can be paid for the natural gas on a heat content basis. Any imposition of discriminatory eco-taxes to be paid by the power plant will give natural gas a commercial advantage.

Note 3. Households are using fossil fuels for cooking and space heating purposes and are supposed to buy the cheapest fuel on offer. In practice however, coal is no longer a competing fuel in this sector. Its use in households has too many disadvantages where handling and storage are concerned. For the greater convenience, households are prepared to pay a premium in favour of natural gas or heating oil (an oil product). Hence, heating oil and not coal is the competing or potentially competing fossil fuel. Therefore, the price charged by the gas company to households for their natural gas deliveries must stay at the same level as the price which is charged or potentially could be charged to households for heating oil. In contrast to the situation where natural gas is sold to power plants, no further adjustment to the said price level is required in as much as there are no significant differences between heating oil and natural gas in relation to the efficiency of heat conversion. Only on account of any imposition of discriminatory eco-taxes would preference be given to the use of natural gas.

Note 4. If the natural gas producer sells its gas to the chemical industry or to the refineries for conversion or transformation into chemical products or fuels the price paid by the plant is derived from the price that is paid in the market for the manufactured products (e.g., chemicals, transport fuels, methanol, hydrogen, etc.).

Note 5. If a gas producer does not sell directly to the end-user but to a gas company, the gas producer's price is derived from the price received by the said gas company from its customers. Between the two prices, there will exist a difference representing the capital and operating costs incurred by the gas company in conditioning and distributing the gas among its customers plus a suitable fee for off take services rendered, such as utilizing underground storage capacity.

Table 3.5   *Geographical Distribution and Volume of Natural Gas Consumption (Billion Cubic Metres) (2001–2011)*

	2001	*2003*	*2005*	*2007*	*2009*	*2011*
US	630	631	623	654	649	690
Canada	88	98	98	96	95	105
Mexico	42	50	56	63	66	69
Australia	22	22	22	27	25	26
Japan	74	80	79	90	87	105
China	27	34	47	70	89	131
Asia Pacific	308	351	398	458	497	591
Russian Federation	366	385	400	422	390	425
EU	452	474	495	482	460	448
OECD	1341	1394	1426	1477	1451	1535
World	2454	2599	2767	2930	2931	3223

Source: BP Statistical Review of World Energy June 2012.

Table 3.6   *Comparison of the Geographical Distribution of Natural Gas Production and Consumption in 2011 (Billion Cubic Metres)*

Country/Region	*Production*	*Consumption*
US	651	690
Canada	160	105
Total North America	864	864
The Russian Federation	607	425
Total Middle East	526	403
China	102	131
Japan	-	105
India	46	61
Asia Pacific	479	591
EU	155	448
OECD	1168	1535
World	3276	3223

The major areas of consumption of natural gas are the North American region, the European Union, the Russian Federation and Asia Pacific (pre-dominantly China and Japan). As shown on Table 3.6 above, the North American region has in 2011 become self-sufficient in natural gas, i.e., indigenous production (864 bcm) is neatly in balance with the indigenous consumption (864 bcm). Within this region, the US is the largest consumer and producer. In 2011 there still was a production shortfall which had to be covered by imports mainly from Mexico and Canada. In the forthcoming years US gas production will increase rapidly as a result of the spectacular development of the production of shale gas. This may lead to an increase of domestic demand (e.g., replacing coal as fuel for the power plants), unless the possibilities of the export of the surplus is being considered.

In the EU, indigenous natural gas production falls far short of satisfying demand. About 34.6 per cent of consumption is covered. The shortfall is made up by importing natural gas by pipeline from Norway and the Russian Federation and by LNG tanker from Algeria, Libya, Nigeria and Qatar.

The Russian Federation is an important consumer country itself, but its current gas production being supported by favourable gas prices is expanding steadily, making enough room for export to the EU by various long-distance pipelines e.g., Nordstream. Furthermore LNG is being shipped to Japan.

Asia Pacific taken as a region consumes more gas as it produces and since a few years the existing shortfall appears to be widening. Within the region, China has surpassed Japan as the biggest gas consumer. Having no indigenous production at all, Japan needs to import gas from gas-exporting countries elsewhere in the region such as Indonesia, Brunei, Malaysia, Australia and the Russian Federation, but also from Qatar. China imports gas mainly from Qatar and Australia. Asia Pacific is also the region in which the natural gas trade involves transportation exclusively by LNG tanker. The LNG trade in this region is dictated by the respective geographical locations of the importing and exporting countries involved and by the interregional distances that have to be coped with.

Table 3.7   Recent and Current Natural Gas Prices 2009–2011
(USD per Million Btu*)

	LNG Japan cif	Average German Import Price
2009	9.06	8.52
2010	10.91	8.01
2011	14.73	10.61

*1 million Btu is the calorific equivalent of 28 cubic metres NG or 0.025 tonnes oil.

3.4.2   MARKETING AND USE OF ASSOCIATED NATURAL GAS

A geographical discrepancy exists between the places of final gas consumption, the location of the producing fields and the gas reserves (the
places of future gas production). In contrast to oil, the geographical
mismatch in the case of natural gas is not easily corrected or overcome by
shipping or piping the natural gas around the world: the inherent physical
constraints of natural gas make this impossible. In contrast to non-
associated gas fields which may be put on hold in anticipation of improved
marketing opportunities and the solving of the transportation problems,
associated gas, which is unavoidably produced in the oil fields, has to be
flared, i.e., burned off in the field, if the gas cannot be utilized in a plant in
the vicinity of the oil field concerned, or re-injected either into the original
reservoir or into another reservoir for one purpose or another. Despite the
recent increase of gas prices, such flaring still takes place in the oil fields
of Nigeria, Siberia and the Middle East. Even after extraction of NGLs,
which is a commercially attractive possibility if the associated gas happens
to be a rich or wet gas, flaring of the remaining gas must still be considered
to be a regrettable waste of a valuable natural resource.

Note. Frequently applied solutions envisage the building of a gas-fired power
station in combination with an aluminium smelter or a water-desalination plant. In
all such cases, the associated natural gas can be supplied at the cost of no more
than that of collecting the gas in the oil field. Associated gas (and non-associated
gas for that matter) may also be converted into liquids in special GTL processing
plant in order to facilitate its transportation (in the form of liquids) to a suitable
market. Such transportation is easier and less expensive than the transportation of
the natural gas itself. In this situation, the producer's gas price is derived from the
price that is paid in the end-market for the liquids. A drawback of any conversion
is that the conversion process has a relatively low efficiency in as much as more
than fifty per cent of the heat content of the natural gas will be lost thereby.

3.5   TAXES

3.5.1   EXPORT DUTIES

An export duty is a duty that is levied on the value of the exported production at the port of export. Unless such a tax is levied on all major export crudes, in which case the global producer price will be raised by the amount of the tax, the cost of the tax must be absorbed by the producer.

3.5.2   IMPORT DUTIES

Import duty is a duty that is levied on the value of the imported oil at the port of import. Such duty has to be paid by the refinery that is importing the oil. The main purpose of an import duty is to protect domestic oil producers, which are bound to sell their production to an inland refinery and get at most paid a price derived from the prices paid by the refinery for imported crude oils after adjustments on account of differences in quality and gravity. If such price turns out to be too low, i.e., if and when world market prices show a tendency to fall below the level at which the domestic producer could still operate commercially, the government of the importing country may contemplate to impose an import duty. Such a measure is a powerful fiscal instrument and had been contemplated by the US government in 1986, at the time OPEC was pursuing a 'flooding-the-market' strategy which caused the world market oil price to tumble.

3.6   ALTERNATIVES FOR OIL PRODUCTS AND NATURAL GAS

3.6.1   INTRODUCTION

Oil products and natural gas have over the decades become essential ingredients for a satisfactory performance of the world economy. In fact, the latter has become completely dependent on their availability. Already for this reason alone, it is opportune to search for or develop other products (hereinafter referred to as alternative products or alternatives) that can take over the functions of oil products and natural gas if for one reason or another oil and/or gas cannot be made available. In this situation coal would be the perfect alternative because in theory and without regard to cost coal (products) can replace oil (products) and natural in all sectors of the economy where currently the latter are used. Even as feedstock for the refineries as well as feedstock for the petrochemical industry, coal can replace both oil and natural gas. Coal can at a cost also replace natural gas as feedstock for manufacturing diesel oil and hydrogen.

Note 1. Starting point for both last mentioned processes is the gasification of the coal. In this process a mixture of carbon monoxide (CO) and hydrogen referred to as syngas is produced. If syngas is further treated with steam, the CO component is converted into hydrogen and CO_2. After removal of the latter, the syngas will then have been completely transformed into hydrogen. In the next step hydrogen can be delivered as such to the end-user (see further in this Chapter). But the syngas can also be further processed for manufacturing hydrocarbons which in turn can be refined into diesel oil, a process that is referred to as the Coal-To-Liquids (CTL) process, also known as the GTL process if methane forms the base material for generating syngas.

Note 2. CTL (or GTL for that matter) involves a catalytic conversion process which is a further development of the Fischer-Tropsch process invented in 1925. In the past the Fischer-Tropsch hydrocarbon synthesis using coal as base material yielded poor quality road transport fuel due to imperfect catalysts and had only found large scale application in Germany during the Second World War and in South Africa during the period that this country was subjected to an oil embargo.

When used in the form as delivered from the coal mine, coal can replace oil products and natural gas as fuel in power plants, in industrial plants for steam generation and even in households for space heating. Furthermore, coal has the advantage of being abundantly available. Its proved reserves are large and geographically speaking widely spread which makes coal less risky from a geopolitical point of view (see Chapter 2). Moreover the costs of production are reasonable in particular when open pit mining is possible. Coal can also be shipped at a moderate cost and can thus be exported at a very competitive price when compared to today's prices of exported oil. But there are drawbacks. Handling, storage and transportation of coal are cumbersome and compare in these respects unfavourably with oil and natural gas, except of course when coal's destination is the power station. But its most prominent drawback and the one which makes coal not the perfect alternative is the generation of CO_2, that follows from using coal as fuel or when coal is gasified. When compared with oil products and natural gas, coal generates (per unit of heat produced) respectively twenty-five per cent and seventy-five per cent more CO_2. In theory and at great cost this drawback can be eliminated by installing at the power plant facilities for the capture and underground storage of CO_2 (CCS-facilities), so as to prevent the CO_2 that is generated from being emitted into the atmosphere. The future of coal and its usefulness to (at least partly) replace oil and natural gas may depend on to what extent these measures prove to be practical and economically justified.

However, looking for alternatives other than coal could become necessary if it is felt that the use of all fossil fuels, coal as well as oil products and gas, is no longer acceptable in the light of increasing atmospheric concentration of CO_2, or if any of such alternatives might offer a real technological advantage over the use of oil products or natural gas.

3.6.2　　　　A REVIEW OF ALTERNATIVES OTHER THAN COAL

3.6.2.1　　　Biomass

Biomass (vegetable material) can be described as a kind of proto-coal, a material that following deep burial and after being exposed to high temperatures and pressure will turn into coal. If not left undisturbed, i.e., if biomass is used as fuel the carbon contained therein would turn into CO_2. This means that in the burning process the carbon which the vegetation perhaps over many years had removed from the atmosphere is returned to it at an instant. If, however, the biomass was allowed to be buried and many million years later to become coal then if that coal, when coming within reach from the surface, would be used as fuel and be burned the same amount of CO_2 would be released into the atmosphere, albeit many million years later.

Biomass is seen and treated as coal and solely or mixed with coal serve the same purposes, i.e., the generation of heat and electricity. Like coal, biomass can be gasified and converted into syngas, which can further be processed as described above in relation to coal. Some types of biomass can be converted into ethanol and diesel oil (see hereinafter). The main drawback is its huge water content.

3.6.2.2　　　Non-fossil Electricity

Non-fossil electricity is electricity that is generated by non-fossil energy sources such as hydropower in various forms, nuclear fission energy and, on a much smaller, local or even regional scale, biomass, wind turbines, photovoltaics, solar power and high temperature geothermal energy (the latter plus hydropower collectively referred to as renewables). With exception of biomass, all renewables can also be described as non-carbon energy sources.

In 2010, global power generation amounted to 21,408 TWh divided between non-fossil electricity and fossil electricity in a 33/67 proportion.

Non-fossil electricity is generated by nuclear fission energy (thirteen per cent), hydroelectric (sixteen per cent) and by the other renewables (four per cent). Fossil electricity is generated by coal (forty-one per cent), oil (five per cent) and natural gas (twenty-one per cent). From these figures, the conclusion can be drawn that if non-fossil electricity were ever to replace fossil electricity (and that seems at the moment the only possibility to push back the generation of CO_2), the capacity of its energy sources will have to be expanded in a drastic manner.

At the moment, it appears that a lack of suitable river sites prevents any large scale expansion of the currently established capacity of hydroelectric. Lack of sufficient space seems to hinder the installation of facilities needed for the other renewables. If a return to coal is not wanted, the generation of large scale non-fossil electricity appears to become a matter of expanding the capacity of nuclear fission energy (with a current market share of thirteen per cent). When such expansion takes place it will be at the expense of coal, the latter being the biggest contributor to CO_2 generation. It cannot be denied that a maximum reduction of CO_2-emissions could be achieved if electricity would exclusively be generated in nuclear power stations but a mix of 80/20 with natural gas would also be very effective for getting CO_2-emissions under control (see Chapter 4 for further discussion).

3.6.2.3   Alternative Fuels for Road Transport

In 2011, the transport sector consumed 46 million barrels per day, which is slightly more than one half of the total world oil consumption in that year (88.0 million barrels per day).Within this sector road transport accounted for 35 million barrels per day. Other transport such as aviation and shipping made up the rest (11.0 million barrels per day). Road transport comprises passenger light duty vehicles (PLDVs) and road freight (trucks). Currently there are 850 million PLDVs and 50 million trucks on the road consuming 22 million barrels per day and 13 million barrels per day respectively.

Currently available alternative fuels for road transport are electricity, biofuels and hydrogen.

Note with reference to electricity. When PLDVs are equipped with an electric motor instead of an internal combustion engine, electricity functions as an alternative transport fuel. The electricity is stored on board of the car in batteries, which from time to time have to be reloaded. Reloading is done by connecting the batteries to the electric grid. While the electric battery car itself does not emit any CO_2 (or any other harmful exhaust gases, such as NOx and SO_2) – and should therefore be ideally suited to operate within urban areas – the overall CO_2-emission associated with using the car depends on the way the power station that supplies the electricity to the grid is being fuelled. If the power station is fuelled by nuclear fission energy, hydropower or other renewables the total CO_2 emission related to the use of an electric battery car is zero. If fossil fuels are energizing the power station then the total CO_2-emission depends on whether coal, oil or gas is supplied.

Note with reference to ethanol and biodiesel. At the moment, two types of biofuel are being manufactured: ethanol and biodiesel. Ethanol (C_2H_5OH) can be blended up to high percentages (eighty-five per cent) with gasoline, but at a higher percentage than thirty per cent, the car engine has to be adjusted. Ethanol is made from corn, wheat and barley (US and other OECD countries) or from sugar cane (Brazil). For some time, research is focused on the possibility to produce ethanol from ligno-cellulosic crops such as eucalyptus, poplar or willow trees and grasses or from waste (e.g., straw). This so-called second generation ethanol should ideally replace corn-, wheat- and barley-based ethanol considering the many environmental and societal drawbacks associated with its use as mentioned above. Biodiesel is comparable with conventional diesel oil and makes it an attractive blending component. Biodiesel is produced mainly from oil-seed crops, including rapeseed, palm oil and sunflowers.

Note with reference to hydrogen. Hydrogen is presently used as rocket fuel and in the refineries for the upgrading of hydrocarbons and for the removal of sulphur from the heavy fractions of the distillation process. However in the context of government policy to reduce CO_2-emissions in the transport sector, the option of using hydrogen as fuel for car engines is still kept open. In this option, hydrogen can be used in two ways: either directly fuelling the car engine in substitution of gasoline or diesel oil (whereby the internal combustion principle can be maintained), or through the intermediary of a fuel cell supplying electricity to an electric motor. Due to its inherent physical constraints, i.e., its low energy density, hydrogen in its gaseous state must during transportation to the filling stations kept under high-pressure. If the car is equipped with a fuel cell there should also be present in the car a tank that is filled with metal hybrides. In these metal hybrides, the gas can be stored at a pressure much lower than the pipeline pressure. When hydrogen is used as fuel (the other option) it must be stored in the car in its liquid state, whereby the hydrogen must be cooled to temperatures below minus 253 degrees Celsius which in turn requires a very special tank. It is very doubtful whether a motor car that is equipped for the use of hydrogen in its gaseous or liquid state can ever satisfy the standard safety regulations and pass any crash tests, not to speak of the difficulties that the average car driver will face when trying to fill up the hydrogen storage devices of his car.

Whether hydrogen is directly or indirectly fuelling cars, in both instances no CO_2 is generated and thus no danger of an emission of CO_2. Whether in the total picture no CO_2 is generated depends on the way in which hydrogen itself is manufactured. Hydrogen can be produced in many ways. The most common way is to produce hydrogen from methane (extracted from natural gas). Hydrogen can also be produced from syngas that in turn is obtained from the gasification of coal or biomass. In both instances CO_2 is produced as a by-product. Finally, hydrogen can be manufactured in a direct manner by the electrolysis of water. Whether or not CO_2 is generated in this process depends on the feedstock intake of the powerstation that is supplying the electricity needed for the electrolysis (see discussion above).

3.7   MARKET OUTLOOK

3.7.1   INTRODUCTION

To assess the future development of the demand for oil and gas, use has been made of one of the scenarios described in *World Energy Outlook 2012*. The selected scenario is referred to as the *New Policies Scenario* and covers the period up to 2035. This scenario assumes cautious implementation of presently stated national targets to reduce greenhouse-gas emissions which seems for the moment at least to form a plausible basis for making estimates and projections. Moreover it seems hardly likely that even in case in the course of time more stringent measures to combat CO_2-emissions are taken, the latter will be directed at the transport sector. To the contrary, it seems only realistic to assume a further growth of oil consumption as projected in the scenario in view of the ever growing number of cars, trucks, planes and ships which to a large extent remain fuelled by oil products. In this context is projected that in 2035 1.7 billion PLDVs and 90 million trucks will be on the road.

The same expectation regarding continuing growth of consumption applies to gas: in particular its consumption in the power generation sector is projected to grow as greenhouse reduction policies give preference to gas for fuelling power stations. If more stringent measures are adopted this will only lead to an increased demand for gas.

Underlying the selected scenario is the projection of the world population growth. The latter determines in first instance the world primary energy consumption, including that of oil and natural gas. According to projections by the United Nations (UNPD, 2011) global population is projected to grow from an estimated 6.8 billion in 2010 to 8.6 billion in 2035.

3.7.2   MARKET OUTLOOK: OIL

Table 3.8   Projected Oil Consumption in the New Policies Scenario (Million Barrels Per Day)

	2015	2020	2030	2035	CAAGR* 2011–2035
North America	22.0	21.2	18.6	17.5	-1.0%
Europe	12.0	11.4	10.4	10.0	-1.0%
Russia	3.2	3.2	3.4	3.5	0.5%
China	11.0	12.7	14.7	15.1	2.2%
India	3.8	4.3	6.2	7.5	3.3%
Japan	4.1	3.7	3.2	3.1	-1.4%
Middle East	7.5	8.1	8.9	9.4	1.4%
World	91.6	94.2	97.7	99.7	0.6%

Source: World Energy Outlook 2012.

* Compound Average Annual Growth Rate.

There is no doubt that production is capable to satisfy the projected consumption. This means that as of the end of 2011 up to and including 2035, 800 billion barrels is projected to have been produced. This leaves about 5100 billion barrels available for the years after 2035, i.e., enough for 140 years of production at an annual rate of 100 million barrels per day.

3.7.3   MARKET OUTLOOK: NATURAL GAS

Table 3.9   Projected Natural Gas Consumption in the New Policies Scenario (Billion Cubic Metres)

	2015	2025	2035	CAAGR* 2010–2035
North America	898	962	1032	0.8%
Europe	550	619	669	0.7%
Russia	448	508	549	0.7%
China	195	390	544	6.6%
India	75	116	178	4.2%
Japan	120	118	123	0.7%

	2015	2025	2035	CAAGR* 2010–2035
Middle East	437	538	640	2.1%
World	3616	4268	4955	1.6%

* Compound Average Annual Growth Rate.

Source: World Energy Outlook 2012.

There is no doubt that production is capable of satisfying the projected consumption. This means that as of end 2011 and up to and including 2035, 98 tcm is projected to have been produced. This leaves about 700 tcm available for the years after 2035, i.e., enough for 140 years of production at an annual rate of 5.0 tcm.

Chapter 4

Government Petroleum Policies

4.1 INTRODUCTION

From the start of the industrial revolution (1750) till today, the primary energy demands of the world economy have been met exclusively or to a large extent by coal, oil and natural gas. First of all came coal (King Coal), later it was joined and even in some sectors partly replaced by oil and natural gas. Somewhat later nuclear fission energy and hydroelectric arrived on the energy scene and made their modest contributions in the power sector. Statistics show that in 2011 coal, oil and natural gas jointly satisfied 87 per cent of the world primary energy consumption (totalling 10.7 billion toe), whereas nuclear energy and hydroelectric contributed 4.9 per cent and 6.4 per cent respectively. Renewables other than hydro counted for 1.6 per cent. Expressed in volumes, oil's contribution amounted to 4.0 billion tonnes and that of natural gas 2.9 billion toe. These figures make abundantly clear that next to coal, oil and natural gas are of vital importance for the functioning of world economy.

Furthermore, as convincingly has been demonstrated in Chapter 3 the remaining recoverable oil and gas reserves (5,871 billion barrels and 790 tcm respectively) are sufficiently large to cover world consumption at present levels far beyond the end of the twenty-first century. As far as coal is concerned its proven reserves at end 2011 (573 billion toe) are on their own sufficient to cover present day's coal consumption for 155 years. Its remaining reserves are far bigger.

It is against this background of economic importance and almost unlimited global availability that governments develop and pursue petroleum policies. In first instance, such policies will be based on their country's own situation regarding petroleum consumption, access to and security of supplies and possible domestic production. In second instance, these national interest policies will be subordinated to the objectives and targets agreed or accepted in the context of a Global Climate Agreement.

4.2   OBJECTIVES OF GOVERNMENT PETROLEUM POLICIES

The primary objectives of a national petroleum policy can briefly be summarized as follows:

   (i) to search for, develop and produce domestic petroleum resources. If successful, the secondary objectives listed herein below will apply;
  (ii) to establish state-owned companies in order to get access to petroleum resources outside the national territory;
 (iii) to stimulate energy saving and an efficient use of energy in order to reduce consumption of energy in general, but including that of petroleum;
  (iv) to aid research into and the development of suitable fossil fuel alternatives in order to reduce dependency on foreign suppliers;
   (v) to make choices between different sources of imported energy, for the purpose of diversification and minimizing geopolitical risks; and
  (vi) to stimulate fuel switching and to give preference to oil, oil products and natural gas over coal in fuelling thermal power plants in order to increase energy transformation efficiency.

Note concerning (ii). France and Italy established in 1953 their respective state-owned companies Entreprise de Recherches et d'Activités Pétrolières (ERAP) and its subsidiary Société Nationale ELF Aquitaine and Ente Nazionale Idrocarburi (ENI) and its subsidiary Agip. Both oil groups were meant to secure access to petroleum resources outside the territory of their respective countries and that in competition with the private sector. The said groups were later privatized. Japan pursued the same policy and established state-owned Japan National Oil Corporation (JNOC). JNOC is expected to acquire petroleum rights in foreign countries in competition or preferably in cooperation with foreign oil groups.

If the search for domestic petroleum resources is successful the following secondary objectives will be pursued:

   (i) institution building;
  (ii) putting a petroleum law and regulations in place;
 (iii) becoming party to international conventions, multilateral or bilateral treaties relating to petroleum operations;

(iv) imposing import duties or quantitative import restrictions on imported oil if needed to protect domestic oil production against low-priced imports;

(v) petroleum taxation;

(vi) state participation in petroleum operations;

(vii) quaranteeing favourable treatment of foreign investments in domestic production;

(viii) to seek cooperation in petroleum matters with other interested governments within the framework of a formal Organization;

(ix) fulfilling international obligations which derive from the international conventions or treaties to which the State has become a party.

With reference to (iv). When domestic production cannot compete with low-priced imports it can be made less expensive by fiscal and/or administrative measures (e.g., abolishing royalty and/or lowering of the rate of the applicable income tax). But domestic production can also be protected against low-priced imports by imposing import duties or quantitative restrictions on imports. Best known example in this respect is the US Mandatory Oil Import Control Program imposed in 1958 and meant at the time to protect the US domestic oil producers against the low-priced imports from the Middle East Gulf area. It should be added that in 1986, when as the result of the 'flooding-of-the-market'-strategy pursued by Saudi Arabia, the world market oil price dropped to about USD 10 per barrel, the US Bush-Administration seriously considered the option to introduce an import duty in order to protect the high cost US domestic production. During the brief period of declining world market prices (1997–2000), which decline started in the beginning of 1997 and reached for the time being its lowest level (viz. USD 10 per barrel) in December 1998, high cost domestic producers everywhere immediately proposed to their respective governments that fiscal burdens be alleviated, e.g., by abolishing royalty, by relaxation of depreciation rules and by lowering of the rate of the applicable income tax(es).

With reference to (vi). Often used arguments in favour of participation by a state entity in petroleum rights and operations are profitability and control or a combination of the two. But even if domestic operations are not likely to be or become profitable, the government concerned may still wish that in the public interest those petroleum operations (in particular exploration) are carried out and designate a state entity for this purpose. As to control, a government may feel that a state entity is needed in order to:

    (a) share in the decision making process, in particular concerning development planning and investments in development;

    (b) gain first-hand experience with the technical, administrative and commercial aspects of petroleum operations; and

    (c) supervise the implementation by the licensee/contractor of all non-technical and non-fiscal provisions of the authorization, among which national interest provisions, such as the employment and training of nationals, the use in the operations of locally manufactured products and of the goods and services of local suppliers.

Note. In the United Kingdom a state oil corporation was established under the Petroleum and Submarine Pipe-lines Act 1975. The corporation was named the British National Oil Corporation (BNOC). The new corporation was authorized in compliance with the directions of the Secretary of State to explore for and obtain petroleum in any part of the world. BNOC was also designated as the official government advisor in petroleum affairs and was given a preferential position in acquiring any license interest that was intended to be transferred. Under the Oil and Pipelines Act 1985, the existence of BNOC was terminated. In Norway, a wholly state-owned company, *Den Norske Stats Oljeselskap* (Statoil) was established on 14 July 1972. In 2001/2004 Statoil became partly privatized and changed its name to Statoil ASA. Instead, a new wholly state-owned company, Petoro A.S., was established on 9 May 2001. The latter's purpose is to manage the State Direct Financial Interest (SDFI) in licenses, a task that Statoil no longer could fulfil because of its part-privatization. In 2007 Statoil merged with Norsk Hydro in 67.3/32.7 proportion. The new company, initially named StaoilHydro, is sixty-seven per cent owned by the Norwegian State, operates world-wide. In 2009 the company returned to its original name of Statoil ASA. In the Russian Federation, state-owned or state controlled companies such as Rosneft (oil) and Gazprom (gas) have been established which also operate outside the territory of the Federation. Other examples of state-owned companies with outside interests and activities are Petronas (Malaysia), China's CNOOC and the state-owned companies of Kuwait (Kuwait Petroleum) and Saudi Arabia (Saudi Aramco) (see further Chapters 2 and 6).

With reference to (viii). The first such Organization and one which was solely dedicated to petroleum matters was the Organization of Petroleum Exporting Countries (OPEC). This Organization was founded on 1 September 1960 by five major oil exporting States, for the stated purpose of coordinating and unifying their petroleum policies and of determining the best means of safeguarding their interests individually, as well as collectively (see further hereinafter).

In 1961 West-European countries formed the Organisation of Economic Co-operation and Development (OECD), the successor of the in 1947 established Organisation for European Economic Cooperation (OEEC). This new Organization comprises thirty free market economies among which the Member States of the former OEEC, the US, Canada, Australia, Japan and later on also South Korea. On 15 November 1974, in a direct reaction and response to the oil crisis of 1973/1974 which was triggered by the total or gradual oil embargo imposed by the Arab Member States of OPEC against the United States and some West-European countries, the OECD founded the International Energy Agency (IEA) and adopted three days later the International Energy Program (IEP).

More broadly based economic cooperation but also including petroleum matters was intended by the European Economic Community (EEC) founded by the Treaty 'Establishing a European Economic Community' signed in Rome on 25 March 1957, effective date 1 January 1958. Much later the EEC was succeeded by the European Community (EC), which was created by the Treaty on the European Union (EU) as one of the three pillars envisaged for this Union (7 February 1992).

Apart from the countries that have joined one of the aforementioned Organizations (OPEC, OECD, EU), there are many other countries (non-OECD, non-OPEC) which on their own and independent from any interstate organization are promoting the search for and the development of their domestic petroleum potential. To this non-organized group belong most of the developing countries but also countries with an economy in transition such as Mexico, Brazil, Russian Federation, India and China. Last mentioned countries possess a viable petroleum industry, but so far only the Russian Federation succeeded to become an important oil and gas exporting country.

4.3   CLIMATE CHANGE RELATED ADJUSTMENTS TO GOVERNMENT PETROLEUM POLICIES

As noted in Chapter 2 the use of fossil fuels has a serious and unavoidable drawback: when being burned or combusted CO_2 is being produced, in such a way that all and any carbon contained in the fossil fuel concerned is turned into CO_2, which then, if not captured and stored away will disappear into the atmosphere.

In the 1990s, the international community under guidance of the United Nations became aware of the fact that said emissions were responsible for the global warming that was going on and that this global warming was projected to continue and reach unacceptable rates if the emission of CO_2 would not be soon curtailed in one way or another. This awareness and concern was shared by most governments but only the Member States of the OECD had been prepared to give those concerns concrete form in the Protocol (to the UN Framework Convention on Climate Change) signed in December 1997 in Kyoto, Japan (Kyoto Protocol). The latter have shown to be prepared to adjust their petroleum policy in such a way that it is no longer solely focused on matters of national interest, but will also take into account any commitment accepted or any pledge made under or in connection with any now existing or future global Climate Agreement. The options open to committed governments are summarized hereinafter.

4.4   UN CLIMATE CONFERENCES, IPCC'S ASSESSMENT REPORTS AND THE KYOTO PROTOCOL

4.4.1   WORLD CLIMATE CONFERENCE (FEBRUARY 1979)

At the level of the UN, serious interest in the possibility of climatic problems resulting from the burning and the combustion of fossil fuels can be traced back to the World Climate Conference convened by the UN World Meteorological Organization (WMO) in February 1979. At this Conference the following statement was issued.

The causes of climatic variations become better understood, but uncertainty exists about many of them and their relative importance. Nevertheless, we can say with some confidence that the burning of fossil fuels, deforestation, and changes in land use have increased the amount of carbon dioxide in the atmosphere by about 15 per cent during the last century and is at present increasing at about 0.4 per cent per year ... It is possible that some effects on a regional and global scale may become detectable before the end of this century and become significant before the middle of the next century. This time scale is similar to that required to redirect, if necessary, the operation of many aspects of the world economy, including agriculture and the production of energy.

In May 1979, the Congress of the WMO approved the World Climate Programme (WCP) which consisted of four components, viz. Climate Data, Climate Applications, Climate Research and the Climate Impact Studies Programme for which the UN Environmental Programme (UNEP) took the responsibility. The next step was taken nine years later, in 1988, when WMO and the UNEP jointly established a new institution named the Intergovernmental Panel on Climate Change (IPCC). The panel formed three Working Groups, namely, I. Scientific Assessment of Climate Change; II. (Economic/Social) Impacts of Climate Change; and III. (Government) Policy Response to Climate Change. Working Group I (WG I) is charged with the task of reporting every six years on the latest scientific insights concerning global warming and its consequences for sea level rise and climate change. WG I issued its Fourth Assessment Report in February 2007. The next Report will appear in 2014.

4.4.2   THE IPCC WG I FIRST ASSESSMENT REPORT (1990)

The IPCC WG I's First Assessment Report was issued in the summer of 1990 in preparation of the Second World Climate Conference held later in the year. In this report, the Working Group gave as its best estimate that by the year 2100 the atmospheric concentration of CO_2 would have risen to twice the pre-industrial level (which would entail a rise to about 550 ppm) and the average temperature to 3.5 degrees Celsius compared to the pre-industrial level. This meant that an additional rise of 3 degrees Celsius by the year 2100 was foreseen considering the 0.5 degrees Celsius increase that already had taken place since the industrial use of the fossil fuels. As to the sea level, a rise of 45 centimetres was predicted.

4.4.3   THE SECOND WORLD CLIMATE CONFERENCE (1990)

Against the background of WG I's First Assessment Report, the Second World Climate Conference convened in Geneva (6–7 November 1990). One hundred and thirty-seven countries took part therein. Just a few days before, on 29 October 1990, the joint Energy/Environment Council of the EC had decided to take actions aiming at reaching stabilization of the total CO_2 emissions by 2000 at 1990 level in the Community as a whole. This initiative of the EC was noted and welcomed by the participants and the Final Declaration of the Conference made reference to it. Since then, the year 1990 became the reference year for formulating CO_2 emission policies. The most important statements contained in the Final Declaration were the following:

> 1. We, the Ministers and other representatives from 137 countries and from the European Communities, meeting in Geneva from 6 to 7 November 1990 at the Second World Climate Conference, declare as follows:
>
> 2. We note that while climate has varied in the past and there is still a large degree of scientific uncertainty, the rate of climate change predicted by the Intergovernmental Panel on Change (IPCC) to occur over the next century is unprecedented. This is due mainly to the continuing accumulation of greenhouse gases, resulting

from a host of human activities since the industrial revolution, hitherto particularly in developed countries. The potential impact of such climate change could pose an environmental threat of an up to now unknown magnitude; and could jeopardize the social and economic development of some areas. It could even threaten survival in some small island states and in low-lying coastal, arid and semi-arid areas.

5. Recognizing that climate change is a global problem of unique character, we consider that a global response … must be decided and implemented without further delay based on the best available knowledge such as that resulting from the IPCC assessment. Recognizing further that the principle of equity and the common but differentiated responsibilities of countries should be the basis of any global response to climate change, developed countries must take the lead. They must all commit themselves to actions to reduce their major contribution to the global net emissions and enter into and strengthen cooperation with developing countries to enable them to adequately address climate change without hindering their national developments goals and objectives.

7. Where there are threats of serious or irreversible damage, lack of full scientific certainty should not be used as a reason for postponing cost-effective measures to prevent such environmental degradation.

8. The potentially serious consequences of climate change, including the risk for survival in low-lying and other small island States and in some low-lying coastal, and arid and semi-arid areas of the world, give sufficient reasons to begin by adopting response strategies even in the face of significant uncertainties. Such response strategies include phasing out the production and use of GFCs, efficiency improvements and conservation in energy supply and use, appropriate measures in the transport sector, sustainable forest management, afforestation schemes … proper land use planning, the use of safe and cleaner energy sources with lower or no emissions of carbon dioxide, methane, nitrous oxide and other greenhouse gases and ozone precursors, paying special attention to new and renewable sources.

10. We agree that the ultimate global objective should be to stabilize greenhouse gas concentrations at a level that would prevent dangerous anthropogenic interference with climate.

12. Taking into account that the developed world is responsible for about 3/4 of all emissions of greenhouse gases, we welcome the decisions and commitments undertaken by the European Community (EC) with its Member States, Australia, Japan, Canada and other developed countries to take actions aimed at stabilizing their emissions of CO_2, or CO_2 and other greenhouse gases not controlled by the Montreal Protocol, by the year 2000 in general at 1990 level, yet recognizing the differences in approach and in starting point in the formulation of the above targets.

16. The specific difficulties of those countries, particularly developing countries, whose economies are highly dependent on fossil fuel production and exportation, as a consequence of action taken on limiting greenhouse gas emissions, should be taken into account.

28. We call for negotiations on a framework convention on climate change to begin without delay after a decision is taken by the 45th Session of the General Assembly of the UN. We urge all countries and regional economic integration organizations to join in these negotiations and recognize that it is highly desirable that an effective framework convention on climate change, containing appropriate commitments, and any related instruments as might be agreed upon on the basis of consensus, be signed in Rio de Janeiro during the UN Conference on Environment and Development.

29. We reaffirm our wish that this convention contain real commitments by the international community.

4.4.4   THE ESTABLISHMENT OF THE UN FRAMEWORK CONVENTION ON CLIMATE CHANGE (1992)

The EC CO_2 stabilization policy, referred to in the Final Declaration, was confirmed by the joint Energy/Environment Council on 13 December 1991 and was put forward as a proposal for global implementation at the UN Conference held in 1992 in Rio de Janeiro. At this conference, the aimed for UN Framework Convention on Climate Change was adopted. According to this convention, it was the intention to convene regularly climate conferences to monitor progress made and review measures taken in reducing the emission greenhouse gases. Annex I Parties to the Framework Convention, comprising the developed countries, committed themselves to adopting policies and measures to return greenhouse gas emissions to their 1990 levels by the year 2000.

Meanwhile the US government became also involved in the CO_2 debate. Its interest in the matter dates from 1989 in which year a meeting of experts was convened by the US President George Bush in Washington to discuss the alleged environmental risk of CO_2 emissions. A few years later, in response to the Framework Convention on Climate Change, his successor, US President Bill Clinton, declared on 21 April 1993 (Earth Day) as follows:

We must take the lead in addressing the challenge of global warming that could make our planet and its climate less hospitable to human life. Today, I reaffirm my personal, and announce our nation's commitment to reducing our emissions of greenhouse gases to their 1990 levels by the year 2000. I am instructing my administration to produce a cost effective plan ... that can continue the trend of reduced emissions. This must be a clarion call, not for more bureaucracy or regulation or unnecessary costs, but instead for American ingenuity and creativity, to produce the best and most energy-efficient technologies.

The first meeting of the Conference of the Parties to the UN Framework Convention took place in 1995 in Berlin. At this meeting, the conclusion (referred to as the Berlin Mandate) was reached that the commitments made by the Annex I Parties would not be sufficient to meet the stated objectives and that further commitments beyond the year 2000 were needed.

4.4.5   THE IPCC WG I'S SECOND ASSESSMENT REPORT (1995)

In the same year (1995), the IPCC WG I issued its Second Assessment Report. In this report, the Working Group adjusted the lower limits of its forecasts slightly downwards. The average temperature was on this occasion estimated further to increase (i.e., in addition to the observed increase of 0.5 degrees Celsius over the past 100 years) by between 1 and 3.5 degrees Celsius, if the atmospheric concentration of CO_2 were to rise to about twice its pre-industrial level. Sea level rise was put between 15 and 95 centimetres. The panel declared to be aware of the fact that there were many uncertainties and many factors that limited its ability to project and detect future climate change. As to the observed 0.5 degrees Celsius increase over the past 100 years, the panel convincingly argued that this rise was unlikely to be entirely natural in origin since it appears to have been quicker than previous temperature changes. The panel concluded that the balance of evidence suggests a discernible human influence on global climate.

4.4.6   THE 1997 KYOTO PROTOCOL

On the strength of IPCC WG I's Second Assessment Report and mindful of the 1995 Berlin Mandate, the Parties to the UN Framework Convention on Climate Change (COP 3) convened again in December 1997 in Kyoto, Japan (1–11 December 1997). The intention was to come to binding commitments for the Annex I Parties with respect to reducing greenhouse gas emissions for the period after the year 2000. This time 159 countries participated in the Conference. The final result was laid down in a Protocol to the Framework Convention. The basic principle is set out in Article 3. In accordance with this Article, the Parties to the Conference shall, individually or jointly, ensure that their aggregate anthropogenic carbon dioxide equivalent emissions of the greenhouse gases listed in Annex A do not exceed their assigned amounts calculated pursuant to their quantified emission limitation and reduction commitment listed in Annex B, and in accordance with the provisions of this Article, with a view to reducing their overall emissions of such greenhouse gases by at least five per cent below 1990 levels in the commitment period 2008 to 2012. The greenhouse gases listed in Annex A comprise carbon dioxide (CO_2), methane (CH_4), nitrous oxide (N_2O), hydrofluorocarbons (HFCs), perfluorocarbons (PFCs) and sulphur hexafluoride (SF_6). However any Annex I Party may use 1995 as its base year for the three fluor compounds. The EU 15 accepted a reduction commitment of 92 per cent for itself and for each of its fifteen Member States, Norway: 101 per cent; the US: 93 per cent; Canada, Hungary, Japan, Poland each: 94 per cent; Australia: 108 per cent; Iceland: 110 per cent; and the Russian Federation: 0 per cent. The EU overall reduction commitment of 92 per cent was subsequently in mutual agreement between the Member States re-distributed as follows: UK: 87.5 per cent; the Netherlands: 94 per cent; Austria: 87 per cent; Germany: 79 per cent; Denmark: 79 per cent; France, Belgium: 92.5 per cent; Italy: 93 per cent, whereas Portugal, Spain, Sweden and Greece are allowed to exceed their 1990/1995 emission levels. The Protocol was signed by eighty-four States, among which the US, on 11 December 1997. According to its rules, the Protocol would enter into force if it was ratified by fifty-five participating States accounting in the aggregate for fifty-five per cent of the 1990 CO_2 emissions. However, the ratification procedures were delayed because the Parties to the Conference wished to await the outcome of further negotiations on detailed rules on how the Protocol should be implemented, in particular with respect to various schemes such as joint implementation, clean development mechanism and emissions trading. These negotiations took place at the UN Climate Conference in Buenos Aires (1998) and subsequently at the COPs held in Bonn (COP 6 2001) and in the same year in Marrakech (COP 7 2001). At these COPs, the rules regarding the way the Protocol should operate were worked out and agreed, thus opening the way for the ratification of the Protocol by the participating States. The EU 15 ratified the Protocol in 2002. On 23 October 2004, this was also done by the Russian Federation. With the Russian ratification, the conditions for entering into force of the Protocol were fulfilled. Accordingly, the Protocol entered into force on 16 February 2005. The US which did sign the Protocol did not proceed to ratification.

As agreed under the Framework Convention, no commitments were imposed on the developing countries, but on the other hand the Kyoto Protocol envisages three schemes set out in Articles 6, 12 and 17 respectively that allow the Annex I Parties to mitigate the financial consequences of fulfilling their commitments under Article 3. Under Article 6, an Annex I Party is allowed to transfer to or acquire from any other such Party emissions reduction units (ERUs) resulting from projects aimed at reducing anthropogenic emissions by sources or enhancing anthropogenic removals by sinks of greenhouse gases in any sector of the economy. Such acquisition of ERUs shall be supplemental to domestic actions for the purposes of meeting a Party's commitments under Article 3. This approach is referred to as 'Joint Implementation' (JI) but is not described as such in this article. In Article 12, a 'Clean Development Mechanism' (CDM) is defined. Under this scheme, Parties not included in Annex I (i.e., the developing countries) will benefit from project activities resulting in certified emission reductions (CERs) and Annex I Parties may use the CERs accruing from such project activities to contribute to compliance with part of their quantified emission limitation and reduction commitment under Article 3. The reason behind CDM is that the costs of projects falling within the scope of the Protocol are generally lower in developing countries than in industrial countries. Article 17 describes the principle of emissions trading. Annex I Parties may participate in emissions trading for the purposes of fulfilling their commitments under Article 3. Any such trading shall be supplemental to domestic actions for the purpose of meeting quantified emission limitation and reduction commitments under that Article.

4.4.7   THE IPCC WG I FOURTH ASSESSMENT REPORT (2007)

In February 2007, the IPCC WG I Fourth Assessment Report was issued under the title, Climate Change 2007: The Physical Science Basis.

In conformity with the previous six years' reports, this latest report contains on the basis of the latest insights facts, predictions and other information concerning global warming and its consequences for sea level rise and climate change.

In the Fourth Report, the following facts, observations and conclusions are presented. Total temperature increase from 1850–1899 to 2001–2005 is 0.76 [0.57–0.95] degrees Celsius and appears to have accelerated during the last fifty years to 0.13 [0.10–0.16] degrees Celsius per decade. This is larger than the corresponding trend for 1901–2000 given in the Third Assessment Report, namely 0.6 [0.4–0.8] degrees Celsius. The global atmospheric concentration of CO_2 has increased from a pre-industrial value of about 280 ppm to 379 ppm in 2005. The latter value exceeds by far the natural range over the last 650,000 years (180–300 ppm) as determined from ice cores. The primary source of the abovementioned increased atmospheric concentration results from fossil fuel use, with land use change providing another significant but smaller contribution. Annual fossil CO_2 emissions increased from an average of 6.4 GtC (23.5 $GtCO_2$) per year in the 1990s to 7.2 GtC (26.4 $GTCO_2$) per year in 2000–2005. CO_2 emissions associated with land use change are estimated to be 1.6 GtC (5.9

$GtCO_2$) per year over the 1990s, although these estimates have a large uncertainty. The global atmospheric concentration of methane has increased from a pre-industrial value of about 715 ppb to 1,732 ppb in the early 1990s, and is 1,774 ppb in 2005. This latter value exceeds by far the natural range of the last 650,000 years (320–790 ppb) as determined from ice cores. It is very likely that the observed increase concentration is due to anthropogenic activities, predominantly agriculture and fossil fuel use, but relative contributions from different source types are not well determined. There exists a very high confidence that the globally averaged net effect of human activities since 1750 has been one of warming, with a radiative forcing of + 1.6 W per square metre. The combined radiative forcing due to increase in CO_2, methane and nitrous oxide is + 2.3 W per square metre. Observations since 1961 show that the average temperature of the global ocean has increased to depth of at least 3,000 m and that the ocean has been absorbing more than eighty per cent of the heat added to the climate system. Such warming causes sea water to expand, contributing to sea level rise. Widespread decreases in glaciers and ice caps and losses from the ice sheets of Greenland and Antarctica have also contributed to sea level rise. All in all, global average sea level rose at an average rate of 1.8 mm per year over 1961–2003. Even if all radiative forcing agents are held constant at year 2000 levels, a further warming trend would occur in the next two decades at a rate of about 0.1 degree C, due mainly to the slow response of the oceans. About twice as much warming (0.2 degree C per decade) would be expected if emissions are within the range of scenarios developed by the Working Group I for the purpose.

Projected Globally Averaged Surface Warming (degrees Celsius) and Sea Level Rise (metres) at the End of the Twenty-first Century

Case	Temperature Change – Best Estimate	Temperature Change – Likely Range	Sea Level Rise
Constant year 2000 concentration	0.6	0.3–0.9	NA
Low Scenario (B1)*	1.8	1.1–2.9	0.18–0.38
Very High Scenario (A1F1)*	4.0	2.4–6.4	0.26–0.59

* B1 and A1F1 Scenarios assume atmospheric CO_2 concentrations to reach in 2100 600 ppm and 1,550 ppm respectively.

Other observations:

- Warming tends to reduce land and ocean uptake of atmospheric CO_2, increasing the fraction of anthropogenic emissions that re-mains in the atmosphere. Depending on the scenario used, this climate-carbon cycle feedback increases the corresponding global average warming at 2100 by more than 1 degree Celsius.
- Increasing atmospheric CO_2 concentration leads to increasing acidi-fication of the ocean, hindering marine organism in forming of $CaCO_3$ for the building of their skeletons and shells and thus reducing the locking up of CO_2.
- Projected warming in the twenty-first century shows scenario-independent geographical patterns similar to those observed over the past several decades. Warming is expected to be greatest over land and at most high northern latitudes, and least over the Southern ocean and parts of the North Atlantic Ocean. Sea ice is projected to shrink in both the Arctic and Antarctic under all scenarios.
- It is considered very likely that hot extremes, heat waves and heavy precipitation events will continue to become more frequent.
- Model studies suggest that to stabilize at 450 ppm CO_2 could require that cumulative emissions over the twenty-first century be reduced from an average of approximately 670 (630–710) GtC {(2,460 (2310–2600) $GtCO_2$)} to approximately 490 (375–600) GtC {1,800 (1370–2200) $GtCO_2$}.
- Average Arctic temperatures increased at almost twice the global average rate in the past 100 years. Arctic temperatures have high decadal variability, and a warm period was also observed from 1925 to 1945.
- Satellite data since 1978 show that annual average Arctic sea ice extent has shrunk by 2.7 (2.1–3.3) per cent per decade, with larger decrases in summer of 7.4 (5.0–9.8) per decade.

Note 1. Arctic sea-ice coverage reached the lowest point of the summer melt on 16 September 2012. On that date, around 3.41 million km^2 of sea were at least fifteen per cet covered in ice. This new low is by far the smallest figure seen in thirty-three years of satellite measurements. The figure is 70,000 km^2 less than the previous record low recorded on 18 September 2007. *Source:* US National Snow and Ice Data Center in Boulder, Colorado.

Note 2. As of October 2012, the atmospheric concentration of CO_2 as measured at the Mauna Loa Observatory, Hawaii, reached 391 ppm.

4.5 THE ROAD TO A NEW GLOBAL CLIMATE AGREEMENT

After the Kyoto Protocol and the associated agreements became effective (16 February 2005), the Member States of the OECD (without the US) and the EU (the Annex I Parties or commitment-States) confirmed their serious intention to take all measures necessary to achieve the individual and overall reduction commitments set out in said Protocol. In this, they were joined without accepting commitments, however, by many other States including the Russian Federation, India and China (the 'non-commitment countries').

Meanwhile it was felt that after the first commitment period of the Kyoto Protocol (2008–2012) the latter should be replaced by a new global Climate Agreement that this time should contain binding commitments for all signatory Parties.

The first steps on the road to such a new Agreement were taken at the 15^e Conference of the Parties to the United Nations Framework Convention on Climate Change (COP-15) held in Copenhagen, Denmark (December 2009). On the basis of the IPCC WGI Fourth Assessment Report, the consensus reached at the Conference was that human society should not be exposed to a global average surface temperature exceeding 2 degrees Celsius above pre-industrial levels. According to the experts, to achieve this goal the atmospheric concentration of CO_2 should be stabilized at 450 ppm (Note: in October 2012 the atmospheric concentration of CO_2 reached 391 ppm as measured at the Mauna Loa Observatory, Hawaii). With respect to 2020, many pledges were made and emission reduction targets announced, but no firm commitments accepted, except by the EU (see hereinafter).

Not much progress towards a new global climate agreement was made at the next Conference (COP-16) held in Cancun, Mexico (December 2010). The 2 degrees Celsius limit was confirmed but it was acknowledged that to achieve this goal a much greater effort in trying to reduce CO_2 emissions was needed.

The next Conference (COP-17) was held in Durban, South Africa (December 2011). This time some serious progress was made. It was decided to start a process of negotiations that should lead to the text of global Climate Agreement to be completed no later than 2015 and ready for adoption and becoming effective as from 2020. It was further decided to extend the Kyoto Protocol to 2017 or 2020 but imposing reduction targets on only the EU, while several other European countries, Australia and New Zealand remained undecided. The Russian Federation and Japan decided not to commit. Canada, who failed to meet its reduction commitments, withdrew altogether from the Protocol. Several national reduction measures were announced.

On the 18th Conference (COP-18) held in Doha, Qatar, the Durban-agreed steps to be taken towards a global Climate Agreement were confirmed. The Kyoto Protocol was extended to 2020, but the Russian Federation, Japan, New Zealand and Canada did not join. This leaves only EU and Australia as Annex 1 Parties to the Protocol, together only responsible for about thirteen per cent of global energy-related CO_2 emissions (*4.0 Gt CO_2 v. 31.2 Gt CO_2*).

Summarizing, as from the end of 2012 and until a Global Climate Agreement will be in effect by 2020, governments of countries burning or combusting fossil fuels, with exception of the EU and Australia, have no other commitment with regard to a reduction of related CO_2 emissions than jointly to fulfil the overall objective of the Copenhagen Accord of December 2009, i.e., jointly trying to prevent that the global average surface temperature will exceed 2 degrees Celsius above pre-industrial levels.

4.6   CLIMATE-CHANGE-RELATED FOSSIL FUEL POLICIES

4.6.1   A REVIEW OF THE OPTIONS

For trying to fulfil voluntary pledges made and intentions announced in the context of the Copenhagen Accord of 2009 or the firm commitments accepted under the extended Kyoto Protocol (only the EU and Australia) governments of fossil fuels burning or combusting countries have the following five options at their disposal:

- Trying to curb the consumption of the fossil fuels. This can be done in multiple ways as follows: (i) by introducing fiscal measures to discourage the end-user from using these fuels, e.g., by imposing a carbon tax and/or by abolishing any road transport fuels subsidies, where such subsidies are given; (ii) by stimulating the efficient use of energy and/or the efficiency of energy transformation in which the fossil fuel concerned takes part; (iii) by setting up a cap-and-trading emission scheme whereby CO_2 emissions limitations (caps) are allocated to power stations and industrial plants accompanied by the right to buy or sell emission rights if respectively exceeding or staying below the cap. A similar scheme is as of 1 January 2005 operated by the EU: the Emissions Trading Scheme (ETS) and the market belonging thereto (see hereinafter in this Chapter).

- Expanding the production of non-fossil electricity. The most effective way to do this is to increase the number of nuclear power stations. Meaningful expansion of the renewables (hydro and the other renewables) is more difficult, because of lack of enough space to install the necessary facilities, lack of suitable sites and lack of storage capacity. However, if such nuclear energy expansion is not wanted (see Note 1 below), the use of coal seems unavoidable although it could be partly replaced by natural gas. To make the use of coal-fired power stations acceptable the latter may have to be equipped with CCS-facilities, including a pipeline leading to the underground storage site.
- Introducing alternatives in the transport sector. The transport sector accounted for a oil consumption of 46 millions barrels per day in 2011 and is by far the biggest market for oil products. Available alternatives are: small-sized nuclear reactors for ships; electricity, hydrogen and biofuels for road transport and aviation (see further Chapter 3).
- Installing small-sized nuclear reactors in industrial plants or equipping such plants like coal-fired power stations with CCS-facilities. Another option is fuel switching, whereby for instance coal is replaced by natural gas or mixed with biomass.
- Replacing fossil fuels in the domestic sector (buildings) by electricity. Whether this contributes to a reduction of CO_2 emissions depends again (as when using electricity for manufacturing hydrogen and for charging the battery of the electric car) on the way in which the electricity concerned is being generated. If non-fossil electricity is made available a significant reduction of CO_2 emissions is to be expected.

Note 1. After the accident at Fukishima Daiichi in March 2011, public acceptance of nuclear energy has become uncertain, introducing the same uncertainty in the feasibility to adopt one or more of the options listed above.

Note 2. The construction and operation of a CCS-system, including transport to and injection in the underground storage site is a very costly business and requires moreover a large input of energy. Whether CCS is commercially acceptable depends on the price that CO_2 stored and not emitted can fetch on the CO_2 market established in the context of an Emissions Trading Scheme.

4.6.2   CONCLUSIONS

Considering the five options listed above it becomes clear that making use of non-fossil electricity is a powerful instrument in trying to reduce energy-related CO_2 emissions. But nuclear fission energy is the most important component of non-fossil electricity. Failing to become accepted by the public (which has become uncertain after the accident at Fukishima Daiichi) would considerably reduce the impact that otherwise non-fossil electricity could have made in this respect. As far as the consumption of oil products and natural gas is concerned, under the present circumstances said consumption will hardly be affected by any of the above listed options being adopted. Indeed, imposing carbon taxes on transport fuels or abolishing fuel subsidies can count on strong sometimes even violent public opposition, in particular in developing countries that are able to produce their own oil.

Should, however, governments at one moment or another decide to adopt a more accommodating attitude towards using nuclear fission energy such change will undoubtedly start with replacing coal in power stations. To this extent, it will make no difference to the overall consumption of oil and natural gas in this sector. It also very unlikely that after coal nuclear energy will also replace oil and gas in this sector and certainly not gas. But a possible squeezing out of oil will not make a big difference because in the power sector the consumption of oil products is already small to modest. The consumption of natural gas in the power sector is more substantial than that of oil but a total replacement of gas is certainly not advisable. To the contrary, reserving a twenty per cent share for natural gas in the power sector appears to be the best option. But nuclear energy may provide electricity (which would then be non-fossil electricity) to electric PLDV's of the road transport sector. For this climate friendly reason it would make the use of electric PLDV's (however cumbersome and not practical) more attractive and give them a better change to compete with PLDV's powered by an internal combustion engine.

4.7   THE ORGANIZATION OF PETROLEUM
             EXPORTING COUNTRIES

4.7.1   ORGANIZATION, STATUTES AND STATED OBJECTIVES

4.7.1.1   Organization

The Organization of Petroleum Exporting Countries (OPEC) embodies a
formal cooperation with respect to petroleum policy between the major
crude oil producing and exporting countries. Already in 1949 Venezuela
had approached the four major oil exporting countries in the Middle East
Gulf area, i.e., Saudi Arabia, Kuwait, Iraq and Iran, with suggestions for
setting up an organization for discussion and exchange of views on the
price competition that was going on in Western Europe and that was
undermining the value of their export crudes. The right moment for
actually founding such an organization came when in August 1960 their
concessionaires took the decision to reduce for a second time in a row the
posted prices of their export crudes. In a fast defensive reaction, the five
major oil exporting countries founded OPEC on 1 September 1960 in
Baghdad.

      OPEC was established as a permanent intergovernmental Organization
with an international status. In accordance with Article 102 of the Charter
of the UN, the Agreement creating OPEC was registered with the UN
Secretariat on 6 November 1962.

      The Organization consists of the following organs:

   (i) the Conference, meeting at least twice a year;
  (ii) the Board of Governors;
 (iii) the Secretariat; and
  (iv) the Economic Commission.

In addition, the Conference will establish from time to time and as required
ad hoc ministerial committees, composed of a variable number of petroleum ministers.

      The Conference is the supreme authority of the Organization, respon-
sible for the formulation of its general policy. It consists of the ministers of
petroleum affairs in the governments of the Member States. The Conference decides upon reports and recommendations submitted by the Board of
Governors or by the aforementioned ad hoc ministerial Committees. It
meets at least twice a year. Binding decisions require unanimity. The Board
of Governors directs the management of the Organization and is responsible for implementing the resolutions of the Conference. The Board

consists of one Governor for each Member State. The Secretariat through the Secretary-General is responsible for maintaining contacts with governments and organizations, it possesses several divisions and departments for collecting information and carrying out studies in the field of energy, finance and economics. The Economic Commission is a specialized body operating within the framework of the Secretariat. It is responsible for assisting the Organization in promoting stability in international oil prices at equitable levels. Ad hoc ministerial committees were established as from the time the Organization was forced, in the light of weak markets and prices, to fix overall production ceilings and individual production quotas for the Member States. The committees were charged with the task to submit recommendations regarding questions of price and production levels and/or to monitor the implementation by the Member States of the resolutions adopted by or agreements made at the Conference, in so far these resolutions and agreements concerned prices, overall production ceilings and Member States' individual production quota. The most important of these committees is the still functioning Ministerial Monitoring Committee (MMC), which was established in 1982. At the time of its establishment, the MMC was composed of four petroleum ministers. Currently all Member States are represented in the Commission. A meeting of the MMC with all its Members present functions therefore as an alternative meeting of the Conference and is in fact deliberately used as such to bring sensitive matters to a solution outside an extraordinary or ordinary meeting of the Conference.

4.7.1.2   The Statutes

According to its Statutes of November 1971, the principal aim of the Organization is the coordination and unification of petroleum policies of the Member States and the determination of the best means of safeguarding their interests individually as well as collectively. In particular the Organization should strive to ensure the stabilization of prices in the international oil markets with a view to eliminate harmful and unnecessary fluctuations. At all times, so is stated in the Statutes, the Organization must give due regard to the interests of the producing nations and to the necessity of securing a steady supply income to the producing countries. At the same time, the Organization must ensure to consuming nations an efficient, economical and regular supply of petroleum and to investors in the petroleum industry a fair return on their capital. The Statutes also formulate the requirements for membership of the Organization. A candidate-State, wishing to qualify for membership, must possess a substantial net export of crude oil, fundamentally similar interests to those of the Member States and must be accepted by a majority of three-fourths of the full members, including the concurrent vote of all five founder Members. Soon after its founding, other oil exporting States joined the Organization: Qatar (1961), Indonesia (1962), Libya (1962), the United Arab Emirates (1967), Algeria (1969) and Nigeria (1971). Ecuador joined in 1963 but withdrew in 1992; Gabon joined in 1975 but withdrew in 1995. Much later Angola joined the Organization and as of 1 January 2007 became the 12th Member State. In October 2007, Ecuador rejoined the Organization.

4.7.1.3   The Solemn Declaration of 1975

A review of the stated objectives of the Organization took place at a meeting of the Sovereigns and Heads of State of the Member States (Algiers, 4–6 March 1975). This review was felt necessary in the light of the adverse reactions that OPEC's actions on prices and takeovers of concessions had caused in the OECD countries. At the end of their meeting, the Sovereigns and Heads of State made public a Solemn Declaration, in which they came out strongly in favour of the New International Economic Order, which was about one year earlier introduced by a Declaration and Programme of Action to that effect respectively contained in UN General Assembly's Resolutions 3201 (S-VI) and 3202 (S-VI) of 1 May 1974 (see Chapter 10).

But the Solemn Declaration had also much to say about oil prices. It was pointed out that an artificially low price for oil in the past has prompted over-exploitation of this limited and depletable resource and that continuation of such policy would have been disastrous from the point of view of conservation and world economy. Very interestingly, an attempt was made to define what the 'right' price should be. The following determining factors were mentioned:

(i) the imperatives of the conservation of petroleum, including its depletion and increasing scarcity in the future;
(ii) the value of oil in terms of its non-energy uses; and
(iii) the conditions of availability, utilization and cost of alternative sources of energy.

With respect of the level of the then prevailing petroleum prices (1975 level), it was pointed out that in spite of the apparent magnitude of the readjustment, the high rate of inflation and currency depreciation had wiped out a major portion of the real value of price readjustment and that the current price was markedly lower than that which would result from the development of alternative sources of energy. Although the Sovereigns and Heads of State did not subscribe to the notion that their export prices were too high, they declared themselves prepared to negotiate the conditions for the stabilization of oil prices so as to enable the consuming countries to make necessary adjustments to their economies. As regards the supply of petroleum, a very sensitive subject in view of the embargoes and supply restrictions which between 20 October 1973 and 18 March 1974 had been imposed against the US and the Netherlands (full embargo) and against France and the UK (partial embargos), the Solemn Declaration, appearing one year after these supply interruptions had been terminated, stated that the Sovereigns and Heads of State reaffirmed their countries' readiness to ensure supplies that would meet the essential requirements of the economies of the developed countries, provided that the consuming countries should not use artificial barriers to distort the normal operation of the laws of demand and supply. In order to achieve this purpose, the Member States declared themselves willing to establish close cooperation and coordination among themselves in order to maintain balance between oil production and the needs of the world market. However this may be, the promised close cooperation and coordination between the Member States was effectuated only after a situation of over-supply had developed in the international oil market and prices started to decline (as from 1981).

4.7.1.4   State Participation

After having settled various fiscal and pricing issues within the framework of the Teheran Agreement of 14 February 1971 (see Chapter 8), OPEC's attention turned to the issue of acquiring interests in the petroleum agreements of the 1930s and other long-term leases or licenses. At an extraordinary meeting of the Conference held on 22 September 1971, a resolution was adopted calling upon the Member States to open negotiations with their concessionaires and licensees in order to reach agreement on the desired participation. All Member States, with the exception of Iran and Indonesia, were involved.

4.7.1.5   OPEC's Long-Term Strategy as Seen in the 1980s

A few years after the Solemn Declaration, OPEC's ideas about what should be the 'right' price for oil in the international market, i.e., the price that should be maintained and supported by collective action, were further worked out by OPEC's six-member Long-Term Strategy Committee

(LTSC). The LTSC presented its report to the 56th extraordinary meeting of the Conference (Taif, Saudi Arabia, 7–8 May 1980), where it was accepted by a majority of the Member States. The recommendations of the LTSC were based on the idea that oil prices should in the long-term approximate the level of the cost of alternatives and that a pricing floor should be established to guarantee continuous advance over time towards that target.

Note. In the view of the LTSC, the proposed pricing floor should combine three elements:

(1) an inflation adjustment based on the change in unit values of export of the OECD Member States;
(2) an exchange rate adjustment in the manner of the Geneva II Agreement (see Chapter 8); and
(3) a rise of the oil prices in real terms proportionately to the growth in real GNP of the aforesaid OECD Member States.

The link laid with the growth in real GNP of the OECD Member States was meant to lay a link with the OECD area's ability to absorb price increases and the tendency to greater energy consumption (i.e., a pricing policy based on what price the market can bear and how much the market needs the oil). The LTSC noted that as markets swing from surplus to shortage, the pricing strategy should be flexible enough to allow prices to go beyond the minimum floor price level, in the light of signals (spot prices or contract prices) received from the market.

The LTSC recommendations on pricing strategy have never been implemented.

4.7.2   OPEC's INTERVENTIONS IN THE GLOBAL OIL MARKET

4.7.2.1   Pricing Policies from 1975 to 2000

After the oil crisis of 1973/1974 had run its course, OPEC remained focused on achieving even higher producer prices, apparently without regard to the global economic effects of such high prices and clearly in contradiction to the principles and objectives proclaimed in the Solemn Declaration. On 1 January 1979 in the aftermath of the Iranian Revolution (December 1978), the official selling price for Arabian Light ex Ras Tanura was fixed at USD 13.335 per barrel, but already six months later, on 1 July 1979, this price was raised to USD 18.00 per barrel. In the following months and years, the official selling price would be raised still more, to reach an all time high of USD 34 per barrel on 1 November 1981. In fact, the market price of Arabian Light ex Ras Tanura was still higher, reaching in 1980 an all time high of USD 36.83 per barrel (or USD 100 per barrel in 2011 USD).

By trying to achieve even higher prices, OPEC became confronted with over-supply and a weak market. This situation was caused by a combination of three factors, namely a decline in world demand, a slow increase in non-OPEC production, and Saudi Arabia's insistence to maintain its production at the exceptionally high level of 10.1 million barrels per day. On the part of Saudi Arabia, this was a deliberate policy meant to force the other Member States to adopt a more restrained price policy. At a meeting in Vienna which in the course of the proceedings was converted into an extraordinary meeting of the Conference (19–20 March 1982), it was decided that as of 1 April 1982 total OPEC production would be bound to an upper limit. On this occasion, the ceiling was fixed at 18 million barrels per day, but after the meeting Saudi Arabia announced a further reduction of its production on a voluntary basis with 0.5 million barrels per day, thereby lowering its ceiling to 7.0 million barrels per day and the overall ceiling to 17.5 million barrels per day. But it was a temporary agreement. The ceiling was to be reviewed a few months later at the 60th meeting of the Conference which was scheduled for 20/21 May 1982 in Quito. At the meeting, the Member States agreed with effect from 1 June 1982 to individual production ceilings. The price for the marker crude was confirmed at the level of USD 34 per barrel. This was the first time in the history of OPEC that a majority of the Member States was prepared to accept a reduction of their output to avoid having to cut their prices. The Conference also decided to establish a Monitoring Ministerial Committee (MMC) which was expected to monitor the market situation and recommend to the Conference the necessary measures to be taken. The MMC would be responsible for checking each country's production level and selling prices.

In the years that followed, OPEC was continuously confronted with overproduction and over-supply and a declining demand for OPEC oil. Internally, OPEC was divided over the strategy that should be followed. The Arab Gulf States led by Saudi Arabia favoured a policy of regulating prices only, without any binding commitments as to how much crude each Member State would be allowed to produce. In contrast, other Member States, Venezuela, Algeria, Libya and Iran in particular, were in favour of a policy directed at obtaining the desired price level by means of regulating production and individual export quotas. Under this policy, the individual quota would be allocated in accordance with the economic needs of the

Member State concerned. On the basis of this criterion only the Member States, which were running a surplus on their current account balance (e.g., Saudi Arabia, Kuwait and Abu Dhabi), should be subject to and accept any such restriction of their production as would be necessary to stay below an agreed overall production ceiling.

In its struggle to support the price structure, OPEC lowered in 1983 the price per barrel of the reference crude to USD 29 bilion. This measure had no effect. In this connection OPEC requested in the second half of 1984 the UK government to persuade BNOC, the UK national oil corporation, to maintain the price of Brent Dated – the benchmark crude for the North Sea area which was connected to the price of oil exported from Member State Nigeria, viz. Bonny Light – at its prevailing level of USD 30 per barrel in order to give Nigeria no cause to breach the OPEC price arrangements. However, BNOC experienced increasing problems in selling its oil against the price at which the company had bought the crude from its licensees (the latter receiving from BNOC the open market price). So when Statoil, the Norwegian state oil enterprise, started in October 1984 to sell its crude at a discount, BNOC reacted by lowering the price of its Brent dated from USD 30 per barrel to USD 28.65 per barrel (meanwhile the open market price had dropped to USD 27 per barrel). Nigeria felt obliged to follow suit and, in contravention of the OPEC price arrangements, lowered the price of its Bonny Light by USD 2.0 to USD 28.0 per barrel. In reaction to the price cutting of Statoil, BNOC and Nigeria OPEC met in Geneva, from 29 to 31 October 1984, which meeting was converted into an extraordinary meeting of the Conference. At this meeting, OPEC decided to support its price structure by lowering the overall production ceiling with effect from 1 November 1984 from 17.5 to 16 million barrels per day and by reconfirming the price of the reference oil at USD 29 per barrel (as had been fixed in the previous year). The decisions taken at this meeting of the Conference were summarized as follows:

> The Conference reviewed with great concern the recent developments in the world oil market following the price cuts undertaken by Statoil of Norway and BNOC of the United Kingdom, as well as by member country Nigeria. The Conference believes that the present oil price structure should be maintained and market stability restored as a means to secure healthy world energy balances and to stimulate world trade. Beneficiaries of such stability are not OPEC countries alone, but the international community at large, producers and consumers alike. The Conference is, therefore, determined to defend the price structure of its marker crude (Arabian Light, 34 degrees API, ex Ras Tanura) at the level of US$ 29/b and to consolidate market stability. For this purpose, the Conference decided to cut as from 1 November 1884 and on a temporary basis the global production ceiling of OPEC from 17.5 to 16 million b/d.

The largest reduction was accepted by Saudi Arabia (647,000 barrels per day). Zero reductions were granted to Iraq and Nigeria. The total production ceiling of 16 million barrels per day was distributed over the Member States in quotas ranging from 137,000 barrels per day for Gabon to 4,353,000 barrels per day for Saudi Arabia. The quotas allocated to the Member States producing more than 1 million barrels per day were as follows: Saudi Arabia: 4.353; Iran: 2.300; Venezuela: 1.555; Nigeria: 1.300; Iraq: 1.200; Indonesia: 1.189 (*source*: MEES, 5 November 1984).

In January 1985, OPEC decided to lower the price of the reference oil to USD 28 per barrel with effect from 1 February 1985. Nevertheless the decline in demand for OPEC oil and in particular that for Saudi Arabian oil continued and became very pronounced in that year as is shown by the diminishing production figures presented in the following Table 4.1.

Table 4.1   Decline in World and OPEC Production (Million Barrels Per Day)

	1979	1980	1985	% change 1979–1985
World	66.0	62.9	57.5	− 13.3
OPEC	31.2	27.2	16.7	− 46.5
OECD	16.5	17.1	20.0	+ 21.0
Former Soviet Union	11.8	12.1	12.0	+ 1.7
Saudi Arabia	9.8	10.3	3.6	− 63.3
Mexico	1.6	2.1	2.9	+ 81.1
Non-OPEC[*]	23.0	23.6	28.7	+ 24.8

[*] Excludes former Soviet Union.

Source: BP Statistical Review of World Energy 2007.

Note. The percentage increase (+ 24.8 per cent) of non-OPEC production (excluding production from the former Soviet Union) was due to production from Mexico, Alaskan North Slope and the North Sea continental shelf. The drastic reduction of Saudi Arabian production must be seen against the background of an overall declining world production.

At the end of 1985, OPEC decided to change its strategy and to concentrate on market share and to ignore price levels for the time being. In this context, it was decided at the 76th meeting of the Conference (Geneva, 7–9 December 1985) 'to secure and defend for OPEC a fair share in the world oil market consistent with the necessary income for Member States' development' (MEES, 16 December 1985). Pricing was not discussed. In order to achieve the desired fair market share, Saudi Arabia started to produce at full capacity. As a result of this 'flooding of the market' strategy, the international producer's price started to collapse, beginning in February 1986 and reaching minimum values in June of that year. Such a sharp drop in the price had not been expected by OPEC. To stop further price erosion, OPEC decided later in the year to abandon the aforementioned 'flooding of the market' strategy. At the 79th meeting of the Conference (Geneva, 6–22 October 1986), Saudi Arabia declared that the price for Arabian Light should not be lower than USD 18 per barrel and that each Member State should adhere to this price. The Conference confirmed, albeit on an interim basis, the return to a system of overall production ceilings and individual production quotas derived therefrom. Only Iraq was free to produce up to its capacity. The matter of a fixed price structure was referred to an already existing ministerial committee of three petroleum ministers which was freshly named the Ministerial Committee on Pricing (MCP). On 14 November 1986 the MCP submitted its recommendations. It was proposed to replace Saudi Arabia's Arabian Light as marker crude by a basket of seven crude oils, among which were also three non-OPEC crude oils, namely West Texas Intermediate, Mexican Isthmus and North Sea Brent dated. According to the proposal, the prices of the OPEC export crude oils should be related to the price of the basket on the basis of quality and API gravity differences and geographic location. The calculated price differentials would result in individual prices above or below USD 18 per barrel. At the 80th meeting of the Conference (Geneva, 20 December 1986), the Member States concluded for the first time in the history of the Organization among themselves a formal agreement on pricing and production levels instead of adopting a Conference resolution about these matters, as had hitherto been the custom. In accordance with the recommendation of the MCP, it was agreed to return promptly to a fixed pricing system at a level of USD 18 per barrel for OPEC's reference price. This price would be based on a basket of seven crude oils, consisting of six OPEC crude oils and only a single non-OPEC export crude oil, Mexican Isthmus. The export crude oils and their individual prices resulting in an average price of USD 18 per barrel for the basket were agreed as set out in Table 4.2 below.

Table 4.2   1987 Spot Prices of the OPEC Reference Basket (USD Per Barrel)

Basket	18.00
Arabian Light	17.52
Sahara Blend	18.87
Minas	17.56
Bonny Light	18.92
Dubai	17.42
Tia Juana Light	17.62
Mexican Isthmus	18.07

Source: MEES 1987

Note. The allocation of the individual prices had been based on the decision that the difference in value between Arab Heavy (outside the basket) and Bonny Light (the lightest oil inside the basket) should not exceed USD 2.65 per barrel.

The Agreement laid down the permitted overall and individual production levels for each quarter of 1987. The overall production ceiling averaged for the whole of 1987 amounted to 16.6 million barrels per day. The Agreement contained very typical provisions, which have been preserved in the later agreements. These typical provisions were the following:

(i) the Member States' production levels would be monitored by a group of high-level marketing representatives from all Member States under supervision of the President of the Conference;

(ii) all Member States should undertake to abide by and adhere strictly and seriously to the production levels as defined in the agreement;

(iii) in case any Member State would violate unilaterally the Agreement and exceed its temporary, allocated production level, in whole or in part, and such violation would be confirmed through the group of marketing experts, under the guidance of the aforesaid President, other Member States may consider themselves free of their obligation under the Agreement; and

(iv) the production levels agreed upon would be temporary and would not constitute a basis for any fair distribution of national quotas in any future negotiations. (MEES, December 1986).

At the 81st meeting of the Conference (Vienna, 25–27 June 1987), OPEC established the production levels for the second half of 1987. The overall ceiling was fixed at 16.6 million barrels per day. The Conference stressed the necessity of cooperation of the oil exporting countries outside OPEC, for instance Norway and the United Kingdom, as an essential prerequisite for a lasting market stability.

As from 1988, world demand for oil started to increase and OPEC could more than proportionally benefit therefrom. This development led to regular upwards adjustments of the overall production ceiling and the national quotas as agreed at successive meetings of the Conference. During the first half of 1990, a new period of overproduction started. The UAE and seven other Member States, among which Saudi Arabia and Kuwait, were to blame for this overproduction by exceeding their quotas despite the fact that these quotas had regularly been increased. Similarly as in 1986 the overproduction led in April 1990 to sharp fall in prices. In June 1990, the calculated spot price of the basket reached a minimum of USD 14.05 per barrel. In an attempt to reverse this trend, the Member States reached at the 87th ordinary meeting of the Conference (Geneva, 26–27 July 1990) a new agreement on production quotas and on an overall production ceiling of 22.491 million barrels per day, but also decided to raise the price of the reference basket from USD 18 per barrel to USD 21 per barrel.

Note. The agreement secured Kuwait's and the United Arab Emirates' acceptance of a quota which would be the same for both Member States, namely 1.5 million barrels per day. This long sought quota parity had earlier been achieved by Iraq in relation to Iran at a level of 3.140 million barrels per day.

A few days after the 87th meeting of the Conference, the Middle East was at war again. On 2 August 1990, Iraq invaded Kuwait and in response to this violation of the international peace, the UN Security Council imposed with effect from 6 August 1990, trade sanctions against Iraq as well as against occupied Kuwait. The July 1990 production and quotas agreement appeared to have lost all its relevance. The trade sanctions had as an immediate effect that the exports of oil and refined products from Iraq as well as from Kuwait came to a halt. The prices on the international oil market started to rise immediately. The calculated basket spot price rose accordingly, reaching its highest value (USD 34.58 per barrel) in October 1990. In contrast to OPEC's pricing policies followed with respect to the two preceding price shocks (1973/1974 and 1979/1980 respectively), OPEC did in 1990 not attempt to maintain the price at the elevated level reached at the time. Instead, the majority of the Member States, amongst which Saudi Arabia, agreed at a meeting of the MMC (Vienna, 29 August 1990) to increase production in excess of the production quotas fixed in

July 1990, in so far as needed to maintain market stability and a regular supply of oil to the customers (i.e., the western countries). In fact, OPEC solved the issue by going back to its basic objectives as stated in the Solemn Declaration of March 1975. OPEC showed thereby to have appreciated the negative economic effects on the world economy of high oil prices. A price explosion was averted that otherwise surely would have taken place. In the months that followed, OPEC proved very successfully in coping with the loss of contributions from Iraq and Kuwait. Already by the first quarter of 1991, OPEC production (without Iraq and Kuwait) had exceeded the July 1990 overall production ceiling (viz. 22.5 million barrels per day) by 1 million barrels per day. Ironically, the production increase achieved by OPEC was so effective that the target price for the basket (USD 21 per barrel) remained unachievable.

In the following years, OPEC managed to cope without the contribution of Iraq. So successfully in fact that, in spite of a steadily growing demand for oil, which became apparent since 1995, problems of overproduction on the part of OPEC Member States kept the target price most of the time out of sight. At the 11th meeting of the MMC (Geneva, 25–29 September 1993), the Committee was confronted with a basket price that had fallen below USD 15 per barrel. In order to halt this slide and to reverse the downward trend, the overall production ceiling for the next six months was fixed at 24.5 million barrels per day. This overall ceiling was distributed amongst the Member States in the form of temporary allocations. At the 95th meeting of the Conference (Vienna, 23–24 November 1993), it was decided to uphold the September 1993 agreement. The November 1993 calculated spot quotation for the basket was USD 14.47.

Price weakness continued unabated because non-OPEC (high cost) production (not bound by production restrictions) was expanding under the umbrella of the favourable price levels which OPEC had set and tried to maintain. Price weakness manifested itself during the last part of 1997 and the whole of 1998. On 31 March 1998, the OPEC Member States finally agreed between them to reduce their overall production by 1.26 million barrels per day with reference to the production actually achieved in February 1998 (namely 31.7 million barrels per day), without altering the individual production quotas that had been established in November 1997. Remarkably, five non-OPEC States, namely Norway, Mexico, Egypt, Oman and Yemen, joined OPEC in this action and pledged to reduce their production in the aggregate by 0.27 million barrels per day (Norway and Mexico each pledged 0.1 million barrels per day). Nevertheless, the producer price continued its decline. The spot quotation for the OPEC reference basket reached in December 1998 its lowest level (USD 9.96

per barrel). After the Member States succeeded at their meeting in March 1999 to agree amongst themselves to bring down the overall level by 1.72 million barrels per day based on the production in February 1999 (i.e., a reduction of 6.4 per cent), the world market price has ever since moved upwards.

Table 4.3 below illustrates the impact of OPEC's intervention in the global oil market over the period 1975–2000.

*Table 4.3   World/OPEC Production (Million Barrels Per Day) and
Spot Prices (USD Per Barrel) 1975–2000*

	1975	1980	1985	1990	1995	1998	2000
World	55.8	62.9	57.5	65.5	68.1	73.6	75.0
OPEC	27.2	27.2	16.7	24.6	27.7	31.2	31.5
% World	48.7	43.2	29.0	37.6	40.7	42.4	42.0
Y.Avg. Price*	11.53	36.83	27.56	23.73	17.02	12.72	28.50
Y.Avg. Price**	-	-	-	-	16.86	12.28	27.6

* 1975–1983: Arabian Light posted at Ras Tanura, 1984–2000: Brent Dated.

** OPEC Reference Basket.

Sources: OPEC Briefings; BP Statistical Review of World Energy 2007.

4.7.2.2   Pricing Policies from 2000 Onwards

The year 2000 can be considered as a real turning point in the global oil market. The demand for oil started to increase quite rapidly as a result of an expanding world economy. In particular, the emerging economies (China, India, etc.) increased their consumption. In first instance, only the international price reacted to the increased demand, production volumes would follow in 2003. OPEC did no longer have to contemplate production cut backs to support a chosen price level, although up to July 2005 at successive meetings of the Conference production quotas for its Member States were established which however were largely ignored, production capacity permitting (see Tables 4.4 and 4.5 hereinafter). In fact, prices moved without its intervention at an elevated level of around USD 25 per barrel, as a matter of fact within a price band (22–28 USD per barrel) that OPEC in March 2000 had set for the price of the OPEC Reference Basket in the context of pursuing pricing policies by means of production adjustments. Meanwhile, the political situation in the Middle East started to become unsettled again. It began with the destruction of the WTC Twin Towers in New York on 11 September 2001 which event led to the War on Terror in Afghanistan. The turmoil increased when on 20 March 2003 Iraq was invaded by a coalition of willing Western States for the purpose of disarming the country and to remove its leader Saddam Hussein. Later tensions developed around Iran and its uranium enrichment programme, which prevented that the political storms could calm down. Remarkably, all this time the export of crude oils from the Middle East Gulf area was never interrupted, not even temporarily. There never was a physical shortage of crude oil from said area. Nevertheless, the financial markets reacted strongly, driven by fears about the political future of the Middle East and the possibility that access to its oil production facilities and oil reserves would at some time in the immediate future be denied to consumers in the OECD countries. As from 2003/2004, prices surged upwards to levels that had not been seen since the second price shock (1979–1985). As from 2005 the price exceeded USD 50 per barrel. In the second half of 2006 and the first half of 2007, prices came down a little and even touched briefly USD 50 per barrel, the level that had been passed in 2005. At this point, OPEC reacted immediately, making it known that they would consider re-introducing production cutbacks if the international price would decline still further, which however did not happen. In fact, the upward trend continued in 2008, but a fallback occurred in 2009, followed again by a period of rising prices easily exceeding 110 USD per barrel for the Brent bench mark in 2011/2012 (see further Chapter 3). Now it appears that OPEC draws the line at USD 100 per barrel, i.e., it will consider production cuts as soon as the international price starts to come down below that price.

Table 4.4   World/OPEC Production (Million Barrels Per Day) and Spot Prices (USD Per Barrel) 2000–2011

	2000	*2003*	*2005*	*2007*	*2009*	*2011*
World	75.0	76.9	81.4	81.7	80.7	83.4
OPEC	31.5	30.8	35.0	35.1	33.9	35.8
%World	42.0	40.0	43.0	43.0	42.0	42.9
Y. Avg. Price[*]	28.50	28.83	54.52	72.39	61.67	111.28
Y. Avg. Price[**]	27.6	28.10	50.64	69.08	61.06	107.46

[*] Brent Dated.

[**] OPEC Reference Basket.

Sources: OPEC Briefings; BP Statistical Review of World Energy 2007.

Note on the OPEC Reference Basket. As mentioned before, Saudi Arabia's Arabian Light was with effect from 1 January 1987 replaced as marker crude for price policy and monitoring purposes by a basket of six OPEC crude oils viz. Arabian Light, Sahara Blend, Minas, Bonny Light, Dubai and Tia Juana Light, and one non-OPEC crude stream, Mexican Isthmus. At the 135th meeting of the Conference held in Isfahan, 16 March 2005, it was decided to change the composition of the Basket (ORB) from the seven crudes as hitherto used to all OPEC 11 crude streams. With effect from 16 June 2005, the Basket was made up of the following crudes: Arabian Light, Sahara Blend, Minas, Iran Heavy, Basra Light, Kuwait Export, Es Sider, Bonny Light, Qatar Marine, Murban and BCF 17 (Venezuela). The Basket has a gravity of 32.7 degrees API, slightly heavier than the previous seven crudes Basket (34.6 degrees API). As of 10 September 2007, the composition of the Basket was changed again, this time to include 'Girassol', the export crude of its new Member State, Angola. As of October 2007, the Basket includes the Ecuadorean crude 'Oriente'. As of January 2009, the Basket excludes the Indonesian crude Minas. As from the same date the Venezuelan crude BCF-17 was replaced by the crude Merey.

Meanwhile OPEC maintained its policy to establish, at successive meetings of the Conference, production allocations for its Member States, at least till November 2007. The last time basic allocations were agreed was at the 136th Extraordinary Meeting of the Conference, 15 June 2005 with respect to the period July 2005 to October 2006. The collective allocation amounted to 28,000 thousand barrels/d. At subsequent Extraordinary or Consultative Meetings production cuts or production increases were agreed reducing or increasing the collective allocation. For the period November 2006 – Januari 2007 the collective allocation was brought back to 26,300 thousand barrels/d, for the period Februari 2007 to October 2007 the collective allocation was further reduced by 500 thousand barrels/d to 25,800 thousand barrels/d. Finally for the period starting November 2007 the collective allocation was increase again and fixed at 27,253 thousand barrels/d.

Table 4.5 records the allocations agreed between July 2003 and July 2005.

Table 4.5   Production Allocations (Thousand Barrels Per Day)
June 2003–July 2005

	2003 (eff. June)	2003 (eff. Nov.)	2004 (eff. Aug.)	2004 (eff. Nov.)	2005 (eff. July)
Algeria	811	782	830	862	894
Indonesia	1,317	1,270	1,347	1,399	1,451

	2003 (eff. June)	2003 (eff. Nov.)	2004 (eff. Aug.)	2004 (eff. Nov.)	2005 (eff. July)
Iran	3,729	3,597	3,817	3,964	4,110
Iraq	-	-	-	-	-
Kuwait	2,038	1,966	2,087	2,167	2,247
Libya	1,360	1,312	1,392	1,446	1,500
Nigeria	2,092	2,018	2,142	2,224	2,306
Qatar	658	635	674	700	726
Saudi Arabia	8,256	7,963	8,450	8,775	9,099
UAE	2,217	2,138	2,269	2,356	2,444
Venezuela	2,923	2,819	2,992	3,107	3,223
OPEC 10[*]	25,400	24,500	26,000	27,000	28,000
OPEC 10[**]	29,495	29,495	31,611	31,611	33,140

[*] Excludes Iraq.

[**] Actual annual OPEC production (excludes Iraq).

Sources: BP Statistical Review of World Energy June 2012; OPEC.

Table 4.5 above shows that during the last years for which production allocations were agreed, actual annual OPEC production (excluding Iraq) constantly exceeded the OPEC collective allocation (excluding Iraq). The same applies to the latest established collective allocations.

4.8 THE EUROPEAN UNION

4.8.1 BACKGROUND

Economic cooperation between European States started when six West-European States, i.e., France, West-Germany, Italy, Belgium, Netherlands and Luxembourg, founded in 1951 the European Coal and Steel Community (ECSC) by the Treaty of Paris. Said Treaty entered into force on 23 July 1952 for a limited duration of fifty years. Shortly thereafter, the same six Member States founded the EEC by the Treaty 'Establishing a European Economic Community' signed in Rome on 25 March 1957, effective date 1 January 1958. Much later and after Denmark, Ireland, Portugal, Spain, Greece and the United Kingdom had joined the EEC, the latter was formally replaced by the European Community (EC). This substitution was effectuated by the Treaty on the European Union (EU) which was signed on 7 February 1992 in Maastricht and entered into force on 1 November 1993. In 1995, 2004 and 2007 respectively three, ten and two more European States joined the EU expanding the membership to twenty-seven States. The EC is one of the two European Communities still remaining after the ECSC on 23 July 2002 had ceased to exist, the other is the European Atomic Energy Community (Euratom). The former's responsibilities and assets have been assumed by the EC.

The original EEC Treaty created a common market for all goods, persons, services and capital, with exception always of coal and nuclear products which were and are governed by their own specific Treaty i.e., ECSC and Euratom. In December 1985, the EEC Treaty was amended by the adoption of the Single European Act. This Act established an internal market intended to be functioning by 1 January 1993. The internal market is described as a place without frontiers, in which the free flow of goods, persons, services and capital is safeguarded in accordance with the provisions of the EEC Treaty. The Act also introduced a new Title (Title VII) in the EEC Treaty containing a statement of the objectives of the Community in environmental matters. Generally, it was laid down that Community environmental policies shall be integrated with Community energy policy.

4.8.2   RESTRICTIONS ON COMMUNITY LEVEL PETROLEUM
           POLICIES

Member States of the EU are sovereign States and while prepared to cooperate with one another with respect to the production and consumption of energy products, including petroleum within the territory under their jurisdiction, they do not wish to surrender their sovereign rights over petroleum resources within said territory, including those located on the continental shelf. To put it differently, they are not prepared to pool said resources for the common good of the Community. Furthermore they wish to decide for themselves which type of energy product to use and consume, whether it should be coal, oil, natural gas, nuclear energy and/or renewables. Finally, Member States insist on the right to independently select the foreign countries from which they want to import their oil and/or natural gas. Currently, the internal consumption of crude oil is for 87.5 per cent supplied by said countries, among them the Russian Federation and Member States of OPEC such as Nigeria and the Middle East Gulf countries. Natural gas is for sixty-five per cent supplied by foreign countries among them again the Russian Federation and Norway (by pipeline) and Algeria, Qatar, Nigeria and Libya (by LNG tanker). To mitigate this dependence on foreign suppliers has always been the central theme of Community level petroleum policies coupled to a policy of stimulating the search for and development of the indigenous petroleum resources. Nevertheless, the Member States wish to draw their own plans, to pursue their own policies and to take their own responsibilities, like entrusting the development of domestic resources and/or the import of oil and/or natural gas to the private sector.

Note. Entrusting petroleum matters to the private sector has not always been the case within the Community, at least not in all Member States. As noted hereinbefore in this Chapter, France, Italy and the UK have experimented with state-owned companies. Norway, an associated Member State, did the same but still operates world-wide with a commercial company by the name of Statoil, in which the Norwegian State owns a sixty-seven per cent interest.

4.8.3   THE SHAPING OF A COMMUNITY LEVEL ENERGY
             POLICY

4.8.3.1   Up to the Oil Crisis of 1973

Up to the outbreak of the first oil crisis in October 1973, Community energy policy was focused on economically protecting and safeguarding the existence of the coal mines and coal production of the Member States, whereby of necessity, due to the worsening economic circumstances, the objective of a common market for hard coal had gradually to be discarded. Due to their relatively low prices, both crude oil and imported hard coal succeeded to penetrate the West-European energy market. The depressed level of the oil prices was caused by the severe competition that went on between and amongst the international oil companies on the West-European market.

Note. As discussed earlier, this competition was also viewed with concern by the governments of the oil exporting countries, in particular by Venezuela, and led in the end to the establishment of OPEC.

4.8.3.2 From the 1973 Oil Crisis up to 1986

During the oil crisis of 1973/1974, the Arab Member States of OPEC either stopped or gradually reduced their exports of oil to the Western countries. This embargo resulted in a drastic increase of the price of oil on the world market. An immediate reaction came not from the EEC, but from the side of the OECD, since not only West-European States were involved. As described before, the OECD established on 15 November 1974 a subsidiary organization by the name of the IEA and adopted three days later the International Energy Programme (IEP).

Note. Every Member State of the OECD may become a member of the IEA. The IEA is charged with the task to execute the IEP. This Programme envisages cooperation between the members of the IEA which is aimed at taking measures to reduce its Members' dependency on the import of oil and to promote a gradual replacement of oil by other energy sources or products. The IEP provides also for a crisis management system that starts functioning as soon as the supply of oil in any significant degree is interrupted. Members are obliged to keep and maintain oil emergency stocks sufficient to substitute for ninety days' imports. During a crisis the members are obliged to share still existing supplies with one another in accordance with the allocation procedures established as part of the IEP. The emergency allocation system is activated either with respect to all participating countries or in respect of any one country (selective trigger) when available supplies are seven per cent or more below consumption during a base period.

The Community was prompted by the events to formulate a coherent energy policy. In 1974 the Council formulated the following policy objectives:

- the need to reduce the dependency on imported energy products, in particular oil;
- the development of nuclear fission electricity;
- the development of the Community's own coal and petroleum resources; and
- stimulating and promoting technical research in the field of energy.

Note. In the aftermath of the oil crisis of 1973, the Community policy makers were of the opinion that hard coal should play an important role in the implementation of the policy to reduce the dependence of the Community on imported oil. Until 1986, the difference in price between Community coal and imported coal on the one side and heavy fuel oil on the other had been large enough in favour of coal to make the transition to a greater use of coal in the industry, as was recommended by the Council, economically feasible. Neverthe-less, for several reasons the policy to promote a greater industrial use of coal failed.

4.8.3.3   Community Policies Objectives: 1986 to 2006

On 16 September 1986, the Council adopted the objectives for the next ten years. Although the Community in that year had been confronted with a fall in oil prices (the Member States of OPEC were engaged in a struggle to obtain a fair market share) as well as with a shocking energy event, namely the accident that on 25 April 1986 took place in reactor number 4 of the nuclear power plant at Chernobyl, Ukraine, the Council nevertheless adhered to and confirmed the long-term objectives of the EC's energy policy based on crude oil/oil products substitution and energy efficiency. But it was conceded that in view of the low level of oil prices and the corresponding attractiveness of imported oil, additional measures might be needed in order to continue following a policy of diversification of the EC's external sources of supply. The emphasis was put on the development of the Community's own energy resources under satisfactory economic conditions and geographical diversification of the Community's external sources of supply and diversification between the different forms of energy; and a search for balanced solutions as regards energy and the environment, by making use of the best available and economically justified technologies and by improving energy efficiency, as well as taking account of the desire to limit distortions of competition in the energy markets by a more coordinated approach in environmental affairs in the Community.

More specifically aimed at the consumption of crude oil and natural gas the following objectives were adopted:

(i) with regard to crude oil: to keep net crude oil imports from third countries within reasonable proportions by maintaining a policy of oil substitution and by continuing and, if need be, stepping-up crude oil exploration and production within the Community, particularly in promising areas not yet exploited. Oil consumption should be kept down to around forty per cent of energy consumption and net oil imports thus maintained at less than thirty-three per cent of total energy consumption in the Community in 1995. (At this point it should be mentioned that already in 1986 this objective had been achieved. It did not prove possible to maintain this percentage in the ensuing years); and

(ii) with regard to natural gas: to maintain the share of natural gas in the energy balance on the basis of a policy aimed at ensuring stable and diversified supplies and continuing and, if need be, stepping-up natural gas exploration and production in the Community.

In January 1996, the EC Commission published a White Paper setting out the framework of an energy policy at Community level for the next ten years. There is almost nothing in this White Paper that relates to the consumption of oil and/ or natural gas, except perhaps that in the Paper it is suggested that the adoption of a CO_2/energy tax would contribute to the goal of sustainable development. However, it is also stressed that any policy based on fiscal measures would need to address their possible effects on the Community's global competitiveness, especially for energy-intensive industries.

Note. In the White Paper, research and technological development are identified as important instruments for supporting the Community's energy policy. For this reason the Community would *inter alia* continue to support a major programme for fossil fuels (JOULE/THERMIE). Said programme aims to promote the efficient use of indigenous resources of energy and reducing environmental emissions, in particular CO_2.

4.8.3.4   From 2006 Onwards

As from 2006, the focus shifted to policies aimed generally at a reduction of CO_2 emissions and more in particular at realizing the decarbonization of the energy system. The first step taken was for the EU to become one of the Annex I Parties to the Kyoto Protocol accepting thereby an eight per cent overall CO_2-reduction commitment with respect to the base year 1990 in the commitment period 2008–2012.

But the EU wanted to do more. In March 2007, the EU Council agreed to cut the Community's own greenhouse gas emissions by at least twenty per cent by 2020 regardless of what other countries do. To attain this goal the EU Council decided to:

(i) save twenty per cent of energy consumption compared with projections for 2020 by improving energy efficiency;
(ii) increase to twenty per cent by 2020 the share of renewable energies in overall energy consumption;
(iii) increase tenfold – to at least ten per cent – the share of biofuels in overall petrol and diesel consumption by 2020, provided that

sustainable 'second-generation' biofuels from non-food crops
(known as cellulosic biofuels) become commercially available;
(iv) develop and promote low- or even zero-emitting technologies,
including CCS technology so that these can make a major
contribution to reducing emissions by 2020.

The EU aims to achieve this for 2020 planned reduction of CO_2 emissions
through actions foreseen in the new integrated energy and climate policy as
set out in the Commission's document 'Energy 2020 A strategy for
competitive, sustainable and secure energy' dated 10 November 2010, with
measures already in place such as the EU Emission Trading Scheme (EU
ETS) (see hereinafter).

Note. The aimed for ten per cent share of cellulosic biofuels in overall gasoline
and diesel consumption is subject to review, because of doubts about their
availability.

At the Extraordinary EU Council of 4 February 2011, the Commission was
requested to prepare the 'Energy roadmap 2050' to reflect the EU's
commitment to reduce greenhouse gas emissions to eighty per cent to
ninety-five per cent below 1990 levels by 2050. The purpose is to arrive at
the end of the road at a decarbonized energy system. In all scenarios natural
gas plays an important role and as far as the transport sector is concerned
electricity is assumed to provide around sixty-five per cent of energy
demand of PLDV's in 2050. This target, if realized, would of course have
severe consequences for the future consumption of gasoline / diesel, but it
would apply in the EU only and be wholly dependent on nuclear electricity
becoming acceptable in a meaningful way.

Note 1 After the accident at Fukishima Daiichi in March 2011, public acceptance
of nuclear energy has become uncertain, introducing the same uncertainty in all
scenarios and projections about the options available to reduce CO_2 emissions.

Note 2. In 2010 the global emission of CO_2 increased to 31.2 Gt CO_2. The EU was
responsible for 3.6 Gt CO_2, which is no more than a 11.5% share of the global
total.

4.8.4   PETROLEUM RELATED EC DIRECTIVES

4.8.4.1   EC Directive 94/22/EC of the European Parliament and of the Council of 30 May 1994

With this Directive the EC introduced legislation aimed to provide the legal instruments for mobilizing and developing the oil and natural gas resources in Member States. The Directive sets out the conditions for granting and using authorizations for the prospecting, exploration and production of the aforesaid resources. The Directive is aimed at ensuring the non-discriminatory access to and pursuit of petroleum operations under conditions which encourage greater competition in this sector, while acknowledging that Member States have sovereignty and sovereign rights over hydrocarbon resources on their territories (see further Chapter 6).

Note. A few years before the introduction of the aforesaid Directive, the Commission on behalf of the European Communities had been the driving force behind the creation of the European Energy Charter. This Charter was on 17 December 1991 signed by forty-nine countries among which the Member States of the EC, the other Member States of the OECD including the US, the countries in central and eastern Europe, the Baltic States and almost all Member States of the CIS (former Soviet Union), including the Russian Federation itself. The Charter was a non-binding political declaration, setting out the objectives, principles and actions which the signatory States declare willing to undertake in the fields of trade and investment in energy products and energy production. A few years later the European Commission, this time acting on behalf of the newly created EC, succeeded in completing a Charter Treaty (signed on 17 December 1994) in which the aforesaid principles and objectives of the Energy Charter were worked out in detail and turned into commitments for the contracting States. For various reasons the Charter Treaty became never effective and has by now lost any relevance.

4.8.4.2   EC Directive 98/30/EC of the European Parliament and of the Council of 22 June 1998

The EC succeeded in creating an internal market in natural gas. The completion of such market took longer than was expected at the time the Single Act was adopted. The completion process took place in two phases. The first phase was formed by two Council Directives, one on the transit of natural gas through grids (Council Directive 91/296/EEC of 31 May 1991) and the other concerning a Community procedure to improve the transparency of gas (and electricity) prices charged to industrial end-users

(Council Directive 90/377/EEC of 29 June 1990) as amended by Commission Directive 93/87/EEC. The final phase was formed by the European Parliament and Council Directive 98/30/EC of 22 June 1998, the final text of which was established at a meeting of the Energy Council on 8 December 1997. The Directive 98/30/EC of 22 June 1998 lays down the rules relating to the organization and functioning of the natural gas sector, including liquefied natural gas, access to the market, the operation of systems, and the criteria and procedures applicable to the granting of authorizations for transmission, distribution, supply and storage of natural gas. Upstream pipeline networks, i.e., any pipeline or pipeline network operated as part of an oil or natural gas production project are not involved and do not form part of the internal market, but LNG facilities owned and/or operated by a natural gas undertaking do.

The internal market in natural gas is not complete in as much as the Commission is working on arrangements that would take away ownership and/or control regarding the gas transportation system from the gas suppliers/ producers. The creation of the internal market should lead to lower prices for the end-user. If this effect leads to an increase of the consumption then a conflict will ensue with the overall Community CO_2-policy of restricting in one way or another the consumption of fossil fuels.

4.8.4.3   Directive 2003/87/EC of the European Parliament and of the Council of 13 October 2003

This Directive establishes a scheme for greenhouse gas emission allowance trading (EU ETS) within the Community in order to promote reductions of greenhouse gas emissions in a cost-effective and economically efficient manner. The Scheme started to operate on 1 January 2005. As of that date any operator of a CO_2 emitting stationary installation needs to be in possession of greenhouse gas emissions permit. For specified periods each Member State shall decide upon the total quantity of allowances it will allocate for that period and the allocation of those allowances to the operator of each installation. For each Member State the total quantity of allowances should remain within the limits of a national allocation plan. For the first specified periods Member States shall allocate the allowances for ninety-five per cent to ninety per cent free of charge. Allowances can be transferred between persons within the Community, i.e., trading in quantities CO_2 is allowed, this creates a market. The operator of an installation shall by April each year surrender a number of allowances equal to the total emissions from that installation during the preceding calendar year. The surrendered allowances are subsequently cancelled. Any operator who does not surrender sufficient allowances by April of each year to cover its emissions during the preceding year shall be held liable for the payment of an excess emissions penalty. To cover this shortfall and to avoid having to pay this penalty the operator will have to buy allowances on the aforesaid CO_2 market.

4.8.4.4 Directive 2009/31/EC of the European Parliament and of the Council of 23 April 2009

This Directive establishes a legal framework for the environmentally safe geological storage of CO_2 to contribute to the fight against climate change. The purpose of such storage is permanent containment of CO_2 in such a way as to prevent and, where this is not possible, eliminate as far as possible negative effects and any risk to the environment and human health. The Directive applies to geological storage in the territory of the Member States, their exclusive economic zones and on their continental shelves within the meaning of the UN Convention on the Law of the Sea. Member States retain the right to determine the areas from which storage sites may be selected pursuant to the requirements of the Directive. This includes the right of Member States not to allow for any storage in parts or in the whole of their territory. Member States shall ensure that no storage site is operated without a storage permit, that there shall be only one operator for each storage site and that no conflicting uses are permitted on the site. The Directive contains elaborate rules on the conditions for issuing storage permits and the contents of said permits, about CO_2 stream acceptance criteria and procedures and about monitoring of the injection facilities and the storage complex for the purpose of detecting significant irregularities, migration of CO_2 and leakage.

Note. The construction and operation of a CCS-system is a costly business, at least till the total authorized quantity of CO_2 has been stored and the storage complex is closed. The operator must be compensated on the basis of the total quantity CO_2 that has been stored and that has not been emitted. The price to be paid to the operator should be the price obtainable on a CO_2 emissions market functioning in the context of an Emissions Trading Scheme.

Chapter 5
Petroleum Legislation of States

5.1   AN OVERVIEW

The drilling of the first oil well in 1859 did not only mark the beginning of the petroleum industry, but also at the same time signalled the beginning of the development of petroleum legislation i.e., legislation specifically designed to regulate the mining of petroleum which requires the drilling of holes into the sedimentary rock in the pores and fissures of which it occurs. This difference with the mining of solid substances like coals and hard rock minerals required a mining legislation that likewise had to be different from the hitherto existing much older mining legislation. A case apart is the mining of oil sands. In so far as these semi-liquid deposits occur at the surface they will be mined like surface occurrences of coals and mineral deposits, i.e., using the open-pit mining method.

Petroleum legislation comprises all laws, regulations, ministerial decrees or decisions, licenses and contracts of work meant to regulate petroleum operations in areas falling under the (natural resources) jurisdiction of the State.

Each country's petroleum legislation is unique in itself, but it is still possible to distinguish between two main categories:

(i) petroleum legislation based on the granting of exclusive licenses; and

(ii) petroleum legislation based on concluding contracts of work.

With reference to (i). The license is an administrative authorization issued by the government acting on behalf of the State, and exercising the latter's sovereign powers over natural resources. The license is either exclusive or non-exclusive. The license is exclusive if it gives the licensee exclusive rights in the sense that as long as the license is valid no other person than the licensee itself is authorized to exercise the rights conferred by the license among which the fundamental right to become owner of the petroleum when and if produced.

Petroleum legislation belonging to category (i) needs for its successful operation a country with a well developed economy and an advanced, sophisticated legal system. Because of this and with a few exceptions, category (i) petroleum legislation has only been adopted and practised by countries that are Member States of the OECD.

With reference to (ii). A contract of work is a contractual relationship (a contract) entered into by a state entity (the state party) on the one part and a commercial petroleum enterprise from the private or public sector (the contractor) on the other. Contracts of work may be categorized into risk contracts and non-risk contracts. Risk contracts are contracts of work under the terms of which the contractor has to invest its own funds in the petroleum operations authorized under the contract. By contrast, a non-risk contract does not require the contractor concerned to supply its own funds; he will be compensated for his efforts regardless of the outcome thereof.

Risk contracts in turn may be divided into:

(i) production sharing contracts, the most common type of risk contract and meant for a complete venture, i.e., a venture including exploration, development (of commercial discoveries) and production operations;

(ii) risk service contracts, also known as technical service agreements, and meant for special production enhancing projects.

Petroleum legislation belonging to category (ii) has universally been adopted and practised by countries with a developing economy, which do not have a readily convertible currency and mostly lack a proper and adequate legal system. The production sharing contract is best suited to their needs when wishing to start exploration and/or further develop domestic petroleum activities. Still, countries with an emerging economy like Brazil, Russia, India and China, known as the BRIC-countries, also prefer to make use of production sharing contracts, albeit for slightly different reasons: what they in particular like about the contracts is the greater degree of state control and petroleum ownership that the latter provide. By contrast, technical service agreements may be very helpful in assisting a developing country to restart or renovate an already existing domestic petroleum industry, e.g., Iraq.

5.2   STRUCTURE

Category (i) petroleum legislation is structured as follows:

(i) There is a petroleum law i.e., an act or decision of a legislative body (or congress) of people's representatives, dealing with petroleum matters. This petroleum law may be set up as a comprehensive law, containing all the principles and important details of the licensing regime and leaving it to the government or the minister responsible for petroleum matters to regulate the minor details, or a basic petroleum law, setting out the main principles of the licensing regime and empowering the government to complete or adjust this regime as needed, creating thereby subsidiary legislation in the form of petroleum regulations and ministerial decrees.

(ii) Specific ministerial decisions taken by the government minister responsible for petroleum affairs pursuant to the petroleum regulations, which *inter alia* may concern the grant of a license, the approval of a work programme or a field development programme.

Category (ii) petroleum legislation is structured much simpler:

(i) There is a petroleum law i.e., an act or decision of a legislative body (or congress) of people's representatives, dealing with petroleum matters. This law contains no more than basic principles, such as the principle that the State is the owner of petroleum *in situ* and that only a state entity is allowed to produce the same for which purpose it is authorized to conclude a contract of work with a foreign oil enterprise.

(ii) The authorized state entity may be the State itself acting under its sovereign powers over natural resources, or an authority representing the State such as a government ministry or a petroleum directorate established within a ministry. The state party may also be a state oil enterprise i.e., a state owned and controlled oil company, usually referred to as the national oil company specially established for the purpose of managing and developing the national petroleum resources. When entering into a contract, the state oil enterprise is acting pursuant to a general authority granted by the petroleum law.

Any petroleum legislation operates in conjunction with any fiscal legislation imposing a tax on income realized by an authorized person, be it a licensee or a contractor, from its petroleum operations.

Petroleum legislation also operates in conjunction with relevant legislation if available. By relevant legislation is meant other legislation that although not specifically directed at petroleum or petroleum operations, nevertheless by the scope and nature of its provisions, also regulates the conduct of petroleum operations. Relevant legislation as described is administered by government ministries and/or by provincial and municipal authorities or administrations. Examples of relevant legislation are environmental and conservation legislation and planning and zoning legislation. In developing countries relevant legislation is not always in existence.

A petroleum law may be a law specifically designed and meant for petroleum matters, but it could also be a special section of a general mining law.

5.3   PRINCIPAL PROVISIONS OF PETROLEUM LAW

5.3.1   DEFINITION OF PETROLEUM

'Petroleum' is commonly defined as all liquid and gaseous hydrocarbons existing in their natural state in the subsoil, as well as other substances produced in association with such hydrocarbons.

Note. In Model Clause 1 of Schedule 4 of the UK Petroleum (Production) (Seaward Areas) Regulations 1988 (as amended), 'petroleum' is defined as follows: 'petroleum' includes any mineral oil or relative hydrocarbon and natural gas existing in its natural condition in strata but does not include coal or bituminous shales or other stratified deposits from which oil can be extracted by destructive distillation.

5.3.2   OWNERSHIP OF PETROLEUM IN SITU

Almost without exception, a petroleum law (or a constitutional law) vests in the State the ownership of petroleum *in situ*, i.e., petroleum as occurring under natural conditions at the surface or in the subsoil of the State concerned.

By contrast, the territorial mining regime of the US vests ownership of natural resources, e.g., coal, hard rock minerals and petroleum, in the public or private owner of the land on the surface or in the subsoil of which the natural resource is located. By contrast, no ownership of petroleum *in situ* is acknowledged under the German Federal Mining Law of 20 August 1980, effective as of 1 January 1982. As a matter of fact, petroleum *in situ* is classified as belonging to the *'Bergfreie Bodenschätze'* ('free minerals') similarly as naturally occurring metal ores, coal, and brown coal have been classified. These free minerals *in situ* have no owner, and are considered to be a *res nullius*. Nonetheless, after Directive 94/22/EC of 30 May 1994 had become effective in the Member States of the EU and Norway it must be assumed that petroleum *in situ* is owned by the German State.

In the international context, it has been established under the rules of the 1982 Convention on the Law of the Sea, that any coastal State has sovereign rights over its part of the continental shelf for the purpose of exploring it and exploiting its natural resources. On the strengths of these sovereign rights and taking into account that petroleum belongs to the natural resources of the continental shelf, coastal States have proclaimed and laid down in their petroleum law to be the owner of the petroleum in the seabed and in subsoil of the continental shelf. The matter of land ownership and associated claim to mineral ownership does not arise in this case because the seabed has no owner.

Apart from a State, a public or private landowner, petroleum *in situ* may have mankind as its owner. Under the 1982 Convention on the Law of the Sea the mineral resources *in situ* of the deep seabed area (the Area as defined in this Convention) have been declared to be the common heritage of mankind. Mineral resources are defined as to include petroleum.

In a parallel development of international law, the issue of state sovereignty over the State's natural resources has been addressed in a more general and principal way, not restricted to the sovereignty of a coastal State over the natural resources of its continental shelf. The first proclamation on this issue can be found in Article 2 of Chapter II of the 1974 UN Charter of Economic Rights and Duties of States. Said article reads:

> Every State has and shall freely exercise full permanent sovereignty, including possession, use and disposal, over all its wealth, natural resources and economic activities.

Note. In States where ownership of mineral resources is vested in the public or private owner of the land on the surface or in the subsoil of which the mineral resources are located, there appears to be a conflict with the principle of the State's sovereign rights over these resources. Accepting aforesaid Article 2 of Chapter II would strictly speaking amount to an expropriation of private mining rights.

5.3.3   CHOICE OF MINING REGIME

The petroleum law must make a choice between the license or the contract of work

5.3.4   DELEGATION OF LEGISLATIVE POWER TO THE
            GOVERNMENT

This subject is only of interest for category (i) petroleum legislation.

5.3.5   PROCEDURES FOR APPLYING FOR AND AWARDING
            EXCLUSIVE AUTHORIZATIONS, THE OPENING-UP OF
            AREAS

These rules include the laying down of (non-discriminatory) criteria for
qualifying as an applicant for an exclusive authorization, be it an exclusive
license or risk contract, the method of choosing between competing
qualified applicants and the procedures leading to the granting of authorizations: e.g., public announcement of the opening-up of areas and
invitation to submit bids, bidding rounds, auctions or cash tender bids,
special invitation, separate negotiations.

5.3.6   SIZE AND SHAPE OF THE AREA FOR WHICH
            AUTHORIZATIONS MAY BE GRANTED

Rules about the size and shape of the areas in respect of which an
(exclusive) license or risk contract will be made available may concern a
geometrical grid, resulting in an opened-up area which is divided into
blocks. If these rules are not part of the petroleum legislation itself they will
be part of a public announcement of areas that are opened-up for
submitting applications.

5.4   COMMON PROVISIONS OF THE EXCLUSIVE
            LICENSE

5.4.1   OWNERSHIP OF PETROLEUM IF AND WHEN PRODUCED

The holder of an exclusive production license has the right to acquire the
ownership of any petroleum that enters into any well that has been drilled
by the former in accordance with all terms and conditions of his license.

Note. As example of a licensee's ownership of petroleum, if and when produced,
may serve the wording used in the UK model offshore production license(to be
found in Schedule 4 of the Petroleum (Production) (Seawards Areas) Regulations
1988 as amended):

> In consideration of the payments and royalties hereinafter provided and the
> performance and observance by the licensee of all terms and conditions hereof
> the Minister, in exercise of the powers conferred upon him by the Act of 1934
> and the Act of 1964 hereby grants to the licensee EXCLUSIVE LICENCE AND
> LIBERTY during the continuance of this licence and subject to the provisions
> hereof to search and bore for, and get, petroleum in the seabed and subsoil under

the seaward area comprising an area of … square kilometres more particularly
described in Schedule 1 to this licence etc.

Another example in this context is provided by the aforementioned German
Federal Mining Law of 13 August 1980. First, petroleum is declared as to
belong to the class of *Bergfreie Bodenschätze* (free minerals). Then the
Law stipulates that any person wishing to search for free minerals needs an
Erlaubnis (an exploration license) and that any person wishing to produce
a free mineral needs a *Bewilligung* (a production license). The exploration
license grants the exclusive right to search for the specified free resources
within the licensed area and to acquire the ownership of any free mineral
that is unavoidably set free in the course of the operations. The production
license grants the exclusive right to search for and to produce the free
minerals described in the license within the *Bewilligungsfeld* (licensed
area) and to acquire the *Eigentum* (the ownership) of the free minerals so
produced.

In Chapter 3, section 3-3 (Production License), third paragraph of the
Norwegian Petroleum Act of 29 November 1996 No. 72 it is stated (after
translation):

> A production licence entails an exclusive right to exploration, exploration
> drilling and production of petroleum deposits in areas covered by the licence.
> The licensee becomes the owner of the petroleum which is produced.

A similar explicit provision about the ownership of petroleum after its
extraction from the subsoil reservoir is found in Article 3.2 of the
Netherlands General Mining Law of 31 October 2002. After having
established that mineral resources *in situ* are owned by the State, the article
goes on stating (after translation) that:

> The ownership of *inter alia* petroleum being produced in accordance with
> the terms of the licence is transferred to the holder of the licence
> concerned.

Summarizing, a transfer of ownership of petroleum takes place from the
owner of the petroleum *in situ* (i.e., either the State or, as the case may be,
the public or private owner of the land overlying the petroleum deposit) to
the holder of an exclusive production license or lease at the moment the
petroleum enters his well.

Of course the validity of this principle becomes questionable if the
petroleum produced from a licensed area, say area A, originates not from
an adjacent open, non-licensed area but from inside the boundaries of an
adjacent licensed area, say area B. When as a direct result of producing
petroleum from area A, petroleum migrates from area B to area A, there

remains less petroleum 'to get' for the holder of the production license for area B. How to solve this problem is discussed hereinafter in this Chapter.

5.4.2   DURATION, SUB-PERIODS

Generally, there is an initial period and one or more extensions. The total license period may reach to thirty or forty years, if development and production forms part of the licensed operations. A license for exploration only shall not extend beyond ten years.

The EC Directive 94/22/EC of 30 May 1994 (which the Member States of the EU and Norway had to implement) does not provide for standard periods. Instead each applied for license is treated as a special case. Seen from this perspective, Member States must ensure that the duration of an authorization does not exceed the period necessary to carry out the authorized operations. However, the competent authorities may prolong the authorization where the stipulated duration is insufficient to complete the operations in question and where the operations have been performed in accordance with the authorization. Member States must also ensure that operators do not retain exclusive rights in the authorized area for longer than is necessary for the proper performance of the authorized operations.

5.4.3   AREA RELINQUISHMENT SCHEDULE

It is a common condition that at certain intervals, for instance at the end of the initial period, part or parts of the original area of the license must be relinquished. Part or parts to be relinquished must of such a shape and size that they are suitable to be offered once more for licensing.

5.4.4   OBLIGATORY EXPLORATION WORK PROGRAMME

During the initial period of the license an obligatory exploration work programme shall have to be carried out. The extension of the license beyond the initial period shall depend on a satisfactory implementation of this condition. The details of such a work programme belong to the particular conditions of a license (see hereinafter) and usually form an element of the competitive bidding for a license. A license may provide for a sanction on the non-fulfilment of the whole or any part of the obligatory work programme. In case of non-fulfilment, the defaulting licensee may have to pay in cash the monetary value of the non-fulfilled programme to the competent authority. Non-fulfilment may also constitute a ground for cancelling the license, but the problem is usually solved in further negotiations on compensatory work between the competent authority and the licensee.

5.4.5 DEVELOPMENT PLAN AND PRODUCTION SCHEDULE

The licensee shall be obliged to prepare a development plan and corresponding production schedule with respect to any commercial discovery that has been made and shall submit such plan and schedule for the approval of the competent authority. Only so approved plans may be carried out.

5.4.6 DISPOSAL OF PRODUCTION

Under prevailing licensing regimes, the licensee is completely free in disposing of its production, except in a case of national emergency.

5.4.7 LIABILITY FOR DAMAGES

The licensee shall have to keep the competent authority indemnified against all claims and demands brought against the authority by any third party in connection with the license or the licensed operations. Under some petroleum legislation, special provisions regarding liabilities for pollution damage caused by the operations are provided. As noted before, where no special rules are provided, liability for damage caused in carrying out the licensed operations is governed by the code of civil law.

5.4.8 METHODS OF WORKING

The licensee will always be obliged to execute all his operations in accordance with the provisions which prescribe the methods that have to be followed or applied in carrying out the authorized operations, such as rules regarding drilling practices and the installation, use, operation and final abandonment of oil/gas installations and pipelines. The licensee will also be obliged to execute the operations in a safe manner, and without harming the health of the workers employed by him in his operations or causing damage to the environment. All these rules and provisions are to be found in the (model) license itself and/or in government regulations or ministerial decrees specifically made for the purpose, all depending on how the petroleum legislation has developed over time.

5.4.9   JOINT EXPLOITATION OF STRADDLING PETROLEUM
               RESERVOIRS

Where a single, continuous petroleum reservoir extends across (the vertical
projection of) the boundary of a production license into the adjacent area
such petroleum reservoir is referred to as a straddling petroleum reservoir.
If in respect of the adjacent area production licenses have been granted
each covering a part of the straddling reservoir the joint exploitation of
such a reservoir by all persons holding such licenses and by the licensee is
usually of benefit to them all and in practice will be carried out on a
voluntary basis. But in principle, the licensees involved in a straddling
reservoir are free to extract petroleum from their part of the reservoir as
long as, and to the extent that, they operate in accordance with the rights
conferred and obligations imposed by their respective licenses. The most
relevant obligation in this respect requires a licensee to ensure that any well
shall be drilled so that any part thereof stays at a safe distance from any of
the boundaries of the licensed area.

Note. See for example Schedule 4 model Clause 20 'Distance of wells from
boundaries of licensed area' (UK offshore petroleum legislation (Petroleum
(Production) (Seaward Areas) Regulations 1988/1995/1996). The said safe
distance here is fixed at 125 metres.

But governments too expect to benefit from joint exploitation in the form
of a more efficient development plan, less waste of capital and a higher
ultimate recovery, which are all factors leading to higher tax revenues, and
in order to ensure that joint exploitation will actually take place will
include in their licenses an obligation for the licensee to this effect.

     The UK offshore petroleum legislation (Petroleum (Production) (Sea-
ward Areas) Regulations 1988/1995/1996) offers an important example of
a statutory requirement to cooperate if and when a straddling reservoir
must be developed. The Schedule 4 model Clause 28 'Unit Development'
reads as follows:

     28(1) If at any time in which this licence is in force the Minister shall be
     satisfied that the strata in the licensed area or any part thereof form part of a
     single geological petroleum structure or petroleum field (hereinafter referred to
     as 'an oil field') other parts whereof are formed by strata in areas in respect of
     which other licences … are then in force and the Minister shall consider that it
     is in the national interest in order to secure the maximum ultimate recovery of
     petroleum and in order to avoid unnecessary competitive drilling that the oil
     field should be worked and developed as a unit in cooperation by all persons
     including the licensee whose licences extend to or include any part thereof the

following provisions shall apply: (2) Upon being so required ... by the Minister the licensee shall cooperate with such other persons (hereinafter referred to as the other licensees) as may be specified in the said notice in the preparation of a scheme (hereinafter referred to as 'a development scheme') for the working and development of the oil field as a unit by the licensee and the other licensees in cooperation, and shall, jointly with the other licensees, submit such scheme for the approval of the Minister ... (4) If a development scheme shall not be submitted to the Minister in time, or if the development scheme so submitted shall not be approved by the Minister, the Minister may himself prepare a development scheme which shall be fair and equitable to the licensee and all other licensees, and the Licensee shall perform and observe all the terms and conditions thereof. (5) If the licensee shall object to any such development scheme prepared by the Minister he may ... refer the matter to arbitration in the manner provided by clause 43 of this licence.

Another example of mandatory cooperation is offered by the Netherlands Mining Law of 31 October 2002. The relevant articles are Articles 23(1) and (2) and Article 42(2), which read (after translation) as follows:

23(1) A person holding a production licence shall refrain from exploiting a reservoir that is reasonably expected to extend beyond the boundary of the licensed area as long as he has not entered into an agreement as prescribed in article 42 (2), unless the Minister decides otherwise. (2) If during or after the exploitation of a reservoir it appears that the latter extends across the boundary of the licensed area the licensee concerned is obliged promptly after the fact has come to his knowledge to inform accordingly the person holding a licence for the adjacent area and to collaborate with that person in preparing and concluding an agreement as prescribed in article 42 (2).

42 (2) If a production licence is in force with respect to an area in which a reservoir is present that is reasonably expected to extend beyond the boundary of the licensed area then the licensee is obliged to collaborate with the person holding a production licence for the adjacent area in preparing and concluding an agreement pursuant to which the production shall be undertaken in mutual consultation, unless the Minister decides otherwise.

According to this example it is not required that the straddling reservoir be developed and produced as a unit, as is required under UK legislation as described above. In the Netherlands example, licensees are free to make a choice out of various forms of cooperative exploitation, which may range from outright unitization to separate development with two operators.

A third example is offered by the Norwegian Petroleum Act of 29 November 1996 No. 72. Chapter 4, section 4-7 'Joint Petroleum Activities' reads (after translation) as follows:

If a petroleum deposit extends over more than one block with different licensees, or onto the continental shelf of another State, efforts shall be made to reach agreement on the most efficient coordination of petroleum activities in connection with the petroleum deposits as well as on the apportionment of the petroleum deposit. This shall apply similarly when, in the case of several petroleum deposits, joint petroleum activities would obviously be more efficient. Agreements on joint exploration drilling shall be submitted to the Ministry. Agreements on joint production, transportation, utilization and cessation of petroleum activities shall be submitted to the Ministry for approval. If consensus on such agreements is not reached within reasonable time, the Ministry may determine how such joint petroleum activities shall be conducted, including the apportionment of the deposit.

The manner in which the licensees involved intend to cooperate, with regard to the exploitation of a straddling petroleum reservoir, should not be a concern of the government. Generally, the government's interest lies in ensuring that a straddling reservoir as a whole is exploited in an optimum manner, resulting in maximum fiscal and other benefits for the State. From this perspective, it would appear that a government would not particularly be interested in how the participating licensees divide the straddling reservoir between themselves. But in a situation where the terms and conditions concerning government take and/or state participation, differ between the participating licenses the government will be keenly interested in these issues. Such a situation may occur if the respective participating licenses have been granted under different licensing rounds involving different conditions.

5.4.10   OBLIGATORY PAYMENTS

The licensee is or may be obliged to make payments to the State other than payments required to be made under the applicable rules of the corporation tax or any special petroleum income tax. Said payments consist of royalty, annual surface rentals, cash bonuses, net, gross or excess profit shares. These payments are all discussed in Chapter 8.

5.4.11   STATE PARTICIPATION

A government may have been authorized to demand as a condition for the grant of a license that the State itself or a wholly state owned enterprise designated for the purpose becomes a participant in such a license and in the venture that is based on the same. Such demand for state participation in the license and the venture based thereon may be fulfilled by the applicant by accepting the State or the designated state enterprise as a co-licensee and establishing a joint venture on the basis of an agreement of cooperation, also known as a state participation agreement. If the State itself is participating in the license, as is for instance the case in Norway, a wholly state owned enterprise may be designated to represent the State in the license and to manage the State's interest. State or designated state enterprise, as the case may be, is hereinafter referred to as the state participant. However, the state participant does not necessarily have to become a co-licensee: the license could be awarded solely to the applicant, everything else (meaning the state participating agreement) remaining the same. If this option is chosen, the former applicant (now 100 per cent license holder) will be solely responsible for exercising the rights and fulfilling the obligations attached to the license (e.g., fulfilling the work commitments, timely applying for renewals and extensions and making submissions for getting approvals, etc.).

However this may, the modalities of the state participation which are to be found in the state participation agreement, concern:

(i) the percentage share state participation (whether fixed for the duration of the agreement or made dependent on factors such as production levels, etc.;

(ii) the timing of the state participant's financial participation becoming effective: i.e., a choice has to be made between the state participant's financial contributions (in accordance with its percentage share participation) to start either from the very beginning of the authorized operations, i.e., at the start of the exploration phase, or not before the first commercial discovery has been made.

If the latter option is chosen it has to be settled whether or not the state participant has to reimburse its percentage share participation of the successful exploration expenditure that led to the commercial discovery.

A text of the required agreement may be provided as part of the model license, if available. Otherwise such agreement is subject to the approval of the competent authority. Its contents are generally very similar to those of the usual joint operating agreement concluded between oil companies from the private or public sector (see Chapter 11).

The percentage share state participation may be fixed in law or regulation as a standard condition of the license or state participation agreement or may be negotiated in the context of a bidding round, and so become a particular condition of the license concerned.

Note. The EC Directive of 30 May 1994 puts restrictions on the influence and power of intervention of the state participant in the management of the operations in the sense that any vote by the state participant shall be based exclusively on transparent, objective and non-discriminatory principles, and shall not prevent the management decisions of its co-licensee(s) from being based on normal commercial principles. Furthermore, the state participant shall not be party to information

nor exercise any voting rights on decisions regarding sources of procurement for
its co-licensee(s).

5.4.12   SETTLEMENT OF DISPUTES (ARISING UNDER A LICENSE)

Since a license creates a direct relationship between the licensee and the
government granting the license in its capacity as representative of the
State, any dispute between the licensee and the government shall in
countries with an advanced, well developed legal system as a rule be dealt
with in accordance with the rules of public administrative law and, in case
no amicable resolution of the conflict appears possible, be finally decided
by a court of administrative law.

Nonetheless, even in aforesaid countries it may be more practical,
when the dispute concerns matters of a highly technical nature to choose
arbitration rather than a court of law as means to settle such disputes. The
petroleum legislation of the UK offers an example.

Schedule 4 Model Clause 43 of the UK offshore petroleum legislation
(Petroleum (Production) (Seaward Areas) Regulations 1988/1995/1996
reads as follows:

> 43 (1) If at any time any dispute, difference or question shall arise between the
> Minister and the Licensee as to any matter arising under or by virtue of this
> licenc or as tot heir respective rights and liabilities in respect thereof then the
> same shall, except where it expressly provided by this licence that the matter or
> thing to which the same relates is to be determined, decided, directed, approved
> or consented to by the Minister, be referreed to arbitration as provided by the
> following paragraph (i.e the arbitration shall be inaccordance with the Arbitra-
> tion Act 1950 by a single arbitrator).

5.4.13   STABILITY OF TERMS

Production licenses are usually granted for long periods. Chances are that
during such a long period license conditions have to be adjusted, not only
for newly to be awarded licenses but also for already existing ones.

If the conditions of a license are set out in a comprehensive petroleum
law or in regulations issued under the authority of a basic petroleum law
they can only be changed if the law is changed, amended or replaced by
another law. Usually such new (amendment) law contains a separate
'Transitional' Section listing which of the conditions incorporated in
already existing licenses are being upheld or 'saved' instead of being
replaced. Apart from that, conditions of already existing licenses are not
affected in the event new regulations (plus may be a new model license) are

issued. As a matter of fact, the new conditions (as possibly contained in a new model) are only incorporated in licenses which will be granted after the effective date of the new regulations. Anyway, the particular conditions of the license are always upheld.

Of more importance, however, than the question of whether or not during the lifetime of the license its conditions can be changed is the question of how much a licensee can rely on the stability of the fiscal regime that is applicable to the licensed operations. In so far this fiscal regime is not part of the conditions of the license but based on other laws it is vulnerable to being changed at any time.

Note. A modern example of protection against any unilateral change of established conditions is provided by the German Federal Mining Law of 13 August 1980. Article 16 of this Law, covering the main aspects of exploration and production licenses, states in its third paragraph that to change or modify any imposed condition after the license had been granted is permissible, provided such change or modification is commercially acceptable to the license holder, technically feasible and is serving the purposes of the license.

5.4.14   PARTICULAR CONDITIONS

Any license document will be completed by describing the conditions that are particular to the license concerned. Following subjects are involved: description of the licensed area, cash bonuses to be paid on certain occasions, duration of the license and the obligatory exploration work programme.

5.5   COMMON PROVISIONS OF THE PRODUCTION SHARING CONTRACT

5.5.1   THE PARTIES

Production sharing contracts are made and entered into on the one part by a state entity, hereinafter 'state party' and on the other by an entity consisting of one or more, mostly foreign oil companies from the private or public sector, hereinafter 'contractor'. This state party may be the State itself, a state authority representing the State, such as a ministry of petroleum or a petroleum directorate established within such a ministry, or, as is more commonly the case, a duly authorized state owned and state controlled oil enterprise.

Note 1. In some host States (e.g., Egypt, Syria), where the contracts are made with a duly authorized state oil enterprise, the government itself is also a party to the contract and will co-sign the same. As a co-signatory of the contract, the government will decide typical governmental matters such as the approval of assignments of interest in the contract and the termination or cancellation of the contract.

Note 2. Where (already) a licensing regime is in existence and the government wishes to switch to production sharing contracts, it is feasible to integrate the desired contracts into specific exclusive licenses relating to the intended petroleum operations and area. This integration can be accomplished either by granting the required license to the state party who then in turn concludes a production sharing contract with a contractor for the purpose of conducting the authorized petroleum operations (exploration and/or development and production) within and with respect to the licensed area, or by granting upon concluding the contract the required exclusive license to the contractor. In both cases, the contract area coincides with the licensed area. Furthermore, the duration of the contract, possible renewals or extensions thereof and area relinquishments are all determined by the corresponding conditions of the (underlying) license and in case the licensing regime involved prescribes separate licenses for the exploration and production stage, the state party or contractor, as the case may be, will have to apply for and need to be granted a production license in the event a discovery of petroleum is declared commercial in order to be able to develop and produce this discovery.

5.5.2   CONTRACT AREA

The area of the production sharing contract is described in the contract. In practice, it is described in terms of blocks with reference to a geographical grid system. The area of a contract may comprise one or more of such blocks.

Alternatively, if the production sharing contract is integrated into a specific exclusive license, the area of the contract coincides with the area of the underlying license, which in turn is also described in terms of blocks with reference to a geographical grid system.

5.5.3   DURATION OF THE CONTRACT AND AREA
RELINQUISHMENT

Distinction is made between an exploration phase and a development/ production phase. The exploration phase is usually divided in sub-periods of two or three years. Parts of the original contract area may have to be surrendered at the end of each sub-period. The contract will be terminated if within the duration of the exploration phase no declaration of commercial discovery is made. At the end of the total exploration period, the area not converted into the areas containing commercial discoveries and earmarked and demarcated for development and production must be surrendered. Development work and production operations in converted areas are bound to specific development and production periods and extensions thereof.

The overall duration of a contract may be fixed at a specified number of years (e.g., thirty years) but should comprise the successive holding/ development and/or production periods (plus possible extensions) and, if so needed, be extended accordingly.

Alternatively, if the production sharing contract is integrated into an exclusive license that is held either by the state party or by the contractor, as the case may be, the conditions of the license regarding duration and renewal or extension of periods, area relinquishment and conversion from exploration license into a production license, if applicable, apply. The holder of the license is responsible for taking action in these matters when required in accordance with the conditions of the license in order to prevent that rights are lost or obligations remain unfulfilled with all the consequences thereof for the status of the license.

5.5.4   OBLIGATORY EXPLORATION WORK

With respect to each sub-period of the exploration phase the contractor will be obliged to carry out a minimum exploration work programme and/or to spend a specified minimum amount of US Dollars on exploration work.

5.5.5   DECLARATION OF COMMERCIAL DISCOVERY OF PETROLEUM

After making a discovery of petroleum, the contractor is obliged to carry out within a specified period a programme of evaluation work in order to decide whether the discovery constitutes a commercial discovery. Only discoveries declared by the contractor to be commercial and as such approved by the state party may be developed and produced in accordance with the rules of the contract, in which case the whole area capable of production from the discovery is turned into a development area. Any such area is considered automatically terminated if within a specified number of years from the date of commercial discovery in said area no oil shall have been lifted as part of a regular programme of lifting in accordance with the lifting schedule.

If in the contract area belonging to a contract which is primarily aimed at the production of oil, a discovery of non-associated gas is made contracts may provide for a postponement of a declaration of commercial discovery and allow the contractor a holding period of say five years with possible extensions, if no outlet for the gas is readily available. During such a holding period the contractor is not obliged to undertake development work with respect to the particular gas discovery, but is expected to investigate, jointly with the state party, the commercial options of development and transportation.

In the 2006 Model Production Sharing Agreement made available in Angola, a more simple approach is adopted: the state party is given the option to keep the gas discovery for itself. Article 29.3 of that Model reads:

> If non-associated natural gas is discovered within the contract area then Sonangol will have the exclusive right to appraise, develop and produce said gas for its own account and risk. If Sonangol so determines and if agreed with contractor within a term determined by Sonangol, the discovery of non-associated natural gas shall be developed jointly by Sonangol or one of its affiliates and contractor.

5.5.6   OPERATORSHIP, PROGRAMMES AND BUDGETS

In principle, the contractor acts as the operator and as such is responsible for and in charge of carrying out the operations in accordance with the programmes and budgets as approved under the rules of the contract. If the contractor is a consortium of companies, one of them shall be appointed as operator. During the exploration phase of the contract, the contractor is responsible for fulfilling the minimum exploration work programme and to spend the minimum expenditure commitments.

But many departures from this basic pattern occur. According to contracts applicable in Egypt and Syria a joint non-profit, non-asset owning operating company (having the contractor and the state party as its shareholders) is established as soon as for the first time a commercial discovery has been declared. This joint operating company is responsible for carrying out the development and production operations and any further exploration work and is funded by the contractor. In other instances, the state party is appointed as the unique operator of the contract area, or much more complicated, may have been given the option to become operator with respect to any individual discovery or field, leaving the contractor in charge of the operations until the state party exercises this option. Such an option may be exercised as from the moment all development costs incurred with respect to the field concerned have been recovered from cost oil generated by the field in question. Whatever choice is made, it all depends on the experience and confidence that the state party in the course of time has gained with the domestic petroleum operations.

The operator, whoever it may turn out to be, is responsible for preparing the annual work programmes and corresponding budgets and any specific plan for evaluation of a discovery and development thereof if commercially warranted. After the proposed programmes and budgets have been approved by the supervisory body, the operator has to carry out these programmes and plans within the agreed budgets and in accordance with the rules of the contract and any applicable petroleum legislation and relevant legislation. In absence of relevant legislation, the necessary operational rules shall be provided by the contract. If so, these regulatory provisions are formulated as duties of the operator. Important duties include the operator's obligation to carry out petroleum operations in a proper and workmanlike manner and in accordance with good oil field practice, to prevent causing damage to the environment, pay for the costs associated with clean-up of any pollution caused, to take appropriate abandonment measures upon termination of the contract, and to fulfil any of the national submitting to the state party copies of all relevant data and information obtained in the course of the operations, such as geological, geophysical and any type of well data, providing all personnel, financial and technical resources required for a proper performance of the operations. An important task of the operator consists in organizing the procedures to be followed in the awarding of major contracts. As a rule, the operator shall be required to award contracts exceeding certain financial limits exclusively by international tender. Exceptions may have to be made with respect to the acquisition of local services and locally manufactured goods

5.5.7   SUPERVISORY BODY

Operations are supervised by the state party directly or exceptionally, by a management committee, consisting of representatives of state party and contractor.

The task of the supervisory body consists in reviewing and approving, in the form as prepared and submitted by the operator:

(i) any declaration of commercial discovery and any plans to develop such a discovery;

(ii) annual programmes of work and corresponding budgets; and

(iii) the award of major contracts.

The supervisory body has the right to propose changes to the submitted work programmes.

Note. The requirement that work programmes, budgets, a declaration of commercial discovery, the corresponding development plan and the award of major contracts shall obtain the approval of the supervisory body is an essential condition of a contract because, as stipulated therein, the operator is only allowed to execute work programmes and development plans and incur costs in connection therewith if these programmes and plans and corresponding budgets and contracts have been so approved. To reinforce this requirement, it is generally expressly stated that no compensation for or reimbursement of costs are given if these costs have been incurred in doing work that was not part of an approved work programme or have been incurred on the basis of a non-approved contract.

Within limits the contractor has the right to change an approved programme in order to adapt the latter to changed circumstances. Similarly the supervisory body may, within pre-determined limits, change an approved programme.

5.5.8   COOPERATION BETWEEN STATE PARTY AND
           CONTRACTOR

The cooperation between state party and its contractor may be formalized by setting up either a jointly owned operating company, in which the parties become shareholder, or a management committee, in which both parties are represented. Such a management committee may also act as a supervisory body (see above). When a management committee is meant to be an organizational instrument for consultation its task consists in discussing and reviewing any proposal prepared by the operator before they are submitted to the supervisory body, in this case the state party, for approval.

5.5.9   OPERATIONS FOR THE SOLE ACCOUNT AND RISK OF THE
           STATE PARTY

A contract may provide for the state party having an option to conduct for its own risk and account certain exploration, appraisal or development drilling operations which are deemed by the contractor not to be economically justified when applying his own economic criteria and yardsticks including the development of any discovery finally not declared to be commercial. If the state party would be interested in a sole risk and account operation, it may have to use the services and facilities of the contractor for which the latter will be compensated. To provide for such operations the contract will adopt the corresponding rules incorporated in standard joint operating agreements made between commercial oil enterprises (see Chapter 11).

5.5.10   FUNDING THE OPERATIONS, US DOLLAR ACCOUNTING

In principle, the costs and expenditures incurred in the authorized operations as well as any losses and risks derived therefrom shall be borne by the contractor and the state party shall not be responsible to bear or repay any of the aforesaid costs and expenditures. But contracts may provide for an option on the part of the state party to share in the funding of the development phase of any particular field as soon as the decision is taken to develop such field. Without exception, however, bearing the costs and risks of exploration work is the sole and exclusive responsibility of the contractor. The latter is generally obliged to provide the funds for the operations in convertible foreign currency (usually US dollars are stipulated). However, the (foreign) contractor is allowed to keep the proceeds of its export sales abroad, at least to the extent that any local payment obligations, such as payment of local taxes and locally incurred costs, have been fulfilled. In this way, the (foreign) contractor is exempted from the generally applicable obligation (imposed on domestic exporters) to surrender foreign currency proceeds to the central bank of the host State (in exchange for local currency). Furthermore, the (foreign) contractor will be allowed to hold bank accounts in convertible foreign currency, to repatriate any surplus foreign exchange and to keep the books of account in US Dollars.

5.5.11   ALLOCATION OF PETROLEUM PRODUCTION

Available petroleum production is divided between the State, the state party and the contractor in accordance with the rules of the individual contract.

Actual figures i.e., the figures to be put in the Model are arrived at after negotiations with applicants and depend on competition, the particular circumstances of the contract and the oil and/or natural gas prospectivity of the contract area. The expectations regarding future oil prices (also impacting on gas prices) play a lesser role because of the built-in flexibility in the sharing of the benefits of the contract, which should ensure that the state party and its government will be the main beneficiaries of a high oil (gas) price level.

Preliminary Note. In what follows hereinafter only the rules of allocation of petroleum production contained in contracts primarily aimed at the production of oil will be described. For contracts primarily aimed at the production of natural gas the same rules will *mutatis mutandis* apply. Nonetheless, in contract areas where oil as well as non-associated natural gas are simultaneously developed and produced the allocation systems may be linked together as will be explained below.

5.5.12   ROYALTY OIL, COST RECOVERY OIL AND PROFIT OIL

The allocation of oil production starts with setting aside a portion of oil destined for the State by way of payment in kind of a royalty (a payment known from the licensing regime). Applicable percentages vary between ten and fifteen per cent, usually made dependent on the level of daily production. The portion remaining after deduction of the royalty oil is (within or without certain limits as determined in the contract) put at the disposal of the contractor for recovery of the costs and expenditures incurred by him in carrying out the petroleum operations. This portion is referred to as cost recovery oil.

Production remaining after royalty oil and cost recovery oil is referred to as profit oil. This portion is shared in complex proportions between the state party and the contractor.

5.5.13   DETERMINATION OF COST RECOVERY OIL

Usually cost recovery oil is bound to a maximum of ten per cent of all oil produced and saved in the contract area after deduction of royalty oil. But instead of using a single percentage figure X, the cost recovery process can be made more complex by dividing production into successive tranches with each tranche higher in the series being assigned a lower cost recovery percentage. But some contracts do not recognize or impose any volume restriction on the production available for cost recovery, in other words total production, after deduction of royalty oil, is put at the disposal of the contractor for cost recovery (as further specified).

If in any given year costs or expenditures are less than the maximum value of the cost recovery oil the difference shall become part of and included in the contract area profit oil. In the event that in any given year costs or expenditures exceed the value of cost recovery crude oil for such year the excess shall be carried forward for recovery in the next succeeding year or years, but in no case after the termination of the contract.

In a contract area where oil as well as non-associated gas are simultaneously being developed and/or produced, the respective allocation systems may be linked in as much as costs incurred with respect to natural gas development operations are allowed to be recovered from oil production and vice versa. This is a powerful incentive to develop non-associated gas reservoirs.

A crucial element of the cost recovery process is the determination of the monetary value of the oil (or the natural gas as the case may be) that is put at the disposal of the contractor for cost recovery. If the price used for the determination of this value is higher than the objective market value, the cost recovery remains incomplete to the disadvantage of the contractor. To meet this problem, a contract will include a description of the market value of the oil or natural gas that is expected to be produced and stipulate to use this value for the calculation of the monetary value of the available cost production.

Not all costs incurred qualify for recovery out of production. Distinction is made between 'recoverable costs' and 'non-recoverable costs'. Non-recoverable costs are costs made by the contractor in deviation from the rules of the contract. In particular, those costs are excluded from recovery which have been incurred in non-authorized work, are the result of gross negligence or wilful misconduct, have been made on the basis of a contract that has been awarded in contravention of the prescribed tender procedures, or which do not appear in an approved budget. Most contracts contain an extensive listing of cost categories that do not qualify for cost recovery and/or contain criteria on the basis of which it shall be judged whether or not costs are acceptable for cost recovery.

Recoverable costs are categorized as exploration costs, capital expenditure, operating costs and abandonment costs. Each cost category, except abandonment costs, may be recovered in accordance with the rules of amortization and depreciation as applicable to such category. Abandonment costs arise at the end of the contract. These costs must be estimated and a quarterly provision should be allowed as part of the recoverable costs.

Cost recovery operates on a quarterly basis, i.e., recognized costs incurred in any quarter are recovered from the cost production available in any such quarter. In the case of under-recovery recognized costs are carried forward to the next quarter.

In order to provide incentives meant to help contractors faced with high cost operations, special cost related deductions (investment credits) may be granted. Such special deductions or credits are expressed as a percentage of the capital expenditure incurred and form part of the recoverable costs.

5.5.14   THE SHARING OF PROFIT OIL

Profit oil is divided between the state party and the contractor in many different ways, the one more complex than the other. A common method uses a series of successive daily production tranches and assigns to each tranche higher in the series a sharing proportion that is more favourable for the state party. The sharing itself concerns the profit oil part of each individual tranche, i.e., each tranche has first to be divided in royalty oil, cost recovery oil and profit oil before the sharing percentages can be applied. A closely related method consists in dividing cumulative oil production in successive tranches and assigning to each tranche a different profit oil split. Over time, as cumulative production increases, the sharing of the profit oil will become more favourable to the state party. But there are still other ways to share profit oil. For instance the sharing proportions applied to profit oil produced in any particular year are determined on the basis of the ratio (the R factor) of the cumulative contract revenues earned by contractor from cost recovery oil and his share of profit oil from inception of such earnings up to the end of the year preceding the year in question to the cumulative contract expenses incurred by contractor from inception thereof to the end of the year preceding the year in question. The sharing of profit oil between the state party and the contractor is made a function of a stepwise increasing value of the R factor in the sense that the higher the value of the R factor the more the sharing proportions change in favour of the state party. The numbers to be filled in are subject to negotiation.

A closely related method of profit production sharing is contained in the 2006 Model Production Sharing Agreement (Angola) and envisages the sharing of profit oil in the current quarter according to the internal rate of return of the income tax paid cash flow (cash flow after income tax) realized by the contractor at the end of the preceding quarter.

5.5.15   PETROLEUM INCOME TAX

As a rule, the contractor is subject to payment of the tax imposed on the income realized by him under the contract. The tax to be paid is a percentage of contractor's taxable income, which consists of the revenues realized by the sale of the cost recovery petroleum and of contractor's share of the profit petroleum less operating costs, depreciation charges and possible tax incentives. Sometimes the state party has also to pay income tax, sometimes the state party is exempted therefrom.

Note. In Indonesia, where the concept of production sharing had originated, the production sharing mechanism was initially meant to replace or absorb the payment of income tax and to exhaust the methods to determine government take. This brought US and European oil companies whose affiliates had entered into such non-income tax paying production sharing contracts in a difficult position in relation to the fiscal authorities in their home countries. Such affiliates were supposed to have been subject to or even to have actually paid income tax in the country where they were operating. The Indonesian government and governments of other host countries that were confronted with these fiscal problems arising in the home countries of the parent companies of their contractors have reacted positively by changing the contracts to the effect that the contractors were made subject to and had to pay tax on the income generated under the contract, while at the same time integrating this tax into the production sharing mechanism in such a way that the overall government take was not affected.

5.5.16   LIFTING AND DISPOSITION OF PETROLEUM

It is the right and obligation of each of the Parties to separately take at the delivery point (in accordance with a lifting schedule) its respective contractual oil entitlements. *Mutatis mutandis* this applies also to the lifting of natural gas entitlements, albeit state party and contractor will dedicate their respective contractual shares to a common outlet.

Note. Oil production may be accompanied by the production of associated natural gas. For the disposal of this gas joint schemes may be developed such as a scheme for selling the gas produced on the domestic gas market, or a scheme for building a gas plant to extract NGLs. Unused gas will have to be flared.

5.5.17   PURCHASE OF STATE PARTY'S SHARE OF THE PROFIT OIL

Where it is foreseen that the state party faces problems with disposing of its share of the profit oil, a contract may require the contractor to purchase any part thereof under normal commercial terms and conditions prevailing in the international oil industry and at the contractual market price in force at the time the oil is lifted. Alternatively, the state party concerned could have been given the right to require its contractor to use his best efforts to arrange the sale of all or part of the state party's share of production on terms and conditions to be agreed between the parties and subject to contractor's right to recover all reasonable costs associated with such marketing and disposal.

5.5.18   DOMESTIC SUPPLY OBLIGATION (OIL)

As a rule, the contractor is allowed freely to export his cost recovery oil and
his share of the profit oil, albeit this freedom under many contracts is
restricted by the imposition of an obligation in one form or another to
supply the domestic market (other than in case of national emergency).
Usually the domestic supply obligation is translated into a right of the state
party to purchase at market price (as defined in the contract) up to fifty per
cent of contractor's oil entitlement. This right is qualified by stipulating
that it will be exercised only after the state party has fully utilized royalty
oil and its share of profit oil and then pro rata among all producers in the
country.

Note. Under the terms of the 2006 Model Production Sharing Agreement (Angola)
the state party, i.e., Sonangol shall have the right to buy from the contractor oil
from the contract area equivalent to the value of the petroleum income tax due by
the contractor to the Ministry of Finance, i.e., fifty per cent of contractor's share
of profit oil.

5.5.19   JOINT EXPLOITATION OF STRADDLING PETROLEUM
                RESERVOIRS

Production sharing contracts usually contain provisions in which attention
is paid to compulsory joint exploitation of straddling petroleum accumulations. The contractors on either side of the boundary are not directly
involved in this matter but have to follow the instructions given by the state
party.

5.5.20   STABILITY OF THE CONTRACTOR'S ECONOMIC POSITION

Apart from the efficiency of the cost recovery mechanism the contractor's
economic position under a production sharing contract is determined by the
percentage and modalities of the petroleum income tax, the percentage of
royalty oil, and the state party's percentage share of profit production. The
question arises as to what guarantees are available with respect to the
stability of these conditions. The volume of royalty oil and the state party's
share of profit production are contractually fixed contributions that have
been agreed and accepted against the background of the payments due
under the income tax law(s) as prevailing at the time the contract was
negotiated and entered into. These contractual payments are assumed to
remain unchanged during the validity of the contract. The petroleum

income tax paying contractor has however no guarantee that the petroleum income tax will similarly remain unchanged during that period.

In the context of a production sharing contract, there are two methods available to achieve the desired stability of the government take and safeguard the economic position of the contractor:

(i) freezing the rate of the applicable petroleum income tax for the duration of the contract; or

(ii) adjusting the contractual payments, such as the sharing of profit oil, in order to counter-balance any negative effects on contractor's economic position caused by a future adverse change of the applicable petroleum income tax.

If the first method is adopted, the contract will provide that petroleum income tax will be levied at the rate existing on the effective date of the contract. Future changes to the rate of the income tax shall then not be applicable to income derived from the contract. Such protection against future changes of the tax rate can only be offered by a contract that is a law in itself (e.g., contracts as applicable in Egypt and Syria) or by a contract made with the State itself.

Note. An example of a stability-of-terms provision is offered by Article 17 of the Russian Federal Law No. 225-FZ 'On Production Sharing Agreements' of 30 December 1995 / 7 January 1999 (PSA Law). This article (in translated form) reads as follows:

1. The terms and conditions of the agreement shall retain their force for the entire duration of its validity. Amendments to the agreement may be made only by agreement between the parties, and at the request of one of the parties in the event of a significant change in circumstances in accordance with the Civil Code of the Russian Federation. Amendments to the terms and conditions of agreements which are introduced by agreement between the parties shall be implemented according to the same procedure as the original agreements, with the exception of the competitive tender.

2. In the event that during the period of validity of the agreement, the legislation of the Russian Federation, the legislation of constituent entities of the Russian Federation and legal acts of local government bodies establish norms which deteriorate the commercial results of the investor under the agreement, amendments shall be made to the agreement which guarantee the investor the commercial results which it could have received under the legislation of the Russian Federation, the legislation of constituent entities of the Russian Federation and legal acts of local government bodies which were in force at the time of

concluding the agreement. The procedure for making such amendments shall be defined by the agreement. This provision for altering the terms and conditions of the agreement shall not apply in the event that the legislation of the Russian Federation introduces changes to standards (norms, rules) for work safety and the protection of subsurface resources, the natural environment and public health, including for the purposes of bringing them into line with similar standards (norms, rules) which are accepted and generally recognized in international practice.

Source of translation: *see Chapter 7*

5.5.21   STATE PARTICIPATION

Although production sharing contracts may be considered to be an alternative to obligatory state participation under a licensing regime, elements of state participation have nevertheless been introduced in the contracts. As a matter of fact, state participation has manifested itself in three different forms, namely in the form of an option (or even commitment) for the state party to contribute to and share the development expenditure (as exemplified by contracts applicable in Tanzania, Libya and China); in the form of establishing a jointly owned operating company (as exemplified by contracts applicable in Egypt and Syria); or by the sharing on a proportional basis of the rights and obligations of the contractor, the state party (or a subsidiary of the state party or a national enterprise designated by the state party), assuming in this manner the position of a co-contractor (as exemplified by contracts applicable in Indonesia and Malaysia).

5.5.22   RECRUITMENT AND TRAINING OF PERSONNEL

Contracts will generally contain clauses requiring contractors to employ by preference nationals of the host country in all categories and functions. Apart from that contractor will be obliged to train all its national personnel for the purpose of improving their knowledge and professional qualification measured against the level of knowledge and professional qualification held by contractor's foreign personnel. The required training of personnel may also extend to and involve the training of the state party's personnel and may take place within the host country or by preference even abroad using the facilities of any one of contractor's foreign affiliated companies. The cost of the training may or may not be partially or wholly recoverable from cost oil. If not, it ranks as a payment of a bonus by contractor.

5.5.23   TRANSFER OF TECHNOLOGY

The required transfer of technology may be part of the training of nationals employed by the contractor or by the state party but is more specifically meant for the benefit of the state party. It is expected that transfer of technology will enable the state party to perform more efficiently the functions assigned to it under the petroleum law as well as under the contract, such as acting as the supervisory body, participating in the activities of a management committee or the board of directors of a joint operating company.

Note. The contracts applicable in China are characterized by the emphasis put on transfer of technology. In these contracts transfer of technology is understood to mean and involve the application and use of the contractor's or rather the contractor's affiliated companies' technology to and for the benefit of the authorized petroleum operations. The use and application of the contractor's technology includes giving training to personnel in handling such technology.

5.5.24   USE OF NATIONAL PRODUCTS AND SERVICES

The contract will contain clauses that impose on the contractor obligations and commitments concerning the use of locally manufactured goods, use of local services and local sub-contractors

Note. A typical example for such type of clause may serve Article 27 of the Angolan Law No. 10 on Petroleum Activities of 12 November 2004. This Law and its Article 27 is applicable *inter alia* to production sharing contracts entered into by Sonangol. Said Article 27 reads (after translation) as follows:

27.1 Licensees, the National Concessionaire *(i.e., Sonangol)* and its associates, and any other entities which cooperate with them in carrying out petroleum operations shall:

(a) acquire materials, equipment, machinery and consumer goods of national production, of the same or approximately the same quality and which are available for sale and delivery in due time, at prices which are no more than 10 per cent higher than the imported items including transportation and insurance costs and custom charges due;

(b) contract local services providers, to the extent to which the services they provide are similar to those available on the international market and their prices, when subject to the same tax charges, are no more than 10 percent higher than the prices charged by foreign contractors for similar services.

Source of translation: *see Chapter 7*

5.5.25   FINANCIAL GUARANTEES

Host governments will insist on being given financial guarantees (say bank guarantees expressed in US dollars) with respect to the fulfilment of the obligatory exploration work programme and/or the exploration expenditure commitment. Sometimes host governments insist on a general performance guarantee to be issued by the parent company of the contractor guaranteeing the fulfilment by contractor of its obligations under the contract.

5.5.26   LIABILITIES

The contractor will be required to indemnify and keep the State and state party harmless against all claims from third parties for loss or damage to property or injury to persons caused by or resulting from the contractor's operations. Exceptions are loss, damage and injury caused by any action of the personnel of the state party or the State (or, alternatively, caused by the proven negligence and wilful default of the state party). In some contracts, it is additionally provided that the state party concerned shall hold the contractor harmless from any claim brought against the contractor by the employees of the state party for their personal injury or damage to personal property due to the fulfilment or non-fulfilment of the contract.

If the contractor consists of more than one oil company each such contractor-company is jointly and severally liable for the performance of all obligations of contractor.

5.5.27   ASSIGNMENT OF INTERESTS

Distinction must be made between external assignments and internal assignments. If the contractor consists of more than one oil company and anyone of the contractor-companies wishes to assign its interest in the contract to the others such an assignment qualifies as an internal assignment. If the contractor or anyone contractor-company wishes to assign its interest in the contract to a third party including an affiliate, such an assignment is an external assignment. Generally, any assignment to third party, that is not an affiliate, needs the prior written consent of the state party or of the government in case the government is a co-signatory of the contract or if the contract had been subject to the latter's approval.

5.5.28   TITLE TO ASSETS

In principle, all movable and fixed assets acquired by the contractor for the authorized operations become the property of the state party. The contractor retains the right to the full and exclusive use of the assets for the operations and shall not have pay for such use. Apart from this, the contractor shall of course have the right to recover the cost of their acquisition out of cost recovery oil in accordance with the rules of the contract. It is generally understood that contractor, so long as such assets are used exclusively for petroleum operations, shall be liable to keep the same in good repair and working order, normal wear and tear excepted. Contracts may differ in the matter of stipulating the exact moment when the assets are acquired by the state party, but in all contracts the ultimate moment of transfer of ownership comes when the contract is terminated.

In the light of this kind of provisions, contractors strive to rent land and buildings and to make use of sub-contractors for drilling and other operations, and, where possible, to lease rather than to purchase equipment and installations.

5.5.29   CONFIDENTIALITY

The contractor is required to keep data and information obtained pursuant to the contract (and which are therefore the property of the state party) confidential and is not allowed to disclose such data and information to third parties that are not affiliates, without the prior written consent of the state party, except:

(i)   when disclosure is needed to permit such a third party to render services under the contract;
(ii) in connection with arranging financing;
(iii) in connection with an assignment of interest; or
(iv) when required under applicable legislation.

5.5.30   SETTLEMENT OF DISPUTES

In view of the international aspect of the contract disputes arising between the state party and its contractor that cannot be resolved by agreement between the two parties are by preference settled by international commercial arbitration in accordance with the rules of the chosen arbitration procedure. The arbitral award is declared binding on the parties. Applicable law (for the purposes of the arbitration) is specified. Usually, English law is chosen, but exceptionally the law of the host State has to be accepted. The contract may contain its own arbitration procedure, prescribing the number of arbitrators (usually three); the way in which these persons shall be selected (their qualifications and nationalities) and shall be appointed (requiring the designation of an international and neutral appointing authority, e.g., the Secretary General of the Permanent Court of Arbitration, for the appointment of a single arbitrator or for that of the third and presiding arbitrator); their task and duties, etc.

Most contracts however refer to established international arbitration procedures, such as the rules of arbitration of respectively the International Chamber of Commerce, the UN Commission on International Trade Law (UNCITRAL) or the International Centre for Settlement of Investment Disputes (ICSID), the latter having been established under the Convention on the Settlement of Investment Disputes between States and nationals of other States. The use of the services of the ICSID is very appropriate in the context of production sharing contracts, because the latter may be considered as a foreign investment agreement and in this manner to fall entirely within the scope and purposes of the aforesaid Convention. Nonetheless, arbitration pursuant to UNCITRAL Rules has become more and more popular.

In some host States, the prevailing production sharing contract recognizes situations in which there may arise a dispute between the Parties (viz. the state party and its contractor) on the one side and the government on the other. Such disputes must be submitted to the regular courts of law of the host State concerned.

5.5.31   AMENDMENT

The contract will stipulate that the same can only be amended by mutual agreement of the Parties but where the original contract had been subject to the approval of the government any agreed amendment is likewise subject to the approval of the government. If a contract has obtained the status of a law, as is the case when a law is required to authorize the government (or the competent minister) to sign the contract, any amendment needs to be approved by law and will involve (again) the legislature.

5.5.32   TERMINATION

The contract will be terminated in accordance with its rules. These rules envisage:

(i) voluntary termination, i.e., the right of the contractor to terminate the contract at any time (without being entitled to any compensation and subject to take the appropriate abandonment measures);
(ii) obligatory termination if no commercial discovery of petroleum has been made during the exploration phase of the contract; and
(iii) termination by the government if the contractor is in breach of any material provision of the contract or if the contractor is declared to be bankrupt.

5.5.33   APPLICABLE LAW

Without exceptions, the contract is governed and construed in accordance with the laws of the host State. To these laws should also belong any relevant provision of an international treaty or agreement to which the host State is a party (e.g., bilateral agreements for the protection of reciprocal investments).

5.5.34   APPROVAL AND RATIFICATION

With a few exceptions, production sharing contracts entered into by the authorized state entity need the approval of the host government before they become effective. In some instances (e.g., Egypt and Syria), where the government itself is a Party to the contract in conjunction with the state party, a special law has to be passed authorizing the minister responsible for petroleum affairs to sign the contract, thereby approving and ratifying the contract and giving it full force and effect of law.

5.5.35   PARTICULAR CONDITIONS

The contract is completed by reaching agreement on the particular conditions of the contract such as the description of the contract area; signature and production bonuses to be paid, exploration work commitments and the actual (percentage) rates and factors to be used in the production sharing mechanism.

5.6   COMMON PROVISIONS OF THE TECHNICAL SERVICE AGREEMENT

Like the production sharing contract the technical service agreement is a contract made between on the one hand a state entity in the latter's capacity as the sole entity authorized to undertake petroleum operations in the country and on the other a foreign oil enterprise as contractor to carry out the contractually specified operations. But the scope and objective of the technical service agreement is much more limited than that of the production sharing contract. It concerns contracts for carrying out special petroleum development projects, where no preceding exploration and/or appraisal work is involved: for instance a contract for the development of a discovery or the rehabilitation of an underperforming oil or gas field; or a contract to apply secondary or tertiary production methods in order to boost production in an otherwise depleted field; etc. Each technical service agreement is unique in the sense that it is tailor-made for a specific project, but it possible to indicate some common provisions as follows.

The contractor is responsible for funding all capital expenditure and operating costs and for the management of the authorized operations. If the contractor succeeds in generating new production or to increase already existing production (i.e., succeeds to achieve incremental production) he is entitled to be repaid in cash (with interest) its funding and to receive in addition thereto compensation also in cash (not in production). Said compensation is related to the quantity of new or incremental production and consists in a single US Dollar amount per unit of production (a fee per barrel) plus all kinds of other cash amounts by way of incentives. The compensation may also be expressed as the market value of a certain portion of the new or incremental production to be received during a fixed number of years. In the latter case, the contract could give the contractor the option to convert the amount of compensation during the period of its validity into the oil and/or gas that is newly or additionally produced under the contract. For this purpose, the oil and/or gas to be so purchased by the contractor is priced at market value. Obviously, whether or not the contractor will make use of such production-for-cash opportunity depends entirely on the terms agreed for the purchase/sale agreement.

Chapter 6

Past and Current License-Based Petroleum Legislation

Preliminary Note. License-based petroleum legislation is in recent times almost exclusively adopted and applied in western countries, i.e., in countries with a developed economy and an advanced. sophisticated legal system, all of which countries happen to be Member States of the OECD. In non-western countries, i.e., in countries with a developing or emerging economy, the present day petroleum legislation is based on and centred around state participation in combination with the contract of work, the latter almost exclusively in the form of the production sharing contract. Nonetheless, all those countries started off with license-based petroleum legislation but as from the 1970s switched to (full) state participation or contract-based petroleum legislation. This transition has been turbulent, in particular where full or majority state participation was at stake as it was in the countries in Northern Africa and the Middle East Gulf area. The industry / government negotiations that led to this transition have made a lasting impact on the relationships between petroleum industry and governments world-wide.

6.1 NON-WESTERN COUNTRIES

6.1.1 THE MIDDLE EAST GULF STATES

6.1.1.1 The Petroleum Agreements of the 1930s

6.1.1.1.1 Introduction

During the 1930s, the governments of seven Middle East Gulf States negotiated and concluded a series of petroleum agreements with major international oil companies (said agreements and companies also referred to respectively as concessions and concessionaires). By these agreements exclusive petroleum rights were granted in respect of large-sized areas, in many instances covering the whole or an important part of the land territory and territorial waters of the Gulf State concerned, and for a very long period (e.g., seventy-five or sixty years). They were further characterized by the absence of mandatory relinquishment of acreage and by the fact that up to their first fiscal revision in 1951 payments required to be made by the concessionaires were restricted to signature and discovery bonuses, annual or monthly sums and royalties, the latter being tied to minimum annual payments. In no petroleum agreement was provision made for state participation.

An early concession had on 28 May 1901 been granted by the then Persian government to William Knox D'Arcy. The concession covered the whole territory of Iran with exception of the five northern provinces and very remarkably provided for the payment of sixteen per cent of the annual net profits. In 1908, oil was discovered in the concession area at Masjid-i-Suleiman (after an earlier discovery near Chiah Surkh in 1904). In 1909, the D'Arcy concession was taken over by the newly incorporated Anglo-Persian Oil Company that went public in order to raise the finance needed for the continuation of the venture. For strategic reasons, the UK government acquired in August 1914, a few days after the outbreak of the First World War, a controlling interest of 51.7 per cent in the concessionaire. In November 1932, the concession was unilaterally cancelled by Reza Shah but after negotiations a revised concession was in April 1933 granted to Anglo-Persian, the former concessionaire. The latter was in 1935 renamed the Anglo-Iranian Oil Company. The newly negotiated concession contained terms which were more in line with those accepted and applied under the petroleum agreements made at around the same the time with the governments of the Arab Gulf States, except that the concession and this was a novelty required a net profit sharing in addition to the payment of a royalty of four gold shillings per ton. The net profit sharing consisted of a twenty per cent tax on dividends distributed to the shareholders of the concessionaire in excess of GBP 671,250. Payments on account of royalty and dividend tax were subject to a minimum annual payment of GBP 750,000 (see further Chapter 8). On this occasion the area covered by the new concession was much reduced and this time comprised an area of 1,00,000 square miles in the South-Western part of Iran. The concession lasted eighteen years. On 20 March 1951, it was nationalized and taken over by the newly established National Iranian Oil Company (NIOC). A new agreement referred to as the Consortium Agreement took in 1954 its place. In its turn, this agreement was replaced with effect from (w.e.f.) 21 March 1973 by the 'Sale and Purchase' agreement.

Another early concession was a concession granted by the government of the Ottoman Empire on 28 June 1914 to the Turkish Petroleum Company (TPC). A few years earlier, this company had been set up in London by British and German interests through the intermediary of the Armenian oil investor Gulbenkian. On 19 March 1914, agreement was reached on a restructuring of the company allowing for the participation of Anglo-Persian in the coming venture. The shareholding in the reconstituted TPC was fixed as follows: Anglo-Persian Oil Company: 50 per cent; Anglo-Saxon Oil Company (Royal Dutch Shell): 25 per cent; German interests represented by the Deutsche Bank: 25 per cent. The Anglo-Persian Oil Company and the Anglo-Saxon Oil Company each transferred a 2.5 per cent beneficiary shareholding to the Armenian oil investor Gulbenkian (since then known as Mr Five Percent). After the dissolution of the Ottoman Empire the concession that on 28 June 1914 had been granted became invalid, but TPC received in compensation for the loss of its concession a new concession from the government of the newly formed Iraqi State. In 1920 the German interest in TPC was transferred to the Compagnie Francaise des Petroles (CFP). On 15 October 1927 oil was discovered in this concession at Baba Gurgur near Kirkuk. In 1928 the concessionaire was restructured in order add a number of American companies, first seven later reduced to two, as shareholders. The newcomers received a combined share of 23.75 per cent at the expense of Anglo-Persian's shareholding. On this occasion the concessionaire was renamed Iraq Petroleum Company (IPC). On 24 March 1931 IPC received a concession, covering the eastern part of Iraq (i.e., the part situated east of the river Tigris). Some years later two more concessions covering the territory of Iraq west of the Tigris were granted respectively transferred to affiliated companies of IPC: in 1938 the one concession was granted to the Basrah Petroleum Company Ltd and in 1942 the other was transferred to the Mosul Petroleum Company Ltd. The concession held by IPC was nationalized by the government on 1 June 1972. The other concessions were acquired in steps by the government, but were finally in 1975 completely in its possession.

In 1925, a concession was granted by the government of Bahrain to a British individual, Major Holmes. On 12 June 1930, this concession was transferred to the Bahrain Petroleum Company, an affiliate of a US oil company incorporated in Canada. In this concession oil was discovered in 1932.

This discovery awakened the interest of the European and American oil companies in the oil potential of the Arabian Peninsula and led to the application for and subsequent grant of concessions in respectively Saudi Arabia (25 May 1933, later substantially extended on 21 July 1939) and Kuwait (23 December 1934). It took some time before oil was discovered in these concessions: Burgan field, Kuwait, 23 February 1938; Damman field, Saudi Arabia, a few weeks later. In 1975, these concessions were completely taken over by the respective governments.

Other States on the Arabian Peninsula followed suit: concessions were granted in the late 1930s in Qatar, Oman and Abu Dhabi. In Qatar, the government took possession of both the onshore and offshore concession in respectively September 1976 and February 1977. In Oman and Abu Dhabi each government acquired w.e.f. 1 January 1974 a sixty per cent state participation in its concessions.

At the time, the petroleum agreements were negotiated none of the Middle East Gulf States possessed any petroleum legislation. All aspects of petroleum operations and the conduct thereof had to be provided for in the agreements themselves in a complete and self-contained form, since it was not possible to make reference to other legislative sources except for the constitutional law or more basically the general sovereign powers of the Head of State.

Most provisions comprised in the petroleum agreements were established in bilateral negotiations between the government of the ME Gulf State concerned and the foreign oil company that at the time applied for a concession. These provisions are hereinafter referred to and described as the 'original provisions'. Later on, new provisions were introduced in the petroleum agreements adopted in these agreements, with exception of the Iranian concession of 1933. As mentioned before, this concession was in 1951 nationalized and in 1954 replaced by a new agreement referred to as the Consortium Agreement.

After the founding on 1 September 1960 of the Organization of Petroleum Exporting Countries (OPEC) revisions regarding government take and state participation were the outcomes of collectively conducted negotiations involving the governments of the OPEC Gulf States on the one side and their respective concessionaires on the other. Oil exporting States, that took no part in these negotiations, but whose concessions or leases comprised a 'most favoured nation' clause, could by virtue of that clause implement the collectively agreed revisions in their concessions or leases. Among those States were Oman, Nigeria, Brunei and Malaysia.

For a review of the petroleum agreements concluded in the 1930s the agreement (Kuwait agreement) made on 23 December 1934 between the Shaikh of Kuwait and the Kuwait Oil Company Limited has been selected as an example. Like all the other petroleum agreements the Kuwait agreement has been revised from time to time, in particular with respect to the government take and state participation. But in the end the Kuwait agreement was on 4 March 1975 completely taken over by the State.

6.1.1.1.2   The Kuwait Agreement of 23 December 1934

6.1.1.1.2.1   Parties

The Agreement is made between the Shaikh of Kuwait in the exercise of his powers as Ruler of Kuwait on his own behalf and in the name of and on behalf of his heirs and successors to whom is or shall be vested for the time being the responsibility for the control and government of the State of Kuwait (hereinafter called 'the Shaikh') and the Kuwait Oil Company Limited, its successors and assigns (hereinafter called 'the Company').

6.1.1.1.2.2   Date of signature

The date of signature is 23 December 1934

6.1.1.1.2.3   Fundamental Law

The Constitution of the State of Kuwait

6.1.1.1.2.4   Agreement Area

Described under Basic Rights

6.1.1.1.2.5   Basic Rights

The Shaikh grants to the Company the exclusive right to explore, search, drill for, produce and win natural gas, asphalt, ozokerite, crude petroleum and their products and cognate substances (hereinafter referred to as 'petroleum') within the State of Kuwait including all islands and territorial waters appertaining to Kuwait as shown generally on the map annexed hereto, the exclusive ownership of all petroleum produced and won by the Company within the State of Kuwait; the right to refine, transport, sell for use within the State of Kuwait or for export and export or otherwise deal with or dispose of any and all such petroleum and the right to do all things necessary for the purposes of those operations. The Company undertakes, however, that it will not carry on any of its operations within areas occupied by or devoted to purposes of mosques, sacred buildings or graveyards or carry on any of its operations, except the sale of petroleum, housing of staff and employees and administrative work within the present town wall of Kuwait.

6.1.1.1.2.6   Duration

The period of this Agreement shall be seventy-five years from the date of signature

6.1.1.1.2.7   Work Programme Exploration and Conduct of Operations

  (i) Within nine months from the date of signature of the Agreement the Company shall commence geological exploration.
 (ii) The Company shall drill for petroleum to the following total aggregate depths and within the following periods of time at such and so many places as the Company may decide:
     (a) 4,000 feet prior to the end of the third year;
     (b) 12,000 feet prior to the end of the ninth year; and
     (c) 30,000 feet prior to the end of the nineteenth year.
(iii) The Company shall conduct its operations in a workmanlike manner and by appropriate scientific methods and shall take all reasonable measures to prevent the ingress of water to any petroleum bearing strata and shall duly close any unproductive holes drilled by it and subsequently abandoned. The Company shall keep the Shaikh and his London representative informed generally as to the progress and its result of its drilling operations but such information shall be treated as confidential.

6.1.1.1.2.8   Obligatory Payments (Up to the Fiscal Revision of 1951)

In consideration of the rights granted by the Shaikh to the Company by this Agreement and of the assistance and protection which the Shaikh hereby undertakes to afford by all means in his powers to the Company and its operations, employees and property the Company shall pay to the Shaikh the following sums:

  (i) Within thirty days after signature of the Agreement Rupees INR 475,000.
 (ii) On each anniversary of date of signature until the Company declares that petroleum has been found in commercial quantities either a royalty of INR 3 for every English ton (2,240 lbs) of Kuwait petroleum won and saved by the Company in Kuwait; or INR 95,000, whichever shall be the greater sum; on each anniversary of the date of signature after the Company has declared that petroleum

has been found in commercial quantities either a royalty as described above or INR 250,000, whichever is the greater sum.

Note. At the time the petroleum agreements were concluded one Rupee was equivalent to USD 0.38 and the market value of one barrel of crude oil was USD 1.00. The royalty rate of INR 3 per ton is therefore equivalent to USD 0.15 per barrel or fifteen per cent of the market value. The signature bonus paid under the Kuwait agreement was the highest, namely INR 475,000, which at the time was equivalent to USD 180,000 or 180,000 barrels of oil.

6.1.1.1.2.9   Ancillary Rights

For the purpose of its operations the concessionaire has the right without hindrance to construct, and to operate power stations, refineries, pipelines and storage tanks, facilities for water supply including boring for water, telegraph and telephone lines and wireless installations, roads, railways, buildings, ports, harbours, harbour works, wharves and jetties, oil and coaling stations with such lighting as may be requisite and any other facilities or works, which the company may consider necessary, and for such purposes to use free of all payments any stone, sand, gravel, gypsum, lime, clay or similar materials or water which may be available, provided always that the inhabitants of the State of Kuwait are not prevented from taking their usual requirements of these materials and that the water supply of the local inhabitants and nomad population who may depend on the same is not endangered. The Company at its discretion but in consultation with the Shaikh may select the position of any such works. The Company may likewise install and operate without hindrance all such means of transportation by land, air and water communication or operation as may be necessary for the effective conduct of its operations hereunder.

The Company is granted free of cost the unrestricted use and occupation of and surface rights over all uncultivated lands belonging to the Shaikh, which the Company may need for the purpose of its operations and in particular the Company shall have the right to select in consultation with the Shaikh an area or areas of land chosen by the Company outside the present town wall of Kuwait with exclusive surface rights upon which to erect oil refineries, storage, terminal and shipping facilities and any other works required for the Company's operations and the Company may with the cognizance of the Shaikh buy or lease for such purposes any lands, houses or buildings with the consent of and on conditions to be arranged with the proprietors thereof, but the terms of such purchase or lease shall not be in excess of those ordinarily current in their respective localities.

The Company shall acquire only such lands, houses and buildings as are necessary for its operations under this Agreement. The Company shall inform the Shaikh from time to time of the land, houses and buildings, which it requires to occupy for its operations and land, houses and buildings previously acquired by the Company from the Shaikh, but found no longer necessary for its operations, shall be returned to the Shaikh free of charge.

6.1.1.1.2.10   Employment of Personnel

The Company shall employ subjects of the Shaikh as far as possible for all work for which they are suited under the supervision of the Company's skilled employees, but if the local supply of labour should in the judgment of the Company be inadequate or unsuitable the Company shall have the right with the approval of the Shaikh which shall not be unreasonably withheld, to import labour, preference being given to labourers from the neighbouring Arab countries who will obey the local laws. The Company shall also have the right to import skilled and technical employees. Any employee imported by the Company who shall by misconduct cause a breach of peace or public disturbance, shall at the request of the Shaikh be dismissed and shall, if it is within the power of the Company to do so, be sent out of Kuwait.

The Company shall pay to the workmen it employs a fair wage, such wage to be decided and stated by the Company at the time the workmen are engaged.

The Company shall provide free of charge medical service for its employees and the Shaikh and his family shall have the right to such medical service and necessary medical supplies free of charge.

6.1.1.1.2.11   Termination (Mandatory)

The Shaikh shall be entitled to terminate this Agreement and all the property of the Company within the State of Kuwait shall become the property of the Shaikh in one of the three following cases:

(1) If the Company shall fail to fulfil its obligations in respect of geological exploration or drilling.

(2) if the Company shall fail within six months after any anniversary of the date of signature of this Agreement to pay to the Shaikh the sums agreed to be due under this Agreement.
(3) if the Company shall be in default under the arbitration provisions of this Agreement.

6.1.1.1.2.12   Termination (Voluntary)

In the event of the Company failing to declare that petroleum has been found in commercial quantities within twelve years of the date of signature of this Agreement the Company shall at its option either pay to the Shaikh the minimum annual payment of INR 250,000 or surrender all rights under this Agreement.

The Company shall have the right at any time after it has drilled the mandatory 4,000 feet or after the expiry of two years from the date of signature of this Agreement – whichever shall be the later date – to give one year's notice in advance to terminate this Agreement and the Company shall on expiry of such notice have no further liabilities except to make payment of all monies which may be due to the Shaikh up to the date of termination.

6.1.1.1.2.13   Force Majeure

Failure on the part of the Company to fulfil any of the conditions of this Agreement shall not give the Shaikh any claim against the Company or be deemed a breach of this Agreement in so far as such failure arises from force majeure, and if through force majeure the fulfilment by the Company of any of the conditions of this Agreement be delayed the period of such delay shall be added to the periods fixed by this Agreement.

6.1.1.1.2.14   Stability of Terms

The Shaikh shall not by general or special legislation or by administrative measure or by any other act whatever annul this Agreement, except as provided in this Agreement in case of termination. No alteration shall be made in the terms of this Agreement by either the Shaikh or the Company, except in the event of the Shaikh and the Company jointly agreeing that it is desirable in the interest of both Parties to make certain alterations, deletions or additions to this Agreement.

6.1.1.1.2.15   Settlement of Disputes

If at any time during the currency of this Agreement any difference or dispute shall arise between the Parties hereto concerning the interpretation or execution hereof, or anything herein contained or in connection herewith or the rights or liabilities of either Party hereunder, the same shall failing any agreement to settle it in any other way, or after consultation with the British Political Resident in Kuwait or the British Political Resident in the Persian Gulf, be referred to two arbitrators, one of whom shall be chosen by each Party, and a referee, who shall be chosen by the arbitrators before proceeding to arbitration.

6.1.1.1.2.16   Audit

If at any time during the currency of the Agreement any dispute shall arise regarding the accuracy of the accounts of the Company in connection with the amounts of the royalty and of other payments due to the Shaikh under this Agreement, the Shaikh shall have the right to appoint, in consultation with the His Majesty's Government, a registered firm of auditors to examine the books of the Company on behalf of the Shaikh in Kuwait and or in London as he may consider necessary. All expenditure incurred in connection with such auditing shall be paid by the Shaikh. The Company shall provide the registered firm of auditors appointed by the Shaikh the necessary facilities to enable them to check the books and registers of the Company and to render every assistance to enable the auditors to thoroughly examine such accounts and in every way assist them to safeguard the interests of the Shaikh.

6.1.1.1.2.17   Protection

The Shaikh shall give to the Company and its employees and property all the protection in his power from theft, highway robbery, assault, wilful damage and destruction, and the Company may appoint in consultation with the Shaikh and itself pay trustworthy guards who shall at all times be Kuwait subjects unless the Shaikh permits otherwise to assists in protecting the property of the Company and its employees. The Company shall erect at its own expense suitable buildings for the accommodation of such guards at such places as the Company shall decide.

6.1.1.1.2.18   The London Representative

The Shaikh shall have the right to appoint from the effective date of this Agreement a Representative in London to represent the Shaikh in all matters relating to this Agreement with the Company in its London office and such Representative shall have full access to the production records of the Company, including the agenda of the Board meetings and shall be entitled to attend the Board's meetings at which the Shaikh's interests are discussed.

6.1.1.2 The Issue of State Participation in Licenses / Agreements

6.1.1.2.1 Introduction

The petroleum agreements concluded in the 1930s did not provide for any form of state participation. But this changed quickly when in 1957 Iran issued its new petroleum law, the Petroleum Law of 29 July 1957. Under the terms of this Law, the, NIOC, was authorized to enter into joint venture agreements with foreign entities but only with respect to acreage situated outside the territory of the Consortium. Under the terms of such an agreement, a joint company was established having NIOC and the foreign entity as shareholders. On the basis of this joint venture concept, the first series of state participation agreements were concluded in 1957 and 1958 and a second series followed in 1964 and 1965. In Egypt, the first state participation agreement was also concluded in 1957. The authorization therefore was given under the terms of the Law No. 86 of 1956. In May 1960, the Egyptian government announced that with respect to operations in the Western Desert it would opt for fifty per cent state participation accompanied by the formation of an Egyptian joint stock company. In 1963 and 1964 the Egyptian government signed a series of participation agreements, known as the Western Desert participation agreements, on the basis of these principles. In Kuwait, state participation was introduced in 1961, Saudi Arabia followed suit in 1965, apparently following the example of Iran. In both cases, the acreage given in concession (with state participation) was situated on the continental shelf of said countries. Libya followed the Egyptian example by offering foreign entities the possibility of entering into joint ventures with the Libyan National Oil Company (LNOC), whereby LNOC would be the holder of the exclusive license underlying the venture concerned.

As could be expected, the governments of the Arab Gulf States which had just settled with their concessionaires various fiscal and pricing issues within the framework of the Teheran Agreement of 14 February 1971 (discussed hereinafter in Chapter 8) turned shortly afterwards their attention to the issue of state participation in their existing and petroleum producing petroleum agreements. At an extraordinary meeting of the OPEC Conference, held on 22 September 1971, a resolution was adopted calling upon the Member States to open negotiations with their concessionaires in order to reach agreement on this issue. In the ensuing negotiations only the governments of the OPEC Arab Gulf States were engaged nonetheless the results thereof had a wider impact and involved other Member States such as Nigeria and other oil exporting States such as Oman, Malaysia and Brunei as well, due to the fact that after the establishment of OPEC, the aforesaid States had introduced in the concessions or leases under their jurisdiction a clause which became known as the 'most favoured nation' clause. The standard text of this clause reads as follows:

> If as a result of changes in the terms of concessions in existence on the effective date or as a result of the terms of concessions granted thereafter an increase in benefits to governments in the Middle East should generally to be received by them the concessionaire will consult with the Emir whether in the light of all relevant circumstances including the conditions in which operations are carried out and taking into account all payments made, any alteration to the terms of this agreement would be equitable to the parties.

On the strength of this clause the aforesaid States could claim all the benefits that resulted from the Gulf States' negotiations.

6.1.1.2.2   *The General Agreement on Participation*

Negotiations on this matter of state participation led to the signing in Riyadh on 20 December 1972 of an agreement called 'the General Agreement on Participation'. Parties to this General Agreement were the same Gulf States and oil companies which had signed the 1971 Teheran Agreement, with the exception of Iran.

Under the terms of the General Agreement, each Arab Gulf State within OPEC acquired with effect from 1 January 1973 a twenty-five per cent undivided interest in the petroleum agreement falling under its jurisdiction and the right to increase this initial interest after five years, as from 1 January 1978, in annual increments of five per cent and with a final increment of six per cent, to a maximum percentage of fifty-one per cent. According to this schedule this final percentage should have been reached on 1 January 1982.

The compensation finally agreed amounted to the updated book value of the concessions. The updated book value was calculated by totalling over the past period of the concession year by year the annual differences between on the one hand capital and exploration expenditures and on the other the amount by which the income tax revenues of the government concerned had been diminished by deductions of capital depreciations and exploration expenditure. By paying its percentage share of the updated book value, the Gulf State concerned effectively paid back its share of the updated past capital and exploration expenditures made by the concessionaire, while withholding the tax relief that the concessionaire should have obtained with respect to that updated expenditure.

In order to allow the concessionaires to adjust themselves to the loss of production capacity the Arab Gulf States were obliged to sell to their co-concessionaires a certain portion of their initial participation share: this portion, referred to as 'bridging oil' was fixed at seventy-five per cent for the first year, at fifty per cent for the second year and at twenty-five per cent for the third year. Besides any Gulf State had the right (but not the obligation) to sell additional volumes to its co-concessionaire. These extra volumes were referred to as 'adjustment oil' or 'put oil'. The Gulf States had been accorded this right in order to provide them with a guaranteed outlet for their share of production in the event they would experience difficulties with the disposal thereof. The volumes of put oil were fixed on an annual basis and expressed as certain annual percentages of the initial interest as well as of each of the successive incremental interests. The concessionaires had to pay for the bridging oil as well as the put oil, if any, the half-way price, i.e., a price, which was equal to the tax paid cost plus half the difference between the tax paid cost and the posted price. The General Agreement has only been effective during the year 1973 and only with respect to the Arab Gulf States Kuwait, Qatar, Abu Dhabi and Saudi Arabia.

6.1.1.2.3   *The Sixty Per Cent to One Hundred Per Cent State Participation*

Meanwhile, state participation at the much higher level of fifty-one per cent was agreed in Libya and Algeria and nationalizations took place in Iraq. In Algeria state participation at a level of fifty-one per cent was introduced as from the moment the Ordinance No. 71–22 of 12 April 1971 became effective. The state participant was Sonatrach, the Algerian state oil company.

To make things more difficult, Iraq refused to implement the General Agreement. In the light of these events those OPEC Gulf States, that had implemented the General Agreement, now demanded a reopening of the negotiations that had led to that Agreement. There resulted a series of bilateral agreements between individual Arab Gulf States and their respective concessionaire(s). According to these bilateral agreements state participation in the respective concessions was fixed at sixty per cent with effect from 1 January 1974. As compensation the concessionaires were paid a certain fixed sum of money, not derived from a formula or explained in any other manner but, taken together with the compensation already paid for the initial twenty-five per cent interest, total compensation proved to be no more than the fiscal book value for the whole sixty per cent interest that in the end was transferred. It was certainly much lower than sixty per cent of the updated book value. However this may be, these bilateral state participation agreements were equally short-lived.

By December 1974, the government of Qatar had already announced its intention to proceed with a complete takeover of the two concessions (onshore and offshore) under its jurisdiction. After protracted negotiations with the respective concessionaires, in particular with regard to the matter of compensation that should be paid, and the future role of the former concessionaires, it was agreed, in September 1976 and February 1977 respectively, that each concessionaire would transfer its forty per cent interest to the government. Apart from the paying of a compensation the settlement included a five-year oil purchase contract at the official government selling price and a service contract in accordance with which affiliates of the former concessionaires rendered technical and personnel services at a fee.

The government of Kuwait cancelled its bilateral 60/40 agreement in March 1975. With the former concessionaires (British Petroleum and Gulf Oil), a settlement was reached along the lines of the Qatar settlement.

The government of Saudi Arabia also decided in 1975 to proceed with a complete takeover of the concession under its jurisdiction. It took a long time (until 1980) before the contractual arrangements were completed.

The government of Abu Dhabi chose to maintain the sixty per cent state participation as agreed with respect to the two concessions (onshore and offshore) under its jurisdiction. The State was represented by its national oil company, the Abu Dhabi National Oil Corporation (ADNOC), owner of the sixty per cent interest. The forty per cent interest in each concession was held by a company (ADPC, onshore, and ADMA, offshore) jointly owned by a number of foreign oil companies as shareholders. Initially, ADPC and ADMA were charged with the operation of their respective concessions under the supervision of a management committee in which their individual shareholders and ADNOC were represented. Later the organizational set up was changed in the sense that ADPC and ADMA lost their role as operator. With respect to each concession this task was taken over by a newly established operating company (ADCO), in which ADNOC took a sixty per cent shareholding. The remaining forty per cent of the shares in ADCO were distributed over the individual shareholders of ADPC (onshore) or ADMA (offshore). ADCO is supervised by a joint management committee, in which ADNOC and the individual shareholders of ADPC or ADMA as the case may be are represented. Interestingly, ADPC itself is no longer represented in the organization of the joint venture.

The government of Oman followed the example of Abu Dhabi and restricted its participation in its petroleum agreement of 7 March 1967 (called the Main Agreement) to sixty per cent (w.e.f 1 January 1974). Non-negotiating Oman could claim its participation on account of having the 'most favoured nation' clause incorporated in said Main Agreement. A few years later, and by means of an agreement referred to as the Transfer Agreement dated 15 May 1980, the state participation was implemented by transferring all assets and operating rights and obligations under the Main Agreement to a new operating company jointly owned by the government and the individual shareholders of the concessionaire. The new company was named Petroleum Development Oman LLC (PDO). The concessionaire itself was renamed Private Oil Holdings Oman Limited (POHOL). The interests transferred to PDO comprised all the interests of the government and the concessionaire in the Main Agreement, including the ownership of all assets belonging thereto, except for the ownership of 'petroleum produced at cost' and the disposal thereof, the financial rights and obligations under the Main Agreement, and the right to terminate the Main Agreement on one year's notice as provided thereunder. Therefore, PDO can be described as an asset owning operating cost company which has to produce and deliver oil (for natural gas special arrangements exist) at cost to the government and POHOL. The government and POHOL are obliged to supply to PDO, if and when required, in a 60/40 proportion, all funds required for the authorized operations. The acquisition of new assets to be owned by PDO is financed by the government and POHOL by providing loans in a 60/40 proportion. The loans have to be repaid by PDO out of funds generated from annual allowances for depreciation included in the cost of operations.

6.1.1.3   The Special Situation in Iran

Iran was not involved in the negotiations concerning state participation and the complete takeover of the concessions because its own concession agreement of April 1933 had (already) on 20 March 1951 been nationalized and taken over by the then newly established NIOC. It had been the former revolutionary government's intention to follow the Mexican example (Note. In Mexico, the licenses and other assets of the foreign oil industry had been nationalized in March 1938) and entrust the domestic petroleum operations to NIOC without allowing any involvement of foreign oil companies. However the revolution failed and after three and a half years of negotiations a new agreement (referred to as the 'Consortium Agreement') was signed on 25 October 1954 by NIOC and Iranian Oil Participants Ltd, a UK corporation. The latter is usually referred to as the Consortium, because its shareholders formed a consortium of major foreign oil companies, among which the former concessionaire, viz. Anglo-Iranian Oil Company, on that occasion renamed British Petroleum, with a percentage share of forty per cent. Pursuant to this new agreement the petroleum operations were continued by the Consortium, acting on behalf of NIOC.

The Consortium Agreement was in substance not very different from the petroleum agreements of the 1930s but nevertheless formally seen as a risk bearing service contract (see Chapter 5). From this point of view, Iran excluded itself from the negotiations leading to the General Agreement on Participation and did not become a party to that agreement. Nonetheless the Iranian government's interest and concern was now focused on revising the Consortium Agreement along the lines of the General Agreement (as if this Agreement applied to Iran) in order to prevent that the state participation demanded and pursued by the other OPEC Gulf States would bring the latter into a better position than Iran in respect of government take and production shares. Subsequently, the Iranian government negotiated and concluded, with effect from 21 March 1973 with the Consortium a new agreement, referred to as the 'Sale and Purchase Agreement', in replacement of the Consortium Agreement. The parties remained the same, i.e., NIOC and Iranian Oil Participants, Ltd.

In reaction to the emergence of bilateral 60/40 state participation agreements, the Sale and Purchase Agreement was initially adjusted in order to copy the effects of the former, but some time thereafter negotiations were started to revise the agreement in a more fundamental manner. The intention was to achieve a combination of a fee paying technical service contract and purchase contract at discounted prices. The negotiations about such for those days novel contract had to be aborted as a result of the outbreak of the revolution in December 1978.

6.1.1.4 The Special Situation in Iraq

Already in 1961 the IPC had been forced to relinquish 99.5 per cent of the area of its concession (which had been awarded on 24 March 1931). On 1 June 1972 the concession was nationalized by the government, some months before the latter signed the General Agreement, which however it refused to implement. This nationalization measure was formally settled on 28 February 1973. IPC's main asset consisted of the Kirkuk field. IPC had to pay GBP 141 million to Iraq and the latter had to deliver 111 million barrels of Kirkuk crude oil over a period of fourteen months.

At the end of 1973, Iraq nationalized forty-three per cent of the share capital of the Basrah Petroleum Company (BPC), which held a concession in the South-Western part of the country. This nationalization of share capital was politically motivated and was connected to the outbreak of the Yom Kippur war (also called the Ramadan war) in the Middle East on 6 October 1973. In January 1975 Iraq concluded with BPC an agreement under which the sixty per cent participation became applicable with retroactive effect from 1 January 1974. As a result thereof Iraq's total interest (direct and indirect) in the operations of BPC amounted to 77.2 per cent with effect from that date. Later in 1975 Iraq decided to take over BPC's remaining forty per cent share in the concession. Negotiations on a settlement took several years.

6.1.1.5 Kuwait (Gulf Continental Shelf)

In Kuwait, a petroleum agreement made on 15 January 1961 between the Emir of Kuwait and Kuwait Shell Petroleum Development Company Ltd, and covering the Kuwaiti part of the continental shelf, provided for optional minority state participation. Pursuant to this agreement the State was given the option to participate for twenty per cent in the agreement as from the moment a commercially viable deposit was discovered. If the State would exercise its option, it would have to reimburse twenty per cent of the expenditure made by the concessionaire up to the effective date of state participation. (Note. The envisaged participation was never realized, since the concession agreement was terminated before a discovery was made.)

6.1.1.6   Saudi Arabia (Red Sea Continental Shelf)

Apparently following the example of Iran, the government of Saudi Arabia represented by Petromin, the Saudi Arabian state oil enterprise, entered in 1965 into a state participation agreement with respect to acreage situated on its part of the Red Sea continental shelf with Auxirap, an affiliate of the French state-owned oil company ERAP. Petromin's participating share amounted to forty per cent; Auxirap's share was sixty per cent. Auxirap was responsible for the conduct and the financing of the exploration work. As soon as a commercial discovery was made a profit-making joint company would be established. The company was liable to pay fifty per cent income tax calculated on the basis of prices required to be posted by the company. The company had to pay royalty at higher rates than were customary at the time (a rate of fifteen per cent increasing to twenty per cent depending on production performance, the latter expressed in daily production rates). The royalty was not credited against income tax but had to be 'expensed', i.e., had to be treated as a cost element deductible from income to arrive at taxable income, in accordance with the then in Saudi Arabia prevailing fiscal treatment of royalties. The joint company would sell the production to its shareholders at a price to be determined by the joint company. At the request of Petromin, Auxirap was obliged to sell Petromin's share. Auxirap had to pay Petromin the price realized in the market but this price was not to be lower than ninety per cent of the company's price.

6.1.2   EGYPT

On 14 September 1914, a UK company named, Anglo-Egyptian Oilfields Ltd, concluded an agreement with the Egyptian government under which the company acquired over the years a growing and large number of 'old style' thirty-year petroleum mining leases (British colonial model). In 1956, these leases and all other assets of this Company were sequestrated and in 1961 formally expropriated.

After World War II, Egyptian petroleum legislation, as set out in section II On Raw Combustibles (Note: raw combustibles include petroleum) of the Law No. 66 of 1953 On Mines and Quarries provided for a licensing regime based on the granting of renewable prospecting licenses which in turn could be converted into one or more long-term (thirty plus fifteen years) mining leases. Under the conditions of the mining lease, the lessee had to pay a royalty at a rate of at least fifteen per cent or twenty-five per cent, depending on which half of the prospecting license area the mining lease derived from. Upon renewal of the mining lease the rate was fixed at twenty-five per cent. The royalty value was defined as the annual average price of similar oil in a recognized market. The government had the preferential right to purchase up to twenty per cent of the petroleum produced from the lease at a price ten per cent less than the recognized market price. (Note. Under the preceding Law No. 137 of 12 August 1948 On Mines and Quarries the granting of licenses for petroleum exploitation was restricted to Egyptian companies only.)

When Law No. 66 was repealed by Law No. 86 of 1956 *On Mines and Quarries*, the former's section II as described above was upheld. Of special interest is Article 50 (a restated Article 69 of the predecessor Law No. 66) pursuant to which the minister responsible for mining matters could be authorized by a special law to enter into an agreement with a company for prospecting for minerals and exploitation of mines subject to special conditions in derogation of the provisions of the Law as shall be determined in the special law granting the authority.

Article 51 declared the provisions of Article 50 to be applicable to raw combustibles and therefore to petroleum. As a consequence, the government was authorized to regulate petroleum operations by means of entering into agreements approved by a special law, in derogation of the provisions of the Law No. 86 (in this case represented by the 'saved' section II of the Law No. 66). In order to represent the government in such agreements, a national oil company named the General Petroleum Authority (GPA) was established in 1956. In February 1957 the first state participation agreement was entered into with International Egyptian Oil Company (IEOC), an affiliate of the Italian state-owned oil company ENI.

In May 1960, the government announced that with respect to acreage in the Western Desert it would opt for fifty per cent state participation accompanied by the formation of an Egyptian joint stock company. In 1963 and 1964, the government concluded a series of participation agreements, known as the Western Desert participation agreements. In these agreements the following principles were incorporated:

(i) An exclusive license for the exploration and production of petro-leum is granted to EGPC and the foreign oil enterprise in equal proportions.

(ii) The exclusive license is granted for a period of thirty years with the possibility of extension by fifteen years.

(iii) The initial license area comprised an exploration area that was divided into exploration blocks.

(iv) After making a commercial discovery in any particular exploration block, the same would be converted into a development area.

(v) Over a period of fifteen years, non-converted exploration blocks had to be surrendered.

(vi) The foreign participant was responsible for the execution of the operations and for the funding thereof till the first commercial discovery was made. Thereafter a joint operating company (JOC) would be established, the shares of which would be held by EGPC and the foreign participant in equal proportions.

(vii) The JOC would be solely responsible for the development of the discovery and for the continuation of the exploration. The JOC would be funded by its shareholders in equal proportions. The JOC would not generate income; it did not sell any production but delivered the same to its shareholders in equal proportions.

(viii) Obligatory payments consisted in the payment of a royalty and a fifty per cent State gross profit share, which comprised the royalty, income taxes, duties and make-up payments. (Note. The fifty per cent State profit share represented the 50/50 profit sharing principle that as of December 1950 had been adopted in the Middle East petroleum agreements.)

(ix) The government received an option to buy up to twenty per cent of the production.

Later on, the principles of the Western Desert state participation agreements were also applied with respect to acreage in the Gulf of Suez (e.g., the Morgan field, Egypt's most prolific field, which in 1965 had been discovered in that area).

As late as 1969, state participation in concession agreements still belonged to the *Preference Items for Concessions in the U.A.R.* as published by the government. Later, in the early 1970s, when state participation was generally implemented in the Middle East Gulf States and in Libya, and in the majority of cases had been followed by nationalization or a 100 per cent takeover of petroleum agreements, the Egyptian government decided to adopt a new concept consisting in merging the principle of state participation as described above with the more exotic principle of production sharing known from Indonesia.

6.1.3   LIBYA

In 1955 a petroleum law was enacted, the Petroleum Law of 1955, which was the first example of a modern petroleum law appearing in the Northern Africa/Middle East region. It provided from the outset the legal framework for petroleum operations in the country which were just about to begin. The law provided for a straightforward licensing regime based on exclusive concessions rather similar to the licensing regime applied at the time in Egypt. Likewise, the Libyan law did away with some peculiarities of the traditional ME petroleum agreements such as the large-sized agreement areas, covering almost whole countries or anyway a large part of the latter, the extra long duration of the agreement and the absence of any mandatory relinguishment of parts of the agreement area.

In 1969 (even before the installation of a new government, the Revolutionary Command Council, under the leadership of Muammar al-Qaddafi), the Libyan government followed again the Egyptian example (namely the Western Desert state participation agreements) and offered foreign oil companies the possibility of entering into joint ventures with the LNOC whereby LNOC would be the holder of the exclusive license underlying the venture concerned. The details of the joint venture are much more complicated than those of the Egyptian example, for instance the respective participating interests in the venture of the two participants are not fixed for the duration of the agreement, but made dependable on production performance.

When some years later, production sharing agreements were adopted in Libya as the standard for petroleum authorizations, many elements of the joint venture agreements were taken over by and incorporated in these new agreements, similarly as what happened in Egypt when that country switched to production sharing agreements.

The new Libyan government did not take part in the negotiations leading to the General Agreement on Participation that was signed in Riyadh on 20 December 1972, and did not join that Agreement at a later stage. Instead, it followed its own policies in this matter and in doing so offered its concessionaires the choice, which had to be made between August 1973 and May 1974, between accepting fifty-one per cent state participation (to be compensated at the fiscal book value) or to be nationalized. The fifty-one per cent share of the production could be bought back at elevated prices. The concession rights and other assets of the concessionaires, which refused to accept fifty-one per cent, were in 1974 nationalized.

Preceding these events, viz. in 1971 and again in 1973, other nationalizations had taken place in Libya. These nationalizations had a political background. In this context British Petroleum fifty per cent interest in Concession No. 65 (the Sarir field) was nationalized on 7 December 1971. This nationalization was settled by an agreement signed on 20 November 1974. Pursuant to this settlement agreement Libya paid the nationalized concessionaire by way of compensation the sum of GBP

17.4 million in cash. On 11 January 1973 Bunker Hunt's fifty per cent interest in the same concession was nationalized. This concession was now completely owned by the Libyan State. A further instance of complete nationalization occurred in 1974 when by virtue of Law No. 11 of 1974 (Decree of Nationalization of 11 February 1974) the concessions held by the US oil company Amoseas, a company jointly owned by California Asiatic Oil Company and Texaco Overseas Petroleum Company, were nationalized. In 1973 the concessionaire had already lost fifty-one per cent of its rights by Law No. 66 of 1973 (Decree of Nationalization of 1 September 1973). The nationalized concessions had been awarded under the terms of the Petroleum Law of 1955. The concession conditions included provision for international arbitration. In accordance with this provision the oil companies submitted the nationalization measures to arbitration, in which however Libya refused to participate on the grounds that the taking of nationalization measures belonged to the sovereign rights of the State and could therefore not be submitted to arbitration. The oil companies obtained an award, in which it was stated that the nationalizations as being in contravention of international law had to be undone [*restitutio in integrum*]. Actually, the award and thereby the restitution was never implemented. The oil companies settled the matter with Libya and under this settlement received as compensation for the loss of their concessions and other assets a volume of crude oil with a value of USD 152 million to be delivered over a period of fifteen months.

After these events, concessions as provided for by the Petroleum Law of 1955 were no longer awarded to foreign oil companies, albeit the Law itself was not repealed. Foreign oil companies were only allowed to undertake petroleum operations on the basis of production sharing contracts to be entered into with the National Oil Corporation (NOC), the designated state oil enterprise which had been established in 1970. NOC is the concessionaire in terms of the Petroleum Law. The first production sharing agreements were signed by NOC on 7 February 1974.

6.1.4   MALAYSIA

The government of Malaysia had incorporated over the years the results of Middle East negotiations in its own licensing regime (i.e., British Colonial Model, and because of that more or less similar to the licensing regime applied at the time in respectively Nigeria, Brunei and Egypt (before the introduction of the state participation agreements in that country). As in Oman, Nigeria and Brunei the interests of Malaysia were formally protected by the presence of the 'most favoured nation' clause in its mining leases and licenses. However, after the signing on 14 February 1971 of the Teheran Agreement by the governments of the OPEC Gulf States the Malaysian government developed and pursued its own concession policies. This new approach was introduced by the Petroleum Development Act 1974 (Act of 1974), which came into force on 1 October 1974 and by virtue of which:

  (i) petroleum agreements were cancelled with effect from 1 April 1975; and
 (ii) ownership in and the exclusive right of exploring for, exploiting, winning and obtaining petroleum, whether onshore or offshore, was vested into a state-owned corporation, which was named Petroliam Nasional Berhad (Petronas).

Note. In vesting the ownership of petroleum into Petronas the new Act constituted a radical departure from the Continental Shelf Act 1966, since the latter had vested all rights with respect to the continental shelf and its natural resources into the Federation to be exercisable by the Government of the Federation.

Since then petroleum operations are regulated by the Act of 1974, as amended by the Petroleum Development (Amendment) Acts of 1975 and 1977, and the Regulations made thereunder. The preceding Petroleum Mining Act 1966 itself was not repealed, merely made non-applicable to Petronas, with exception of the provisions regarding getting permission to enter upon lands for carrying out petroleum operations (see further Chapter 7).

6.1.5   NIGERIA

Originally, petroleum operations in Nigeria were regulated by the Minerals Oils Act of 1958. This Act was an enabling petroleum law providing for a licensing regime of which the terms and conditions as applicable to the licenses and leases were set out in the license or lease document itself. This licensing regime was referred to as the British Colonial Model and as said before was also applicable at the time in Malaysia, Brunei and Egypt. The Mineral Oils Act 1958 was repealed and replaced by the Petroleum Act 1969 which was formerly known as Decree No. 51 of 1969 and issued as such by the then Federal Military Government with effect from 27 November 1969. When the Federal Military Government was succeeded by the Federal Government some consequential changes to the text had to be made: the 'Commissioner' became the 'Minister' and so on.

The Act with its four Schedules relating respectively to 'Licenses and Leases'; 'Rights of Pre-emption'; 'Repeals'; and 'Transitional and Savings Provisions'; and the Petroleum (Drilling and Production) Regulations belonging thereto were meant to modernize the previous licensing regime without affecting its concept and principles. As part of the modernization and in contrast to the preceding Mineral Oils Act they comprise taken together all the relevant (standard) terms and conditions applicable to the licenses and leases. The Act starts off with declaring that the entire ownership and control of all petroleum in, under or upon any lands to which the Act applies shall be vested in the State and that the Minister (of Petroleum Resources) may grant licenses to explore for petroleum (non-exclusive exploration licenses), licenses to prospect for petroleum (exclusive prospecting licenses) and leases to search for, win, work, carry away and dispose of petroleum (exclusive oil mining leases). The Minister shall exercise general supervision over all operations carried on under said licenses and leases. Furthermore the Minister is empowered to make regulations regarding any aspect of petroleum operations carried out under licenses or leases granted by him under the Act. In particular, the aforesaid Petroleum (Drilling and Production) Regulations are from time to time amended by the Minister to introduce or change important subjects such as rates of royalty and the utilization of associated gas. Another aspect of the modernization exercise consisted in providing for only a rather restricted duration of prospecting licenses (five years) and oil mining leases (twenty years plus renewals).

Although Nigeria had become a Member State of OPEC in July 1971, it was not directly involved in the negotiations that had started end 1971 between the governments of the Arab Gulf States within OPEC and their concessionaires on the subject of state participation in their existing and on-going petroleum agreements. Nigeria did also not join later in the General Agreement on Participation that in the end was signed in Riyadh on 20 December 1972. There was however no need for the Nigerian government to take part in the Middle East negotiations on participation, since the country's interests were adequately protected by the 'most favoured nation' clause included in its financial agreement of 25 April 1967 made with Shell-BP.

Nevertheless, as a Member State of OPEC, the Nigerian government closely followed the negotiations on state participation and in the course of time implemented the results obtained under the first stage multi-lateral and second stage bilateral negotiations by concluding with Shell-BP a series of agreements to this purpose. Said series opened with the Heads of Agreement made on 11 June 1973. Said Heads of Agreement were based on the General Agreement on Participation albeit the Heads provided for an initial participating interest of thirty-five per cent instead of twenty-five per cent. By a Letter Agreement dated 16 April 1974, the terms of the Heads were revised to the effect of increasing the State's participating interest and fixing it, w.e.f. 1 April 1974 at fifty-five per cent (instead of sixty per cent w.e.f. 1 January 1974 as had been agreed with the Arab Gulf States within OPEC. The State's participating interest was vested in NNPC by the Nigerian Petroleum Corporation Act of 1977 and by the same Act NNPC was authorized to acquire an additional five per cent participating interest w.e.f. 1 July 1979. (Note. Nigeria followed in this matter the example of Oman and Abu Dhabi.)

Pursuant to the Acquisition of Assets (British Petroleum Company Ltd.) Act of 1979 whereby BP's shares in Shell-BP were extinguished and this restructured company (now a Shell company) was left in possession of a participating interest of twenty per cent, NNPC acquired a further direct twenty per cent interest in the licenses and leases w.e.f. 1 August 1979.

The 80/20 division of interests between NNPC and the restructured leaseholder and the issues that in the meantime had arisen between the parties involving the proper compensation for the initial thirty-five per cent and the additional five per cent interest and for quantities of buy-back oil with respect to 1973 and 1974 were finally settled in a Participation Agreement dated 22 August 1984. Subsequently, by the Assignment Agreement of 30 June 1989, NNPC transferred out of its eighty per cent interest a ten per cent interest to Shell and a five per cent interest to each of two new participants, Elf and Agip, thereby creating a new joint venture comprising four participants. At a later stage, NNPC sold another five per cent interest to Elf, retaining fifty-five per cent for itself.

6.1.6   VENEZUELA

Although one of the founding Member States of OPEC, Venezuela did not take part in the negotiations on the subject of state participation in existing and on-going concession that were organized in 1971/1972 by the Arab Gulf States within OPEC. Without going through the intermediate stages of partial state participation as envisaged by the multi-lateral General Agreement on Participation and the subsequent bilateral 60/40 state participation agreements, the government terminated all concessions w.e.f. 1 January 1976. Following the examples set by Kuwait, Qatar and Saudi Arabia, agreements were made with the former concessionaires which comprised service agreements and oil purchase contracts with respect to the latter's former concession areas.

6.2   WESTERN (OECD) COUNTRIES

Preliminary Note. The license-based petroleum legislation adopted and applied by western countries operates within the framework of an advanced and sophisticated legal system, which guarantees more or less that conflicts, disputes or disagreements arising in petroleum matters between industry and government will get a judicial review and not be solved or ended in unilateral action from the side of the government.

Like any other form of petroleum legislation the western license-based petroleum legislation is based on the (internationally recognized) principle that the ownership of petroleum *in situ* belongs to the State, with however one, notable exception: within the boundaries of the land territory of the United States the ownership of petroleum *in situ* belongs to the public or private owner of the land overlying the petroleum resource.

     Western license-based petroleum legislation is also characterized by the close attention paid to the issues of safety and health, the protection of the environment, more specifically the marine environment of the continental shelf, and the prevention of harmful or wasteful methods of operation. All this has resulted in the issue of a large body of subordinated legislation (government regulations, ministerial decrees) that provide for the necessary rules and instructions in this respect. Being very much of a technical nature, this body of legislation is constantly reviewed, renewed or adjusted when this is required by the introduction or adoption of new production techniques and technologies (e.g., onshore hydraulic fracturing of natural gas containing shales) or in the aftermath of great disasters offshore like oil spills resulting from blow-outs or gas explosions on platforms or drilling ships, or oil spills resulting from a stranding or collision accident happening to an oil tanker. Well known disasters struck respectively the semi-submersible drilling rig Sedco 135-F in the Bay of Campeche of the Gulf of Mexico, spill date 3 June 1979–23 March 1980, total discharge 3 million barrels; the oil tanker 'Exxon Valdez' in Prince William Sound, Alaska on 24 March 1989, total discharge 260,000–750,000 barrels; and the Deepwater Horizon platform in the Gulf of Mexico, spill date 20 April–15 July 2010, total discharge 4.9 million barrels. A different kind of disaster, a gas explosion destroying a platform and causing a great loss of life, but not resulting in an oil spill, was suffered by the Piper Alpha offshore production platform situated in the North Sea, 190 km north-east of Aberdeen. The explosion took place on 6 July 1988. This incident led to a large scale investigation into the causes of the incident and subsequent recommendations to improve the safety on offshore platforms (Lord Cullen report).

6.2.1 THE UNITED STATES

6.2.1.1 Introduction

According to the US legal system for the mining of mineral resources within the boundaries of the land territory of the United States, said mineral resources to which oil is reckoned to belong, are the property of the public or private owner of the land on which or beneath which the mineral resource is located. In essence this legal system is no more than property law extending the ownership of land to the mineral resources on or beneath the surface.

On account of this property right mineral acquisition rights could be obtained from the public or private owner of the land concerned. Any person interested to acquire and produce or mine a desired mineral resource could apply for and obtain a right (lease) permitting such acquisition. Usually the only obligation imposed by the lessor on the lessee was to pay a royalty in cash to the former.

The most important public owner of land and the mineral resources belonging thereto was and is the federal government. In accordance with the Constitution federal lands (and their mineral resources) are put under the legislative power of Congress.

Note. Congress was assigned in the Constitution the power to 'to dispose of and make all needful Rules and Regulations respecting the Territory or other Property of the US'.

In pursuance of this constitutional legislative power the Congress has enacted *inter alia* acts dealing with the federal mineral property. In fact, the Constitution must be considered to be a rather elementary mining law forming the fundament of all mining and petroleum legislation for federal lands.

The first drilling for oil in 1859 introduced a completely different method of mining, because in this case the mineral resource to be mined consists of a mixture of liquid and gaseous substances which is stored in the pores and fissures of sedimentary rock and which has to be extracted therefrom by drilling holes from the surface into the rock.

Lawmakers, regulators, legal theorists, landowners and oil producers in the US (and Canada) were forced to reconcile the migratory character of petroleum with the hitherto prevailing principles of mineral property rights.

To come to a solution, distinction was made between the ownership of petroleum *in situ* and the ownership of petroleum as it emerged at the wellhead at the surface. Initially, there were two views. According to the most radical view, because of its migratory character petroleum could not be owned by the owner of the land overlying the petroleum deposit concerned in the same way as solid minerals which are fixed at the place of their deposition, are owned: in other words the normal rules of land-related ownership applicable to solid minerals cannot be applied to petroleum. In this view, ownership of petroleum can only be obtained by and when taking possession of petroleum, i.e., only after succeeding in extracting petroleum from its place of accumulation and conveying the same to the wellhead at the surface. The other view is that as long as petroleum remains *in situ* there is no difference with solid minerals, i.e., petroleum *in situ* belongs to the owner of the land overlying the petroleum deposit but that as soon as the petroleum starts moving in the direction of wells that were drilled on the adjacent plot and actually leaves (the subsoil of) his plot such owner will lose his *in situ* ownership. It is the latter view that apparently has prevailed. (Source: Canadian Oil and Gas Law, Part II, §31 Theories of Ownership in the US.)

Of course no problem of ownership of petroleum *in situ* exist with respect to the petroleum resources in the subsoil of the continental shelf. In accordance with the 1958 Convention on the Continental Shelf (which in 1964 became law in the United States) as confirmed by its successor Convention on the Law of the Sea of 1982, the US Federal Government may claim sovereign rights over (its part of) the continental shelf for the purpose of exploring it and exploiting its natural resources (among which petroleum).

Against this background, US petroleum legislation has developed along three lines: firstly, there is legislation emanating from the federal government and directed at petroleum operations taking place on federally owned land territory (including land in respect of which the federal government has retained (after the transfer of ownership of the land) the title to minerals); secondly, there is petroleum legislation emanating from the respective Union States. The latter legislation regulates petroleum operations either carried out on land owned by the Union State concerned or carried out on privately owned lands which have retained their mineral property rights, and thirdly there is legislation emanating from the federal government and regulating petroleum operations taking place on that part of the continental shelf that belongs to the United States in the sense as described above.

Note. The aforesaid federally owned land territory consists for the largest part of the public domain lands which are made up of areas that were transferred by the thirteen original Union States to the federal government or were ceded to the federal government by foreign governments. The remainder of the federally owned land territory consists of: (1) 'acquired lands', which are lands acquired by the US by private contract; (2) 'Indian lands'; (3) 'reservations other than Indian reservations', such as the Naval Petroleum Reserves, National Parks, National Forests and other protected environmentally sensitive areas which were created from public domain lands.

6.2.1.2 Federal Legislation for Public Domain Lands

The first federal legislation meant to promote the mining of *inter alia* petroleum on the public domain was the Mineral Leasing Act of 15 February 1920, throughout the years many times amended. The Act authorizes the Secretary of the Interior under such necessary and proper rules and regulations as he may prescribe to grant to any applicant qualified under this Act a prospecting permit, which shall give the exclusive right, for a period not exceeding two years, to prospect for oil and gas upon not to exceed 2,560 acres of land wherein such deposits belong to the United States and are not within any known geological structure of a producing oil and gas field (non-KGS-lands) upon condition that the permittee shall begin drilling operations within six months from the date of the permit, and shall, within one year from and after the date of the permit, drill one or more wells to a depth not less than 2,000 feet unless valuable deposits of oil or gas shall be sooner discovered. The Secretary of the Interior may, if he shall find that the permittee has been unable with the exercise of diligence to test the land in the time granted by the permit, extend any such permit for such time, not exceeding two years, and upon such conditions as he shall prescribe. The applicant shall prior to filing his application for permit, locate the lands sought in the application in a reasonably compact form.

Upon establishing to the satisfaction of the Secretary of the Interior that valuable deposits of oil or gas have been discovered within the limits of the land embraced in any permit, the permittee shall be entitled to a lease for 1/4 of the land embraced in the prospecting permit: provided that the permittee shall be granted a lease for as much as 160 acres of said lands, if there be that number of acres within the permit. The area to be selected by the permittee, shall be in compact form. Such leases shall be for a term of twenty years upon a royalty of five per centum in amount or value of the production and the annual payment in advance of a rental for USD1 per acre, the rental paid for any one year to be credited against the royalties as they accrue for that year, with the right of renewal (upon such reasonable terms and conditions as may be prescribed by the Secretary of the Interior, unless otherwise provided by law at the time of the expiration of such periods). The permittee shall also be entitled to a preference right to a lease for the remainder of the land in his prospecting permit at a royalty of not less than 12 1/2 per centum in amount or value of the production, and under such other conditions (as) are fixed for oil or (gas) lease(s) in this Act, the royalty to be determined by competitive bidding or fixed by such other method as the Secretary may by regulations prescribe: provided that the Secretary shall have the right to reject any or all bids.

All permits and leases of lands containing oil or gas, made or issued under the provisions of this Act, shall be subject to the condition that no wells shall be drilled within 200 feet of any of the outer boundaries of the lands so permitted or leased, unless the title to adjoining lands have been vested in private owners, and to the further condition that the permittee or lessee will, in conducting his explorations and mining operations, use all reasonable precautions to prevent waste of oil or gas developed in the land, or the entrance of water through wells drilled by him to the oil sands or oil-bearing strata; or the destruction or injury of the oil deposits.

All unappropriated deposits of oil or gas situated within the known geologic structure of a producing oil or gas field (KGS-lands) and the unentered lands containing the same, not subject to preferential lease, may be leased by the Secretary of the Interior to highest responsible bidder by competitive bidding under general regulations to qualified applicants in areas not exceeding 640 acres and in tracts which shall not exceed in lengths 2 1/2 times their width, such lease to be conditioned upon the payment by the lessee of such bonus as may be accepted and of such royalty as may be fixed in the lease, which shall not be less than 12 1/2 per centum in amount or value of the production, and the payment in advance of a rental of not less than USD 1 per acre per annum thereafter during the continuance of the lease, the rental paid for any year to be credited against the royalties as they accrue for that year. Leases shall be for a period of twenty years, with the preferential (right to renewal) upon such reasonable terms and conditions as may be prescribed by the Secretary of the Interior, unless otherwise provided by law at the time of the expiration of such periods. Whenever the average daily production of any oil well shall not exceed 10 barrels per day, the Secretary of the Interior is authorized to reduce the royalty on future production when in his judgment the wells cannot be successfully operated upon the royalty fixed in the lease. The above provisions shall apply to all oil and gas leases made under this Act.

6.2.1.3   Union State Petroleum Legislation

Union States (States) enact petroleum laws with respect to privately owned land and state-owned land on which or beneath which petroleum has accumulated, except in cases where the federal government had been the previous owner of the land and has kept the mineral property for itself before transferring the ownership of the land. Making rules and regulations for state-owned land and its petroleum resources is based on the State being the owner of this resource. Making rules and regulations for privately owned land and its petroleum resources is based on the police power of the State. Within this setting it is any State's priority and duty to ensure that the exploration for, development and production of petroleum seen as an industrial activity are carried out in a safe manner, without causing damage to the environment or endangering the health of the population. But state intervention in petroleum operations has gone further and has extended to the technical methods in which the petroleum resources discovered beneath the land are being exploited by their owner or lessee.

In the early days of the industry, exploitation of a petroleum deposit consisted in drilling as many wells as could be accommodated within the (restricted) space available to the landowner or its lessee. This approach resulted in a poor recovery of petroleum because over-produced wells went prematurely to water and a significant part of the petroleum remained behind in the reservoir. Moreover the driving mechanism (also referred to as reservoir energy) was spoilt and wasted. As a form of self-regulation, the buyers of the oil in those days, i.e., the refining companies also referred to as the oil companies, frustrated by the production fluctuations caused by the wasteful extraction methods adopted by the oil producers, stepped in and tried to acquire as many leases and surrounding producing property as possible. In this way the average size of a lease increased, which allowed to apply more efficient production methods requiring less wells to be drilled. This resulted in a saving of capital and at the same time in the improvement of the ultimate recovery of petroleum. Nevertheless, States were generally not satisfied with the way petroleum resources were exploited by their owners and lessees and in the course of time all of the major producing States enacted conservation laws that allowed intervention in the way private petroleum property was exploited, thus directly affecting the economic interests of the landowner and its lessee.

Note. Such intervention goes far beyond the police power of States. It represents an infringement of the property rights of the owner or its lessee. It appears that the only right left to the owner or its lessee is the right to decide not to exploit the petroleum deposit beneath his land.

The principles of these conservation laws were broadly the same: any waste of oil and gas was prohibited. 'Waste' includes the waste of reservoir energy and the location and spacing and operation of oil and gas wells in a manner in which reduces the ultimate recovery of oil or gas from a particular petroleum deposit. A state authority (a Commissioner of Conservation) is appointed which is authorized to limit and pro-rate the production of oil or natural gas from any field (pool); to regulate the spacing of wells, and to establish drilling units. In the context of state conservation laws a drilling unit is understood to mean the maximum area which may be efficiently and economically drained by one well. The unit is considered to constitute a developed area as long as a well is located thereon which is capable of producing oil and gas in paying quantities. Separate ownerships within such a drilling unit have to be integrated (and are made subject to pooling orders). The owner of each tract is assigned a share of the production of the well draining the unit. If demand for oil or gas (in any particular Union State) exceeds production capacity, the production of any well shall be restricted to the Maximum Efficient Rate (MER) of production, in order to prevent that reservoirs are being damaged by excessive production. The MER is based on the physical characteristics of the producing reservoir. On the other hand, if production capacity exceeds demand production limitation will be introduced based on the total production allocated to each Union State. The total applicable to an individual State will be distributed over its individual producers whereby exceptions will be made and exemptions be granted for special cases, such as secondary recovery projects and marginal wells, which may continue to produce at full capacity.

Note 1. Up to now demand for oil in the US exceeds domestic production capacity, but the deficit is narrowing. Nevertheless there has been a period (first half of 1990) that domestic production, in particular the small producer, was in danger of having to shut down because of the low prices prevailing on the global oil market as a result of over-supply.

Note 2. The principles of the conservation laws, except for the imposition of a MER, are a thing of the past. Pooling orders and well spacing have been replaced by modern unitization agreements (discussed in Chapter 11).

6.2.1.4   Federal Legislation for the Outer Continental Shelf Lands

6.2.1.4.1   Introduction

In 1945, US President Harry S. Truman proclaimed that the Government of the United States regarded the natural resources of the subsoil and the seabed of the continental shelf beneath the high seas, but contiguous to the coasts of the US, as appertaining to the US, subject to its jurisdiction and control. In the accompanying press release the continental shelf is described as submerged land which is contiguous to the continent and which is covered by no more than 100 fathoms (600 feet) of water. Since then the international level Convention on the Continental Shelf (27 April 1958) became effective as law in the United States in 1964, eleven years after passage of the Outer Continental Shelf Lands Act (see below). The successor Convention on the Law of the Sea of 1982 has still not be ratified by the US. In this Convention, the outer limit of the continental shelf is defined in a complete different way as this has been done in the 1958 Convention, this time much in favour of the coastal State. The United States can only claim the new outer limit, if this part of the 1982 Convention is recognized as to belong to customary international law.

6.2.1.4.2   The Act of 7 August 1953 as Amended

On the basis of the Presidential Proclamation the Act of 7 August 1953 was enacted, known as the Outer Continental Shelf Lands Act. Over the years, the Act has substantially been modernized by amendment but the main principles have been maintained.

6.2.1.4.2.1   Definitions

(a) The term 'outer Continental Shelf' means all submerged lands lying seaward and outside of the area of lands beneath navigable waters and of which the subsoil and seabed appertain to the United States and are subject to its jurisdiction and control.
(b) The term 'minerals' includes oil, gas, sulphur, geopressured-geothermal and associated resources, and all other minerals which are authorized by an Act of Congress to be produced from 'public lands' as defined in the Federal Land Policy and Management Act of 1976.

(c) The term 'lease' means any form of authorization which is issued or maintained (*when earlier issued by any State*) under this Act and which authorizes exploration for, and development and production of, minerals.

(d) The term 'Secretary' means the Secretary of the Interior, except that with respect to the administration and grant of leases the term 'Secretary' means the Secretary of Energy.

Note 1. Although in the Act no specific reference is made to international law, the seaward boundary of the outer continental shelf lands must be considered to be determined by the seaward limits agreed in the context of the 1982 Convention of the Law of the Sea (effective date 16 November 1994). Under international law these limits apply even if a particular coastal (federal) State has not (yet) ratified the Convention as is the case with the US. On the other hand, the predecessor of the 1982 Convention, namely the 1958 Convention on the Continental Shelf, became in 1964 effective as law in the US and it appears that its wording has been incorporated in the Act.

Note 2. The functions and regulatory powers with respect to the administration and grant of leases were transferred to the Secretary of Energy by the Act of 4 August 1977, whereby the Congress created the Department of Energy and set up the Federal Energy Regulatory Commission (FERC).

6.2.1.4.2.2   Congressional Declaration

Section 3 of the Act clarifies the national policy for the Outer Continental Shelf, as follows:

It is hereby declared to be the policy of the United States that:

(1) the subsoil and seabed of the outer continental shelf appertain to the United States and are subject to its jurisdiction, control, and power of disposition as provided in this Act;

(2) this Act shall be construed in such a manner that the character of the waters above the outer Continental Shelf as high seas and the right to navigation and fishing therein shall not be affected;

(3) the outer Continental Shelf is a vital national resource reserve held by the Federal Government for the public, which should be made available for expeditious and orderly development, subject to environmental safeguards, in a manner which is consistent with the maintenance of competition and other national needs;

(4) since exploration, development, and production of the minerals of the outer Continental Shelf will have significant impacts on coastal and non-coastal areas of the coastal States, and on other affected States, and, in recognition of the national interest in the effective management of the marine, coastal, and human environments – (A) such States and their affected local governments may require assistance in protecting their coastal zones and other affected areas from any temporary or permanent adverse effects of such impacts; (B) the distribution of a portion of the receipts from the leasing of mineral resources of the outer Continental Shelf adjacent to State lands will provide affected coastal States and localities with funds which may be used for the mitigation of adverse economic and environmental effects related to the development of such resources; and (C) such States, and through such States, affected local governments, are entitled to an opportunity to participate, to the extent consistent with the national interest, in the policy and planning decisions made by the Federal Government relating to exploration for, and development and production of, minerals of the outer Continental Shelf;

(5) the rights and responsibilities of all States and, where appropriate, local governments, top reserve and protect their marine, human, and coastal environments through such means as regulation of land, air, and water uses, of safety, and of related development and activity should be considered and recognized; and

(6) operations in the outer Continental Shelf should be conducted in a safe manner by well-trained personnel using technology, precautions, and techniques sufficient to prevent or minimize the likelihood of blow-outs, loss of well control, fires, spillages, physical obstruction to other users of the waters or subsoil and seabed, or other occurrences which may cause damage to the environment or to property, or endanger life or health.

Note. The importance of (4) and (6) above becomes very clear in the light of the disaster that struck the platform Deepwater Horizon in the Gulf of Mexico whereby between 20 April and 15 July 2010 a total discharge of 4.9 million barrels took place.

6.2.1.4.2.3   The System of Leasing and Its Administration

(i) The Secretary shall administer the provisions of this Act relating to the leasing of the outer continental Shelf and shall prescribe such rules and regulations as may be necessary to carry out such provisions. The Secretary may at any time prescribe and amend such rules and regulations as he determines to be necessary and proper in order to provide for the prevention of waste and conservation of the natural resources of the outer Continental Shelf, and the protection of correlative rights therein, and not withstanding any other provisions herein, such rules and regulations shall, as of their effective date, apply to all operations conducted under a lease issued or maintained under the provisions of this Act. The regulations prescribed by the Secretary shall include provisions:

(a) for the suspension or temporary prohibition of any operation or activity, including production, pursuant to any lease or permit:
  – at the request of a lessee, in the national interest, to facilitate proper development of a lease or to allow for the construction or negotiation for use of transportation facilities; or
  – if there is a threat of serious, irreparable, or immediate harm or damage to life (including fish and other aquatic life), to property, to any mineral deposits (in areas leased or not leased), or to the marine, coastal, or human environment, and for the extension of any permit or lease affected by suspension or prohibition under (a) or (b) by a period equivalent to the period of such suspension or prohibition, except that no permit or lease shall be so extended when such suspension or prohibition is the result of gross negligence or wilful violation of such lease or permit, or of the regulations issued with respect to such lease or permit.

(b) with respect to cancellation of any lease or permit;

(c) for the assignment or relinquishment of a lease;

(d) for unitization, pooling, and drilling agreements;

(e) for the subsurface storage of oil and natural gas from any source other than by the Federal Government;

(f) for drilling or easements necessary for exploration, development, and production;

(g) for the prompt and efficient exploration and development of a lease area; and

(h) for the compliance with the national ambient air quality standards pursuant to the Clean Air Act to the extent that activities authorized under this Act significantly affect the air quality of any State.

(ii) The issuance and continuance in effect of any lease, or of any assignment or other transfer of any lease, under the provisions of this Act shall be conditioned upon compliance with regulations issued under this Act.

(iii) Whenever the owner of a non-producing lease fails to comply with any of the provisions of the Act, or of the lease, or of the regulations issued under this Act, such lease may be cancelled by the Secretary, subject to the right of judicial review as provided in this Act, if such default continues for the period of thirty days after mailing of notice to the lease owner.

(iv) Whenever the owner of any producing lease fails to comply with any of the provisions of this Act, of the lease, or of the regulations issued under this Act, such lease may be forfeited and cancelled by an appropriate proceeding in any United States district court having jurisdiction under the Act.

(v) Rights-of-way through the submerged lands of the outer Continental Shelf, whether or not such lands are included in a lease maintained or issued pursuant tot his Act, may be granted by the Secretary for pipeline purposes for the transportation of oil, natural gas, sulphur, or other minerals, or under such regulations and upon such conditions as may be prescribed by the Secretary, or where appropriate the Secretary of Transportation, including assuring maximum environmental protection by utilization of the best available and safest practices for pipeline burial and upon the express condition that oil or gas pipelines shall transport or purchase without discrimination, oil or natural gas produced from submerged lands or outer Continental Shelf lands in the vicinity of the pipelines in such proportionate amounts as the Federal Energy Regulatory Commission, in consultation with the Secretary of Energy, may, after a full hearing with due notice thereof to the interested parties, determine to be reasonable, taking into account among other things, conservation and the prevention of waste.

(vi) Except for field pipelines, every permit, license, easement, right-of-way, or other grant of authority for the transportation by pipeline on or across the outer Continental Shelf of oil or gas shall require that the pipeline be operated in accordance with following competitive principles: (1) the pipeline must provide open and non-discriminatory access to both owner and non-owner shippers. (2) upon specific request of one or more owner or non-owner shippers able to provide a guaranteed level of throughput the Federal Energy Regulatory Commission may, upon finding, after a full hearing with due notice thereof to the interested parties, that such expansion is within technological limits and economic feasibility, order a subsequent expansion of throughput capacity of any pipeline for which the permit, license, easement, right-of-way, or other grant of authority is approved or issued after the date of enactment of this subparagraph.

(vii) The lessee shall produce any oil or natural gas, or both, obtained pursuant to an approved development and production plan, at rates consistent with any rule or order issued by the President in accordance with any provision of law. If no such rule or order has been issued, the lessee shall produce such oil or gas, or both, at rates consistent with any regulation promulgated by the Secretary of Energy which is to assure the maximum rate of production which may be sustained without loss of ultimate recovery of oil or gas, or both, under sound engineering and economic principles, and which is safe for the duration of the activity covered by the approved plan. The Secretary may permit the lessee to vary such rates if he finds that such a variance is necessary.

(viii) No lessee shall be permitted to flare natural gas from any well unless the Secretary finds that there is no practicable way to complete production of such gas, or that such flaring is necessary to alleviate a temporary emergency situation or to conduct testing or work-over operations.

6.2.1.4.2.4   Grant of Leases by the Secretary

(1) The Secretary is authorized to grant to the highest responsible qualified bidder or bidders by competitive bidding, under regulations promulgated in advance, any oil and gas lease on submerged lands of the outer Continental Shelf which are not covered by leases maintained under this Act. The bidding shall be by sealed bid and, at the discretion of the Secretary, on the basis of:

(i) cash bonus bid with a royalty at not less than 12.5 per centum fixed by the Secretary in amount or value of the production saved, removed or sold;

(ii) variable royalty bid based on a per cent in amount or value of the production saved, removed or sold, with either a fixed work commitment based on dollar amount for exploration or a fixed cash bonus as determined by the Secretary, or both;

(iii) cash bonus bid, or work commitment bid based on a dollar amount for exploration with a fixed cash bonus, and a diminishing or sliding royalty based on such formulae as the Secretary shall determine as equitable to encourage continued production from the lease area as resources diminish, but not less than 12.5 per centum at the beginning of the lease period in amount or value of the production saved, removed or sold;

(iv) cash bonus bid with a fixed share of the net profits of no less than thirty per centum to be derived from the production of oil and gas from the lease area;

(v) fixed cash bonus with the net profit share reserved as the bid variable;

(vi) cash bonus bid with a royalty at no less than 12.5 per centum fixed by the Secretary in amount or value of the production saved, removed or sold and a fixed per centum share of net profits of no less than thirty per centum to be derived from the production of oil and gas from the lease area;

(vii) work commitment bid based on a dollar amount for exploration with a fixed cash bonus and a fixed royalty in amount or value of the production saved, removed or sold;

(viii) cash bonus bid with royalty at no less than 12.5 per centum fixed by the Secretary in amount or value of production saved, removed, or sold, and with suspension of royalties for a period, volume, or value of production determined by the Secretary, which suspensions may vary based on the price of production from the lease; or

(ix) any modification of bidding systems authorized in (i) through (vii), or any other systems of bid variables, terms, and conditions which the Secretary determines to be useful to accomplish the purposes and policies of the Act, except that no such bidding system or modification shall have more than one bid variable.

(2) The Secretary may, in order to promote increased production on the lease area, through direct, secondary, or tertiary recovery

means, reduce or eliminate any royalty or net profit share set forth in the lease for such area.

(3) The Secretary of Energy shall submit any bidding system authorized in 1(viii) above to the Senate and the House of Representatives. The Secretary may institute such bidding system unless either the Senate or the House of Representatives passes a resolution of disapproval within thirty days after receipt of the bidding system.

(4) Not later than thirty days before any lease sale the Secretary shall submit to the Congress and publish in the Federal Register a notice:

(i) identifying any bidding system which will be utilized for such lease sale and the reasons for the utilization of such bidding system; and

(ii) designating the lease tracts selected which are to be offered in such sale under the bidding system mentioned in 1(i) above and the lease tracts selected which are to be offered under any one or more of the bidding systems mentioned in 1(ii) through 1(viii) above and the reasons such lease tracts are to be offered under a particular bidding system.

(5) An oil and gas lease issued pursuant to a lease sale shall:

(i) be for a tract consisting of a compact area not exceeding 5,760 acres, as the Secretary may determine, unless the Secretary finds that a larger area is necessary to comprise a reasonable economic production unit;

(ii) be for an initial period of five years; or not to exceed ten years where the Secretary finds that such longer period is necessary to encourage exploration and development in areas because of unusually deep water or other unusually adverse conditions, and as long after such initial period as oil or gas is produced from the area in paying quantities, or drilling or well reworking operations as approved by the Secretary are conducted thereon;

(iii) require the payment of amount or value as determined by one of the bidding systems set forth in 1 above;

(iv) entitle the lessee to explore, develop, and produce the oil and gas contained within the lease area, conditioned upon due diligence requirements and the approval of the development and production plan required by this Act;

(v) provide for suspension or cancellation of the lease during the initial lease term or thereafter in accordance with the provisions of the Act;

(vi) contain such rental and other provisions as the Secretary may prescribe at the time of offering the area for lease; and

(vii) provide a requirement that the lessee offer twenty per centum of the crude oil, condensate, and natural gas liquids produced on such lease, at the market value and point of delivery applicable to Federal royalty oil, to small or independent refiners.

(6) Following each notice of a proposed lease sale and before the acceptance of bids and the issuance of leases based on such bids, the Secretary shall allow the Attorney General, in consultation with the Federal Trade Commission, thirty days or a shorter period if so agreed to review the results of such lease sale. The Attorney General may, in consultation with the Federal Trade Commission, conduct such antitrust review on the likely effects the issuance of such leases would have on competition as the Attorney General, after consultation with the Federal Trade Commission, deems appropriate and shall advise the Secretary with respect to such review. The Attorney General, after consultation with the Federal Trade Commission, may make such recommendation to the Secretary, including the non-acceptance of any bid, as may be appropriate to prevent any situation inconsistent with the antitrust laws.

(7) No bid for a lease may be submitted if the Secretary finds, after notice and hearing, that the bidder is not meeting due diligence requirements on other leases.

(8) No lease issued under this Act may be sold, exchanged, assigned, or otherwise transferred, except with the approval of the Secretary. Prior to any such approval, the Secretary shall consult with and give due consideration to the views of the Attorney General.

6.2.2 THE UNITED KINGDOM

6.2.2.1 Introduction

Petroleum legislation in the United Kingdom consists of Acts (formal laws) and subsidiary legislation in the form of implementing and supplementary

Regulations made under such Acts. To said Regulations model clauses are scheduled for incorporation in the license to be granted.

The Petroleum Act 1998 of 11 June 1998 is the latest Petroleum Act empowering the Secretary of State to make such Regulations, and the model clauses belonging thereby. In the long period preceding the Act's enactment, the Secretary of State's powers rested on the Petroleum (Production) Act 1934. Both Acts refer to the Continental Shelf Act 1964.

Licenses for exploration and production can be applied for landward areas or for seaward areas (the offshore). These two areas are separated by the low water line. The seaward areas comprise the territorial sea and such part of the continental shelf as falls to the United Kingdom under international law. The UK North Sea continental shelf has been demarcated in accordance with boundary treaties made with the opposite North Sea coastal States.

For the purposes of offshore licensing, the seaward areas are covered by a grid consisting of units measuring twelve minutes longitude by ten minutes latitude (about 200 to 250 square km), each unit comprising 120 sections. Licenses are granted with respect to tranches (contiguous blocks) or individual blocks, depending on what is on offer in any particular round of licensing. Each block is bounded by minute lines of latitude and longitude and therefore comprising a whole number of sections

Offshore licensing is organized in successive rounds of licensing. Should the Secretary of State wish to introduce new or partly new model clauses for incorporation in the licenses to be granted in any particular round of licensing, then the prevailing regulations must either have to be amended or be completely replaced by new regulations before announcing the round. In fact, each of the rounds held so far has been preceded by the issue of amendment regulations or by new regulations. In any case, the model clauses which are scheduled to any regulation will be different for different rounds.

Once a license has been granted, its terms and conditions can only be altered or new conditions be inserted through enactment of an Act, which provides for such a retroactive change or insertion. In the past, such changes with retroactive effect were enacted by the Petroleum and Submarine Pipelines Act 1975 and by the Oil and Gas (Enterprise) Act 1982.

6.2.2.2   The Petroleum Act 1998

This Act (Part I) was meant to consolidate and confirm the existing procedures around the granting licenses and the making of Regulations. Its purpose was not to change retroactively the model clauses incorporated in existing licenses. In addition, the Act (Parts II and III) consolidated provisions regarding offshore installations (abandonment, decommissioning, etc.) and submarine pipelines, subjects previously dealt with in several different Acts.

Part I: Petroleum

Section 1. Meaning of 'Petroleum'

'Petroleum' (a) includes any mineral oil or relative hydrocarbon and natural gas existing in its natural condition in strata; but (b) does not include coal or bituminous shales or other stratified deposits from which oil can be extracted by destructive distillation.

Section 2. Rights to petroleum vested in Her Majesty

(a) Her Majesty has the exclusive right of searching and boring for and getting petroleum to which this section applies.
(b) This section applies to petroleum which for the time being exists in its natural condition in strata in Great Britain or beneath the territorial sea adjacent to the United Kingdom.

Section 3 Licenses to search and bore for and get petroleum

(1) The Secretary of State, on behalf of Her Majesty, may grant to such persons as he thinks fit licenses to search and bore for and get petroleum to which this section applies.
(2) This Section applies to: (a) petroleum to which section 2 applies; and (b) petroleum with respect to which rights vested in Her Majesty by section 1 (1) of the Continental Shelf Act 1964 (exploration and exploitation of the continental shelf) are exercisable.
(3) Any such license shall be granted for such consideration (whether by way of royalty or otherwise) as the Secretary of State with the consent of the Treasury may determine, and upon such other terms and conditions as the Secretary of State thinks fit.

Section 4 Licenses: further provisions

(1) The Secretary of State shall make regulations prescribing; (a) the manner in which and the persons by whom applications for licenses under this part of this Act may be made; (b) the information to be included in or provided in connection with any

such application; (c) the fees to be paid on any such application; (d) the conditions as to the size and shape in respect of which licenses may be granted; (e) model clauses which shall, unless he thinks fit to modify or exclude them in any particular case, to be incorporated in any such liceence.

(2)–(5)   *(formalities).*

6.2.2.3   The Petroleum (Production) (Seaward Areas) Regulations 2008

Preliminary Note. As mentioned before, model clauses for incorporation in licenses reached the end of their development in the Petroleum (Production) (Seaward Areas) Regulations 1988/1995/1996, which were issued in connection with the 17th round of licensing. However, on the occasion of the 21st round of licensing (February 2003), a new type of license was introduced: viz. a 'Promote License'. The promote license allows the holder thereof to assess and study the prospectivity of the license area without having to accept burdensome work commitments. The duration of the license is two years but may be converted into a regular license if the licensee offers a substantive work programme. Later on, on the occasion of the 22nd round of licensing (February 2004) again a special type of license was introduced, viz. the 'Frontier License'. This license was meant for exploration activities in the Atlantic Margin west of the Shetlands. A frontier license is granted for relatively large areas for an initial term of six years and another six years for development.

With the coming of the Petroleum Licensing (Production) (Seaward Areas) Regulations 2008 and the model clauses scheduled thereto (meant to apply to the 25th and subsequent rounds of licensing for seaward areas), the text of the model clauses has been reorganized for the sake of clarity and simplicity in that all model clauses contain a fixed pattern of consecutive periods of validity of the license (Initial Term, Second Term, Third Term and a further Term) and a fixed scheme for surrendering parts of the licensed areas, leaving the actual figures to be stipulated in a Schedule 5 to the license. Other particulars are also found in Schedules to the license: Schedule 1 describing the licensed area; Schedule 2 containing the payments to be made as consideration for the grant of the license; Schedule 3 describing the exploration work programme to be carried out during the Initial Term.

1. Introduction

The Secretary of State, in exercise of the powers conferred on him by section 4 of the Petroleum Act 1998, makes the following regulations.

1. These Regulations made be cited as the Petroleum Licensing (Production) (Seaward Areas) Regulations 2008 and shall come into force on 6th April 2008.
2. In these Regulations: 'production license' means a license to search and bore for, and get, petroleum in strata in the seabed and in the subsoil in a seaward area; and 'seaward area' has the meaning given by regulation 3 (1) (a) of the Petroleum (Production) (Seaward Areas) Regulations 1988.
3. For the purposes of Section 4 (1) (e) of the Petroleum Act 1998 the model clauses prescribed for production licenses in seaward areas are those set out in the Schedule.

2. Schedule: Model Clauses for Seaward Area Production licenses

(1) Interpretation

(1) 'the Act' means the Petroleum Act 1998;
(2) Any obligation which are to be observed and performed by the Licensee shall at any time at which the Licensee is more than one person be joint and several obligations;
(3) 'the Minister' means the Secretary of State for Business, Enterprise and Regulatory Reform;
(4) 'Petroleum' includes any mineral oil or relative hydrocarbon and natural gas existing in its natural condition in strata but does not include coal or bituminous shales or other stratified deposits from which oil can be extracted by destructive distillation;
(5) 'Initial Term' means the period specified as such in Schedule 5 to this license;
(6) 'Second Term' means the period specified as such in Schedule 5 to this license;
(7) 'Third Term' means the period specified as such in Schedule 5 to this license;
(8) 'Mandatory Surrender Area' means the area specified as such in Schedule 5 to this license;
(9) 'Drill-or-Drop Period' means the period (if any) specified as such in Schedule 5 to this license;

(10) 'Early Surrender Area' means the area (if any) specified as such in Schedule 5 to this license;

(11) Éarly Surrender Period' means the period (if any) specified as such in Schedule 5 to this license;

(12) 'Work Programme' means the programme set out in Schedule 3 to this license.

(2) Grant of License

In consideration of the payments hereinafter provided and the performance and observance by the Licensee of all terms and conditions hereof, the Minister in exercise of the powers conferred upon him by the Act hereby grants to the Licensee exclusive license and liberty during the continuance of this license and subject to the provisions hereof to search and bore for, and get, petroleum in the seabed and subsoil under the seaward area more particularly described in Schedule 1 to this license provided that nothing in this licenses shall affect the right of the Minister to grant a methane drainage license in respect of the whole or any part of the licensed area or affect the exercise of any rights grante under any such methane drainage license.

(3) Term of License

This license, unless sooner determined under any of the provisions hereof, shall continue for the Initial Term, for the Second Term and for the Third Term. On expiry of the Third Term this license shall determine unless extended as provided hereunder.

(4) Initial Term

(Detailed provisions where in Schedule 5 a Drill-or Drop Period, a Promote Period or an Early Surrender Area and an Early Surrender Period are specified).

(5) Option to continue license into a Second Term

Before the expiry of the Initial Term the licensee may give notice to the Minister that he desires this license to continue in force in relation to part of the licensed area ('the Continuing Part') and will determine this license in relation to such part of the licensed area as shall be described in the notice ('the Surrendered Part'). The Surrendered Part must consist in an area which when taken together with any area previously surrendered is no less than the Mandatory Surrender Area but the licensee shall not be obliged to surrender so much of the Licensed Area that following such surrender the Licensed Area comprises less than 30 Sections.

(6) Extension of the Intial or Second Term

Before the expiry of either the Initial Term or the Second Term the the Licensee may give notice to the Minister that he desires the term in question to be extended for a further period.

(7) Option to continue the License into a Third Term

Before the expiry of the Second Term the licensee may give notice to the Minister that he desires this license to continue as to a part of the licensed area ('the Producing Part'). If such notice is given this license shall continue in force after the expiry of the Second Term in the event that before such expiry the Minister has given its consent (*to relevant works erected or carried out by the licensee for getting petroleum from the licensed area*); or has approved a development and production programme and such approval is still in force upon expiry of the Second Term or has served a programme on the licensee and such programme is still in force upon expiry of the Second Term. Where this license continues in force it shall so continue during the Third Term.

(8) Power further to extend term of License

Where this license is continued in force to the end of the Third Term, the Minister, on application being made to him before the expiry of such period, may in his discretion agree with the licensee that this license shall continue in force thereafter for such further period as the Minister and the licensee may agree and subject to such modification of the terms and conditions of this license (which modification may include making provision for any further extension of the term of this license) as the Minister and the licensee may then agree is appropriate.

(9) Right of licensee to determine license or surrender part of licensed area

Without prejudice to any obligation or liability imposed by or incurred under the terms of the license the licensee may at any time by giving notice to the Minister to that effect determine this license or surrender any part of the licensed area being a part which complies with 9. below.

(10) Areas surrendered

Any area surrendered by the licensee shall be bounded by minute lines of latitude extending not less than two minutes of longitude and minute lines of longitude extending not less than two minutes of latitude, consist of not less than 30 sections and have boundaries which whether they run north and south or east and west either coincide with the corresponding boundaries of the block or are not less than 2 sections distant from those boundaries.

(11) Payment of consideration for license

The licensee shall make to the Minister as consideration for the grant of this license payments in accordance with Schedule 2 to this license (*i.e., initial payment and annual payments measured by the number of square km comprised in the licensed area*).

Note. Previous royalty payments have with effect from 1 January 2003 been abolished.

(12) Keeping of accounts

  (1) The licensee shall keep within the United Kingdom full and correct accounts of (a) the quantity of petroleum in the form of gas won and saved; (b) the quantity of petroleum in any other form won and saved; (c) the name and address of any person to whom any petroleum has been supplied by the licensee, the quantity so supplied, the price thereof or other consideration therefor and the place to which the petroleum was conveyed pursuant to the agreement for such supply; and (d) such other particulars as the Minister may from time to time direct.
  (2) The quantities of petroleum stated in such accounts may exclude any water separated from the petroleum.
  (3) Such accounts shall state separately the quantities of petroleum used for the purposes of carrying on drilling and production operations and pumping to field storage, and the quantities not so used, and in the case of petroleum not in the form of gas shall state the respective quantities of petroleum of each specific gravity.

(13) Working Obligations

  (i) The licensee shall before the expiry of the Initial Term of the license carry out the Work Programme.
  (ii) At any time the Minister may serve a notice on the licensee requiring him to submit to him an 'appropriate' exploration work programme with respect to a specified period that should fall within the term of the license.

Note. For the purpose of this provision an 'appropriate' programme is described as one which any person who, if he had the competence and the resources needed to exploit the rights granted by this license to the best commercial advantage and were seeking to exploit those rights in this manner, could reasonably be expected to carry out during the period specified in the notice:

(iii) If the Minister notifies the licensee that he is of the opinion that the programme submitted by the licensee does not satisfy the relevant requirements, the latter must either submit the matter to arbitration or submit to the Minister a further programme that satisfies the relevant requirements.

(14) Development and Production Programmes

1. The licensee shall not:

(a) erect or carry out any relevant works for the purpose of getting petroleum from the licensed area or for the purpose of transporting to a place on land petroleum produced from that area, or

(b) get petroleum from that area,

except with the consent in writing of the Minister or in accordance with a programme which the Minister has (finally) approved or served on the licensee as the case may be.

2. The licensee shall submit to the Minister a programme specifying (a) the relevant works which the licensee proposes to erect or carry out for either of the purposes described under (1); (b) the proposed location of the works; (c) the maximum and minimum quantities of petroleum in the form of gas and the maximum and minimum quantities of petroleum in other forms, which, in each calendar year or in each such period as may be specified by the Minister the licensee proposes to get as mentioned under (1) (a) above.

3. The Minister may give notice to the licensee that the Minister approves the programme or approves the programme subject to certain conditions or rejects the programme on one or both of the following grounds, namely: that the carrying out any proposal included in the programme would be contrary to good oilfield practice; that the proposals included in the programme made pursuant to (2) (c) are not in the national interest.

4. The consent of the Minister referred to in (1) above may be given subject to conditions.

(The consequences of a rejection of a programme are worked out in great detail)

(15) Commencement and abandonment and plugging of Wells

The Licensee shall not commence or recommence the drilling of any Well or abandon any Well without the consent of the Minister.

(16) Distance of Wells from Boundaries of Licensed Area

No well shall, except with the consent in writing of the Minister, be drilled or made so that any part thereof is less than 125 metres from any of the boundaries of the licensed area.

(17) Control of Development Wells

The licensee shall not suspend work on drilling a development well or having suspended it shall not begin it again except with the consent of the Minister and in accordance with the conditions, if any, subject to which the consent is given.

(18) Avoidance of Harmful Methods of Working

1. The licensee shall execute all operations in or in connection with the licensed area in a proper and workmanlike manner in accordance with methods and practice customarily used in good oilfield practice and without prejudice to the generality of the foregoing shall take all steps practicable in order:
   (i) to control the flow and to prevent the escape or waste of petroleum discovered in or obtained from the licensed area;
   (ii) to conserve the licensed area for productive operations;
   (iii) to prevent damage to adjoining petroleum bearing strata;
   (iv) to prevent the entrance of water through wells to petroleum bearing strata except for the purposes of secondary recovery; and
   (v) to prevent the escape of petroleum into any waters in or in the vicinity of the licensed area.
2. The licensee shall not flare any gas from the licensed area; or use gas for the purpose of creating or increasing the pressure by means of which petroleum is obtained from that area, except with the consent in writing of the Minister and in accordance with the conditions, if any, of the consent.

(19) Appointment of Operators

The licensee shall ensure that another person (including, in the case where the licensee is two or more persons, any of those persons) does not exercise any function of organizing or supervising all or any of the operations of searching or boring for or getting petroleum in pursuance of this license unless that other person is a person approved by the Minister and the function in question is one to which that approval relates.

(20) Fishing and Navigation

The licensee shall not carry out any operations authorised by this license in or about the licensed area in such a manner as to interfere unjustifiably with navigation or fishing in the waters of the licensed area or with the conservation of the living resources of the sea.

(21) Training

The Minister may from to time give to the licensee instructions as to the training of persons employed or to be employed whether by the licensee or by any other person, in any activity which is related to the exercise of the rights granted by this license and the licensee shall ensure that any instructions so given are complied with.

(22) Unit Development

1. If at any time at which the license is in force the Minister shall be satisfied that the strata in the licensed area or any part thereof form part of a single geological petroleum structure or petroleum field (hereinafter referred to as 'an oil field') other parts whereof are formed by strata in areas in respect of which other licenses granted in pursuance of the Act are then in force and the Minister shall consider that it is in the national interest in order to secure the maximum ultimate recovery of petroleum and in order to avoid unnecessary competitive drilling that the oil field should be worked and developed as a unit in cooperation by all persons including the licensee whose licenses extend to or include any part thereof the following provisions shall apply.
2. Upon being so required by notice in writing by the Minister the licensee shall cooperate with such other licensees in the preparation of a scheme (hereinafter referred to as 'a development scheme') for the working and development of the oil field as a unit by the licensee and the other licensees in cooperation, and shall, jointly with the other licensees, submit such schemes for the approval of the Minister.
3. If no development scheme shall be submitted to the Minister within the period stated in the notice, or if the development scheme so submitted shall not be approved by the Minister, the latter may himself prepare a development scheme which shall be fair and

equitable to the licensee and the other licensees, and the licensee shall perform and observe all the terms and conditions thereof; and if the licensee shall object to any such development scheme prepared by the Minister he may refer the matter to arbitration.

(23) Directions as to Oil Fields across Boundaries

Where the Minister is satisfied that any strata in the licensed area or any part thereof form part of an oil field, other parts whereof are in an area to which the Minister's powers to grant licenses pursuant to the Act do not apply and the Minister is satisfied that it is expedient that the oil field should be worked and developed as a unit in cooperation by the licensee and all other persons having an interest in any part of the oil field, the Minister may from time to time by notice in writing give to the licensee such directions as the Minister may think fit, as to the manner in which the rights conferred by the license shall be exercised.

(24) The 1988 / 1995 / 1996 model clauses contain at this place in the text a clause headed 'Disposal of Production'. In this clause it is stated that:

1. The licensee shall ensure that all petroleum won and saved from the licensed area other than petroleum used therein for the purpose of carrying on drilling and production operations or pumping to field storage and refineries shall be delivered on shore in the United Kingdom, unless the Minister gives notice of his consent in writing to delivery elsewhere and in such case the licensee shall ensure compliance with any conditions subject to which that consent is given.
2. Any conditions imposed by the Minister on such a consent may include provision:
   (i)   as to the place of delivery;
   (ii) as to the price to be obtained for the petroleum to which such consent relates;
   (iii) as to the time within which and the manner in which payment of the price is to be made; and
   (iv) requiring payment to be made to a person resident in the United Kingdom.

Apparently, this model clause has lost its relevance and has therefor been deleted.

(25) Indemnity against Third Party Claims

The licensee shall at all times keep the Minister effectually indemnified against all actions, proceedings, costs, charges, claims and demands whatsoever which may be made or brought against the Minister by any third party in relation to or in connection with this license or any matter or thing done or purported to be done in pursuance thereof.

(26) Restrictions on Assignment, etc.

The licensee shall not, except with the consent in writing of the Minister and in accordance with the conditions, if any, of the consent, do anything whatsoever whereby under the law (including the rules of equity) of any part of the European Union or of any other place, any right granted by this license or derived from a right so granted becomes exercisable by or for the benefit of or in accordance with the directions of another person.

(27) Power of Revocation

If any of the events specified in this clause shall occur then and in any such case the Minister may revoke this license and thereupon the same and all the rights thereby granted shall cease and determine but subject nevertheless and without prejudice to any obligation or liability incurred by the licensee or imposed upon him by or under the terms and conditions of this license. The specified events include among others: any payment of consideration for the license being in arrear or unpaid for two months; any breach or non-observance by the licensee of any of the terms and conditions of this license; the bankruptcy of the licensee; any breach or non-observance by the licensee of the terms and conditions of a development scheme; if the licensee is a company, the licensee's ceasing to direct and control either its operations under the license or any commercial activities in connection with those operations from a fixed place within the United Kingdom; if the licensee is a company and there is a change in the control of the licensee; and the Minister serves notice in writing on the licensee stating that the Minister proposes to revoke the license unless such a further change in the control of the licensee as specified in the notice takes place within the period of three months beginning with the date of service of the notice and that further change does not take place within that period.

(28)Arbitration

If at any time any dispute, difference or question shall arise between the Minister and the licensee as to any matter arising under or by virtue of this license or as to their respective rights and liabilities in respect thereof then the same shall, except where it is expressly provided by this license that the matter or thing to which the same relates is to be determined, approved, or consented to by the Minister, be referred to arbitration by a single arbitrator who, in default of agreement between the Minister and the licensee and, in case of arbitration in relation to a development scheme, other licensees affected by that scheme, as to his appointment, shall be appointed by the Lord Chief Justice of England for the time being.

6.2.2.4   Special Legislation for Offshore Installations, Submarine Pipelines and the Protection of the Marine Environment

UK offshore petroleum operations are not only regulated within the framework of model clauses for production licenses but also by legislation directed all aspects of offshore installations and submarine pipelines, e.g., the Petroleum Act 1998. Furthermore, there have been enacted a number of Acts, which are relevant to the conduct of offshore petroleum operations, such as the Mineral Workings (Offshore Installations) Act 1971, as amended, and its regulations, which regulate activities on offshore installations, the Act, which provides for the prevention of pollution caused by oil, and the Gas Act 1986 (concerning the supply of gas in the UK through pipes). The latter Act has to be brought into line with the EU Directive concerning the completion of the internal market for natural gas (the EC Directive 98/30/EC of 22 June 1998). Finally, the United Kingdom is a Member State of the EU and Party to a number of Conventions concerning the protection of the marine environment, in particular that of the North Sea. As such the United Kingdom has adopted and from time to time will have to adopt new petroleum and environmental regulation in order to implement corresponding EC Directives or decisions taken by Commissions established under the rules of the respective Conventions. In this connection is OSPARCON of particular importance.

Note regarding BNOC. After the Petroleum and Submarine Pipe-lines Act 1975 had created the British National Oil Corporation (BNOC), the requirements regarding participation by the corporation in the licenses were stipulated as a particular condition in the *London Gazette* notice of the offshore licensing round concerned. Under the 5th round (1976/1977) and in the 6th round (1978/1979) a fifty-one per cent participation of BNOC in the license, if so desired by this corporation, was made obligatory. Under the 7th (1980/1981), 8th (1982/1983) and 9th (1984/1985) rounds the licensee was required to give BNOC the option to buy at market price up to fifty-one per cent of any petroleum produced under the license. The same purchase-option was acquired by BNOC with respect to the offshore licenses which had been granted under the first four offshore licensing rounds which preceded the corporation's establishment under the Act of 1975. On 13 March 1985 the UK government announced its intention to terminate the existence of BNOC. The main reason for the government's decision was of a political nature: the then Conservative government did not believe in the merits of state participation. But there was also a pragmatic reason for the decision. The corporation encountered increasing difficulties in selling its oil production. Its share of UK North Sea oil production had increased to about sixty per cent, the sum of 12.5 per cent royalty oil (licensees were obliged to pay royalty in kind if so demanded by the State), 51 per cent participation oil and 51 per cent purchase-option oil. In 1984 UK production amounted to 2.3 million barrels per day. A sizable part of the corporation's share had to be sold back to the licensees who had a buy-back option, but at that time still about 800,000 barrels per day had to be sold by the corporation on the open market. BNOC's total sales of about 1.3 million barrels per day, including 250,000 barrels per day royalty oil, put the corporation in a strong position to influence the development and level of the price of oil on the global market. The official price established by BNOC for the North Sea marker crude, Brent-Blend (end 1983/beginning 1984 fixed at USD 30 per barrel) had a direct impact on the price of the crude oil, Bonny-Light, exported from Nigeria and through the Bonny-Light price the BNOC price (to the discomfort of the corporation) became linked to the OPEC price system. In the second half of 1984 OPEC requested the UK government to persuade BNOC to maintain the price of Brent-Blend at its prevailing high level in order to give Nigeria no cause to breach the OPEC price arrangements. However, BNOC experienced increasing problems in selling its oil against the price at which it has bought the oil from its licensees (the latter received from BNOC the official price). When then, in October 1984, Statoil, the Norwegian state oil company, started to sell its oil at a discount, BNOC in its turn was forced to lower the official price of Brent-Blend from USD 30 per barrel to USD 28.65 per barrel (meanwhile the open market price had dropped to USD 27 per barrel). Nigeria felt obliged to follow suit and, in contravention to the OPEC agreement on pricing, lowered the price of its Bonny-Light by USD 2 per barrel to USD 28 per barrel. A price crisis was the result (see Chapter 3). BNOC did not succeed in solving its difficulties, whereupon the government decided to withdraw the corporation as intermediary trader and allow the licensees to sell their oil themselves. BNOC had suffered grate losses on the reselling of the oil, but about eighty per cent were compensated, at least as far as the UK Treasury was concerned, by the fact that the licensees had to pay income taxes calculated on the official price they were receiving from BNOC.

A few years before taking the decision to terminate the existence of BNOC, the government had already taken away some important privileges that the corporation had received when it was established. The Act of 1975 had designated BNOC as the official government adviser in petroleum affairs.

BNOC was given a preferential position in acquiring any license interest that was intended to be transferred and no decision on approving such assignment was given before BNOC had made it known whether it would be interested in acquiring for itself the interest involved. Moreover, the Act exempted BNOC from paying the Petroleum Revenue Tax. In 1979 all these privileges were abolished.

The termination of BNOC had been anticipated and the ground therefore was prepared by the Oil and Gas (Enterprise) Act of 1982. Pursuant to this Act, BNOC was authorized to establish 'equity oil subsidiaries', to transfer its petroleum exploration and production rights to such subsidiaries and to dispose of its shares in them. Under this procedure a subsidiary under the name 'Britoil' was established, which later was privatized. In 1988 Britoil was bought by British Petroleum.

After the existence of BNOC was terminated in 1985 (Oil and Pipelines Act 1985), the existing purchase options were inherited by the Oil and Pipeline Agency (OPA) and the arrangement in the form of a particular condition was continued under the 10th round, but only in respect of petroleum other than natural gas, i.e., the licensees under that round were required to grant OPA an option to buy up to fifty-one per cent of the petroleum other than natural gas produced under the license. This condition was not repeated in later rounds, since the government in June 1988 put an end to all forms of state participation.

Note regarding British Petroleum. In August 1914, just after the outbreak of the First World War, the UK government was authorized to purchase 51.7 per centum of the shares in the Anglo-Persian Oil Company. The latter was a private sector company that had gone public on 19 April 1909. The company was the sole owner of a concession in former Persia that on 18 May 1901 had been granted to William Knox D'Arcy. The acquisition of the shares, for which the government paid GBP 2 million, afforded the government a controlling interest in the company, but at the time it was emphasized by the government that the acquisition was made for strategic reasons only, namely to secure the supply of fuel oil to the Royal Navy, and that it had no intention of interfering in commercial matters. In 1933, this concession was unilaterally cancelled by the Persian government and a new concession was negotiated and finally granted in April 1933 to the former concessionaire which in 1935 was renamed the Anglo-Iranian Oil Company. In the wake of a revolution under the leadership of Mossadegh, the 1933 concession was nationalized on 20 March 1951 and taken over by the newly established NIOC. It had been the then revolutionary government's intention to entrust the domestic petroleum operations to NIOC without allowing any involvement of foreign oil companies. However the revolution failed and after 3.5 years of negotiations a new agreement was signed on 25 October 1954 by NIOC and Iranian Oil Participants Ltd, a UK corporation, also known as the Consortium.

The Anglo-Iranian Oil Company obtained a share of forty per cent in the consortium and was on that occasion renamed British Petroleum. Much later, the UK government started gradually to reduce its shareholding in British Petroleum. In 1977 an interest of 35.2 per cent was sold. In 1987, the government tried to sell the remaining shareholding, but did not completely succeed. In December 1995, the remaining 1.8 per cent was sold for GBP 518 million.

6.2.3   NORWAY

6.2.3.1   Introduction

Petroleum legislation in Norway consists of Acts (formal laws) and subsidiary legislation in the form of implementing and supplementary Regulations.

The Act currently in force is the Act of 29 November 1996, No. 72 as amended. With effect from 1 July 1997, this Act replaced its predecessor, the Act of 22 March 1985, No. 11 (1985 Act). Like its predecessor, the Act is a comprehensive petroleum law exclusively directed at the regulation of offshore petroleum operations. In its turn, the 1985 Act was preceded by the Act of 21 June 1963 No. 12 and the Regulations issued under this Act. In stark contrast to its successors the 1963 Act was of the nature of an enabling law, leaving the main provisions of the petroleum regime to be set out in Regulations. The Regulations concerned were the Royal Decrees of 9 April 1965 and 8 December 1972 respectively, both 'relating to exploration for and exploitation of petroleum on the Norwegian continental shelf'

After the 1985 Act entered into force, the scope of the 1963 Act was restricted to 'scientific research and exploration for and exploitation of sub-sea natural resources other than petroleum resources' and the aforesaid Royal Decrees were both terminated. In contrast to the 1963 Act, the 1985 Act was a comprehensive petroleum law, containing the main provisions of the petroleum regime and leaving only details to be settled by regulation to be issued by the King. The numerous licenses, among which there are very important ones as far as production volumes are concerned, which were granted under either the 1965 Royal Decree or the 1972 Royal Decree remained in existence but became 'automatically' governed by the provisions of the 1985 Act, except as was provided in the said Act itself. For instance, as far as to their duration was concerned, the terms of the preceding Decrees were maintained. The same procedure was followed when the present Act was introduced.

Licenses are granted in licensing rounds. Up to and including the 3rd round licenses were granted under the 1965 Royal Decree. As from the 4th round up to and including the 9th round licenses were granted under the 1972 Decree. As from the 10th round licenses were granted in accordance with the 1985 Act and as from 1 July 1997, the effective date of the present Act licenses are granted in accordance with this Act.

The main reason to replace the Act of 1985 was for Norway to implement the relevant provisions of the EC Directive 94/22/EC of 30 May 1994 (hereinafter referred to as the EC Directive), to which it was committed by reason of its membership of the Agreement on the European Economic Area (EEA) of 2 May 1992. The occasion was used to pay more attention to procedures relating to plans for development and production and plans for decommissioning and disposal of facilities, to clarification and codification of existing practices. Nonetheless, the 1996 Act itself has on a number of occasions and on a number of points been amended (see hereinafter).

Since the 1996 Act is a comprehensive petroleum law, the standard rights and obligations of a licensee are mainly found in this Act and to a lesser extent in the regulations made under the Act and in the special legislation concerning safety, working conditions and pollution control.

The few conditions particular to the individual license are to be found in the license itself (e.g., the actual size and geographic location of the licensed area, the duration, the actual obligatory work programme and the adjustment of the undivided interests of the individual licensees in case of state participation) and further in the associated agreements. The standard conditions of a license will change and new terms will be imposed, if and when the Act and the regulations based thereon will be changed provided always that conditions may be 'saved' under the transitional provisions of any new Act. Changing or replacing the prevailing Act is within the power of the Norwegian Parliament (the *Storting)*. Changing or replacing regulations supplementing or implementing the Act is delegated by the Act to the King but any new regulations made by the King may also contain saving provisions. Still it may be expected that all persons, who undertake petroleum activities on the Norwegian continental shelf, shall at any time operate more or less under the same terms and conditions, the only differences between them consisting in the aforesaid particular conditions of their licenses, among which most prominently the percentage state participation.

Apart from national legislation, there exists relevant international legislation. In the first place should be mentioned the 1982 Convention on the Law of the Sea the rules of which determine Norway's rights and obligations as a coastal State. Next in importance comes the 1992 Convention for the Protection of the Marine Environment of the North-East Atlantic (OSPARCON), to which Norway is a party. The requirements and rules of this Convention and the decisions taken by the Commission established under it are of direct relevance to the conduct of the Norwegian offshore petroleum operations which take place within the Area of the Convention in as much these requirements, rules and decisions will have to be implemented and made applicable to the licenses and their holders through regulations made under the Act.

6.2.3.2 The Act of 29 November 1996 No. 72 (as Amended)

1. Chapter 1: Introductory Provisions

Section 1 - 1. The Norwegian State has the proprietary right to subsea petroleum deposits and the exclusive right to resource management.

Section 1 - 2. Resource management is executed by the King in accordance with the provisions of this Act and decisions made by the Storting (Parliament). Resource management of petroleum resources shall be carried out in a long-term perspective for the benefit of the Norwegian society as a whole. In this regard the resource management shall provide revenues to Norway and shall contribute to ensuring welfare, employment and an improved environment, as well as to the strengthening of Norwegian trade and industry and industrial development, and at the same time take due regard to regional and local policy considerations and other activities.

Section 1 - 3. None other than the State may conduct petroleum activities without the licences, approvals and consents required pursuant to this Act. Provisions otherwise in the Act and regulations issued pursuant to the Act shall apply to such activities insofar as they are appropriate.

Section 1 - 4. The Act applies to petroleum operations in connection with sub-sea petroleum deposits under Norwegian jurisdiction. The Act also applies to petroleum activities inside and outside the realm and the Norwegian continental shelf to the extent that such application follows from international law or from agreement with a foreign State.

This Act does not apply to Svalbard, including its internal waters and territorial sea.

The King may issue further regulations to supplement or delimit the provisions of this Section.

Note 1. The Norwegian North Sea continental shelf is demarcated up to 64 degrees north latitude pursuant to a boundary treaty made with the United Kingdom (the Agreement of 10 March 1965 relating to the delimitation of the continental shelf between the two States). Up in the North, in the Barents Sea, the territorial waters were divided between Norway and the former Soviet-Union, much more recently the adjacent continental shelf was demarcated between Norway and the Russian Federation by their Boundary Treaty of 15 September 2010.

Note 2. The territory of Svalbard to which 4. above refers includes all islands and their internal waters and territorial sea making up the Archipelago of Svalbard as described in Article 1 of the Treaty of Svalbard signed on 9 February 1920. Said Treaty recognized and confirmed Norway's full and absolute sovereignty over the Archipelago and the waters belonging thereto but made this sovereignty subject to an equal rights and treatment regime in favour of ships and nationals of the Contracting States in respect of hunting and fishing and in respect of maritime, industrial, commercial, mining activities. From the moment the concept of the continental shelf had been formulated and described under the terms of the 1958 Convention on the Continental Shelf the Norwegian government took the position that the Treaty did not apply to the continental shelf of Svalbard as defined in the said Convention. When later the continental shelf was described in terms of the 1982 Convention of the Law of the Sea the Norwegian government shifted its position and claimed that the continental shelf of Svalbard formed part of the Norwegian continental shelf and for this reason was beyond the territorial reach of the Svalbard Treaty:

Section 1-5. Norwegian law other than this Act, including provisions relating to licences, consents or approvals required according to the legislation, shall also be applicable to petroleum activities. This applies unless otherwise warranted by an Act, a decision by the King, international law or agreement with a foreign State. Notwithstanding the above, other Norwegian law shall not apply to mobile facilities under foreign flag other than those that are permanently placed, unless otherwise stipulated by an Act or by a decision made by the King in Council.

Section 1-6 In this Act the following (*essential*) definitions shall apply:

   a) Petroleum, all liquid and gaseous hydrocarbons existing in their natural state in the subsoil, as well as other substances produced in association with such hydrocarbons.
   b) Continental shelf, the seabed and subsoil of the marine areas extending beyond the Norwegian territorial sea, throughout the natural prolongation of the Norwegian land territory to the outer

edge of the continental margin, but no less than 200 nautical miles from the base lines from which the breadth of the territorial sea is measured, however not beyond the median line to another State, unless otherwise can be derived from the rules of international law for the continental shelf beyond 200 nautical miles from the base. lines, or from an agreement with the relevant State.

(*Note.* This definition conforms to the definition of the continental shelf included in the 1982 Convention on the Law of the Sea, see Chapter 9).

2. Chapter 2: Exploration License

Section 2-1. The Ministry may grant to a body corporate a license to explore for petroleum within limited areas of the seabed or its subsoil. Exploration license may also be granted to a physical person domiciled in an EEA State. The exploration license gives the right to explore for petroleum. It does not give exclusive right to exploration in those areas that are mentioned in the license or any preferential right when production licenses are granted. Exploration license is granted for three years, unless another period of time is stipulated (*details to be provided by means of regulations*).

Section 2-2 The exploration license shall state the area covered by the license. The exploration license does not give any right to exploration in areas covered by production licenses, unless otherwise decided by the Ministry in accordance with Section 3-11.

3. Chapter 3: Production License etc.

Section 3-1 Prior to the opening of new areas with a view to granting production licenses, an evaluation shall be undertaken of the various interests involved in the relevant area.

Section 3-2 Offshore areas inside the outer boundary of the continental shelf are divided into blocks of 15 latitude minutes by 20 longitude minutes in size, unless adjacent land areas, common boundaries with the continental shelf of other States, or other circumstances warrant otherwise.

Section 3-3 The King in Council may, on conditions to be further stipulated, grant production licenses. A production license may cover one or several blocks or parts of blocks. Production license may be granted to a body corporate established in conformity with Norwegian legislation and registered in the Norwegian register of Business Enterprises or to a physical person domiciled in a State of the European Economic Area (EEA).

A production license entails the exclusive right to exploration, exploration drilling and production of petroleum deposits in areas covered by the license. The licensee becomes the owner of the petroleum which is produced.

The King may stipulate as a condition for granting a production license that the licensees shall enter into agreements with specified contents with one another.

Note. Production licenses are accompanied by model agreements, which have to be executed by the licensee within a certain period after the license has been granted. The so-called associated agreements are the joint operating agreements, formerly known as the state participation agreements, the personnel training agreements and the frame agreements for research and development.

Section 3-4 Cooperation agreements entered into with a view to applying for a production license shall be submitted to the Ministry. The Ministry may require alterations to be made in such agreements.

Section 3-5 Prior to the granting of a production license, the Ministry shall, as a rule, announce the area for which applications for production licenses may be submitted.

The announcement shall be published through notification in *The Norwegian Gazette* (*Norsk Lysingsblad*) and the *Official Journal of the European Communities*. The notification shall stipulate a time limit for the filing of applications of not less than ninety days, and it shall contain such information as decided by the Ministry.

The granting of a production license shall be done on the basis of factual and objective criteria, and the requirements and conditions stated in the notification. The King is not obliged to grant any production license on the basis of the applications received.

The King may grant production licenses without announcement. Prior to such granting of a production license, the licensees of production licenses in all adjacent areas shall be given the opportunity to apply for a production license for the area in question. Notification shall be published in *The Norwegian Gazette* (*Norsk Lysingsblad*) and the *Official Journal of the European Communities* indicating the blocks which are affected. (*Details set out in regulations*).

Note. The above section 3-5 implements the provisions of Article 3 of the EC Directive 94/22/EC of 30 May 1994.

Section 3-6 The King may decide that the Norwegian State shall participate in petroleum activities according to this Act (see Section 11-1 to and including Section 11-10).

Section 3-7 When granting a production license, the Ministry shall appoint or approve an operator. Change of operator must be approved by the Ministry. If the Ministry appoints or approves an operator who is not a licensee according to the production license, the provisions concerning the obligations of the licensee established in or pursuant to this Act shall apply correspondingly to the operator unless otherwise specifically provided.

Section 3-8 The King may impose on the licensee a specific work obligation for the area covered by the production license.

Note. In practice, applicants for a production license will propose a work programme and the license will be granted, everything else being equal, to the applicant that made the best proposal in this regard.

Section 3-9 The production license shall be granted for up to 10 years. If the production license is granted for a shorter period of time, the Ministry may subsequently extend the license period within the ten-year limit.

A licensee who has fulfilled the work commitment according to Section 3-8 and the conditions otherwise applicable to the individual production license may demand that the license shall be extended after the expiry of the period stipulated above. The extension period shall be stipulated in the individual production license, and shall as a general rule be up to 30 years, but may in specific cases be up to 50 years.

When granting a license, the King shall stipulate what part of the area covered by the production license the licensee may demand an extension for pursuant to the second paragraph. The size of the area stipulated according to the preceding sentence shall as a rule constitute 50 per cent of the area covered by the production license, notwithstanding that the licensee shall be entitled to keep at least one 100 square kilometres. The Ministry may on application consent to the licensee keeping more than the area stipulated when the license is granted according to this provision. (*Details set out in regulations*).

The Ministry may, on application from the licensee and when particular reasons so warrant, extend the production license in excess of the extension according to the second paragraph. Application for extension must have been submitted no later than five years prior to the expiry of the production license, unless otherwise approved or decided by the Ministry. The Ministry stipulates the conditions for such particular extension.

Section 3-10 The Ministry may on application from a licensee approve that part of the area covered by the production license is partitioned off and issue a separate production license for the area partitioned off. (*Details set out in regulations*)

Section 3-11 Right for others to exploration.

Section 3-12 Right for others to place facilities, etc.

Section 3-13 Natural resources other than petroleum resources etc.

Section 3-14 The licensee may during the period mentioned in Section 3-9, first paragraph, with three months notice, relinquish parts of the area covered by the production license. Thereafter, relinquishment of parts of the area may take place at the end of each calendar year, provided notice of such relinquishment has been given at least three months in advance. The Ministry may require the obligations stipulated according the production license and the conditions on which it has been granted to be fulfilled prior to relinquishment. (*Details set out in regulations*).

Section 3-15 The licensee may during the period mentioned in Section 3-9, first paragraph, with three months notice, surrender a production license in its entirety. Thereafter, surrender may take place at the end of each calendar year provided notice of such surrender has been given at least three months in advance. The Ministry may require the obligations stipulated according to the production license and the conditions on which it has been granted to be fulfilled prior to surrender.

4. Chapter 4: Production etc. of Petroleum

Section 4-1 Production of petroleum shall take place in such a manner that as much as possible of the petroleum in place in each individual petroleum deposit, or in several deposits in combination, will be produced, in accordance with prudent technical and sound economic principles and in such a manner that waste of petroleum or reservoir energy is avoided.

Section 4-2 If a licensee decides to develop a petroleum deposit, the licensee shall submit to the Ministry for approval a plan for development and operation of the petroleum deposit. The plan shall contain an account of economic aspects, resource aspects, technical, safety related, commercial and environmental aspects, as well as information as to how a facility may be decommissioned and disposed of when the petroleum activities have ceased. The plan shall also comprise information on facilities for transportation or utilization comprised by Section 4-3.

Section 4-3 Specific license to install and to operate facilities for transport and utilization of petroleum.

Section 4-4 The Ministry shall, prior to or concurrently with approval pursuant to Section 4-2 or a licence being granted pursuant to Section 4-3, approve the production schedule. A production schedule other than that which follows from Section 4-1 may be stipulated if warranted by resource management considerations or other significant social considerations.

Burning of petroleum in excess of the quantities needed for normal operational safety shall not be allowed unless approved by the Ministry.

Upon application from the licensee, the Ministry shall stipulate, for fixed periods of time, the quantity which may be produced, injected or cold vented at all times. The Ministry shall base this stipulation on the production schedule on which the development plan is based, unless new information on the deposit or other circumstances warrant otherwise.

When so required due to important interests of society, the King in Council may, for an individual petroleum deposit or several petroleum deposits, stipulate other production schedules than those stipulated or approved pursuant to the first and third paragraph, and may in this connection order improved recovery. If the decision according to this paragraph is to the effect that production shall be reduced in relation to the production schedule stipulated or approved, the Ministry shall endeavour to apportion to a reasonable extent the reduction proportionally between the relevant petroleum deposits. In the event of such apportionment, special considerations shall be given to long-term agreements for the supply of gas and to petroleum deposits which in part are situated on the continental shelf of another State.

Section 4-5 The Ministry may decide that exploration drilling or development of a deposit shall be postponed.

Section 4-6 The Ministry may make a decision to require preparation, commencement or continuation of production, and hereunder, that on-going production shall be continued or increased, when this is economically beneficial to society, when necessary to develop an efficient transportation system or to ensure efficient utilization of the facilities comprised by Sections 4-2 and 4-3. Such a decision may also be made if it is efficient for reservoir engineering reasons, or when it is desirable that two or more petroleum deposits are produced in conjunction with each other, or when warranted by other significant social reasons.

Section 4-7 If a petroleum deposit extends over more than one block with different licensees, or onto the continental shelf of another State, efforts shall be made to reach agreement on the most efficient coordination of petroleum activities in connection with the petroleum deposit as well as on the apportionment of the petroleum deposit. This shall apply similarly when, in the case of several petroleum deposits, joint petroleum activities would obviously be more efficient. Agreements on joint exploration drilling shall be submitted to the Ministry. Agreements on joint production, transportation, utilization and cessation of petroleum activities shall be submitted to the Ministry for approval. If consensus on such agreements is not reached within reasonable time, the Ministry may determine how such joint petroleum activities shall be conducted, including the apportionment of the deposit.

Note. Petroleum operations involving petroleum reservoirs extending into the continental shelf of another State will be regulated by the terms of a specific agreement to be concluded with that other State. With respect to the United Kingdom the framework for such an interstate petroleum development agreement was set out in the Agreement of 10 March 1965. The most important interstate agreement following from this Boundary Treaty was the interstate agreement of 16 October 1979 providing for the joint exploitation of the Statfjord Field Reservoirs (Norwegian production licence No. 037, awarded on 10 August 1973 under the last phase of the 2nd round).

Section 4-8 The Ministry may decide that facilities comprised by Sections 4-2 and 4-3 and which are owned by the licensee, may be used by others, if so warranted by considerations for efficient operation or for the benefit of society, and the Ministry deems that such use would not constitute any unreasonable detriment of the licensee's own requirements or those of someone who has already been assured the right of use. Nevertheless, natural gas undertakings and eligible customers domiciled in an EEA State shall have a right of access to upstream pipeline networks, including facilities supplying technical services incidental to such access. The Ministry stipulates further rules in the form of regulations and may impose conditions and issue orders relating to such access in the individual case.

Section 4-9 Extended operator responsibility for the overall operation of upstream pipeline network etc.

Section 4-10 The licensee shall pay a fee for a production licence, after expiry of the period stipulated pursuant to Section 3-9 first paragraph first sentence, calculated per square kilometre (area fee).The licensee shall furthermore pay a fee calculated on the basis of the quantity and value of petroleum produced at the shipment point of the production area (production fee). Nevertheless production fee shall not be paid for petroleum produced from deposits where the development plan is approved or where the requirements to submit a plan for development and operation are waived after 1 January 1986. When granting a production licence, a non-recurring fee (cash bonus) may be levied and there may be stipulated a fee which shall be calculated on the basis of production volume (production bonus). (*Details set out in regulations*)

Section 4-11 The King decides where and in which way landing of petroleum shall take place.

Section 4-12 The King may decide that the licensee shall make deliveries from his production to cover national requirements and provide transportation to Norway. The King may further decide to whom such petroleum shall be delivered. A price shall be paid for the petroleum delivered, which shall be determined in the same way as the price which forms the basis for calculation of the production fee, with the addition of transportation costs.

Section 4-13 In the event of war, threat of war or other extraordinary crisis, the King may decide that a licensee shall place petroleum at the disposal of the Norwegian authorities.

5. Chapter 5: Cessation of Petroleum Activities

Section 5-1 The licensee shall submit a decommissioning plan to the Ministry before a licence according to Section 3-3 or Section 4-3 expires or is surrendered, or the use of a facility is terminated permanently. The plan shall contain proposals for continued production or shutdown of production and disposal of facilities. The decommissioning plan shall be submitted at the earliest five years, but at the latest two years prior to the time when the use of a facility is expected to be terminated permanently.

Section 5-2 Notification of termination of use

Section 5-3 The Ministry shall make a decision relating to disposal and shall stipulate a time limit for implementation of the decision. In the evaluation on which the decision is based, emphasis shall, inter alia, be attached to technical, safety, environmental and economic aspects as well as to consideration for other users of the sea. The Ministry may stipulate specific conditions in connection with the decision. The licensee and the owner are under obligation to make sure that a decision relating to disposal is carried out, unless otherwise decided by the Ministry. The obligation to carry out the decision relating to disposal is applicable if this decision is made or is to be implemented after the expiry of the licence. If the decision is to the effect that the facility shall continue to be used in the petroleum activities or for other purposes, the licensee, owner and user are jointly obliged to make sure that future decisions on disposal are carried out, unless otherwise decided by the Ministry.

Section 5-4 Whoever is under obligation to implement a decision relating to disposal according to Section 5-3 is liable for damage or inconvenience caused wilfully or negligently in connection with disposal of the facility or other implementation of the decision. If the decision is for abandonment the licensee or owner shall be liable for damage or inconvenience caused wilfully or inadvertently in connection with the abandoned facility unless otherwise decided by the Ministry. In the event of decisions for abandonment, it may be agreed between the licensees and the owners on one side and the State on the other that future maintenance, responsibility and liability shall be taken over by the State based on an agreed financial compensation.

Section 5-5 In the event that the State requires removal of a facility, any liens, charges and encumbrances thereon shall lapse.

Section 5-6 The State has a right to take over the licensee's fixed facility when the licence expires, is surrendered or revoked, or when the use of such facility has been terminated permanently. The King decides with binding effect if and to what extent compensation shall be paid for the takeover.

6. Chapter 6: Registration and Mortgaging

7. Chapter 7: Liability for Pollution Damage

Section 7-1 Pollution damage means damage or loss caused by pollution as a consequence of effluence or discharge of petroleum from a facility, including a well, and the costs of reasonable measures to avert or limit such damage or such loss, as well as damage or loss as a consequence of such measures. Damage or loss incurred by fishermen as a consequence of reduced possibilities for fishing is also included in pollution damage.

Ships used for stationary drilling are regarded as a facility. Ships used for storage of petroleum in conjunction with production facilities are regarded as part of the facility. The same applies to ships for the transport of petroleum during the time when loading from the facility takes place.

Section 7-2 The provisions of this chapter are applicable to liability for pollution damage from a facility when such damage occurs in Norway or inside the outer limits of the Norwegian continental shelf or affects a

Norwegian vessel, Norwegian hunting or catching equipment or a Norwegian facility in adjacent sea areas. With regard to measures to avert or limit pollution damage it is sufficient that damage may occur in such an area. The provisions of this chapter are also applicable to pollution damage from facilities used in petroleum activities according to this Act, when the damage occurs in onshore or offshore territory belonging to a State, which has acceded to the Nordic Convention on Environment Protection of 19 February 1974.

Section 7-3 The licensee is liable for pollution damage without regard to fault. The provisions relating to the liability of licensees apply correspondingly to an operator who is not a licensee when the Ministry has so decided in connection with the approval of the operator status. If there are several licensees under the licence and one of them is the operator, or if the Ministry has made a decision according to the first paragraph, claims for shall initially be directed to the operator. If any part of the compensation is left unpaid on the due date by the operator, this part shall be covered by the licensees in accordance with their participating interest in the licence. If someone fails to cover his share, this shall be allocated proportionately between the others. If it is demonstrated that an inevitable event of nature, act of war, exercise of public authority or a similar *force majeure* event has contributed to a considerable degree to the damage or its extent under circumstances which are beyond the control of the liable party, the liability may be reduced to the extent it is reasonable, with particular consideration to the scope of the activity, the situation of the party that has sustained damage and the opportunity for taking out insurance on both sides. In the event of pollution damage from a facility located in an area outside the Norwegian continental shelf, the party who has approval from the competent authority to conduct the activities to which the facility is connected is regarded to be a licensee.

Section 7-4 The liability of a licensee for pollution damage may only be claimed pursuant to the rules of the Act. Liability for pollution damage cannot be claimed against:

(i) anyone who by agreement with a licensee or his contractors has performed tasks or work in connection with petroleum activities;

(ii) anyone who has manufactured or delivered equipment to be used in the petroleum activities;

(iii) anyone who undertakes measures to avert or limit pollution damage, or to save life or rescue values which have been endangered in connection with the petroleum activities, unless the measures are performed in conflict with prohibitions imposed by public authorities or are performed by someone other than public authorities in spite of express prohibition by the operator or the owner of the values threatened; or

(iv) anyone employed by the licensee or by someone mentioned under items (i), (ii) or (iii).

Section 7-5 The licensee cannot claim recourse for pollution damage against someone exempted from liability pursuant to the rules of Section 7-4, unless the person in question or someone in his service has acted wilfully or by gross negligence. Recourse liability may be mitigated to the extent that this considered reasonable in view of manifested conduct, economic ability and the circumstances in general.

Section 7-6 If pollution damage occurs in a petroleum activity and the activity has been conducted without a licence, the party that has conducted the petroleum activity shall be liable for the damage regardless of fault. The same liability rests on others who have taken part in the petroleum activity and who knew, or should have known, that the activity was conducted without a licence.

Section 7-7 Public announcement. Preclusive notice

Section 7-8 Legal action for compensation for pollution damage shall be brought before the courts in the court district where the effluence or discharge of petroleum has taken place or where damage has been caused.(*If the matter is more complicated the Ministry decides where the action shall be brought*).

8. Chapter 8: Special Rules relating to Compensation to Norwegian Fishermen

Section 8-1 This chapter applies to compensation for financial losses incurred by Norwegian fishermen as a result of the petroleum activities occupying fishing fields or resulting in pollution and waste, or as a result of damage caused by a facility or actions in connection with the placing of a facility. This Chapter does not apply to pollution damage as mentioned in Section 7-1.

Section 8-2 Occupation of a fishing area.

Section 8-3 Pollution and waste.

Section 8-4 Joint and several liability.

Section 8-5 If a facility or an action in connection with the placing of such facility causes damage and the injured party does not have a right to compensation pursuant to the provisions of Section 8-2, the licensee shall, regardless of fault, be liable for damages in respect of the financial losses suffered by fishermen as a result of the damage.

9. Chapter 9: Special Requirements to Safety.

Section 9-1 The petroleum activities shall be conducted in such manner as to enable a high level of safety to be maintained and further developed in accordance with the technological development.

Section 9-2 Emergency preparedness.

Section 9-3 The licensee shall initiate and maintain security measures to contribute to avoiding deliberate attacks against facilities and shall at all times have contingency plans to deal with such attacks. The licensee shall place facilities at the disposal of public authorities for drills and shall participate in such drills to the extent this is necessary.

Section 9-4 Around and above facilities there shall be a safety zone unless otherwise decided by the Ministry. In the event of accidents and emergencies the Ministry may establish or extend safety zones. The extent of zones referred to in the first and second sentences shall be determined by the King. This provision is not applicable to pipelines and cables.

Note. Article 60 of the 1982 Convention on the Law of the Sea authorizes coastal States to establish reasonable safety zones around artificial islands, installations and structures, not exceeding however a distance of 500 metres around them. Article 60 refers exclusively to installations and structures which – just like artificial islands which are also mentioned – extend above the surface of the sea and appears to exclude any submarine construction such as submarine pipelines and submarine production installations from qualifying for the establishment of a safety zone around them. The provisions of this section 9-4 are in line with said Article 60 in as much as the definition of 'facility' in section 1-6 does not mention sub-sea facilities other than pipelines and cables for which however an exception is made in this Section:

Section 9-5 Suspension of the petroleum activities, etc.

10. Chapter 10: General Provisions.

Section 10-1 Petroleum activities according to this Act shall be conducted in a prudent manner and in accordance with applicable legislation for such petroleum activities. The petroleum activities shall take due account of the safety of personnel, the environment and of the financial values which the facilities and vessels represent, including also operational availability.

Sections 10-2 through 10-6 (*Miscellaneous provisions*)

Section 10-7 The licensee to provide such security as approved by the Ministry for fulfillment of the obligations, which the licensee has undertaken as well as for possible liability in connection with the petroleum activities.

Section 10-8 Licensees who jointly hold a licence are jointly and severally responsible to the State for the financial obligations arising out of petroleum activities pursuant to the licence.

Section 10-9 If liability in respect of a third party is incurred by anyone undertaking tasks for a licensee, the licensee shall be liable for damages to the same extent as, and jointly and severally with, the perpetrator and, if applicable, his employer. Liability for pollution damage is governed by the rules of Chapter 7.

Section 10-10 Commission of Inquiry (to be appointed in case of a serious accident)

Section 10-11 Training (*of civil servants*).

Section 10-12 Transfer of a licence or participating interest in a licence for petroleum activities may not take place without the approval of the Ministry. The same applies to other direct or indirect transfer of interest or participation in the licence, including, *inter alia*, assignment of shareholdings or other ownership shares, which may provide decisive control of a licensee possessing a participating interest in a licence. Transfer of a group of licensees' right of ownership to fixed facilities may not take place without the approval of the Ministry.

Section 10-13 In the event of serious or repeated violations of this Act, regulations issued pursuant hereto, stipulated conditions or orders issued, the King may revoke a licence granted pursuant to this Act. If an application for a licence contains incorrect information or if information of significance has been withheld, and it must be assumed that the licence would not have been granted had correct or complete information been available, the licence may be revoked in relation to the licensee concerned. A licence may be revoked if the security which the licensee is obliged to provide pursuant to Section 10-7 has become significantly weakened, or if the company or other association holding the licence is dissolved or enters into debt settlement proceedings or bankruptcy proceedings.

Section 10-14 Revocation of a licence, surrender of rights or lapse of rights for other reasons do not entail release from the financial obligations which follow from this Act, regulations issued pursuant hereto or specific conditions. If a work obligation or other obligation has not been fulfilled, the Ministry may demand payment, in full or in part, of the amount which the fulfilment of the obligations would have cost. The amount shall be determined by the Ministry with binding effect.

Section 10-16 Enforcement measures.

Section 10-18 The King may issue regulations to supplement and implement this Act, including inter alia provisions relating to working conditions, confidentiality and relating to the licensee's obligation to make information on the activities pursuant to the Act available to the public. The King may also issue regulations relating to the duty to provide information for the fulfilment of Norway's obligations pursuant to the EEA agreement. In connection with individual administrative decisions, other conditions than those mentioned in this Act may be stipulated, when they are naturally linked with the measures or the activities to which the individual administrative decision relates.

11. Chapter 11: Management of the State Direct Financial Interest (SDFI).

Preliminary Note. This Chapter 11 is re-arranging state participation in response to the provisions relating to state participation contained in the EC Directive.

Section 11-1 The State participates in petroleum activities under this Act in that the State reserves a specified share of a licence granted pursuant to this Act and in the joint venture established by a joint operating agreement in accordance with the licence.

Section 11-2 The commercial aspects in relation to the participating interests which the State owns or reserves for itself shall be managed by a limited company owned by the State as sole owner. The company shall be a licensee in respect of the participating interests it manages on behalf of the State. In individual joint venture the company shall have rights and duties as a licensee according to rules stipulated in or pursuant to this Act with appurtenant regulations.

Note. The company in question is Petoro AS which was founded on 9 May 2001.

The revenues resulting from the management of the participating interests shall belong to the State. The operating expenses, investments and other expenditure incurred to or relating to the management of the participating interests shall be covered by appropriation from the State. Funds for the operation of the company shall be provided by the State.

Section 11-3 The State is directly liable for any obligations incurred by the company by contract or otherwise. Claims against the State shall be made to the company.

Section 11-6 The Board of Directors shall see to it that the participating interests are subject to sound management in accordance with commercially sound priciples and allocated funds and authorisations issued to the company and the activitie it manages.

Section 11-7 (*List of matters to be submitted by the Board of Directors to the General Assembly*) The Board of Directors shall in addition submit to the General Assembly (a) all matters that must be assumed to comprise principal or political aspects of significance or that may entali significant socio-economic or social effects; and (b) any decision made by the management committee of a joint venture in which the company participates, that will constitute a violation of conditions and requirements specified in the licence as regards the State's production policy or the State's financial interests.

Note. The Norwegian State participation in production licences has a long and complicated history. It was introduced as early as 1969. With respect to licences granted in that year and in 1971 by virtue of the Royal Decree of 1965, the State was given the choice between either to acquire an undivided interest (varying from 5 per cent to even 40 per cent) in the licence or to receive a percentage share (varying from 10 per cent to 17.5 per cent) in the net income of the licensee. After the Royal Decree of 1972 entered into force and after the establishment of a wholly state- owned company named *Den Norske Stats Oljeselskap* (Statoil) on 14 July of that year licensees were obliged to accept Statoil as a co-licensee and to enter into a joint operating agreement (model agreement attached) with this company. Under most licences granted since then Statoil's (initial) fifty per cent interest share in the licence could be increased at the expense of the undivided interest shares of the other licence holders. A notable exception in this respect forms production licence PL 037, covering the Norwegian part of the Statfjord field (blocks 33/9 and 33/12). This important licence was granted on 10 August 1973, under the last phase of the 2nd round. In this licence Statoil retained its initial and final fifty per cent interest. Where in a licence an increase of Statoil's initial share is provided for, such an increase is within pre-determined limits at the option of Statoil: in this respect distinction should be made between on the one hand pre-9th round 1972 licences, where the limits are determined on a sliding scale and on the other post-8th round licences comprising 9th round 1972 licences and 1985 licences, i.e., the latter being licences issued under the terms of the Act of 1985, where the limit is set by the Ministry at the time of approving the required development plan on the basis of a pre-determined number stipulated in the licence concerned. Under the rules of the aforesaid pre-9th round 1972 licences the Statoil interest is increased from fifty to fifty-one per cent upon Statoil joining or concurring with a statement of commerciality. Such statement in turn triggers the declaration of commerciality to be issued by the operator, which marks the start of Statoil's financial contributions. The sliding scale used in these licences relates a range of estimated peak values of the daily production from the licensed area to the value of Statoil's percentage interest (higher than fifty per cent) at any such peak values. Such a sliding scale and the modalities of its implementation are set out in the associated joint operating agreement. Generally, the sliding scale starts at sixty, sixty-two, or sixty-five per cent from a zero daily production and results in a Statoil interest in the licence of respectively seventy-five or eighty per cent at a daily peak production of 200,000 barrels oil equivalent or more. Such increase becomes effective upon the approval of the Ministry of the production profile of the commercial field in which Statoil is going to participate. Under the aforesaid post-8th round licences Statoil's proportional financial contributions will commence on the date of approval of the development plan when the initial undivided interests of the licence holders are adjusted on the basis of the limit set by the Minister. All costs incurred by Statoil's co-licensees prior to the start of Statoil's financial contributions i.e., the cost of exploration, appraisal and evaluation of the first commercial discovery under the aforesaid licences, are for the account of said co-licensees.

With effect from 1 January 1985, an arrangement was made between the State and Statoil in accordance with which the State acquired a direct undivided interest in almost all licences, in which Statoil was holding such an interest. From Statoil's initial 50 per cent in such licences, 30 per cent was transferred to the State and 20 per cent retained by Statoil. Any future increase of Statoil's interest in the licence in question had to be completely transferred to the State. The State's share, called the State Direct Financial Interest (SDFI), was represented and managed by Statoil, which exercised on behalf of the State all rights and obligations attached to the SDFIs, albeit the State remained directly responsible for the funding of its share.

This was the situation till this Act entered into force and introduced a new approach to state participation i.e. the SDFIs would be entrusted to a newly established wholly-owned state owned state company by the name of Petoro A.S.(9 May 2001). At about the same time (June 2001) an intial public offering of 18.2 per cent of Statoil shares took place. In 2004 a further 4.6 per cent of Statoil shares were sold, and in 2005 about 0.8 per cent, leaving in the end the State with a 76.33 per cent shareholding interest in Statoil, which in the process changed its name to Statoil ASA. Prior to the intial offering, 15 per cent of the SDFIs were sold to Statoil and 6.5 per cent to Norsk Hydro and other Norwegian offshore operators. The balance of 78.5 per cent SDFIs was transferred to the custody of the aforesaid Petoro A.S. By selling a total of 21.5 per cent of the SDFIs to Norwegian partly private companies like Statoil and Norsk Hydro, Petoro A.S. as a licensee is only holding a minority interest in the licences in which it is represented. As far as Statoil was concerned the company merged in 2007 with Norsk Hydro and formed a new 67.3/32.7 company which was temporarily named StatoilHydro. Through its majority shareholding in both Statoil and Norsk Hydro the State holds an overall majority interest of 67 per cent in the new company. In 2009 this company got its final name: Statoil ASA (Statoil's name before the merger with Norsk Hydro) and is trading under the name of Statoil.

In successive rounds of licensing SDFI is a minority interest e.g. 25 per cent and sometimes there is no SDFI at all. Still, when the new Statoil with a 67 per cent state shareholding participates in a licence the indirect state participation may already be higher than the SDFI, if any, in the licence concerned.

12. Chapter 12: Entry into Force and Amendment of Laws.

Note. This Act entered into force on 7 July 1997 and has since then been amended by the following Acts: the Act of 14 December 2001 No. 98; of 28 June 2002 No. 61; of 20 December 2002 No. 88; of 27 June 2003 No. 68; of 7 January 2005 No. 2; of 30 June 2006 No. 60 and of 26 January 2007 No. 3.

6.2.4   THE EUROPEAN COMMUNITY (EC)

Preliminary Note. Member States of the EU have sovereignty and sovereign rights over petroleum resources located within their territory, which include those parts of the continental shelf to which they, if they are coastal States, are entitled under the rules of 1982 Convention on the Law of the Sea. Member States have not shown to be willing to give up this position and, for instance, to be prepared to pool their domestic resources for the common good of the Community. Currently, the Community's consumption of crude oil is for 87.5 per cent supplied by foreign countries, among them the Russian Federation and Member States of OPEC like Nigeria and the Middle East Gulf countries. Natural gas is for sixty-five per cent supplied by foreign countries among them again the Russian Federation and Norway (by pipeline) and Algeria, Qatar, Nigeria and Libya (by LNG tanker). To mitigate this dependence on foreign suppliers has always been the central theme of Community level petroleum policies coupled to a policy of stimulating the search for and development of the indigenous petroleum resources. Against this background and in support of the above sketched Community level policies the EC Directive 94/22/EC of 30 May 1994 was adopted.

Apart from that and prompted by the disaster that struck the Deepwater Horizon platform in the Gulf of Mexico in March 2010, as a result of which 4.9 million barrels were discharged into the waters of the Gulf, the Community adopted on 21 February 2013 the tekst of a Directive on safety of offshore oil and gas operations. Such type of Directive does not infringe on Member States' sovereign rights over petroleum resources, since any major accident relating to offshore oil and gas operations will not only affect the Member State on whose continental shelf the accident took place but also other Member States with coastal waters: in other words safety of offshore petroleum operations has been declared to be a matter for the Community.

6.2.4.1 The EC Directive 94/22/EC of 30 May 1994

1. Introduction

On 30 May 1994 the European Parliament and the EC Council adopted the Directive 94/22/EC (OJ No. L 164/3) on the conditions for granting and using authorizations for the prospecting, exploration and production of hydrocarbons in the EC Member States.

2. Preamble of the Directive

As stated therein:

(a) steps must be taken to ensure the non-discriminatory access to and pursuit of activities relating to the prospection, exploration and production of hydrocarbons under conditions which encourage greater competition in this sector and thereby to favour the best prospection, exploration and production of resources in Member States and to reinforce the integration of the internal energy market;

(b) for this purpose it is necessary to set up common rules for ensuring that the procedures for granting authorizations for the prospecting, exploration and production of hydrocarbons must be open to all entities possessing the necessary capabilities;

(c) authorizations must be granted on the basis of objective, published criteria; and the conditions under which authorizations are granted must likewise be known in advance by all entities taking part in the procedure;

(d) Member States must retain the options to limit the access to and the exercise of these activities for reasons justified by public interest and to subject these activities to the payment of a financial contribution or a contribution in hydrocarbons, the detailed arrangements of the said contributions having to be fixed in such a way as not to interfere in the management of entities;

(e) these options must be used in a non-discriminatory way and steps must be taken to avoid imposing on entities, conditions and obligations which are not justified by the need to perform this activity properly;

(f) the activities of entities must be monitored only to the extent necessary to ensure their compliance with these obligations and conditions.

3. Main Provisions

Article 2

1. Member States retain the right to determine the areas within their territory to be made available for the exercise of the activities of prospecting, exploring for and producing hydrocarbons.

2. Whenever an area is made available for the exercise of the activities set out in paragraph 1 Member States shall ensure that there is no discrimination between entities as regards access to and exercise of these activities. However, Member States may refuse on grounds of national security, to allow access to and exercise of these activities to any entity which is effectively controlled by third countries or third countries nationals.

Article 3

1. Member States shall take the necessary measures to ensure that authorizations are granted following a procedure in which all interested entities may submit applications in accordance either with paragraph 2 or 3.

2. This procedure shall be initiated: (a) either at the initiative of the competent authorities by means of a notice inviting applications to be published in the Official Journal of the European Communities, at least 90 days before the closing date for applications; (b) or by means of a notice inviting applications to be published in the

Official Journal of the European Communities following submission of an application by an entity without prejudice to Article 2 (1). Other interested entities shall have a period of at least 90 days after the date of publication in which to submit an application. Notices shall specify the type of authorization, the geographical area or areas in part or all of which an application has been or may be made and the proposed date or time limit for granting authorization.

3. Member States may grant authorizations without initiating a procedure under paragraph 2 where the area for which authorization is requested: (a) is available on a permanent basis; or (b) has been the subject of a previous procedure according to paragraph 2 which has not resulted in the grant of an authorization; or (c) has been relinquished by an entity and does not fall automatically under (a).

4. A Member State may decide not to apply the provisions of paragraph 1 if and to the extent that geological or production considerations justify the granting of the authorization for an area to the holder of an authorization for a contiguous area.

Article 4

Member States shall take the necessary measures to ensure that: (a) if the geographical areas are not delimited on the basis of a prior geometric division of the territory, the extent of each area is determined in such a way that it does not exceed the area justified by the best possible exercise of the activities from the technical and economic points of view. In case of authorizations granted following the procedures laid down in Article 3(2), objective criteria shall be established to this end and shall be made available to the entities prior to the submission of applications; (b) the duration of an authorization does not exceed the period necessary to carry out the activities for which the authorization is granted. However, the competent authorities may prolong the authorization where the stipulated duration is insufficient to complete the activity in question and where the activity has been performed in accordance with the authorization; (c) entities do not retain exclusive rights in the geographical area for which they have received an authorization for longer than is necessary for the proper performance of the authorized activities.

Article 5

Member States shall take the necessary measures to ensure that:

1. authorizations are granted on the basis of criteria concerning in all cases: (a) the technical and financial capability of the entities; (b)

the way in which they propose to prospect, to explore and/or to bring into production the geographical area in question; and, where applicable; (c) if the authorization is put up for sale, the price which the entity is prepared to pay in order to obtain the authorization; (d) if, following evaluation under the criteria (a), (b) and, where applicable, (c), two or more applications have equal merit, other relevant objective and non-discriminatory criteria, in order to make a final choice among these applications. The competent authorities may also take into account, when appraising applications, any lack of efficiency and responsibility displayed by the applicants in operations under previous authorizations. Where the competent authorities determine the composition of an entity to which they may grant an authorization, they shall make that determination on the basis of objective and non-discriminatory criteria. Where the competent authorities determine the operator of an entity to which they may grant an authorization, they shall make that determination on the basis of objective and non-discriminatory criteria;

2. the conditions and requirements concerning exercise or termination of the activity which apply to each type of authorizations by virtue of the laws, regulations and administrative provisions in force at the time of submission of the applications, whether contained in the authorization or being one of the conditions to be accepted prior to the grant of such authorization, are established and made available to interested entities at all times. In the case provided for in Article 3(2)(a) they may be made available only from the date starting from which applications for authorization may be submitted;

3. any changes made to the conditions and requirements in the course of the procedure are notified to all interested entities;

4. the criteria, conditions and requirements are applied in a non-discriminatory manner; [and]

5. any entity, whose application for an authorization is unsuccessful is, if the entity so wishes, informed the reasons for the decision.

Article 6

1. Member States shall ensure that the conditions and requirements referred to in Article 5(2) and the detailed obligations for use of a specific authorization are justified exclusively by the need to ensure the proper performance of the activities in the area for which an authorization is requested, by the application of paragraph 2 or by

the payment of a financial contribution or a contribution in hydrocarbons.

2. Member States may, to the extent justified by national security, public safety, public health, security of transport, protection of the environment, protection of biological resources and of national treasures possessing artistic, historic or archaeological value, safety of installations and of workers, planned management of hydrocarbon resources (for example the rate at which hydrocarbons are depleted or the optimization of their recovery) or the need to secure tax revenues, impose conditions and requirements on the exercise of the activities set out in Article 2(1).

3. The rules for payment of contributions referred to in paragraph 1, including any requirement for State participation, shall be fixed by Member States in such a way as to ensure that the independence of management of entities is maintained. However, where the grant of authorizations is subject to the State's participation in the activities and where a legal person has been entrusted with the management of this participation or where the State itself manages the participation, neither the legal person nor the State shall be prevented from assuming the rights and obligations associated with such participation, equivalent to the importance of the participation provided that the legal person or the State shall not be party to information nor exercise any voting rights on decisions regarding sources of procurement for entities, and that any vote by the State or the legal person shall be based exclusively on transparent, objective and non-discriminatory principles, and shall not prevent the management decisions of the entity from being based on normal commercial principles. However, The option to oppose a decision shall be exercised in a non-discriminatory manner, particularly regarding investment decisions and sources of supply of entities.

4. Member States shall ensure that the monitoring of the entities under an authorization is limited to that necessary to ensure compliance with the conditions, requirements and obligations referred to in paragraph 1. In particular, they shall take the measures necessary to ensure that no entity is required, by any law, regulation or administrative requirement, or by any agreement or undertaking, to provide information on its intended or actual sources of procurement, except at the request of the competent authorities and exclusively with a view to the objectives set out in Article 36 of the Treaty.

(*Note*: this Article 36 allows Member States to prohibit or restrict the import or export of goods for reasons of public security, protection of health, etc.).

Note. State participation is addressed in the Directive since the modalities thereof could have a discriminating effect and distort competitiveness in the sector. As stated in Article 6(3) state participation may be imposed as a condition of the authorization but there should be no interference with the management of the other participants. As formulated in the Directive, the State participant should not prevent the management decisions of the other participants from being based on normal commercial principles There are only two EC Member States viz. Denmark and The Netherlands, and one EEA Member State, viz. Norway, left where state participation is in force, and for which the provisions of the Directive might be relevant. However the Danish and Norwegian regimes provide for minority state participation only. In the Netherlands, under the terms of the Mining Law of 31 October 2002, it is either fifty per cent (old regime licences) or forty per cent (new regime licences), but anyway no majority. In all three cases, the state participant although only having a minority interest may claim the right to oppose *a decision by the holders of an authorization which would not respect the conditions and requirements specified in the authorisation, regarding deple-tion policy and protection of the financial interests of the State.*

Chapter 7

Past and Current Contract-Based Petroleum Legislation

Preliminary Note. Since the 1970s, contract-based petroleum legislation is the prevailing petroleum legislation in non-western countries. The production sharing contract (PSC) is in this context the most widely used form of contract. Although the PSC underwent decades of development in different countries, models of the PSC as offered by Governments to the petroleum industry (for further negotiation) are nonetheless becoming rather similar, undoubtedly due to the world-wide sharing and exchange of information between Governments. Because of this, the more detailed description of the PSC in this Chapter is restricted to those countries which in one way or another have contributed significantly to the development and adoption of the PSC, countries such as Indonesia, because in this country the concept of the PSC originated and underwent its first development; Egypt, because this country was the first to follow Indonesia's example; Malaysia, because of its regional connection with Indonesia; Angola, because this country is a Member of OPEC and has been inspired by and further developed the Indonesian and Egyptian PSC; Brazil, because this country has introduced a rather innovative type of PSC; and finally, the Russian Federation because this country applies (to a certain extent) the PSC to develop massive petroleum resources. In passing, mention is made of Peru and Libya, because those countries became acquainted with the concept of the PSC at the initiative of Occidental Petroleum Corporation, one of the oil companies which at the time were known as the Independents; the Philippines, because the form of PSC adopted in that country was rather peculiar, substituting proceeds sharing for production sharing; Nigeria, because this country like Angola, is also a Member of OPEC and a very important exporter of petroleum; and finally China, which in an early, unsuccessful stage, also experimented with the PSC.

7.1   INDONESIA

7.1.1   BACKGROUND

Production sharing contracts were adopted by the Indonesian government in replacement of the exclusive licenses that had been terminated by virtue of Government Decree No. 44 of 26 October 1960. This Decree determined that oil and natural gas are part of the national riches under the control of the State. Exploration and exploitation were declared to be the responsibility of the State which for this purpose could delegate this responsibility to national state enterprises. These enterprises had to be established by law. Such laws established their authority to undertake the exploration and exploitation of petroleum. The Decree authorized the competent minister to designate enterprises which should assist the national state enterprise in fulfilling its task, if so needed. Then existing exclusive licenses had in fact been nationalized and the former licensees (referred to as concessionaires) were only allowed to continue exercising their rights for a period as short as possible and to be determined by government regulation. The affected concessionaires were accorded a preferential right in obtaining a contract of work to be entered into with the designated state enterprise in respect to the area of their former (and suspended) petroleum agreement.

A new state oil enterprise named *Perusahaan Pertambangan Minyak dan Gas BumiNegara (Pertamina)* was established by Law No. 8 of 1971, in replacement of the state enterprise P.N. Pertamina. The latter dated from 1968 and was on this occasion liquidated. The stated objective of the new Pertamina (as laid down in Article 5 of Law No. 8 of 1971) was to develop and carry out the exploitation of oil and natural gas in the widest sense of the word for the maximum prosperity of the people and the State as well as for creating national strength. Pertamina's tasks are described (Article 13) as consisting in carrying out oil and natural gas exploitation for the acquisition of maximum prosperity for the people and the State and in supplying and serving the domestic demand for oil and natural gas. For the implementation of its tasks Pertamina was permitted (Article 12) to cooperate with another party in the form of a 'Production Sharing Contract'. The terms and conditions of such cooperation would be regulated by a government regulation; and any resulting production sharing contract would become effective as of the moment of approval by the President. In the 'Elucidation' annexed to the Law, it is stated that in this cooperation the most favourable terms for the State have to be sought. Furthermore it is stated that every production sharing contract, which has been approved by the President, will be notified to Parliament.

Initially, the production sharing contracts were seen as income tax replacing agreements. The contractor was liable to pay income tax but contractor's income taxes were considered to be part of Pertamina's share of the profit oil and the latter was responsible for its payment. In order to satisfy all formalities, a contractor received tax receipts from the tax authorities enabling the contractor to demonstrate (mainly vis-à-vis the tax authorities of its home country) that it not only had been subject to income tax but that the tax had also been paid.

Note. Indonesia offers an example of a State where nationalization of foreign petroleum rights was not intended as a means of establishing a state-controlled and state-managed domestic petroleum industry (in contrast to the objectives of the nationalization measures that had been taken in Mexico (1938) and in Iran (1951)). For the Indonesian government the expropriation of foreign held rights meant the first step (together with the establishment of national state enterprises) in a restructuring of the petroleum regime whereby the granting of exclusive licenses would be replaced by the awarding of contracts of work, in this case production sharing contracts, to foreign oil enterprises. Now it must be said that the concept of production sharing was not new to Indonesia. Its origin can be traced back to the Netherlands-Indies Mining Law of 1899, as amended in 1919, which law had in the colonial past been in force in Indonesia. In accordance with Article 5a of this colonial mining law, the competent minister could be authorized by special law to enter into contracts with an oil enterprise granting the latter (the contractor) the exclusive right to search for and produce petroleum within a certain territory and for a certain number of years. A contractor was obliged to pay a royalty and a proportional part of the gross profit (revenues less costs and losses carried forwards). The proportion was related to the annual capital expenditures. The government had the right to demand that royalty and profit share be paid in oil or oil products, provided the oil or oil products so received would be used by the government for its own needs. Clearly, it is only a small step from this type of contract to the production sharing contract that was now adopted in Indonesia.

7.1.2   THE ORIGINAL INDONESIAN MODEL

The early Indonesian production sharing contracts stood at the basis of the concept's further development and evolution that took place not only in Indonesia itself but also in all other non-Western States that followed Indonesia's example and made this concept the centre piece of their petroleum regime.

The original model is summarized in Pertamina's *Summary of Indonesian Oil Contracts*, 2nd edition, January 1972, in which the data of all contracts concluded between 1969 and 1971 are represented.

The main provisions are the following:

   (i) Duration of contract thirty years including a period of ten years for exploration.

(ii) Contract is automatically terminated if within the ten year exploration period the contractor does not succeed in discovering petroleum.

(iii) During the ten year exploration period, at regular intervals, parts of the contract area have to be relinquished.

(iv) Pertamina is responsible for the management of the operations. The contractor is responsible to Pertamina for the execution of the operations and provides the necessary funds therefore.

(v) If petroleum is discovered which in the judgment of Pertamina and its contractor (alternatively: in the judgment of the contractor after consultation with Pertamina) can be produced commercially then the contractor will commence development.

(vi) The contractor is responsible for the preparation of annual work programmes and corresponding budgets. Any such programme and budget are submitted for approval to Pertamina. Pertamina's agreement to a proposed work programme shall not be unreasonably withheld; *(In an actual contract it is stated that when considering work programmes and budgets proposed by contractor, Pertamina will give due consideration to the fact that its contractor carries the risk of and provides the necessary funds for the petroleum operations.)*

(vii) If Pertamina wishes to propose a revision as to certain specific features of the submitted work programme and budget Pertamina and its contractor shall meet and endeavour to agree on the revisions proposed by Pertamina. In any event, any part of the work programme as to which Pertamina has not proposed a revision shall in so far as possible be carried out as prescribed therein.

(viii) It is recognized by both parties that the details of a work programme may require changes in the light of changing circumstances. The contractor is authorized to make such changes provided they do not change the general objective of the work programme.

(ix) Pertamina shall periodically consult with contractor with a view to the fact that contractor is responsible for carrying out the work programme adopted pursuant to the contract.

(x) The contractor is obliged to execute a work programme in a workmanlike manner and by any appropriate scientific methods.

(xi) Up to a maximum of forty per cent of available crude oil production may be taken by the contractor in repayment of costs incurred. In this context and for this purpose 'costs' mean expenditures as paid, without application of depreciation or amortization rules, even when the purchase or acquisition of capital assets is concerned.

(xii) The balance of crude oil remaining after the contractor has taken his entitlement to cost oil (at least sixty per cent of total production) is split sixty per cent to Pertamina and forty per cent to the contractor (main producing areas) or sixty-five per cent to Pertamina and thirty-five per cent to contractor.

(xiii) Up to twenty-five per cent of total crude oil production had to be supplied to the domestic market. The actual amount that had to be delivered within the said twenty-five per cent limit was a certain fraction of the Indonesian domestic consumption. This fraction was arrived at by dividing total contract production by total Indonesian production (all contract areas taken together). The domestic supply obligation was shared between Pertamina and its contractor in the same proportions as profit oil was divided between them. If the system of dividing daily production in tranches was applicable, up to twenty-five per cent of each tranche had to be delivered to the domestic market. The contractor received USD 0.20 per barrel for crude oil delivered to the domestic market.

(xiv) Pertamina is fully entitled to take its share of profit oil in kind. If Pertamina elects to take any part thereof, it shall so advise contractor not less than ninety days prior to the commencement of each semester of each year provided that such election shall not interfere with the proper performance of any crude oil sales agreement which the contractor has executed prior to the notice of such election. If Pertamina does not take its share of the profit oil in kind the contractor is obliged to market Pertamina's share to the best of its abilities. If however Pertamina can realize a better price for contractor's cost oil, it can exercise an option to market this portion of the production itself.

(xv) The contractor is entitled to retain abroad the proceeds of the sale of all crude oil from the venture, except for the proceeds of Pertamina's share of the profit oil sold by contractor.

(xvi) The valuation of the crude oil production for the purpose of the contract is based on realized prices f.o.b. point of export in Indonesia as paid by third parties, or, if there are no such third party sales and prices, a price shall be derived from prices paid by third parties for crude oil of similar type and quality.

(xvii) The contractor is subject to Indonesian income taxes and all other taxes, including all dividend withholding taxes or taxes imposed on the distribution or remittance of income or profit by contractor. However, all such present and future taxes are to be paid and assumed by Pertamina out of its share of the profit oil. The contractor will receive official receipts from the tax authorities evidencing that all taxes due by him had been paid; (*In the 1980s the Indonesian government was persuaded to change the income tax paying procedure and to accept direct payment of income taxes by the contractor, due to the difficulties which US oil companies experienced in their dealings with the US Internal Revenue Service (IRS) in getting the tax payments made by Pertamina on behalf of contractor accepted and recognized for the purpose of the US foreign tax credit.*)

(xviii) If associated natural gas cannot be commercially exploited it has to be flared or put at the disposal of Pertamina for the latter's account. If natural gas can commercially be exploited, Pertamina and its contractor may decide to participate in a gas project. Costs and revenues will then be treated on the same basis as in the case of crude oil; (*As was customary in the early contracts there are no specific provisions made for natural gas; in those days markets for natural gas had still to be developed.*)

(xix) Pertamina is entitled to request its contractor to offer a five per cent undivided interest in the contractor's side of the contract to an Indonesian enterprise (Indonesian participant) to be designated by Pertamina. Pertamina should make its request within three months after the contractor's first declaration of commercial discovery. The Indonesian participant must repay five per cent of the costs incurred by contractor up to that moment. Repayment should be made in cash or kind. If in kind, fifty per cent of the Indonesian participant's share of production would be reserved for that purpose and the amount to be repaid would be increased by fifty per cent.

7.1.3   FURTHER DEVELOPMENTS OF THE INDONESIAN PSC

The first amendment to the Original Model took place in reaction to the dramatic increase of the international oil price at the end of 1973, beginning 1974. This amendment concerned the introduction of a system of successive daily production tranches. Each daily production tranche was divided in cost oil (tied to a maximum of forty per cent of the tranche) and profit oil. For each tranche higher in the series the split of the profit oil portion became more favourable to Pertamina. In fact, the original profit oil split of 65/35 was under the new system only applicable up to 75,000 barrles per day (the bottom tranche); the profit oil in the next tranche, which ranged from 75,000 barrles per day to 200,000 barrles per day, was divided 67.5/32.5; and profit oil in the upper tranche, i.e., that part of the production in excess of 200,000 barrles per day, was divided 70/30. In addition, an excess profit charge was introduced payable in cash with respect to each barrel of net profit oil. In this context, net profit oil meant the profit oil remaining after satisfying the domestic supply obligation. The excess profit charge amounted to a certain percentage of the difference between the at the time prevailing selling price of USD 12 per barrel and a base price which was fixed at USD 5 per barrel. The intention was to replace the respective 65/35; 67.5/32.5 and 70/30 proportions, in which net profit oil was divided, by a new 85/15 proportion but only in respect of the aforementioned price difference. As a result the amount of the excess profit charge (surcharge) payable by contractor per barrel net profit oil in respect of the bottom tranche can be calculated as: $(.35 - .15) \times (USD12 - USD 5)$ = USD 1.40. For the next tranche it would be $(.325 - .15) \times (USD 12 - USD 5)$ = USD 1.225 and then for the upper tranche $(.30 - .15) \times (USD 12 - USD 5)$ = USD 1.05.

During the 1980s, the Indonesian production sharing contract was simplified. According to the new pattern, production is not divided in tranches and no excess profit sharing is applicable. Total production is made available for cost recovery. Recoverable costs are described in fiscal terms, whereby a distinction is made between costs that have to be written off over a number of years and costs that have to be written off in the year in which they have been incurred. The contractor may claim an investment credit equal in value to twenty per cent of the capital expenditure, and this credit has to be recovered from production by priority. The recovery of the investment credit is restricted. The recovery of the credit is only allowed if the sum of Pertamina's sixty-six per cent share of profit oil and fifty-six per cent (the combined tax rate) of the contractor's thirty-four per cent share therein (hence in the aggregate eighty-five per cent of profit oil) is at least equal to the value of forty-nine per cent of total production. If a contract concerns development in deep water entailing higher capital expenditures, the contractor receives an incentive in the form of an increased investment credit. The percentage figure of the credit is 50 per cent in respect of any water depth between 200 metres and 350 metres and is 100 per cent in respect of a water depth of 350 metres or more. The domestic supply obligation (DSO) on the basis of USD 0.20 per barrel is maintained albeit during the first five years of production oil may be sold to the domestic market at market value. The DSO is limited to twenty-five per cent of total production and is shared between Pertamina and its contractor in the same proportion as in which the profit oil is shared between them, namely 66/34. The contractor must satisfy its DSO out of its share of the profit oil. If there is not enough profit oil (due to the claim on cost recovery production) then the contractor's DSO is correspondingly reduced.

In 1989, a new model production sharing contract was developed and made available to interested foreign oil companies. On this occasion, distinction is made between First Tranche Petroleum, a portion amounting to twenty per cent of total production, and the remaining portion of eighty per cent. The 80 per cent portion is meant for recovery of recoverable costs, a basic investment credit of 17 per cent in respect of expenditure made for offshore production installations and submarine pipelines and an additional investment credit of 110 per cent in respect of offshore installation located in waters deeper than 200 metres. The previous restriction on the recovery of the investment credit (i.e., a minimum limit put on the combined Pertamina and government share of revenue) was abolished. Any production remaining after costs and credits have been recovered from the eighty per cent portion, is shared between Pertamina and its contractor in various proportions depending on the particular category (marginal fields, enhanced recovery, etc.), to which the oil production belongs, and, within the various categories, on production volumes. The first tranche petroleum is shared between the parties in the same manner as the profit oil.

By Government Regulation No. 35 of 1994 new production sharing terms were introduced to stimulate investments in remote and frontier areas.

7.1.4   LAW NO. 22 OF 2001

Law No. 22 of 23 November 2001 was the first law concerning oil and natural gas that was promulgated since the Law No. 8 of 1971. It restated the principle that the exploitation of oil and natural gas must be capable of contributing maximally to the people's prosperity and welfare; it declared that the Law No. 44 of 1960, the Law No. 2 of 1962 and the Law No. 8 of 1971 were no longer suitable for the development of petroleum mining business; and that in the light of national and international developments, it was necessary to amend legislation concerning oil and natural gas mining so as to be capable of creating transparent, competitive, efficient and environmental friendly oil and natural gas business activities as well as boosting the growth of national potential and role.

1. Chapter I Definitions

'Mining concession' means the authority delegated by the State to the government to manage exploration and exploitation activities.

'Upstream business activities' mean the business activities focused or based on exploration and exploitation business activities.

'Business entities (BE's)' mean companies established in and operating under the laws of Indonesia.

'Permanent establishments (PE's)' mean companies established outside Indonesia which undertake activities within Indonesia and are obliged to comply with the laws of Indonesia.

'Joint cooperation contract' means a production sharing contract or other models of joint cooperation contract in exploration and exploitation activities, which are more in favour of the State and whose output is maximally used for improving people's welfare.

'Executing Agency (EA)' means an Agency established by the government for the purpose of controlling the upstream business activities.

'Working area' means a certain region within the Indonesian mining jurisdiction used for exploration and exploitation.

2. Chapter II Principles and Objectives

The carrying out of oil and natural gas-related business activities (*which include upstream as wel as downstream business activities*) shall be based on the principles of *inter alia* benefit, equitable distribution, collective prosperity and public welfare, security, safety, legal certainty as well as the environmentally friendly principle, and shall (*as far as relevant for upstream business activities*) aim at: a. guaranteeing effective, efficient, highly competitive and sustainable exploration and exploitation of state-owned oil and natural gas; b. guaranteeing the efficient and effective supply of oil and natural gas as a source of energy and material for domestic requirements; c. supporting and promoting the national capacity so as to be more capable of competing nationally, regionally and internationally; d. increasing state income in order to contribute maximally to the national economy and developing as well as strengthening the position of Indonesian industry and trade; e. creating job opportunities, enhancing public welfare and prosperity, as well as the conservation of the environment.

3. Chapter III Control and Concession

Oil and natural gas constitute national assets controlled by the State. The control by the State shall be executed by the government as the holder of the mining concession. As such holder the government shall establish the EA.

Upstream business activities comprise exploration and exploitation, and shall be carried out and controlled through joint cooperation contracts. The joint cooperation contracts shall at least contain the following provisions: a. the ownership of natural resources belong to the government up to the delivery point; b. the control over operational management is exercised by the EA; c. capital and risks shall be wholly borne by BE's or PE's.

The government shall give priority to the exploitation of natural gas for the domestic need and has the task of preparing strategic petroleum reserves to support the supply of fuel oil in the country. PE's shall only be allowed to undertake upstream business activities.

4. Chapter IV Upstream Business Activities

The upstream business activities shall be carried out by BE's or PE's on the basis of joint cooperation contracts with the EA. Every joint cooperation contract shall contain at least the following principal provisions: state revenue, working area and return, obligation to disburse funds, transfer of ownership of produced oil and natural gas, period and conditions of the extension of the contract; obligation to supply oil or natural gas to meet the domestic need; expiration of the contract; plan for development of field; etc. (*a copy of the joint co-operation contract signed and approved must be sent to the commision on oil and natural gas affairs of the House of Representatives in order to provide legal certainty to the parties to the contract*).

The working area to be offered to BE's or PE's shall be stipulated by the minister. The minister shall stipulate BE's or PE's authorised to undertake exploration and exploitation business activities in the working area offered by the minister. Every BE or PE shall be given only one working area. If BE's or PE's manage more than one working area they must establish a separate statury body for each working area.

The period of validity of the joint cooperation contract is 30 years at the maximum. BE's or PE's can apply for an extension of this period by 20 years at the maximum. The contract period is divided into a period for exploration and a period for exploitation. The exploration period shall be 6 years and can be extended for a period of 4 years at the maximum. BE's and PE's shall be obliged to return gradually part or all of their working areas to the minster. BE's or PE's having been given approval for field development but remaining passive for a period of up to 5 years after the expiration of the exploration period shall be obliged to return their whole working area to the minister.

Guidances, procedures and requirements for the joint cooperation contracts, stipulation and offereing of working areas, alteration and extension of joint cooperation contracts as well as the return of working areas, shall be further stipulted in governemnt regulations.

Data obtained from the general survey and/or exploration and exploitation shall be state property controlled by the government. Data obtained by BE's or PE's in their working areas can be used by the latter for the duration of their joint cooperation contracts. The confidentialty of the aforesaid data shall be upheld for a specified period. Further details shall be provided by government regulation.

The plan for the development of the first field in a working area shall have to obtain the approval of the minister on the basis of advice from the EA, after consulting with the relevant provincial government.

In developing and producing oil and natural gas fields, BE's or PE's shall be obliged to optimize and utilize the same in accordance with good technical norms. Details will be provided by government regulation.

BE's and PE's shall supply maximally 25 per cent of their portion resulting from the production of oil and natural gas to the domestic market. Details are provided by government regulation.

5. Chapter VI State Revenue

BE's or PE's undertaking upstream business activities shall pay state revenue in the form of taxes and non-tax state receipts. The state revenu in the form of taxes shall consists of taxes, import duty and regional taxes and levies. The non-tax state receipts shall consist of state portion, state levies in the form of several kinds of contributions, and bonuses. Provisions stipulating the amounts of the non-tax state receipts will be taken up in the joint cooperation contracts.

6. Chapter VIII Part Two Supervision

Responsibilty for supervising over jobs and the performance of oil and natural gas related business activities with regard to the compliance with provisions of law in force shall be at the competent ministry. The supervision over the carrying out of upstream business activities based on joint cooperation contracts shall be exercised by the EA and be done in such a way that that the exploitation of oil and natural gas resources belonging to the State shall render a maximal benefit and revenue to the State in order to increase the public welfare accordingly.

The EA shall have the following tasks: giving advice to the minister in matters like *inter alia* the preparation and offering of working areas and joint cooperation contracts; signing joint cooperation contracts; assessing plans for the development of the first field in a working area and conveying the same to the minister for approval; approving working plans and budgets. The EA shall constitute a state-owned statutory body.

7. Chapter XI Transitional Provisions

The status of Pertamina which was established on the basis of Law No. 8 of 1971, shall be changed into a state limited liability company.

All rights, obligations and consequences resulting from the production sharing contracts between Pertamina and other parties and from contracts connected with the said production sharing contracts, shall transfer to the EA. All such contracts shall remain effective up to their respective expiration.

Law No. 44 of 1960, Law No.15 of 1962 and Law No. 8 of 1971 shall remain effective as long as they do not contravene or are replaced by new regulations on the basis of this law.

7.1.5   RECENT PSC TERMS (AFTER 2001)

The Law No. 22 of 2001 allows the government wide discretion in determining by regulation the specifics concerning the various elements of the non-tax receipts: state portion (of production), the state levies and the bonuses. Within this context, the government issues from time to time new regualtions, focusing on specific aspects of the production sharing mechanism, such as detailed rules about costs and cost recovery, investment credits, etc. whereas actual figures to be put in the individual joint cooperating contract (First Tranche Oil, Profit Oil split, etc., signature bonus and production bonuses) are left to negotiation between the EA and the foreign company in question. This flexibility allows the government to make PSC's that can address special cicumstances in special regions. More importantly, this flexibilty allows the government to support the natural gas business. The latter is fastly growing in the sector of producting and exporting of LNG. In this sector, Indonesia has become a major exporter of LNG to Japan and South Korea.

7.2 EGYPT

7.2.1 BACKGROUND

On the basis of Articles 50 and 51 of the Law No. 86 of 1956 *On Mines and Quarries*, the minister responsible for petroleum matters could be authorized by special law to enter into an agreement with a foreign oil company for prospecting for and exploiting petroleum, subject to special conditions in derogation of those provisions of the Law No. 86 which envisaged a license-based regime. Soon after Law No. 86 came into force the government started to make use of its powers to regulate petroleum operations on the basis of petroleum agreements instead of old-style licenses and mining leases.

Initially, the type of agreement chosen was the state participation agreement, meant to regulate petroleum operations in the Western Desert and later also in the Gulf of Suez. Later on, in May 1970, the concept of production sharing was introduced in Egypt on the occasion of concluding a typical Indonesian style production sharing contract between EGPC and the North Sumatra Oil Development Corporation (NOSODECO), a Japanese company. Thereafter, as of July 1973, EGPC concluded a great number of agreements on this Indonesian pattern, albeit some features of the preceding license-based regime and state participation were retained, like the grant to EGPC of an exclusive mining lease (concession) covering the whole country and the establishment of a Egyptian stock company jointly owned by EGPC and contractor upon making the first commercial discovery. At the same time, the more important of the earlier state participation agreements (e.g., the participation agreement under the provisions of which the Morgan field in the Gulf of Suez was produced) were converted into production sharing contracts.

7.2.2 PRINCIPAL PROVISIONS OF THE EGYPTIAN PSC

The principal features of an Egyptian style production sharing contract are as follows. As the concession holder, EGPC is liable to pay a royalty in respect to each individual production sharing contract, and is made the sole owner of any petroleum produced under such contract. After commercial discovery, development leases are created within the limits of which petroleum must be developed and produced. Upon the first commercial discovery, an Egyptian joint stock company is established to act as operating company of commercial petroleum. This operating company is jointly owned by EGPC and the contractor and has a board of directors of eight members, four of whom are designated by EGPC and four by the contractor. Its object is to act as the agency through which EGPC and the contractor carry out the development operations under the contract. The joint company also acts as the agency to carry out all aspects of the exploration work, including the preparation of the exploration work programmes and budgets, but does not own any right or title to petroleum produced or in any other asset or property obtained or used in connection with the contract or any development lease. The joint company does not carry any responsibility or liability in respect of the operations carried out by it. Any of the company's decisions shall be understood to be the result of the decisions of EGPC and the contractor or of the contractor alone as may be required under the contract. Under this organizational set-up the contractor has no operational task anymore (after the first commercial discovery) but remains nevertheless fully responsible for the funding of the operations. The contractor is obliged to share the profit production with EGPC, as the sole owner of the concession. The contractor is liable to pay income tax, but EGPC is responsible for paying the tax on behalf of the contractor.

Since their inception in 1973, the Egyptian style production sharing contracts have not much changed, except as regards the percentage shares of cost recovery and the sharing of the profit production. Cost production percentages range around 40 per cent; the contractor's profit production share may range between 25 per cent and 12.5 per cent. Actual percentages depend on the petroleum potential of the exploration acreage on offer and on market conditions, i.e., on the prevailing or expected producer prices for exported oil.

A major change came about when the need arose to become more specific about the contractor's position regarding the development of natural gas reserves. Contracts concluded before 1988 contained a 'standard' provision regarding natural gas, also known from the Indonesian contracts. This standard provision simply stated that, if natural gas would be produced or would be capable of being produced, EGPC and its contractor should study all possible economic alternatives for its use. The standard clause further provided for the production sharing principles being applicable to natural gas, if and when sold for export. Natural gas not exported as LNG, and not used in the petroleum operations, would remain the property of the State and at the free disposal of EGPC. In 1988, the standard clause was made more specific by the introduction of an integrated treatment of crude oil and natural gas development as far as cost recovery out of production is concerned.

Note. When production sharing contracts became generally applied in Egypt, Syria followed suit. The concept was adopted in an almost identical form. The Syrian government was in this matter assisted by officials from EGPC's concession department. A difference however was introduced. This concerned a variation in the payment of royalty. Under the Egyptian PSC, EGPC as the concession holder had been made responsible for paying this royalty out of its own resources. Under the Syrian PSCs, the royalty took the form of setting aside a part of the production in favour of the State, thereby reducing the production on which the contractor and state party could lay a claim by way of cost production and profit production.

7.3   PERU

In 1971, a simple form of production sharing was introduced in Peru. It had been the Occidental Petroleum Corporation, one of the so-called Independents, which acquainted the country with the concept. Under the terms of the Peruvian style contract, the production as made available by the contractor was divided in two equal shares between Petroperu, the Peruvian national state oil company and the contractor. The latter was liable to pay income tax. As of 1985, production sharing contracts were replaced by risk service agreements. Under the rules of this type of agreement the contractor is paid a fee expressed in US dollars per barrel produced.

7.4   THE PHILIPPINES

By Presidential Decree of 22 December 1972, 'on the promotion of petroleum exploration and production in the Philippines', new conditions for service contracts were published. The proposed contracts are concluded between the Petroleum Board (the state party) and a foreign oil company (the contractor) and appear to be similar to the Indonesian style production sharing contracts but with this difference that the sales proceeds of the production are shared between the parties instead of the production itself.

Note. Sales proceeds sharing instead of production sharing comes very close, at least substantially, to the holding of an exclusive production license.

7.5   LIBYA

In Libya, production sharing contracts were adopted and applied as of 1974. Not surprisingly, it was the same oil company that had been instrumental in introducing the concept in Peru, namely Occidental

Petroleum Corporation, who signed on 7 February 1974 the first production sharing contract with the Libyan National Oil Corporation, NOC. This state corporation had been established in 1970. Up to that time, exclusive petroleum rights had been granted in the form of concessions under the terms of the Petroleum Law of 1955. Upon the introduction of production sharing contracts, the Petroleum Law was not abolished but its scope and application was restricted to the petroleum activities of NOC. Exclusive oil rights were reserved for and only granted to NOC. The latter became authorized to enter into production sharing contracts with interested foreign oil companies, provided any proposed and negotiated agreement was submitted to the governmental authorities (the former General People's Committee) for approval.

Note. Although for the time being the contracts are not relevant any more, a brief description of the Libyan PSC is still a matter of interest. The pattern is rather similar to that of the Peruvian style contract but there were some important differences. For instance, the production was similarly divided into two parts but not in equal proportions. The applied proportions were much more favourable to NOC, such as for instance 81/19 or 85/15. Because of this disproportionate division the Libyan contractor was exempted from having to pay any income taxes (nor royalties for that matter). There was also a difference in the matter of funding of development work. After a commercial discovery was made (in a block) NOC would contribute to the operating costs and development costs to be incurred up to the date of export. These costs would be shared between NOC and the contractor in the same proportion as the production would be shared, say 81/19 or 85/15. Under the earlier contracts, NOC's contributions to development expenditure were treated as loans which had to be paid back by the contractor over a number of years, repayment to start when a certain level of production had been reached or a certain quantity of petroleum had been produced. For instance, as soon as the cumulative production, all blocks taken together, would have reached the level of 100 million barrels, the contractor concerned was obliged to start repayment of NOC's contributions at a rate of five per cent per year. In other contracts, in particular those concerning non-associated natural gas, no repayment are required.

A peculiar feature of the early Libyan contracts concerned the supervision of the operations. This supervision was not done by NOC but by a management committee consisting of two members representing the Libyan State and the contractor respectively. In fact, the management committee established by the nationalization decree of 1 September 1973 acted as management committee for the purposes of the production sharing contracts then introduced. Later on, this was changed in the sense that the two Libyan members were appointed by NOC. Decisions are taken by simple majority; hence NOC was placed in firm control as if it would have been itself and acted as the supervisory body.

Later on, without changing the pattern of the original contracts dating from 1974, the terms concerning the production sharing proportions, NOC's contributions to development expenditure and repayment obligations, if any, were varied to make contracts economically favourable or less favourable, depending on whether non-associated gas or crude oil was involved, on the prospects of finding commercial petroleum in a particular contract area and on the level or expected level of the international oil price. So introduced the Libyan model contract of 15 April 1989 a production sharing mechanism whereby a relation is made between the sharing proportions and the status or completeness of the cost recovery. Under this mechanism, the sharing proportion becomes more in favour of the state party depending on whether 'pay-out' has been achieved. The completeness of the cost recovery is indicated by the continuously changing value of a fraction representing the ratio between the contractor's cumulative cash-in (i.e., the proceeds from the sale of cost production and the contractor's share of profit production) and the contractor's cumulative cash-out. It will be clear that until production starts the value of this fraction is zero and that at payout time the fraction equals one.

Note. It will be appreciated that the status of existing contracts is uncertain.

7.6   MALAYSIA

7.6.1   BACKGROUND

Up to the signing on 14 February 1971 of Teheran Agreement by the governments of the OPEC Gulf States, the Malaysian government had closely followed the continuing negotiations on government take that took place with the governments of the OPEC Gulf States and their concessionaires and had incorporated the results of these negotiations in its own licensing regime, Malaysia's position in these matters being protected by the presence of a 'most favoured nation' clause in its licenses and leases. Thereafter, however, the Malaysian government developed and pursued its own concession policies, which in this case meant that the government followed the example given years earlier (in 1960) by Indonesia and decided to nationalize the then existing petroleum licenses and agreements and to make only production sharing contracts available to the foreign petroleum industry.

The new policy was introduced by the Petroleum Development Act 1974, which came into force on 1 October 1974 and by virtue of which:

(i) petroleum agreements were cancelled with effect from 1 April 1975; and

(ii) ownership in and the exclusive right of exploring for, exploiting, winning and obtaining petroleum, whether onshore or offshore, was vested into a state-owned corporation, by the name of Petroliam Nasional Berhad (Petronas).

Note. In vesting the ownership of petroleum into Petronas, the new Act constituted a radical departure from the Continental Shelf Act 1966, since the latter had vested all rights with respect to the continental shelf and its natural resources into the Federation to be exercisable by the Government of the Federation.

Since then, petroleum operations are regulated by the Act of 1974, as amended by the Petroleum Development (Amendment) Acts of 1975 and 1977, and the Regulations made thereunder. The prime minister is authorized to make regulations to give effect to the provisions of the Act.

In consideration for having received the ownership of petroleum resources and these exclusive rights, Petronas is liable to make payments to the Federal Government or any State Government as agreed. Petronas had been granted complete freedom to set the form, terms and conditions of any new agreements, including those that were meant to replace the petroleum agreements that were cancelled. Petronas was and is under no obligation to submit finally agreed terms to the government for approval. Since on the side of the State only Petronas is involved in the making of the new agreements, changes and amendments to the latter can be arranged by Petronas and its contractor in mutual agreement without the intervention of any other state authority or of the legislature.

The new Act of 1974 was preceded by the Petroleum Mining Act 1966, which was not repealed, merely made non-applicable to Petronas, with exception of the provisions regarding getting permission to enter upon lands for carrying out petroleum operations. The Petroleum Mining Act 1966 provided for an Appropriate Petroleum Authority authorized to grant licenses or to enter into petroleum agreements. Such licenses or petroleum agreements, as were in existence at the time, were 'saved' by the Act of 1974 but for only a limited period. The Act declared that such licenses and agreements would continue for six months from the coming into force of the Act or for such extended period as the prime minister would allow. Considering that the Act of 1974 had left it to the same prime minister to decide when the Act should come into force, the continued validity of existing licenses or agreements was entirely put within the discretionary powers of the prime minister.

Note. As originally written, the Act of 1974 provided for a compulsory acquisition of licenses and agreements without offering the dispossessed titleholders any compensation at all, let alone 'adequate' compensation as demanded under the Constitution, and in this respect was clearly in conflict with the latter. The discrepancy was recognized and the Act of 1974 was retroactively amended by the Petroleum Development (Amendment) Act 1977. After this amendment, the Act of 1974 provided for adequate compensation to be paid to the person who would have lost its license or petroleum agreement as a result of the termination of these rights under the rules of the Act. This adequate compensation was allowed to take the form of a single sum; periodical payments or such form as would be agreed under any arrangement agreed between the former holder of the license or petroleum agreement and another person designated by the Federal Government. With this amendment, which was made effective as of 1 October 1974, the effective date of the Act, the latter was reconciled with the Constitution.

The time during which existing licenses and petroleum agreements were suspended was meant to be used for the negotiation of new arrangements with Petronas. Such arrangements were considered to qualify as adequate compensation for the rights that were lost under the Act of 1974. Since Petronas had been given the exclusive rights to explore and exploit, the new arrangements could only take the form of contracts of work. As a matter of fact, Petronas decided to adopt for these contracts the production sharing principle. In the end all licenses and agreements were terminated with effect from 1 April 1975. Temporary contractual arrangements were made to bridge the period between the termination date and the coming into force of the new arrangements. The negotiation of the first production sharing contracts took a long time. They were finally signed on 30 November 1976.

From the outset it was Petronas' policy, like in Indonesia, that these contracts should have as their objective and be so designed as to serve the national interest of Malaysia and to contribute to the economic development of the country. This policy is reflected in various provisions of the contracts. It also allows Petronas to introduce new types of risk contract if it feels that the latter may better address special circumstances like enhancing the recovery from mature oil fields. It has also prompted Petronas to pay from the outset special attention in the contracts to natural gas. Like in Indonesia but much earlier, this sector is built on the production and export of LNG to Japan and South Korea, and has grown in recent years to very important gas business.

7.6.2   PSC TERMS

The production sharing mechanism is composed of the following elements. Very typical for Malaysian contracts is that part of the production is set aside as royalty production. This fraction may not exceed either ten per cent of crude oil won and saved (royalty oil) or ten per cent of the natural gas available for commercial sale (royalty gas). Royalty production is taken by Petronas to enable the latter to settle cash payments to the Federal and State Governments due to these governments under the Act of 1974.

A maximum of fifty per cent of the crude won and saved (cost oil) and a maximum of sixty per cent of the proceeds of the sale of the natural gas (cost gas) is reserved for the purpose of recovering by the contractor of all costs relating to crude oil operations and to natural gas operations separately. It is important to note that costs are recoverable on a cash-out, expensed basis, no depreciation of amortization of capital expenditure being required. The cost recovery procedures with respect to oil operations is kept separate and independent from those with respect to natural gas operations, no 'integration' is permitted, except that the cost of using associated gas for oil operations and the cost of extracting NGL's from the natural gas produced is considered part of the crude oil related cost and as such recoverable from cost oil.

The remaining portion of the crude oil won and saved is called profit oil and the remaining portion of the proceeds of the natural gas sold is called profit gas. The profit oil is divided between Petronas and its contractor on the basis of successive production tranches, coupled to the level of cumulative production. To give an example: incremental sharing proportions may range from 50/50 to 70/30 in favour of Petronas. As soon as cumulative production exceeds 80 million kilolitres (about 50 million barrels) profit oil is shared in a 70/30 proportion. The proceeds of profit gas may be divided between Petronas and contractors in a 50/50 proportion, but as soon as the cumulative quantity sold exceeds a certain value, say sixty billion cubic metres the proportion changes to 70/30 in favour of Petronas. Actual numbers and figures are a matter of negotiation.

In contrast with the Indonesian example, a contract does not provide for a domestic supply obligation, but instead Petronas has been given the right to purchase from its contractor up to fifty per cent of the quarterly cost oil at a price equal to the cost oil value.

Petronas is allowed to request an increase or decrease of the production rate of any oil field located in the production area for the following purposes and reasons: for optimizing oil and gas recovery; to minimize wastage of natural gas; for safety or operational reasons; or in the national interest. Similarly in the national interest Petronas may request its contractor to develop for Petronas' account and benefit any petroleum reservoir considered by the contractor to be sub-economical or to execute on this basis such works or build such facilities as Petronas may desire.

The contract contains provisions specifically focused on natural gas, associated as well as non-associated. If non-associated gas is found in substantial quantities the contractor is allowed to hold the gas field, after agreeing with Petronas the extent thereof, for a period not exceeding five years. Before the expiry of the holding period the contractor has to submit for the approval of Petronas a development plan. Failure to do so shall render the gas field to be relinquished to Petronas, unless Petronas agrees to extend the holding period. Any such extension may not exceed five years. If during the holding period contractor would come to the conclusion that exploitation of the gas field is not commercially justified the gas field must be surrendered to Petronas. Contractors must develop the gas field within four years from the date on which the development plan had been approved by Petronas, albeit a development period longer than four years could also be approved by Petronas. Failing to develop within the agreed development period renders the gas field surrendered to Petronas, except in a situation of force majeure.

As far as associated natural gas is concerned the contract requires that this natural gas is used by priority for optimizing oil production. Such use includes re-injection for pressure maintenance. Associated gas that cannot be used for these purposes must be re-injected in suitable underground reservoirs, but if there are no such reservoirs the gas may be flared. Before any gas is flared any NGL's should be extracted from the associated gas if commercially feasible.

Contractors are not allowed to sell their cost gas and share of profit gas save on a joint dedicated basis with Petronas to an outlet for natural gas which can be developed on terms that render the production and delivery of the gas economically acceptable to both parties.

Another characteristic feature of the Malaysian contracts is the provision for state participation. The applicable model contract provides for an unspecified sharing of contractor's rights and obligations as between the foreign company and Carigali, a wholly owned subsidiary of Petronas. The foreign company is obliged to enter into an agreement of cooperation with Carigali and this agreement must be approved by Petronas.

Note. The principles of such agreement are set out in the model contract. The percentage participation interest is a matter of negotiation and will be specified in the agreement. An important principle to be incorporated into the actual agreement concerns Carigali's exemption from having to contribute to the cost of exploration work and from being responsible for fulfilling the minimum exploration work obligations. In case of a commercial discovery Carigali is free to decide whether or not to participate in the development thereof. Under the terms of the contract Carigali and its foreign partner are treated collectively as one party, which also applies to arbitration. Disputes between Carigali and its foreign partner are settled as provided for in their joint operating agreement.

A Malaysian contract is further characterized by containing a number of 'national interest' provisions. In this context, the contract contains elaborate rules in the matter of procurement of equipment, materials, services and supplies, the employment of expatriates and the training of contractors' and Petronas' personnel.

Note. In the matter of procurement contractors have by priority to purchase from domestic manufacturers and suppliers. If the required products and services are not available in Malaysia contractors may order, after having received Petronas' approval therefore, these goods and services from outside Malaysia. All procurement of equipment, etc. shall be on an arm's length basis and shall, unless otherwise approved by Petronas, be obtained as a result of competitive bidding. Before employing foreign employees contractors have first to obtain the written approval of Petronas for such employment. Foreign employees may not be employed in positions which can be fulfilled by nationals. Contractors' national employees should be trained to take over the positions held by foreign employees. Contractors are obliged annually to submit, the details of all salaries, benefits and privileges accorded to each classified category of contractors' personnel (both foreign and national).

Contractors are subject to the Petroleum (Income Tax) Act 1967, as amended with effect from 1 April 1975 by the Petroleum (Income Tax) (Amendment) Act 1976 (No. 1) and (No. 2). In contrast with the Indonesian example, the production sharing mechanism that was introduced by the new contracts was not seen as an income tax replacing or absorbing arrangement and the contracts were not meant to exhaust the methods to determine government take. The aforesaid Petroleum (Income Tax) Act 1967, designed and meant to impose a tax on income from petroleum operations, was maintained, albeit the Act had to be amended (with effect from 1 April 1975) in some respects in order to cater for the peculiarities of the production sharing contracts.

7.7 ANGOLA

7.7.1 BACKGROUND

The State of Angola became independent in November 1975. In petroleum policy and strategy matters, the government was guided by and followed the Indonesian and Malaysian examples. In 1976, a national oil company was formed under Decree No. 57 of 9 June 1976. This company was named Sociedade Nacional de Combustivel de Angola, Empresa Pablica (Sonangol EP). Two years later, a new petroleum law was enacted (Law No. 13 on Petroleum Activities of 26 August 1978). This Law, which was set-up as a framework law leaving details to be filled in by government regulations, declared all onshore and offshore petroleum deposits to be the property of the People of Angola and all the exploration and exploitation rights to be transferred to Sonangol. As from the coming into force of the Law all then existing petroleum rights were cancelled and transferred to Sonangol. Any foreign company possessing the necessary technical capabilities and financial capacities, and wishing to explore within the national territory, was permitted to do so but only in association with Sonangol and within the areas comprised in the licenses granted to Sonangol. Such association could be in the form of a 51/49 joint venture (this possibility was restricted to the onshore) or in that of a production sharing contract (this possibility was available for both the onshore and the offshore).

With effect from 1 January 2007 Angola became the 12th Member State of OPEC.

7.7.2 LAW NO. 10 OF 2004

In 2004, Law No. 13 of 1978 was replaced by Law No. 10 of 12 November 2004. It is stated in the new Law that such replacement was due in view of the natural growth of the Angolan oil industry which implied the need for adoption of new concepts and practices in petroleum concessions. But it is also stated that the fundamental principle of state ownership of petroleum resources enshrined in the Constitutional Law and the regime of a sole concessionaire and mandatory association for petroleum concessions is maintained. In this context the new Law envisages to safeguard *inter alia* the protection of the national interest, the promotion of the development of the employment market and the valorization of mineral resources, the protection of the environment, the rational usage of petroleum resources and the increase of the Country's competitiveness on the international market.

1. Chapter I Definitions and Statement

'Foreign Associate' means a corporate entity incorporated abroad and which in its capacity as foreign investor associates itself to the National Concessionaire (in the form of either a joint venture or a production sharing agreement);

'National Concessionaire' means the entity to which the State grants mining rights;

'Mining Rights' means the set of powers granted to the National Concessionaire;

'Operator' means the entity that carries out petroleum operations in a given petroleum concession.

Petroleum deposits existing in the surface and subsurface areas of the Angolan national territory, inland waters, territorial waters, exclusive economic zone and continental shelf are an integral part of the public property of the State.

2. Chapter II Principles of Organisation and Execution of Petroleum Operations

The National Concessionaire is Sociedade Nacional de Combustivel de Angola, Empressa Publica – (Sonangol, E.P.) as the holder of mining rights. Mining rights shall be granted to the National Concessionaire either directly or, when wishing to associate itself with third parties, by means of a concession decree. Petroleum operations may only be carried out under a prospecting licence or petroleum concession. Prospecting licences shall be issued by the supervising Minister, whereas the Government shall be responsible for granting concessions for the exercise of mining rights. The duration of concessions shall comprise two periods: an exploration period for exploration and appraisal and a production period for development and production. The duration of each of the concession periods shall be defined in the concession decree. The duration of each of the concession periods may exceptionally be extended upon the request of the National Concessionaire. The powers to grant such an extension rest with the supervising Minister. Concession areas are defined by the supervising Minister.

Any company that wishes to carry out petroleum operations in the territory of Angola outside the scope of a prospecting licence, may only do so in association with the National Concessionaire. Such association may take the form of a corporation, a consortium or a production sharing agreement. In a corporation or in a consortium the participating interest of the National Concessionaire shall, as a rule, exceed 50 percent.

The risk of investing in the exploration period shall be borne by the entities which associate themselves with the national Concessionaire.

These entities shall not be entitled to recover the capital invested in the event that no economically viable discovery is made.

The operator shall be appointed in the relevant concession decree upon proposal of the National Concessionaire and shall be an entity of recognized capacity, technical knowledge and financial capability.

The operator shall notify the supervising Ministry and the Ministry of Finance, through the National Concessionaire, of the contracts and sub-contracts entered into with third parties for carrying out petroleum operations, under the terms to be defined by said Ministries.

The mining rights granted hereunder carry the obligation to explore and produce petroleum in a rational manner, in accordance with the most appropriate technical and scientific practices used in the international petroleum industry and in accordance with the national interest.

The National Concessionaire and its associates shall be subject to the specific obligations described above, together with the general obligations to preserve petroleum deposits or reserves, the breach of such obligations shall be subject to the penalties established by la wand regulations.

The petroleum operations shall be carried out in accordance with applicable law and the generally accepted practices in the international oil industry relating to safety, hygiene and health at work.

In carrying out their activities the licensees, the National Concession-aire and its associates shall take the precautions necessary to protect the environment, in order to preserve the same, namely in respect of health, water, soil and subsoil, air, the preservation of biodiversity, flora and fauna, ecosystems, landscape, atmosphere and cultural archeological and artistic heritage.

For the above purposes the licensees, the National Concessionaire and its associates shall submit to the supervising Ministry within the required time frames, the plans required by applicable law speciffying the practical measures which should be taken in order to prevent harm to the environment, including environmental impact studies and audits, plans for reha-bilitation of the landscape and structures or contractual mechanisms and permanent management and environmental auditing plans.

Licensees, the National Concessionaire and its associates shall be obliged to repair the damage they cause to third parties in the course of petroleum operations, unless they can show to have acted without fault.

Except when, in the event of a national emergency, the output of petroleum is requisitioned by the Government, the State shall not be liable for losses or damage of any type or nature, including, but not limited to, losses and damage to property or compensation payable to persons for death or accident, caused by or resulting from any petroleum operation carried out hereunder by the licensees, the National Concessionaire or its associates or by any entity acting on behalf of the same.

Licensees, the National Concessionaire and its associates, and any other entities which co-operate with them in carrying out petroleum operations shall (a) acquire materials, equipment, machinery and consumer goods of national production, of the same or approximately the same quality and which are availble for sale and delivery in due time, at prices which are no more than 10 per cent higher than the imported items including transportation and insurance costs and custom charges due, and (b) contract local service providers, to the extent to which the services they provide are similar to those available on the international market and their prices, when subject to the same tax charges are no more than 10 per cent higher than the prices charged by foreign contractors for similar services.

3. Chapter V Petroleum Concessions

In the event that the National Concessionaire wishes to associate itself with any other entity in order to carry out petroleum operations in a given area jointly, the concession shall be granted by means of a concession decree and shall be deemed effective on the date of the execution of the contract in question. If the National Concessionaire wishes to associate itself as aforesaid it shall apply for authorisation to carry out an open tender to define the entities with which it shall associate. If the open tender procedure fails for one reason or another the status of associate may be awarded by direct negotiation. A proposal for direct negotiation will be made known by public notice. If within 15 days from the date of the notice other entities declare an interest in the same concession area, a tender shall be held limited to the interested companies.

The concession decree is the formal instrument of the Government whereby it awards a given petroleum concession to the National Concessionaire. The concession decree shall cover the following issues, amongst others (a) award of mining rights; (b) definition and description of the concession area; (c) duration of the concession and the different phases and periods; (d) identity of the operator.

In the event of the National Concessionaire being associated with third parties for the purpose of carrying out petroleum operations, the concession decree shall contain the following: (a) the authorisation for the National Concessionaire to enter into such association; (b) the identity of its associates; and (c) the approval of the contract in question.

4. Chapter VI Petroleum Operations

Exploration is carried out on the basis of annual plans.

Discovery of any petroleum deposit will immediately be reported to the supervising Ministry. The National Concessionaire may declare a commercial discovery when it deems that in the course of prospecting, exploration and appraisal activities, there exists an economically exploitable petroleum deposit. In the event of the National Concessionaire being associated with third parties through a production sharing agreement the declaration of commercial discovery shall only be signed by its associates. Following the aforesaid declaration the National Concessionaire and its associates shall draw up a general development and production plan, which shall be submitted (within some specific deadlines) by the National Concessionaire to the supervising Ministry for review and approval (within 90 days after having received the plan). At any time the general development and production plan may be amended on the express and duly substantiated request of the National Concessionaire. The general development and production plan may not be carried out before approval by the supervising Ministry.

The National Concessionaire shall immediately notify the supervising Ministry as soon as: (a) it discovers in the concession area a petroleum deposit capable of commercially viable development which extends beyond the areaof the siad concession; (b) it discovers in the concession area a petroleum deposit which can only be commercially developed in conjunction with a petroleum deposit existing in an area adjacent to the said concession; (c) it considers that a commercial discovery in the concession should, for technical and economic reasons, be developed jointly with a commercial discovery in an area adjacent to the concession in question. In the event of the two areas being covered by petroleum concessions the supervising Ministry may by notice addressed to the National Concessionaire and its associates, determine that the petroleum discovered shall be developed and produced on a joint basis. The entities involved shall co-operate in the preparation of a plan for this purpose.

The demarcation of petroleum areas in which the commercially exploitable petroleum deposits are located, shall be deemed definitive with the approval of the general development and production plan. At the end of the exploration period any areas which have not been definitively demarcated shall cease to be part of the concession area and shall be deemed relinquished in favor of the State.

Commercial production may only begin after submitting a report on the execution of the general development and production plan and after having been granted authorisation by the supervising Ministry.

The National Concessionaire and its associates shall prepare annual production plans to be submitted to the supervising Ministry for approval. Any amendment of the production plans shall require the prior approval of the supervising Ministry which, on its own initiative and provided such is justified by the national interest, to ensure the efficient use of reservoirs, facilities and/or transport systems, may determine an increase, reduction or maintenance of the scheduled production volumes and shall, in such cases, give the National Concessionaire a reasonable period for submitting additional production plans.

The natural gas produced from any petroleum deposit shall be exploited, and flaring of the same is expressly forbidden, except flaring for short periodsof time when required for purpose of testing or other operating reasons. The deveopment plans for petroleum deposits shall always be devised in such a way as to allow for the use, preservation or commercial exploitation of associated gas.

The definitive plugging of any producing well requires the prior submittal of the plan fort his to the supervising Ministry for review and approval.

At least one year prior to the termination of the concession or the date of abandonment of any area included therein, the National Concessionaire shall prepare and deliver to the supervising Ministry a plan providing for the cases of decommisioning the wells, facilities, equipment for the rehabilitation of the landscap and continuation of the petroleum operations.

At any time, by giving prior notice of at least 90 days, the Government may request the National Concessionaire and its associates, to supply to an entity apponted by the same at the delivery pont, from their respective share in output a quantity of petroleum aimed at satisfying the domestic consumption requirements of the Republic of Angola.

The participation of the National Concessionaire and its associates in aforesaid supply shall not exceed the proportion between the annual output derived from the concession area and the total annual output of petroleum in the Republic of Angola nor exceed 40 per cent of the total output from the concession area in question.

The value of the petroleum being supplied shall be calculated in accordance with the rules on the valuation of petroleum for fiscal purposes and shall be paid in internationally convertible currency.

The associates of the National Concessionaire shall without prejudice to the domestic supply obligation and to the Government's right to requisition the output of petroleum in the event of a national emergency, dispose freely of thier share of the petroleum produced under this law and other applicable legislation.

The point of transfer of ownership of the petroleum produced shall be situated outside or beyond the wellhead, and the metering point for petroleum produced shall be located prior to the point where ownership is transferred.

Entities that carry out petroleum operations in national territory shall be required to employ only Angolan citizens in all categories and functions, except ifthere are no Angolan citizens in the national market with the required qualifications and experience, under terms to be regulated. National and foreign workers employed by the entities referred to above who occupy identical professional categories and carry out identical functions shall enjoy the same rights of remuneration and the same working and socal conditions, without any form of dicrimination. The duties of recruitment, integration and training of Angolan personnel employed by the aforesaid entities shall be established by Government decree.

Any dispute that may arise between the National Concessionaire and its associates which relate to strictly contractual issues shall be resolved by agreement between the parties according to the principles of good faith and of equity and balance between the interests of the parties. Should no agreement be reached, disputes shall be resolved by resorting to arbitration under the terms set forth in the agreement in question.

Source of translated text: *Angolan Law Firm Miranda and Partners*

7.7.3 THE 2008 MODEL PSC

In 2008, a new Model PSC was made available to the interested industry, the key terms of which have to be settled by open tendering or by direct negotiation as stipulated in the Petroleum Law. These negotiable key terms include the duration of respectively the Initial Exploration Phase, the Optional Exploration Phase, and the Production Period; minimum exploration work obligations and expenditures, the maximum percentage Cost Recovery Crude Oil and the percentages applicable in the scale linking contractor's rate of return to the sharing of Development Area Profit Oil.

Contracting Parties

The contracting Parties are Sociedade Nacional de Combustiveis de Angola – Empresa Publica (Sonangol E.P.) and Contractor.

Creation of development areas, production period

Following each commercial discovery the extent of the whole area within the contract area capable of production from the deposit or deposits identified in the discovery well and its related appraisal wells, if any, shall be agreed upon by Sonangol and contractor. Each agreed area shall then be converted automatically into a development area effective from the date of commercial discovery. There shall be a production period for each development area which shall be [....] years from date of commercial discovery in said development area. The production period may be extended. Any development area is considered automatically terminated if within 3 years from the date of commercial discovery in said development area, the first lifting of oil from the said development area has not taken place as part of a regular program of lifting in accordance with the lifting schedule.

Recovery of contractor's costs and expenditures

Except as otherwise provided for, the costs and expenditures incurred in the petroleum operations, as well as any losses and risks derived therefrom, shall be borne by the contractor, and Sonangol shall not be responsible to bear or repay any of the aforesaid costs and expenditures.

Under the Petroleum Activities Tax Law, contractor shall recover all exploration, development, production and administration and services expenditures (*meant here expenditures as recognized under the Tax Law, i.e. fiscal costs*) incurred under this contract by taking and freely disposing of up to a maximum amount of [....] percent per year of all crude oil produced and saved from development areas and not used in petroleum operations. Such crude oil portion is hereinafter referred to as 'cost recovery crude oil'.

If in any year recoverable costs are less than the maximum value of the cost recovery oil, the difference shall become part of and included in the 'development area profit oil'. If in any year recoverable costs exceed the value of cost recovery crude oil from the relevant development area for such year, the excess shall be carried forwards for recovery in the next succeeding year or years, but in no case after termination of the contract. If development expenditures for a development area are not fully recovered within 5 years after commencement of commercial production or within 5 years after the year in which development expenditures are incurred whichever later occurs, then contractor's percentage share cost recovery oil shall be increased from year 6, based on a method agreed upon by Sonangol and contractor but not exceeding 65 per cent.

Production Sharing

The total crude oil produced and saved in a quarter from each commercial discovery and its development area and not used in petroleum operations less the cost recovery crude oil from the same development area shall be referred to as 'development area profit oil' and shall be shared in the current quarter between Sonangol and the contractor according to a scale linking contractor's after tax rate of return for each development area as achieved at the end of the preceding quarter to varying percentage shares for Sonalgol and the contractor, in as much the higher contractor's rate of return proves to be, the smaller the contractor's percentage share of the the development area profit oil will be.

Note. The above described system of production sharing can be summarized as follows. The overall agreed percentage portion of 'cost recovery crude oil' is distributed among the different development areas, in as much the agreed percentage is applied to the production generated by each of them. This means that as soon as production is established in any development area that production is split in two portions: a portion 'cost recovery crude oil' and a remaining portion 'development area profit oil'. Recovery of exploration expenditure is not tied to a specific development area and can be recovered from any portion cost recovery crude oil available. In contrast, development expenditure can only be recovered from the portion cost recovery crude oil that is allocated to the development area in which this expenditure was incurred. Hence, it is possible that in one development area recoverable costs are less the portion of cost recovery crude oil allocated to that area, thus increasing the portion of 'development area profit oil', while in another development area the costs exceed the portion of cost recovery crude oil, if any, and in so far being development expenditure they cannot be transferred to another development area where there is an excess cost recovery crude oil.

Contractor's obligation to purchase Sonangol's share of production

Sonagol shall have the right to require contractor to purchase any part of Sonangol's share of production under normal commercial terms and conditions in the international petroleum industry and at the market price in force at the time the crude oil is lifted as established in the Law.

Sonangol's right to buy an income tax- based share of contractor's crude oil

Sonangol shall have the right to buy from the contractor crude oil from the contract area equivalent in value to the petroleum income tax due by the contractor, i.e., 50 per cent of contractor's share of development area profit oil.

Sharing of domestic supply obligation

The fulfillment of the obligation to satisfy the domestic consumption requirements of the Republic of Angola as stipulated in the Law, shall be shared between Sonangol and contractor in proportion to their respective net shares of production (contractor's net share being its portion of cost recovery crude oil plus its share of development area profit oil less the income tax-based quantities delivered to Sonangol.

Associated and non-associated natural gas

Contractor shall have the right to use in the petroleum operations associated natural gas produced from the development areas. Any surplus associated natural gas shall be made available free to Sonangol whenever the latter so determines.

If non-associated natural gas is discovered within the contract area then Sonangol will have the exclusive right to appraise, develop and produce the said gas for its own account and risk, but if Sonangol so determines and if agreed with contractor the discovery of non-associated gas shall be developed jointly by Sonangol or one of its Affiliates and contractor.

Sole risk operations by Sonangol

Sonangol may give a sole risk notice in respect of operations which involve: deeper drilling in any exploration well; the drilling of an exploration well (but no more than 2 such wells in any year); the drilling of an appraisal well which is a direct result of a successful exploration well; the development of any discovery which is a direct result rom a successful exploration well and/or appraisal well sole risk operation; the development of a petroleum deposit discovered by a successful exploration well and/or appraisal well carried out by contractor as part of a plan approved by the Operating Committee, if 36 months have elapsed since such successful well was completed and contractor has not commenced the development of such deposit. After receiving the sole risk notice contractor gets some specified periods of time to notify Sonangol whether or not it elects to undertake the proposed operation by including it as part of the petroleum operations.

Operating Committee

The operating committee is the body through which the parties co-ordinate and supervise the petroleum operations. The operating committee shall be composed of 4 members, 2 of whom shall be apponted by Sonangol and the other 2 by contractor. The chairman is appointed by Sonangol from among its representatives. Each member shall have one vote and the chairman shall in addition have a tie breaking vote. Decisions are taken by a simple majority of the votes present or represented, but unanimity is required for the important matters such as the approval work plans; the proposed general development and production plan; lifting schedule; etc.

Ownership of assets

Physical assets purchased by contractor for the carrying out of work plans and budgets become the property of Sonangol when purchased in Angola or if purchased abroad when landed in Angola. Such physical assets should be used in petroleum operations provided that contractor is not obligated to make any payments for the use of such assets during the term of the contract. This provision shall not apply to equipment leased from and belonging to third parties (or contractor).

Note. The 2004 Petroleum Law was accompanied by the Law No. 13 on Taxation of Petroleum Activities of 24 December 2004. This Law applies to all entities, whether Angolan or foreign, performing petroleum operations in Angolan territory, as well as in other territorial or international areas within the tax levying jurisdiction of the Republic of Angola, as recognized by international law or agreements. The main tax charges introduced by the Petroleum Tax Law (Article 4) are a petroleum production tax and a petroleum income tax. The petroleum production tax (the equivalent of a royalty) is not applicable to PSC's. The petroleum income tax is levied on the taxable income which consists of revenues generated by the petroleum operations less operating costs and less depreciation charges at the rate of 16.666 per cent in respect of costs incurred for exploration operations, the drilling of development wells and for production, transportation and storage facilities. For PSC's the tax rate is fifty per cent (section III, Article 41), which boils down to an income tax levied at a rate of fifty per cent of contractor's share of development area profit oil.

7.8   THE PEOPLE'S REPUBLIC OF CHINA

In August 1982, China invited foreign oil enterprises to apply for production sharing contracts with respect to the Chinese part of the continental shelf. The basis for the contracts was laid down in the *Regulations of the People's Republic of China on Exploitation of Offshore Petroleum Resources in Cooperation with Foreign Enterprises*, which had been made public on 30 January 1982.

The new Regulations followed the by now classic Indonesian and Malaysian approach: the ownership of petroleum *in situ* on the continental shelf was vested in the State. The Chinese National Offshore Oil Corporation (CNOOC), which had been established at the same time, was given the exclusive right to search for and exploit such petroleum. CNOOC should undertake the licensed activities in cooperation with foreign oil enterprises. The Regulations contained the main principles on the basis of which this cooperation should take place. The standard chosen appeared to be the application of a production sharing mechanism characterized by two special features: (1) the production sharing concept is applied to each individual field, and (2) CNOOC is given the option to participate in the development of any such field with a share of up to fifty-one per cent. Development cost oil as generated by a particular field is divided between the contractor and CNOOC in proportion to both parties' individual contributions to the costs of development. Remaining oil (which means oil remaining after royalty oil (12.5 per cent), tax oil (5 per cent) and cost oil (up to 50 per cent of production) is divided between the contractor and CNOOC as participant on the one hand and CNOOC as state party on the other in the proportion $(X)/(1-X)$. The X-factor is determined on the basis of successive tranches of levels of daily production, each tranche having its own X-factor. Actual X-factors are fixed in negotiations with applicants.

7.9   NIGERIA

As one of the Member States of OPEC, Nigeria's interest was primarily focused on the introduction of OPEC style state participation with respect to the oil mining leases under its jurisdiction. With respect to new exploration acreage the Nigerian government had shown in one instance to be prepared to experiment with the concept of production sharing. In 1972 a production sharing agreement was concluded with a US oil company, but this agreement remained an isolated event.

Note. In May 1970 the Egyptian NOSODECO contract was signed. Undoubtedly, this contract had stood model for the Nigerian 1972 contract. For instance the cost oil allocation (a fixed forty per cent) and the division of the profit oil was very similar to the Egyptian example. Nevertheless, in three important aspects the Nigerian contract deviated from the Egyptian example. First, the Nigerian contract did not have an autonomous contract area. Instead, the contract area coincided with the area of two oil prospecting licenses granted to and held by the state party (in this case the Nigerian National Petroleum Corporation, NNPC). Being the license holder made NNPC under the applicable petroleum legislation responsible for maintaining the licenses in good standing, for fulfilling any area relinquishment obligations and also for the conversion of the prospecting licenses into oil mining leases in the event of a commercial discovery. Second, the Nigerian contract provided for setting aside a portion of the production (a portion referred to as tax oil) for the payment of the special Petroleum Profits Tax, whereas the Egyptian contract did not provide for the delivery of tax oil, since the contractor's income taxes were paid by EGPC on the former's behalf out of EGPC's share of profit oil. Under the Nigerian contract profit oil amounted to what remained of the production after deduction of cost oil (a fixed forty per cent) and tax oil (fifty-five per cent of the production remaining after cost oil, the percentage figure representing the then prevailing rate of the Petroleum Profits Tax). The so remaining profit oil portion is divided between NNPC and its contractor in proportions of 65/35 (lower tranche, up to and including 50,000 barrles per day) and 70/30 (upper tranche, in excess of 50,000 barrles per day). Thirdly, under the Nigerian contract the contractor remained throughout the duration of the contract responsible for carrying out the operations, no joint operating company was established (after making a commercial discovery) as was and still is the practice under Egyptian contracts.

Not before the early 1990s did the Nigerian government again offer oil companies the opportunity to enter into production sharing agreements with NNPC. This change in policy took place in connection with opening up for exploration the Nigerian continental shelf. In fact, prospecting licenses were on offer to be formally acquired by NNPC. Oil companies interested in starting an exploration venture could apply or make a bid for a production sharing contract with respect to NNPC's licenses covering the exploration acreage of their choice. As the licensee, NNPC is responsible for keeping the licenses in good standing and, in case of commercial discovery, for timely converting the prospecting licenses in oil mining leases. The contractor has to work in accordance with the rules provided for in the licenses, possible future oil mining leases and the applicable petroleum legislation (see Chapter 6).

The production sharing mechanism is composed of the following elements. A portion of oil (royalty oil) is reserved for NNPC in order to allow the latter to pay the royalty due to the State under the terms of any offshore oil mining lease (rates depend on water depth and are ranging between twenty per cent (shallow water) and 0.0 per cent (water depth in excess of 1,000 metres). A further portion of production is allocated to the contractor for recovery of the operating and capital costs incurred by him in accordance with rules of accounting incorporated in the agreement. The next portion, referred to as tax oil, is allocated to NNPC in order to allow the latter to pay on behalf of itself and contractor the petroleum income tax due under the Petroleum Profits Tax Act (PPT). In this case, taxable income consists of the difference between the proceeds and deductible costs of the total venture, as calculated in accordance with the rules of the PPT. However this may be, the contractor must be seen (vis-à-vis the tax authorities of the home country of its parent company) as having been subject to the PPT or as having actually paid its share of the PPT imposed. For this reason the PPT paid by NNPC to the government is allocated between the parties on the basis of actual proceeds received and actual costs incurred. The remaining production is divided between NNPC and its contractor in proportions depending on levels of cumulative production.

7.10   THE RUSSIAN FEDERATION

7.10.1   AN OVERVIEW

In the Russian Federation, the concept of the production sharing contract for petroleum operations was introduced by Presidential Decree 2285 of 24 December 1993. The production sharing contract was meant to offer an attractive alternative for the licensing system still provided for by the many times amended Federal Law No. 2395-1 of 21 February 1992 *Concerning the Subsoil* (the Subsoil Law), with the aim to promote foreign investment in exploration for and production of petroleum.

Note. Under the terms of the aforesaid Decree 2285, three production sharing contracts (viz. Kharyaga, Sakhalin I and Sakhalin II) were signed. These contracts enjoy a protected status unless otherwise agreed.

The above mentioned Subsoil Law is a license-based, general mining law. As indicated before, it has been amended on several occasions, most notably by integrating the PSA within its structure, but in principle the Law has remained the same.

    The production sharing agreement was formally adopted by the Federal Law No. 225-FZ of 30 December 1995 *Concerning Production Sharing Agreements*, which entered in force on 11 January 1996 (PSA Law). This Law was amended by Federal Law No. 19-FZ of 7 January, 1999 *Concerning the Introduction of Amendments and Additions to the Federal Law No. 225-FZ* and many times since then, in particular, however, in 2003 by the Federal Law No. 65-FZ of 6 June 2003 (PSA Tax Law).

    The said PSA Tax Law reconciled the PSA Law with the Tax Code of the Russian Federation by means of appending a Chapter 26.4 to section VIII of Part Two of this Tax Code. This Chapter establishes a special tax regime which is to be applied in the context of investors operating under the terms of a production sharing agreement. As said before, the Law also introduced amendments and additions to the PSA Law itself.

    Operations in offshore areas beyond the twelve-mile territorial sea limit are separately governed by the Federal Law No. 187 *On the Continental Shelf of the Russian Federation* of 30 November 1995.

7.10.2   FEDERAL LAW NO. 2395-1 OF 21 FEBRUARY 1992 (AMENDED)

Scope of the Law

The subsoil is the part of the Earth's crust located below the soil layer and, where there is no such layer, below the ground surface and the bottom of water reservoirs and channels, extending to the depths accessible for geological study and development.

The Law regulates the relations arising in connection with the geological study, use and protection of the subsoil of the territory of the Russian Federation, its continental shelf, and also in connection with reclamation of the waste products from mining works and related recycling products, peat, sapropel and other specific mineral resources, including underground waters, the natural brine of drowned rivers and lakes. The Law contains the fundamental legal and economic principles for the overall rational utilization and protection of the subsoil, and provides for the protection of the interest of the State and the citizens of the Russian Federation and of the rights of users of the subsoil.

General Provisions

The legislation of the Russian Federation concerning the subsoil is based on the Constitution of the Russian Federation and consists of this Law and other Federal Laws and other regulatory legal acts, and also the laws and other regulatory legal acts of the constituent entities of the Russian Federation as are adopted in accordance with this Law.

The Law shall have force in the entire territory of the Russian Federation, and shall also regulate the relations of the use of the subsoil on the continental shelf of the Russian Federation in accordance with federal legislative acts concerning the continental shelf and the regulations of international law.

The laws and other regulatory legal acts of constituent entities of the Russian Federation cannot contradict this Law.

The relations connected with the use and protection of land, water sites, plant and animal life and the atmosphere arising when using the subsoil shall be regulated by the relevant legislation of the Russian Federation and the legislation of the constituent entities of the Russian Federation.

Property Rights with respect to the Subsoil

Subsoil within the borders of the territory of the Russian Federation including underground space and minerals contained in the subsoil, energy and other resources is state property. Questions of ownership, using and disposition of the subsoil shall be under the joint jurisdiction of the Russian Federation and the constituent entities of the Russian Federation. Minerals extracted from the subsoil under the terms of the license can be federal state property, the property of the constituent entities of the Russian Federation, or municipal, private and in other forms of property.

The State Subsoil Fund

The State Subsoil Fund shall be comprised of plots which are in use in the form of geometricized blocks of the subsoil, and plots of the subsoil which are not in use, within the territory of the Russian Federation and its continental shelf. The ownership, use and disposition of the State Fund of the subsoil within the territory of the Russian Federation shall be exercised in the interests of the peoples living in the corresponding territories and of all the peoples of the Russian Federation jointly by the Russian Federation and the constituent entities of the Russian Federation.

Plots of the Subsoil of Federal Value

For the purpose of ensuring defence of the country and the safety of the State, certain parts of the subsoil may receive the status of plots of the subsoil of federal value. A list of plots of federal value is officially published.

Use of the Subsoil

The use of the subsoil shall be granted for: (1) regional geological study, including regional geological- geophysical works, geological survey, engineering and geological researches, paleontologic research and other worksfocused on general geological studying of the subsoil, geological works on earthquake prediction, etc; (2) geological studying, including searches and the assessment of mineral deposits and also geological studying and assessment of suitablity of the the plots of the subsoil for construction and operation of the underground constructionwhich are not connected with mining; (3) investigation and mining (*also translated as prospecting and extraction of commercial minerals*), including reclamation of waste materials from mining and the related recycling products; (4) the construction and operation of underground installations which are not connected with mining; (5) the formation of specially protected geological sites which are of scientific, cultural or other significance.

The use of the subsoil may be granted simultaneously for geologic studying, investigation and mining. Thus, investigation and mining, except for investigation and mining on the plot of the subsoil of federal value, can be carried out both during geological studying of the subsoil, and after its completion.

Plots of Subsoil Granted for Use

According to a license to use the subsoil for mining, the construction and operation of underground installations which are not associated with mining, formation of specially protected geological sites, and also according to the production sharing agreement in case of investigation and production of raw mineral substance, the plot of the subsoil shall be granted to the user in the form of a mining allotment - the geometricized block of the subsoil.

The preliminary boundaries of a mining allotment shall be established when a license for the use of the subsoil is granted. Following the development of a technical project and the receipt of a favourable opinion on the project from a State expert commission, and after this project has been agreed with the State mining supervision bodies and State bodies for the protection of the natural environment, documents defining the revised boundaries of the mining allotment (with characteristic sectional views and a list of grid references) shall be included in the license as an integral part thereof.

Any user of the subsoil which has received a mining allotment shall have the exclusive right to use the subsoil within the boundaries of that allotment in accordance with the license which has been granted. Any activities connected with using the subsoil within the borders of the mining allotment, can be performed only with the consent of the aforesaid user.

Limitations on the Use of the Subsoil

The use of an individual plot of the subsoil may be limited or prohibited in the interest of national security and the protection of the natural environment. The use of the subsoil in the territories of inhabited localities, suburban zones, and industrial, transport and communications facilities may be partially or completely prohibited in cases where such use could create a danger to human life or health or cause damage to economic objects or the natural environment.

Periods of Use of Subsoil

The subsoil shall be granted for use for a specified period or without limitation of period. When the use of plots of the subsoil are granted for a specified period, the following periods are applicable: for geological studies – for the term of up to 5 years or for the term of up to 10 years in case of geological studies on plots of the subsoil of domestic sea waters, the territorial sea and the continental shelf; for mining – for the term needed for working off of the mineral deposit, estimated to start from the technical and economic assessment of field development of the minerals, which provide for rational use and protection of the subsoil. The periods of use may be extended on the initiative of the user if needed to complete searches and the assessment or field development or accomplishment of liquidation measures, provided that the user has complied with the conditions which are stipulated in the license.

The License for the Use of Subsoil

The granting of the use of the subsoil is drawn up by special State permission in the form of a license in the standard form with the State Emblen of the Russian Federation and with textual, graphical and other appendices which form an integral part of the license and which determine the main conditions for the use of the subsoil.

Granting the use of the subsoil on the terms of the production sharing agreement is drawn up in the license to use the subsoil. The license certifies the right to use the specified plot (plots) of the subsoil on the terms of the agreement determining all of the necessary conditions of using the subsoil according to the Federal Law 'concerning production sharing agreements' and the legislation of the Russian Federation on the subsoil.

Note. With the above provision, the PSA has been anchored or integrated in the Law. In other words the PSA- conditions have become license – conditions.

The license is the document certifying the right of the holder on using the plot of the subsoil within specified borders in accordance with the stated purpose and during the fixed term provided that the holder complies with the conditions which have been stipulated in advance. Between representatives of public authorities and the user of the subsoil the agreement can be signed which establishes conditions of using such plot, and also obligations on both sides on accomplishment of the said agreement.

The license certifies the right to carry out work involving the geological study of the subsoil; field development of minerals; reclamation of the waste products from mining works and related recycling products; use of the subsoil for the purpose of the construction and operation of underground installations, not connected with mining, formations of specially safeguarded geological sites, collection of mineralogical, palaeontological and other geological specimens.

Contents of the License to Use Subsoil

The license to use the subsoil on the terms of a production sharing agreement shall contain the relevant data and the conditions provided for by the specified agreement.

The Procedure for Granting Licenses to Use the Subsoil

Procedure and conditions of carrying out tenders or auction for the right to use plots of the subsoil under the terms of production sharing agreements are determined in accordance with the legislation of the Russian Federation.

7.10.3   FEDERAL LAW NO. 225-FZ OF 30 DECEMBER 1995
             (AMENDED)

Scope

This Federal Law establishes the legal basis of the relations arising in the course of making Russian and foreign investments in the searches, investigation and production of raw mineral materials in the territory of the Russian Federation, and also on the continental shelf and/or within the exclusive economic zone of the Russian Federation under the terms of production sharing agreements.

General Provisions

This Federal Law regulates the relations arising in the process of the conclusion, execution and termination of production sharing agreements, and defines the main legal conditions of such agreements.

The relations arising in the course of the searches, investigation and production of raw mineral substances, the sharing of extracted production and also its transportation, processing, storage, conversion, use, implementation of disposition or otherwise, are regulated by the production sharing agreement concluded according tot his Federal Law.

The rights and obligations of parties to a production sharing agreement which are of a civil legal nature, are determined according to this Federal Law and the civil legislation of the Russian Federation.

The production sharing agreement (hereinafter referred to as 'the agreement') is the agreement according to which the Russian Federation grants to the subject of business entity (hereinafter referred to as 'the investor'), on a paid basis and for a specified period exclusive rights to searches, investigation and production of raw mineral substances on the plot of the subsoil specified in the agreement, and to carry out the works connected with it, and the investor undertakes to carry out the specified work at its own expense and risk. The agreement determines all necessary conditions connected with using the subsoil, including conditions and procedure for the division of the extracted production between the parties to the aggreement according to the provisions of this Federal Law. Conditions of using the subsoil, established in the agreement, shall be in conformity with the legislation of the Russian Federation.

Right to use the plot of the subsoil can be limited, suspended or stopped in accordance with the conditions of the agreement signed in accordance with the legislation of the Russian Federation.

Lists of plots of the subsoil with respect to which the rights of use on a production sharing basis may be granted according to the provisions of this Federal Law (hereinafter referred to as 'the List'), shall be established by Federal Laws.

Drafts of the specified Federal Laws, and also drafts of Federal Laws concerning modification and additions to these specified Federal Laws, shall be submitted to the State Duma of the Federal Assemby of the Russian Federation accompanied by the conclusions of the Government of the Russian Federation and decisions of legislative (representative) bodies of the constituent entities of the Russian Federation in whose territories the corresponding plots of the subsoil are located.

To the List shall be added plots of the subsoil which for reasons of feasibility are so included by the Government of the Russian Federation.

No more than 30 per cent of reserves of commercial minerals which have been explored and recorded on the State balance sheet may be granted on a production sharing basis.

The basis for inclusion in the List is the lack of the possibility of geological studying, investigation and mining under any condition of use of the subsoil provided for by legislation of the Russian Federations other than the terms of the production sharing agreement. Confirmation of lack of such possibility shall be the holding of an auction for the granting of the right to use the plot of the subsoil on conditions other than production sharing in accordance with the Law of the Russian Federation 'about the subsoil' and the recognition of the auction as being void owing to the absence of participants. In case of such confirmation the plot of the subsoil in question can be included in the List if the following conditions are satisfied: the development of the plot can provide jobs and promote town-forming, and termination of development would have negative social consequences; the development is necessary for drawing into economic circulation of minerals which are situated on the continental shelf of the Russian Federation and in the region of the Far North and comparable districts and lie in areas where there are no human settlements, transport and other infrastructure; the development requires the use of special high cost technology for production of difficult, considerable reserves of commercial minerals which occur under dificult mining-and geological conditions.

The Parties to the Agreement

Parties to the agreement are on the one part the Russian Federation (hereinafter 'the State'), on behalf of which the Government of the Russian Federation is authorized to act; and on the other investors – a legal entity or a consortium of legal entities created on the basis of a joint venture agreement without having the status of a legal entity which invest its own, borrowed or attracted resources (property and/or property rights) in searches, investigation and production of raw mineral substances and are users of the subsoil under the terms of the agreement. If a consortium of legal entities not having the status of a legal entity acts as investor under the agreement, participants in such consortium shall have joint and several rights and obligations under the agreement.

Using Plots of the Subsoil on the Terms of the Agreement

The right to use plots of the subsoil on the terms of a production sharing agreement is granted to the investor on the basis of the agreement signed according to this Federal Law. The plot of the subsoil is granted to the investor for use in accordance with the terms of the agreement. Thus the license to use the plot of the subsoil which certifies right to use the plot of the subsoil specified in the agreement, is issued to the investor according to the procedure established by the legislation of the Russian Federation 'About the subsoil', within 30 days from the date of signing of the agreement.The specified license is issued for the duration of the agreement and is subject to prolongation or renewal or termination in accordance with the terms of the agreement. In the event that the investor is a consortium of legal entities which does not have the status of a legal entity, the license in question is issued to one of the participants in the consortium in which respect the license will indicate that this participant will speak on behalf of the consortium and also indicate all other participants.

Duration of the Agreement

The duration of the agreement is established by the parties in accordance with the legislation of the Russian Federation, as in force on the date of signing the agreement. At the initiative of the investor and on condition that the investor has fulfilled the obligations which it undertook, the validity of the agreement is prolonged for such a period as is sufficient to complete the economially reasonable production of raw mineral substances and to ensure the rational use and protection of the subsoil. The conditions and the procedure for such prolongation are determined by the agreement. In case of prolongation of the agreement the corresponding license to use the subsoil is subject to renewal for the duration of the agreement by the authorities which have granted this license.

Procedure for Signing Agreements

The agreement can be concluded with the winner of the auction which is carried out according to the procedure established by the legislation of the Russian Federation and within the time limits agreed by the parties. The winner of the auction is the participant of the auction who has offered the highest price for the right to conclude the agreement.

Agreements shall be concluded on the basis of the provisions established by the legislation of the Russian Federation. The agreements connected with the use of plots of the subsoil located on the continental shelf of the Russian Federation and (or) within the exclusive economic zone of the Russian Federation, and also changes and additions made to specified agreements shall be affirmed by separate Federal Laws.

The agreement shall be signed on behalf of the State by the Government of the Russian Federation.

Conditions Applicable to the Carrying Out of Works

The works and types of activity which are envisaged by the agreement (hereinafter referred to as 'works under the agreement') shall be carried out according to programmes, projects, plans and budgets which shall be approved in accordance with the procedure determined by the agreement. Works under the agreement are carried out subject to complying with the requirements of the legislation of the Russian Federation, and also subject to complying with the standards approved in accordance with the established procedure (regulations, rules) with respect to safe conduct of works, protection of the subsoil, the environment and public health. In this respect, the agreement shall impose on investor obligations such as: - the granting to Russian legal entities a preferential right to participate in works under the agreement as contractors, suppliers, carriers or in another capacity based on agreements (contracts) with investors; - to employ citizens of the Russian Federation, the number of which shall at least account for 80 per cent of the total of all workers employed; and to employ foreign workers and specialists only during the intial stages of the works under the agreement or in the absence of citizens of the Russian Federation having the required qualifications; - to acquire equipment, devices and materials necessary for geological studying, production, transportation and processing of commercial minerals of Russian origin of which the value amounts to not less than 70 per cent of the overall value of equipment, devices and materials which are acquired (including acquisitions under lease agreements, leasing and on other grounds) in each calendar year for carrying out the works under the agreement, and the purchase costs and costs of using which are compensated to the investor by compensatory production. In this respect, for the purposes of this Federal Law, equipment, devices and materials shall be deemed to be of Russian origin if they are made by Russian legal entities and/or citizens of the Russian Federation in the territory of the Russian Federation from units, parts, designs and accessories, at least for 50 per cent in value terms made in the territory of the Russian Federation by Russian legal entities and/or citizens of the Russian Federation; - implementing measures directed at prevention of adverse effects of specified works on the environment and also measures to remedy the consequences of such effects; insuring liability to pay compensation for damage in case of accidents which have caused the adverse effects on the environment; - removing all construction, installations and other property upon termination of the works under the agreement, and clearing the territory in which the works under the agreement were carried out.

The parties must also stipulate in the agreement that at least 70 per cent in value term of technological equipment for mining, and for the transportation and initial processing (if this provided for by the agreement) of the extracted minerals, acquired and / or used by the investor for carrying out the works under the agreement, shall be of Russian origin. This provision shall not apply to the use of main pipeline transport facilities, the construction and acquisition of which is not provided for in the agreement.

To the extent that above listed provisions conflict with the principles of the World Trade Organisation, in case the Russian Federation would join his organisation, said provisions lose force or shall be brought into accord with these principles within time limits and according to the procedure which are provided for in documents of the World Trade Organisation and the agreement on the accession of the Russian federation to the World Trade Organisation.

When carrying out works under the agreement at sites which are located in the territories of traditional accommodation and economic activity of indigenous small ethnic minority communities, the investor shall take, as stipulated by the legislation of the Russian Federation, measures for protection of primordial habitat and the traditional lifestyle of these communities, and also provide payment of the appropriate compensations in the instances required and according to the procedures which are established by the Government of the Russian Federation.

The carrying out of works under the agreement, including accounting according to the specific provisions of this Federal Law, shall be organised by the investor or on its instructions by the operator of the agreement. As such operator of which the scope of activity shall be limited to the organisation of the specified works, can act a branch or legal entity created by the investor for these purposes in the territory of the Russian Federation, or a legal entity which is engaged by the investor for these purposes, or foreign legal entities which carries out activities in the territory of the Russian Federation. Investor is liable to the State for the operator's actions with its assets as if such actions were the investor's own.

Upon completion of specific stages of searches and investigation of mineral deposits the investor shall return plots of the territory which it has been transferred to it for use in accordance with the terms of the agreement. The sizes of the returned plots, and also the procedure, times and conditions of their return are determined by the agreement.

Geological, technical and economic information regarding sites at which works under the agreement are carried out and at which mining is planned shall be made available for state examination according to the procedure and volume established by the legislation of the Russian Federation.

For the purpose of co-ordinating activities relating to carrying out the works under the agreement provision shall be made for stablishing a managing committee which shall be composed of an equal number of representatives from each party. The numerical composition, the rights and obligations of the managing committee and also the procedure for its work is determined by the agreement. The procedure for appointment of the representatives of the State in the managing committee, their powers and also the procedures for preparation and acceptance of decisions by the appointed persons on behalf of the State is established by the Government of the Russian Federation.

Production Sharing

1. Extracted production shall be shared between the State and the investor according to the agreement which shall provide for conditions and the procedure for:
   - determinations of total volume of extracted production and its value;
   - determinations of the part of the extracted production possession of which is tranferred to the investor for compensation of

its cost incurred in carrying out the works under the agreement (hereinafter referred to as 'compensatory production'). In this respect the ultimate level of compensatory production shall not exceed 75 percent, or in case of extraction on the continental shelf, 90 per cent. The composition of the costs for which the investor can be compensated out of compensatory production, is determined by the agreement in accordance with the legislation of the Russian Federation;

– division between the State and the investor of profit production which is understood to mean extracted production less that part of the production the monetary equivalent of which is used to discharge the taxes on mining, and less compensatory production;

– transfers by the investor to the State of that part of the extracted production that belongs it in accordance with the terms of the agreement or its monetary equivalent;

– receipt by the investor of that part of the extracted production that belongs to it in accordance with the terms of the agreement.

2. In some cases the sharing of extracted production between the State and the investor can take place according to another procedure than the one described in 1. above. In this case the agreement shall provide for conditions and the procedure for:

– determination of total volume of extracted production and its value;

– division between the State and investor of the extracted production or the monetary equivalent thereof and determination of the shares belonging to the State and the investor respectively. The sharing proportions are determined by the agreement depending on geologo-economic and cost estimates of the plot of the subsoil, the engineering design, indicators of the technical-and- economic assessment of the agreement. In this respect the share of the investor of the extracted production shall not exceed 68 per cent;

– transfers to the State of that part of the extracted production that belongs to it in accordance with the terms of the agreement or its monetary equivalent;

– receipt by the investor of that part of the extracted production that belongs to it in accordance with the terms of the agreement.

The signing of the agreement containing specified conditions and procedure for the sharing of extracted production shall be stipulated by the conditions of the auctions.

3. The agreement can provide for only one method of sharing the extracted production. The agreement cannot provide for transition from one method of sharing extracted production to the other, nor for replacement of one method of sharing extracted production by another.

Right of Ownership of the Investor to Extracted Production

That part of the extracted production that according to the sharing conditions of the agreement is the share of the investor, shall be owned by the investor. Raw mineral substances of which the investor became the owner in accordance with the terms of the agreement can be exported from the customs area of the Russian Federation on conditions and according to the procedure which are specified in the agreement, without quantitative export restrictions, except as specified by the provisions of the Federal Law 'About state regulation of foreign trade activity'.

Distribution of the State Share of Extracted Production

Distribution of the monetary equivalent of the extracted production and also other income received by the State as a result of the sharing of extracted production, between the Russian Federation and the constituent entities of the Russian Federation in which territory the plot of the subsoil granted for use is located, is carried out according to the procedure established by the Federal Laws. Similar income received from agreements with respect to plots of the subsoil of domestic sea waters, the territorial sea, the continental shelf of the Russian Federation is transferred to the federal budget.

Right of Ownership to Property and Information

1. Property which is newly created or acquired by the investor and which is used by it for carrying out the works under the agreement, shall be owned by the investor, unless otherwise provided for by the agreement. The ownership of specified property can pass from the investor to the State from the date that the value of the said property has been fully compensated; or from the date of termination of the agreement; or from another date approved by the parties subject to conditions and according to the procedure which is provided for by the agreement. In this respect, for the duration of the agreement the

investor is granted the exclusive right to use that property without charge for work under the agreement, and the investor bears the burden of maintaining the property used by it and the risk of the property's accidental destruction or accidental damage.

2. All primary geological, geophysical geochemical and other information, data concerning its interpretation and derived data, and also samples of rock formations, including core samples, reservoir liquids obtained by the investor as a result of carrying out the works under the agreement, shall be owned by the State. Subject to compliance with the confidentiality terms provided for by the agreement, the investor has the right to use freely and without charge such information, data and samples for the purpose of carrying out the works under the agreement.

Transportation, Storage and Processing of Raw Mineral Substances

1. The investor shall have the right of free access to pipeline transport facilities on a contractual basis, and also the right of free use on a contractual basis of pipeline and other forms of transport facilities, facilities for storage and processing of raw mineral substances without any discriminatory conditions.

2. In carrying out works under the agreement the investor has the right to construct facilities for the storage, processing and transportation of raw mineral substances, the ownership of which is determined by the agreement taking into account the other provisions regarding ownership rights of the ageement.

Taxes and Payments during the Validity of the Agreement

1. In the context of the performance of an agreement, the special procedure for the calculation and payment of taxes and levies which is established by the Tax Code of the Russian Federation and other legal acts of the Russian Federation concerning taxes and levies, shall apply.

Note. The Tax Code was amended in 2003 by the Federal Law No. 65-FZ of 6 June 2003 by introducing: 'Chapter 26.4. The System of Taxation in the context of Operating under Production Sharing Agreements'.

2. In the context of the performance of the agreement the investor pays one-time payments for the use of the subsoil upon the occurrence of events specified in the agreement and license (bonuses); annual payments for an agreed plot of water and for plots of the seafloor

which are payable according to the procedure established by the agreement in accordance with the legislation of the Russian Federation as at the date of signing of the agreement; the fee for participation in tender (auction); the fee for the issue of a license; regular payments for using the subsoil (rentals); compensation for expenses incurred by the State on searches and investigation of minerals, compensation for the damage caused as a result of carrying out works under the agreement in places of traditional accommodation and economic activity of small groups indigenous people of the Russian Federation. The amount of the specified payments and also the time limits for their payment are determined as part of the conditions of the agreement. In this respect, the procedure for determination of the aforesaid compensations is established by the Government of the Russian Federation.

Stability of Conditions of the Agreement

1. Conditions of the agreement remain in force during the enire duration of the agreement. Changes in the agreement are only allowed by agreement of the parties, and also at the request of one of the parties in the event of an essential change of circumstances according to the Civil Code of the Russian Federation. Agreed changes in the conditions of the agreement become effective in the same way as the original agreement.
2. If during the term of the agreement the legislation of the Russian Federation, the legislation of the constituent entities of the Russian Federation and legal acts of local government bodies will establish regulations which deteriorate the commercial results of the activities of the investor under the agreement, changes shall be made to the agreement which provide to the investor commercial results which could have been received by it in case of application of the legislation of the Russian Federation, the legislation of the constituent entities of the Russian Federation and legal acts of local government bodies in force on the date of signing the agreement. The procedure for the introduction of such changes is determined by the agreement.
   The provisions for changes of conditions of the agreement shall not apply if the legislation of the Russian Federation makes changes to standards (regulations, rules) with respect to the safe conduct of works, protection of the subsoil, environment and public health, including changes for the purpose of bringing those standards into

line with similar standards (regulations, rules) accepted and generally recognized in international practice.

State Safeguards of the Rights of the Investor

1. Protection of the property and other rights acquired and excercised by it according to the agreement is guaranteed to the investor.
2. Regulatory legal acts of federal executive bodies, and also the laws and other regulatory legal acts of constituent entities of the Russian Federation and legal acts of local government bodies shall not apply to the investor if the specified acts set limitations on the rights of the investor acquired and exercised by it according to the agreement, except for instructions of the relevant organs of the supervision, which are issued in accordance with the legislation of the Russian Federation for the purpose of ensuring the safe conduct of works, protection of the subsoil, environment, public health, and also for the purpose of ensuring public and state security.

Dispute Resolution

Disputes between the State and the investor connected with execution, the termination and invalidity of the agreementshall be resolved in accordance with the terms of the agreement in court, in arbitration court or with reference to a Tribunal (including international arbitral institutions).

Sources of translated text: Ernst & Young; CIS Legislation Data Base (translation computer program)

7.11   BRAZIL

7.11.1   LAW NO. 12.351 OF 22 DECEMBER 2010

On 22 December 2010, the Government promulgated the Law No. 12.351 for the specific purpose of developing the areas of the pre-salt petroleum reservoirs (and areas of strategic interest as well) under the regime of production sharing, and for the establishment of a Social Fund.

The definitions and main provisions of this Law in the matter of production sharing are the following:

1. Definitions

'Operator' means: Petroleo Brasileiro S.A. (Petrobras);

'Cost Oil' means: in case of a commercial discovery, that part of the production which corresponds with all costs and investments made under the contract in carrying out exploraton, appraisal, development, production activities and de-commissioning of installation subject to the limits, provisions and conditions established in the contract;

'Profit Oil' means: that part of the production that shall be divided between the Union and the contractor and that is made up of the difference between the total volume of the production and the parts of the production related to cost oil, royalties and, if applicable, an additional special charge;

'Contractor' means Petrobras or the consortium established by Petrobras with the winner of the bidding procedure;

2. The Main Provisions are:

Exploration for and production of oil and natural gas shall take place on the basis of contracts made by the Union in accordance with a regime of production sharing;

Petrobras shall be the operator in all blocks in respect of which a production sharing contract has been made and on this basis shall be assured of a minimum participation in the consortium formed with the winner or winners of the bidding procedure. This minimum percentage is determined by the Ministry of Mines and Energy ('the Ministry'), which may be not lower than 30 per cent.

The Union shall not assume any risks in connection with the exploration, appraisal, development and production activities arising under the production sharing contracts;

All costs and investments necessary for the execution of the production sharing contract shall be borne by the contractor with the right of restitution, in case of commercial discovery, out of cost oil.

On behalf of the Union, the Ministry shall sign the production sharing contracts either directly with Petrobras if the latter does not have to follow a bidding procedure, or otherwise in accordance with the rules of a bidding procedure.

Interested parties need to participate in a competitive bidding procedure if they want to become a partner of Petrobras in a production sharing contract. Such procedure is organised by the Agencia Nacional do Petroleo, Gas Natural e Biocombustiveis (ANP). Only a single item decides the bidding: the winner is the bidder who offers the highest percentage share of profit oil in favour of the Union, taking into account the minimum percentage profit oil determined beforehand by the Ministry. The winner is required to establish a consortium with Petrobras and with the Public Enterprise.

The Public Enterprise is a state-owned enterprise who takes part in the consortium for the purpose of representing and protecting the interests of the Union, but shall not assume any risk nor be responsible for any costs or investments related to exploration, appraisal, development and development activities and de-commissioning of exploration or production installations, arising under the contract.

The rights and obligations of Petrobras and the other contractors shall be in proportion to their participating interest in the contract.

For the management of the operations an operating committee is established, composed of representatives of the Public Enterprise and those of the other members of the consortium. The Public Enterprise appoints one half of the representatives, including the president, the other representatives are appointed by the other members.

Government receipts derived from the regime of production sharing consist of (1) royalties; and (2) a signature bonus.

The royalty amounts to 15 per cent of the value of the production, do not form part of cost oil but are deducted from the total volume of the production in calculating profit oil. The royalty has to be paid by the contractor on a monthly basis as from the date of the start of commercial production. The royalty value shall be established by the competent authority on the basis of market value.

A signature bonus shall have to be paid to the Union on the date of signing of the contract, the amount of which shall be fixed in the contract. The bonus shall not be included in cost oil. Furthermore a participation charge at the rate of 1 (one) percent of the value of the production is payable if the contract area is situated on land. Like the royalties, this charge may not be included in cost oil but is deductible from the total volume of production in calculating profit oil.

Chapter 8

Petroleum Taxation

8.1   AN OVERVIEW

The oldest charge with which the oil and gas producer, as holder of a license or lease, became confronted was a payment in kind or cash to the owner of the petroleum *in situ*, be it the State or exceptionally the owner of the land beneath which the petroleum deposit is located. This payment is known as royalty and has always been expressed as a percentage of the extracted oil and/or natural gas volumes. In addition, the licensee had to pay area rentals and various cash bonuses. Apart from these license-related obligatory payments, the oil and gas producer had to pay taxes (income taxes) on the income earned with its petroleum activities, just like any other commercial enterprise making profits.

This all changed after the 1970s, when producer prices, due to and triggered by political events, started to rise in an unprecedented manner and, in particular in the oil exporting countries of the Middle East Gulf area and Northern Africa, a spectacular gap opened up between the cost of production and the producer price (of exported oil). In reaction thereto and starting in the Middle East Gulf area, host governments sought for ways and means to increase the government take (i.e., the sum of royalty and income taxes) that could be achieved from the petroleum operations undertaken inside their territories. In western countries, the income tax imposed on holders of a production license in their capacity of a commercial enterprise producing petroleum for profit (hereinafter referred to as 'corporation tax') was and still is not suitable for dealing with the peculiarities of the extractive petroleum industry, and higher royalty rates alone were not sufficient to achieve any substantial increase of the government take. To cope with this situation, governments of western oil or gas producing and even exporting countries introduced completely new special petroleum income taxes, supplementary taxes or net or gross profit sharing arrangements, and windfall profit taks, all operating in conjunction with the corporation tax.

As from the same time, non-Western countries outside the Middle East Gulf area, adopted and developed production sharing contracts, which from the outset were meant to improve state control over a national asset, but proved also be very useful in achieving a greater government take simply by adjusting the production sharing proportions in favour of the state party. Production sharing however did not exempt the contractor from having to pay corporation tax or a special petroleum income taks on profits earned with its contract, although the tax rates are not at the level of rates with which licensees have to cope.

The rise of international oil price in the 1970s, which caused all this activity around petroleum income taxation, reached in 1980 its peak at a value of almost USD 37 per barrel, which is about USD 100 per barrel in today's money. Thereafter, the price started to decline, reaching its lowest value of about USD 13 per barrel in 1998. Governments reacted by relieving the tax burden somewhat by abolishing royalties for instance, or improved the production sharing mechanisms in favour of the contractor. After 2000, the international oil price started to climb again and currently appear to stabilize at a level of USD 102 per barrel for Brent and USD 95 per barrel for West Texas Intermediate at Cushing. However high this price level appears to be, it is a level that the petroleum industry needs in order to be financially capable to move to extreme areas like extreme deep water areas or the Arctic.

8.1.1 LICENSE-RELATED TAXATION (WESTERN COUNTRIES)

Holders of an exclusive production license producing petroleum for profit are obliged to make the following payments to the State by way of tax:

Royalty

The royalty is a payment expressed as a percentage of the oil and/or natural gas volumes that are produced by the licensee and which is payable in cash or kind to the owner of the petroleum *in situ*. The royalty is the most basic and oldest known petroleum tax. Royalty is a deductible item for the purposes of the income tax and for the producer it is a cost element decreasing the profitability of its business.

Important elements in the calculation of the royalty are:

(a) the royalty rate, expressed at a percentage of the volumes produced;
(b) if payable in kind, the place where the royalty petroleum must be delivered;
(c) if payable in cash, the place where the royalty value is assessed taking the base value as starting point;
(d) the value chosen as the base value.

As a rule, a theoretical arm's length market value is taken as the base value. If the wellhead is selected as the place of assessment of the royalty value, all capital and operating costs involved in treating, handling and transporting the oil or natural gas production from the wellhead to the market place may be deducted from the theoretical arm's length market value.

Area rentals

Area rentals are a payment in cash which is expressed as an annual amount per square km. Usually, the amount increases the longer the license is kept. Area rentals are deductible items for the corporation tax, similarly as the royalty.

Cash bonuses

Cash bonuses are payments in cash which are due to be paid on the occurence of certain events, e.g., on the day the license is granted, or when the production for the first time reached a certain level. It may also be the (huge) cash payment due to be paid by the successful applicant if the license in question is put up for sale. Most bonuses are not deductible for the income tax.

State net profit share

State net profit share is a levy which is expressed as a percentage share of the net profit. The net profit is the income remaining after payment of corporation tax. The rules of calculation of the state net profit share will be laid down in regulations or in the license. The payment of this share will be an allowable deduction (in the same way as royalty or rentals are) in calculating the taxable income under the rules of the corporation tax. A well known example of a net profit share is the net profit share that is allowed to be offered in the bidding procedure for competitive leases to be granted with respect to the US outer continental shelf under the terms of the US Outer Continental Shelf Lands Act of 7 August 1953, as amended.

State gross profit share

State gross profit share is a levy which is expressed as a percentage share of the gross profit. The gross profit is the income before payment of corporation tax, i.e., gross proceeds less operating costs and depreciation. The sharing of the gross profit takes the place of a special petroleum income tax. The rules of calculation of the gross profit and the State's share thereof will be laid down in the regulations or in the license. The gross profit as defined does not have to be identical to taxable income as defined for the purposes of the corporation tax. As a matter of fact, the sharing of gross profit allows for flexibility and adjustment of the fiscal burden when needed in the light of changing circumstances. For instance, it offers the opportunity to change the State's percentage share and/or to introduce incentives in the form of special cost allowances reducing the amount of the gross profit that has to be shared with the State. Gross profit sharing under a licensing regime had its origin in the 50/50 profit sharing principle that was introduced in Saudi Arabia in December 1950 in respect to its petroleum agreement. This principle meant that the total sum of income tax and all other payments to the State including royalty should not exceed 50 per cent of the gross profits of the concessionaire concerned (this matter is further discussed hereinafter).

State share of excess profits

State share of excess profits is a levy which is calculated on a unit basis as a percentage share of the difference between a certain base price, which is indexed for inflation, and the actually realized sales price. The cash payment is in itself a deductible item in calculating and determining taxable income under the rules of the income tax (in the same way as royalty, rentals and state net profit share are). A well-known example is the US windfall profit tax, which was in effect from 1980 to 1988:

Corporation tax

Corporation tax is a levy on income earned by the holder of an exclusive production license in its capacity of a commercial enterprise from production of petroleum under the terms of its license. The corporation tax is calculated as a percentage of such holder's taxable income. The impact of the tax is determined by the manner in which this taxable income (revenues less allowable deductions and less incentives) is described and calculated and by the applicable percentage rate.

The calculation of the taxable income depends on the following important factors:

    (i) the definition of 'income' and in this context the use of transfer prices instead of prices actually realized in a sales transaction;

  (ii) the treatment of and accounting for stock changes;

 (iii) the description of cost items and type and scope of expenditure allowed to be deducted from sales revenues in calculating taxable income;

 (iv) the modalities (rates, progression and timing) of the writing off of the cost of acquisition of capital assets;

  (v) the treatment of exploration expenditure;

(vi) the treatment of losses incurred in other operations (i.e., in non-petroleum operations or in operations carried out in other licenses);

(vii) the carry forward of losses suffered in previous periods, etc.; and

(viii) additions to the general reserve to meet future liabilities, in particular making deductions to cover the future costs of abandonment of offshore installations or fields generally.

Special petroleum income tax

Special petroleum income tax is a levy on income realized by a licensee from selling its oil and natural gas production. Such tax is introduced when the generally applicable corporation tax is considered not adequate for the extractive petroleum industry.

Concurrency of income taxes and profit sharing

If the licensee is liable to pay the generally applicable corporation tax, any other payment to the State, such as the royalty, area rentals, the state net profit share and excess profit tax, if applicable, is allowed to be deducted from taxable income for the purposes of the corporation tax, in the same way as any recognized and undisputed costs may be deducted from taxable income. Where the corporation tax is applied concurrently with a special petroleum income tax, or concurrently with a gross profit sharing arrangement, special provisions will have to be made to mitigate the impact of these payments. For instance, a special petroleum income tax may be allowed as a deduction in calculating the taxable income under the rules of the generally applicable corporation tax (as is the case in the United Kingdom) or it may be the other way around (as in the case of the special hydrocarbon tax in Denmark, where said tax is levied on the net income (income after payment of the corporation tax) of the licensee). The special petroleum tax may also have to be paid in addition to and independently from the corporation tax (as in Norway). A state gross profit share (which has for instance to be paid by the licensee in the Netherlands) has to all intent and purposes the same effect as a special petroleum income tax. In the Netherlands, where petroleum income is also subject to the corporation tax, the latter is considered as a prepayment of the state gross profit share.

8.1.2   CONTRACT-RELATED TAXATION (NON-WESTERN COUNTRIES)

A commercial enterprise working as a contractor under the terms of a production sharing contract concluded with a state entity of a non-western country is liable to pay tax on its income realized from its operations under the contract. However, on the revenue-side the contractor's taxable income is different from that of a licensee in calculating corporation tax, in that the revenues comprise the sales proceeds of only a part of the production, namely that part of the production that is taken by the contractor for recovery of its costs as prescribed in the contract, and the part that the contractor takes as its share of the profit production.

Usually, the tax levied on contractor's income is not the income tax generally applicable to commercial enterprises in the country, but rather a petroleum income tax specifically designed for taxing income derived from petroleum operations under a production sharing contract.

8.1.3   PETROLEUM RELATED DUTIES (ALL COUNTRIES)

8.1.3.1   Export Duty

This type of levy is calculated as a percentage of the value of exported petroleum and assessed at the point of export. Export duties are rarely imposed on oil or natural gas production. If imposed, it would not change the producer price obtainable for the exports on the world market. Hence, its effect would be to lower the price to be received by the exporting producer.

8.1.3.2   Import Duty

This type of levy is calculated as a percentage of the value of imported petroleum or as a fixed sum per unit of petroleum (weight or volume) and assessed at the point of import. The duty has to be paid by the buyer of the imported production. Import duties make imports artificially more expensive. Such duties are levied if a government of an importing country wishes to protect its domestic oil producers against imports offered at a price with which the domestic producers cannot compete.

8.2   PAST AND CURRENT TAXATION (LICENSES)

8.2.1   THE MIDDLE EAST GULF COUNTRIES

8.2.1.1   Obligatory Payments

The Middle East petroleum agreements of the 1930s (also referred to as concessions if the context so allows) initially only envisaged obligatory payments consisting of signature bonuses, discovery bonuses, certain annual or monthly payments and royalties tied to minimum sums. The concessionaires were exempted from paying any taxes or other impost of every kind, including income taxes, customs duties, import or export taxes.

In contrast, the 1901 D'Arcy concession provided for the payment of sixteen per cent of the annual net profits; whereas the 1933 revised Anglo-Persian concession required a net profit sharing in addition to the payment of a royalty of 4 gold shillings per ton. The net profit sharing consisted of a twenty per cent tax on dividends distributed to the shareholders of the concessionaire in excess of GBP 671,250. Payments on account of royalty and dividend tax were subject to a minimum annual payment of GBP 750,000.

8.2.1.2   The 50/50 Profit Sharing

At the end of December 1950, the first revision of the fiscal regime (whereby Saudi Arabia took the lead) took place. By Royal Decree of 27 December 1950, Saudi Arabia introduced and imposed an income tax at a rate of fifty per cent of the income earned by the concessionaires. The Aramco concession till then providing for exemption from paying income tax had to be revised in this respect. At the time the revision was agreed (30 December 1950), it was also agreed that the total sum of income tax and all other payments to the State should not exceed fifty per cent of the net income of the concessionaire, the so called 50/50 profit sharing principle. Initially, the net income had to be calculated after deduction of foreign income taxes, but in October 1951 it was decided that the net income to be shared had to be the net income before foreign tax.

In 1955 the concessions were revised in two respects:

(i) the concessionaires were obliged to publish the price at which they were ready to sell their production FOB port of export to all comers, which price was referred to as the posted price; and

(ii) the rate of the royalty was increased to 12.5 per cent.

The royalty was calculated by applying the newly agreed rate to the posted price reduced by a temporary percentage discount and a marketing allowance.

Note. In 1958, the government of Venezuela increased the rate of its income tax from twenty-six per cent to forty-five per cent. Up to that time, actually since 1943, concessionaires in that State had been subject to an income tax at a rate of 26 per cent, a royalty at a rate of 16.67 per cent and an additional charge meant as a make-up payment and calculated to increase the total sum of the payments to the State to 50 per cent of the concessionaires' net oil income. It is important to note that the 16.67 per cent royalty had to be expensed and was not considered to be a pre-payment of the income tax as was the case in the Gulf States at that time. The Venezuelan system amounted to a 50/50 profit sharing arrangement and as such it had been adopted by the Gulf States, albeit with a different treatment of the royalty necessitated by the fact that in the Gulf States the rate of the applicable income tax was fifty per cent. After having increased the rate of the income tax to forty-five per cent, while concomitantly repealing the make-up payment, the Venezuelan State received more than fifty per cent of the net income of a concessionaire, succeeding thereby to receive more from its concessionaires than any Gulf State did.

After years of unchanged posted prices, the concessionaires lowered in February 1959 their prices by USD 0.18 per barrel and for a second time, in August 1960, by USD 0.10 per barrel. The total reduction amounted therefore to USD 0.28 per barrel.

Table 8.1   Posted Prices (USD Per Barrel) 1953–1960

	1953	1954	1955	1956	1957	1958	1959	1960
Arabian Light ex Ras Tanura (34°)	1.82	1.93	1.93	1.93	2.00	2.08	1.90	1.80
Irani crude ex Bandar Mashur (34°)		1.91	1.91	1.91	1.98	2.04	1.86	1.77
Iraqi crude ex Fao (34°)	1.79	1.90	1.90	1.85	1.92	1.97	1.80	1.72
Kuwaiti crude ex Mina-al- Ahmadi (34°)	1.64	1.72	1.72	1.72	1.78	1.85	1.67	1.59

The concessionaires had been forced to reduce their posted prices in the struggle for outlets in the West-European market. In that region, the concessionaires were confronted with each other's exports, with oil exported from Venezuela and, as from 1955, with oil exported from the Soviet Union. To counter the competition, the concessionaires were forced to sell their crude oils below the applicable posted prices. Since the 50/50 profit sharing system was calculated on the basis of posted prices, selling below the posted price caused the concessionaires to lose the corresponding fiscal relief. Unable to continue with this practice, the concessionaires decided, as mentioned above, in February 1959 and again in August 1960, to adjust their posted prices to market realities. As mentioned before the price adjustments triggered and caused the establishment of OPEC on 1 September 1960 by the governments of Saudi Arabia, Iran, Iraq, Kuwait and Venezuela. After this event the 50/50 profit sharing arrangement based on posted prices was further developed in continuing negotiations between the governments of the OPEC Gulf States and their respective concession-aires. These practically, permanently ongoing negotiations were focused on two issues, namely:

(i) the rate and fiscal treatment of royalties;
(ii) the level of the posted prices and the rate of the income tax.

With reference to (i). For fiscal purposes, royalties were no longer considered to form a part of the State's fifty per cent profit share and as such a pre-payment on account of income tax. Instead royalties were treated as an expense deductible from gross income in calculating and determining taxable income. Over the period 1964–1966 the concessions were revised to the effect that as of 1964 royalties had to be expensed. At the same time a new system of discounts in respect of the posted price (i.e., 8.5 per cent in 1964, 7.5 per cent in 1965, 6.5 per cent in 1966 and to be reconsidered in the years thereafter in the light of the then prevailing market situation) was agreed as quid pro quo for the acceptance of the increase of the government take and the deviation from the 50/50 profit sharing principle. Not surprisingly, the fact that in Venezuela (and in all Western countries) the royalty had always been expensed for the purpose of the corporation tax was used by OPEC to its advantage. As part of the total overhaul of the OPEC fiscal system set in motion by the 1971 Teheran Agreement, the rate of the royalty was on 1 July 1974 increased from 12.5 per cent to 14.25 per cent. On 1 October 1974 this rate was further increased to 16.67 per cent, to be raised again on 1 November 1974 to 20 per cent. By way of small compensation the posted price of 34° Arabian Light was lowered with effect from that date from USD 11.651 per barrel to USD 11.251 per barrel.

With reference to (ii). In 1966, the government of Saudi Arabia concluded an agreement with its concessionaire to the effect that the posted price would also be applicable for fiscal purposes where sales to third parties were concerned. Hitherto posted prices were only applied for fiscal purposes in connection with sales to affiliated companies.

In October 1970, the Gulf States raised the rate of the income tax from fifty per cent to fifty-five per cent. Following adoption of OPEC Resolution XXI 120 on the 21st meeting of the Conference (December 1970) calling for a settlement and conclusion of all ongoing negotiations on fiscal matters and issues, governments and concessionaires negotiated and concluded on 14 February 1971 in Teheran an agreement on posted price levels and the rate of income tax (the 1971 Teheran Agreement). Under the terms of the Teheran Agreement the income tax rate was raised to fifty-five per cent, and the concessionaires undertook to increase their posted prices in various ways and at various dates. All existing allowances were abolished. The 1971 Teheran Agreement was meant to settle in a binding manner the matter of government take and financial obligations of the concessionaires for a period from 15 February 1971 to 31 December 1975. As part of the agreement, the OPEC Gulf States declared they would not take any action in the Gulf to support any OPEC Member State which might seek or demand any increase in government take above the terms then agreed.

Note. With Libya, which was not a party to the 1971 Teheran Agreement, a separate agreement (the Tripoli Agreement, 2 April 1972) along the lines of the former was made. The 1971 Teheran Agreement was immediately adopted by other oil exporting States, among which were the OPEC Member State Nigeria as well as non-OPEC Member States, such as Oman, Malaysia and Brunei. It should be recalled that the licenses and concession agreements then current in those oil exporting countries contained a 'most favoured nation' clause.

The next increase (by 8.49 per cent) of the posted prices took place on 20 January 1972. It was not the result of the 1971 Teheran Agreement, but that of the Geneva Agreement signed on that date. The latter was supplemental to the 1971 Teheran Agreement and provided for a further increase of the posted price in compensation for the devaluation of the US dollar that occurred soon after the 1971 Teheran Agreement had become effective. In February 1973 the US dollar devalued by ten per cent. OPEC concluded that the 1972 Geneva Agreement (Geneva I) did not adequately respond to these drastic changes. Negotiations were resumed and led to a revision of Geneva I subsequently called Geneva II. The latter contains a calculation of a new posted price as of 1 June 1973.

On 16 October 1973, after the outbreak of the Yom Kippur war (also referred to as the Ramadan war), the OPEC Gulf States decided unilaterally to increase the posted prices, considering themselves no longer bound by the terms of the 1971 Teheran Agreement and Geneva II. The posted prices were raised by no less than seventy per cent. Soon thereafter, with effect from 1 January 1974, the posted prices were raised again (by the respective governments), on this occasion by almost 130 per cent. The Table 8.2 indicates the movements of the posted price (USD per barrel) for 34° Arabian Light resulting from the implementation of the 1971 Teheran Agreement and Geneva II and as of 16 October 1973 and 1 January 1974 from the unilateral actions of the governments.

Table 8.2   Posted Prices Arabian Light (USD Per Barrel) 1971–1974

15 February 1971 Teheran	20 January 1972 Geneva I	1 January 1973 Teheran	1 June 1973 Geneva II	16 October 1973	1 January 1974
2.180	2.479	2.591	2.898	5.119	11.651

Until the end of 1974 the posted prices were maintained at their level as fixed on 1 January 1974. Actually, on 1 November 1974 a small downwards adjustment (from USD 1.651 to USD 11,251) took place, in compensation for the sharply increased royalty and income tax rates. The latter had on 1 October 1974 been increased to 16.67 per cent (as to the royalty) and 65.65 per cent (as to the income tax). On 1 November 1974 the rates were further increased: the royalty rate to twenty per cent and the income tax rate to eighty-five per cent. In respect of the production that could be bought back by the concessionaires under the terms of the state participation agreements a government selling price was introduced, which was set at ninety-three per cent of the posted price, now called the fiscal price. As of 1 January 1975 the official government selling price became the only price that was published, this time by the governments themselves. The fiscal price remained in use for the calculation of royalty and income tax. Application of the new rates on the basis of these fiscal prices resulted in an average government take of ninety-one per cent of the difference between the fiscal price and the cost of production.

At the 42nd meeting of the Conference (Vienna, 12–13 December 1974) it was decided to fix the average government take per barrel calculated with respect to 34° Arabian Light, the marker crude, at USD 10.12, valid for the period 1 January 1975 to 30 September 1975. Taking into account a fiscal price of USD 11.251 per barrel the calculations must have assumed a cost of production (for Arabian Light) of USD 0.13 per barrel. However this may be, after the aforesaid meeting of the Conference the developments of the OPEC fiscal regime lost their meaning since by that time in most Gulf States the concessions had completely been taken over by the State.

8.2.2   UNITED KINGDOM

8.2.2.1   Obligatory Payments

The licensee is obliged to make the following payments:

  (i) an initial payment, which is the payment of a prescribed sum per
      block or per square km comprised in the licensed area;
 (ii) annual payments, which are payments to be made annually of a
      prescribed sum per square km comprised in the licensed area.

With reference to (i) and (ii). The rates of respectively the initial payment
and the annual payments are set out in Schedule 2 to the license.

Note. Previously existing royalty payments were definitively abolished with effect
from 1 January 2003.

8.2.2.2   Payments under Income Tax Laws

Currently, a licensee is liable to pay tax on its income from its operations
under the license under the rules of two types of income taxes, the
corporation tax (CT) and the supplementary corporation tax (SCT).
Holders of older licenses (see below) are also liable to pay a special
petroleum income tax. CT and SCT are imposed under the rules of the
Income and Corporation Taxes Act 1970 (amended). SCT was introduced
in the 2002 Finance Act. The special petroleum income tax is imposed
under the rules of the Oil Taxation Act 1975 (amended), and is referred to
as the Petroleum Revenue Tax (PRT).
     Whereas CT and SCT are imposed on the aggregate income realized by
the licensee from petroleum produced under all and any of his licenses
and/or under all of its participating interests in licenses, PRT is imposed on
petroleum income realized by each person participating in a separate field
('oil field'), except that pursuant to the 1993 Finance Act, oil fields, in
respect of which the development programme has been approved after 16
March 1993, are exempt from paying PRT.
     For the purposes of CT and SCT, the carrying on of the authorized
petroleum activities must be treated as a separate trade, distinct from all
other activities carried on as part of the trade (Oil Taxation Act 1975). This
separation of activities for tax purposes is called the 'ring fencing' of
activities. The existence of the ring fence around petroleum activities
means that losses, which would qualify for being claimed under the

corporation tax, cannot be claimed against income arising from petroleum activities, unless the losses arose from these activities. However, losses incurred in carrying on petroleum activities can be offset against income arising from other activities.

For the purposes of CT and SCT, gross profit is the value of the petroleum disposed of calculated on the basis of prices realized in arm's lengths sales plus 100 per cent of the market value of the change in stocks. All amounts of PRT (see below) paid by a participant in a field may be deducted by him from his taxable petroleum income. Other allowable expenditures include exploration and appraisal costs, intangible development drilling costs, operating expenditure and the cost of closing down a field, including the cost of demolishing an offshore installation. Further details of implementation are from year to year announced in the annual Finance Acts.

The rates of CT and SCT are set annually in the Budget and currently amount for licensees thirty per cent and thirty-two per cent respectively.

For older oil fields, i.e., oil fields for which development consent was given before March 1993, PRT has to be paid. Taxable income (assessable profit) is calculated on a chargeable period of six calendar months basis and separately with respect to the income and expenditures attributable to each person participating in any oil field. It consists in the difference between gross profit plus tariff and disposal receipts on the one hand and allowable expenditures, the supplementary amount (i.e., an 'uplift' on expenditures qualifying to be uplifted) and the cash equivalent of the oil allowance (a proportional part of the gross profit) on the other. Gross profit is the value of the petroleum disposed of calculated on the basis of prices realized in arm's lengths sales plus fifty per cent of the market value of the change in stocks.

The oil allowance is fixed for each field separately and expressed in long tonnes per chargeable period with a cumulative limit. The oil allowance was initially fixed for all offshore fields at 250,000 tonnes with a cumulative limit of 5 million tonnes. For offshore fields situated north of 55 degrees latitude, and approved for development between 31 March 1982 and 16 March 1993 the allowance was doubled to 500,000 tonnes per chargeable period with a cumulative limit of 10 million tonnes. With effect from 1 July 1988 the oil allowance for fields in the Southern Basin (i.e., fields situated between 52 and 55 degrees latitude) was halved to 125,000 tonnes with a cumulative limit of 2.5 million tonnes.

Allowable expenditure includes all expenditure incurred for exploration and exploitation of the field, abandonment costs, but only insofar as they are related to safety and the prevention of pollution, the cost of transport to the United Kingdom and any unrelievable field losses. The supplementary deductible amount or 'uplift' is available in the form of an amount of thirty-five per cent of the qualifying capital expenditure (i.e., the pre-production expenditure and further some production enhancing expenditure). The 'uplift' may only be applied as a deduction until the payout time of the field has been reached. The total tax payable with respect to a field is limited to eighty per cent of the amount by which the adjusted profit for the six months' chargeable period exceeds fifteen per cent of the accumulated qualifying capital expenditure at the end of that period. This so called 'safeguard' is available for a period, which is half as long again as the payback period. The assessable profit may be further reduced by the allowable losses carried forward from the previous chargeable period. The adjusted profit for a chargeable period amounts to the difference between gross profit on the one hand and non-qualifying expenditure on the other.

Note. 'Uplift' and 'safequard' are thought to be not relevant anymore since by now most PRT-paying fields must be past their payback period.

Similarly as the rates for CT and SCT, the rate for PRT is determined in the annual Budget on the basis of the estimated profitability of the petroleum production operations. At the introduction of the tax under the terms of the 1975 Oil Taxation Act the rate was set at forty-five per cent. With effect from 1 January 1979 the rate was increased to sixty per cent and with effect from 1 January further increased to seventy per cent. On 1 January 1983, the rate reached its highest level ever: seventy-five per cent. With effect from 30 June 1993 the rate was lowered to fifty per cent. The frequent changes were all due to and dictated by the fluctuations of the price of oil on the world market.

8.2.3   NORWAY

8.2.3.1   Obligatory Payments

The licensee is required to make the following payments:

  (i) cash bonuses, production bonus;
 (ii) area fee; and
(iii) a production fee (royalty).

When granting a production license a non-recurring fee (cash bonus) may be levied and furthermore a fee may be stipulated which is calculated on the basis of production volume (production bonus).

The licensee shall pay a fee (area fee) for a production license, after expiry of the initial period, calculated per square km.

The licensee shall pay a fee calculated on the basis of the quantity and value of petroleum produced at the shipment point of the production area (production fee). With regard to petroleum which is injected, exchanged or stored prior to being delivered to be taken ashore or used for consumption, the production fee shall be calculated on the basis of the quantity and value of the petroleum at the shipment point for the original production area at the time when the petroleum according to contract is delivered to be taken ashore or used for consumption. Nevertheless, a production fee shall not be paid for petroleum produced from deposits where the development plan is approved or where the requirement to submit a plan for development and operation is waived after 1 January 1986.

The King may decide that the area fee and the production fee shall not be paid wholly or partly, or that the duty to pay such fees shall be postponed.

Note. As a matter of fact, royalty on natural gas for all fields was abolished in 1992. With effect from 1 January 2000 royalty on crude oil from a series of important royalty paying oil fields were either abolished or phased out over a three- or six-year period.

8.2.3.2 Payments under Income Tax Laws

The licensee deriving income from the exploitation of subsea petroleum deposits and from pipeline transportation is liable to pay tax on such income in accordance with the Act of 13 June 1975 No. 35 relating to the Taxation of Subsea Petroleum Deposits, etc. (the Petroleum Taxation Act). Last amended by Act of 29 June 2007 No. 51.

The Act governs the taxation of exploration for and extraction of subsea petroleum deposits, and activities and work relating thereto, hereunder pipeline transportation of extracted petroleum in internal Norwegian waters, territorial sea and on the continental shelf (or in areas outside these seas or outside Norwegian juridiction to the extent that Norway has the right to impose taxes on aforesaid petroleum activities according to international law or special agreement with a foreign State).

8.2.3.3   Payments under the Common Tax Act (as modified for the purpose)

Income earned from the above described petroleum activities shall be liable for tax pursuant to the provisions of the common Tax Act, taking into account the special rules on the assessment of taxable income set forth in this Law.

These special rules are the following: Gross income shall be determined on the basis of the norm price. The norm price shall be established by the Ministry and shall correspond to the price at which petroleum could have been traded between independent parties in a free market. Expenses incurred in acquiring pipeline and production facilities, including the installations which form part of, or are related to such facilities, may be depreciated at a maximum rate of 16.67 per cent per annum, with the first year of the depreciation period being the year in which such expense was incurred. Expenses incurred in acquiring operating assets may be depreciated at a maximum rate of 33.33 per cent per annum, with the first year of the depreciation being the year in which such expense was incurred, provide that the purpose is production, transportation by pipeline and processing of gas to be liquefied by cooling in a new large-scale cooling facility located in certain counties and municipalities as specified in the Law. Losses may be deducted from income in subsequent years without time-limit. One-half of the losses sustained in non-petroleum activities inside Norway may also be deducted.

Under no circumstance shall any deduction be granted in respect of provisions for the payment of future expenses for the removal of facilities used in extraction, processing or pipeline transportation.

8.2.3.4   Payment of the Special Tax to the State

Taxpayers who are involved in extraction, processing and pipeline transportation within the above described areas shall pay a special tax to the State on income from such activities. The special tax shall be calculated at such rate as is resolved by the Storting for each year.

The special tax shall be assessed on such income from the above specified activities in conformity with the basis for the assessment of the common income tax. Deductions are not granted for any loss resulting from other activities than extraction and pipeline transportation. The special tax is payable on net income as calculated under the common tax but corrected for uplift. The uplift shall be 7.5 per cent of the cost price of operating assets. The cost price of the operating asset shall be included when calculating the taxable income for four years, beginning with the first year of depreciation thereof. The uplift shall be deducted when calculating the special tax.

The special tax shall not be deducted upon assessment of the other income tax.

8.3 PAST AND CURRENT TAXATION (CONTRACTS)

8.3.1 INDONESIA

In the 1980s, the Indonesian government was persuaded to change the income tax paying procedure and to accept direct payment of income taxes by the contractor, due to the difficulties which US oil companies experienced (in their dealings with the US Internal Revenue Service [the IRS]) in getting the tax payments made by Pertamina on behalf of contractor accepted and recognized for the purpose of the US foreign tax credit. The IRS considered and treated the Indonesian production sharing agreements as royalty paying agreements in respect of which no income tax in the sense as understood under US fiscal rules was paid. Under the terms of the revised contracts the contractor had to pay itself the income tax and dividend tax then levied at a combined rate of fifty-six per cent in respect of its profits (i.e., the value of the contractor's share of profit oil). On that same occasion, cost recovery rules were brought in line with cost deduction schedules as applicable under customary western style corporation tax. In recent years the combined tax rate fell to forty per cent.

8.3.2 ANGOLA

Contractors are liable to pay a special petroleum income tax under the terms of the Law No. 13 on Taxation of Petroleum Activities of 24 December 2004. This Law applies to all entities, whether Angolan or foreign, performing petroleum operations in Angolan territory, as well as in other territorial or international areas within the tax levying jurisdiction of the Republic of Angola, as recognized by international law or agreements. The main tax charges introduced by the Petroleum Tax Law are a petroleum production tax and a petroleum income tax. The petroleum production tax (the equivalent of a royalty), however, is not applicable to production sharing contracts. The petroleum income tax is levied on the taxable income assessed as set forth in this Law generated by the following activities: exploration, development, production, storage, sales, exportation, treatment and transportation of petroleum. For the purpose of assessing the taxable income the crude oil produced shall be valued at the market price calculated on the basis of the actual FOB prices obtained through arm's length sales to third parties in accordance with the rules set forth in this Law.

Taxable income shall be the profit assessed at the end of each fiscal year and as far as production sharing agreements are concerned be assessed for each development area separately and independently from other development areas. Hence, in each development area taxable income shall be the profit petroleum resulting from the deduction – from the total amount of petroleum produced in the area – of the cost recovery petroleum and of the receipts of Sonangol in accordance with the provisions of the relevant production sharing agreement.

The assessment of tax costs shall be undertaken in accordance with the following rules: the lifting and the right to freely dispose of cost recovery petroleum is limited to a maximum percentage of the total amount of petroleum produced and saved in each development area as set forth in the corresponding production sharing agreement; exploration expenses shall be recoverable from the unused balance of cost recovery petroleum within each development area after recovery of expenses for production, development, and administration and services subject to the applicable maximum amount of cost recovery petroleum; exploration expenses shall not be entered into the accounts as fixed assets and shall not be amortized; expenses for production, development and administration and services in each development area shall only be recovered using cost recovery petroleum produced in the same area. Development expenses shall be entered into the accounts as fixed assets and once the investment allowance (if provided for by the production sharing agreement) has been added, shall be amortized at an annual rate of twenty-five per cent; production expenses in each development area shall only be recoverable using cost recovery petroleum produced in the same area and shall be entered into the accounts as expenses. Production and development expenses which are common to more than one development area shall be shared among said development areas in proportion to the annual output of each development area; administration and service expenses, part of which shall be entered into the accounts a fixed assets and be amortized at an annual rate of twenty-five per cent, shall be allocated to the expenses for exploration, development and production according to a method set forth in the Law.

For production sharing agreements the tax rate is fifty per cent.

Source of translation: Miranda, Correia, Amendoeira & Associados, Sociedade de Advogados.

8.3.3   THE RUSSIAN FEDERATION

The Federal Law No. 65-FZ of 6 June 2003 which entered into force on 9 June 2003 (usually referred to as the PSA Tax Law) appended a new Chapter 26.4 to section VIII.1 of Part Two of the Tax Code of the Russian Federation. This Chapter establishes a special tax regime which is to be applied in the context of investors operating under production sharing agreements which have been concluded in accordance with the Federal Law No. 225-FZ of 30 December 1995 'Concerning Production Sharing Agreements', provided that the agreements were concluded after an auction was held for granting the right to use the subsoil on a basis other than production sharing, and the auction had been declared void; and provided that in case of a 'non-standard' agreement (i.e., an agreement providing for a single, all-in split of production, without a cost recovery procedure) the State's share of the total volume of extracted production is not less than thirty-two per cent; and provided further that the agreement provides for an increase of the State's share of profit production in the event that the economics of the investor's operations improves.

The special tax regime shall be applied during the entire period of validity of the agreement.

The special tax regime provides for the payment of the aggregate of taxes and levies established by the tax and levy legislation of the Russian Federation to be replaced by the sharing of extracted production as envisaged in the agreement, with exception of taxes and levies the payment of which is envisaged by this Chapter.

In the context of a 'standard' agreement, an investor shall pay the following taxes and levies:

- Value Added Taks (VAT)
- Tax on the profits of organisations (profits tax)
- Tax on the extraction of commercial minerals (mineral production tax (MPT)
- Unified social tax
- Payments for the use of natural resources
- Charges for negative impact on the environment
- Charges for the use of water
- State duty, custom levies, land taxs, excise duty.

The amounts paid by the investor in respect of all of the above listed taxes and levies with exception of MPT and profits tax are recoverable by the investor under cost recovery provisions of the agreement. Investors are exempt from the payment of regional and local taxes and levies.

In the context of a 'non-standard' agreement, the investor does not have to pay MPT or profits tax, but has only to pay:

The unified social tax, - State duty, - custom levies, - VAT, - charges for negative impact on the environment. The investor shall be exempted from the payment of regional and local taxes and levies.

Investors operating under 'standard' agreements are liable to pay profits tax with respect to the profit earned from their operations. For the purposes of calculating the tax base of the profits tax all expenses made by the investor in operations under the agreement are divided into (1) expenses which are reimbursable out of compensatory production (reimbursable expenses), and (2) expenses which are not so reimbursable, but are accepted for reduction of the tax base. These expenses are specified as consisting of financing costs, bonuses, MPT and expenses in connection with participating in an auction. The taxable profit shall be taken to be the value of profit production belonging to the investor in accordance with the agreement, reduced by the expenses specified above.

The rate of the profits tax current at the time of signing the agreement is the rate that will apply for the duration of the contract. The current rate of the profits tax is 24 per cent.

The MPT was introduced by Federal Law No. 126-FZ of 8 August 2001, by means of adding Chapter 26 (Articles 334 to 346) to the Tax Code. The tax was meant for royalty/tax concessions under the terms of the Federal Law 'About the subsoil'. The PSA Tax Law confirms that under a production sharing agreement MPT is payable on oil and gas condensate at a rate of 340 roubles per tonne multiplied by a coefficient Cp which reflects the movement in world oil prices. This tax rate shall be applied with a coefficient of 0.5 until the maximum level of commercial extraction of oil and gas condensate, which may be established in any given agreement, is reached. Once the maximum level has been reached the tax rate shall be applied with a coëfficient of 1. The MPT is not a reimbursable expense, but belongs to the expenses that reduce the tax base of the profits tax.

Source of translated text: Ernst & Young.

Chapter 9

Petroleum and the 1982 Convention 'On the Law of the Sea'

9.1   ORIGIN AND INITIAL DEVELOPMENT

After the end of the Second World War, drilling technology and techniques had progressed to the point where drilling offshore beyond the shallow coastal waters became feasible. This meant that in a technical sense offshore petroleum operations were ready to move beyond the limits of the territorial sea and coastal State jurisdiction. At that moment, the breadth of the territorial sea and hence the seaward extent of the territorial sovereignty of the coastal State was not internationally agreed. Maritime nations, among them the US, adhered to the three-mile limit which was historically derived from the range of shore-based cannon. The importance and significance of this range followed from the doctrine brought forward by Hugo Grotius in the seventeenth century, stating that claims to sovereignty over the contiguous sea was justified on the basis of defending the coastal zone against aggressors but that the coastal State should be able, if challenged, to support the claimed sovereignty by military force. In practical terms Grotius' doctrine led to the theory that the seaward limits of territorial sovereignty should coincide with and could not exceed the range of shore-based cannon. In 1728 the Italian jurist Galiani proposed to fix this range at three miles, but this limit was only supported and put in practice by the seafaring nations such as the US. Under the auspices of the League of Nations an attempt to achieve uniformity in this matter was made at the 1930 Hague Codification Conference, but no agreement could be reached. Beyond the seaward limits of the territorial sea the domain of the high seas begins. In respect of the high seas four freedoms were internationally recognized: the freedom to navigate; the freedom to fish; the freedom to lay cables and pipelines; and the freedom of overflight. The possibility of exploring for and of exploitation of mineral resources of the seabed and the subsoil of the area of the high seas had never been considered. Attention had always been focused on the superjacent waters and on the commercial use that could be made of these waters, in practice amounting only to navigation and fishing. The question of where the jurisdiction lay over the natural resources underneath the high seas had to be solved before the industry could move with confidence into the domain of the high seas.

9.2   THE 1945 TRUMAN PROCLAMATION

In 1945 the US tried to solve the problem by simply unilaterally claiming the sovereignty over the resources of the subsoil and the seabed of the continental shelf beneath the high seas but contiguous to the coasts of the US. The claim is stated in the Proclamation issued on 28 September 1945 by the US President Harry S. Truman as follows:

> Now, therefore, I, Harry S. Truman, President of the USA do hereby proclaim the following policy of the USA with respect to the natural resources of the subsoil and seabed of the Continental Shelf. Having concern for the urgency of conserving and prudently utilizing its natural resources, the Government of the USA regards the natural resources of the subsoil and seabed of the Continental Shelf beneath the high seas, but contiguous to the coasts of the US as appertaining to the US, subject to its jurisdiction and control. In cases where the Continental Shelf extends to the shores of another State, or is shared with an adjacent State, the boundary shall be determined by the US and the State concerned in accordance with equitable principles. The character as high seas of the waters above the Continental shelf and the right to their free and unimpeded navigation are in no way thus affected.

The Proclamation restricts the natural resources jurisdiction of the US to its continental shelf. Remarkably, the Proclamation does not contain a definition or description of what area of the seabed constitutes a continental shelf. However, in the accompanying press release the continental shelf is described as submerged land which is contiguous to the continent and which is covered by no more than 100 fathoms (600 feet) of water. The Proclamation was a declaratory statement, on the basis of which natural resources in unknown quantities were acquired at no costs at all. In the preamble of the Proclamation practical and economic arguments and reasons are listed meant to justify this acquisition. In this connection reference is made to the long-range worldwide need for new sources of petroleum and other minerals; the expectation that such resources underlie many parts of the Continental Shelf off the coasts of the USA and that with modern technological progress their utilization is already practicable, or will become so at an early date; the requirement of recognized jurisdiction over these resources in the interest of their conservation and prudent utilization, when and as development is undertaken; and the view of the US government that the exercise of jurisdiction over the natural jurisdiction over said natural resources by the contiguous nation is reasonable and just. In support of this view the following arguments were brought forward:

(i) the effectiveness of measures to utilize or conserve these resources is contingent upon cooperation and protection from the shore;

(ii) the continental shelf may be regarded as an extension of the land mass of the coastal nation and thus is naturally appurtenant to it;

(iii) the said resources frequently form a seaward extension of a pool or deposit lying within the territory; and

(iv) self-protection compels the coastal nation to keep close watch over activities off its shores, which are of the nature necessary for the utilization of the said resources.

Note. The prolongation-argument, i.e., the argument that the continental shelf should be regarded as an extension of the land mass of the coastal State and thus naturally appurtenant to it, carries enough weight to support and justify the proclaimed jurisdiction. All other arguments that are mentioned in the preamble are in fact superfluous. They only serve to make clear why in the first place the US was keen and found it necessary to proclaim such jurisdiction. The prolongation-argument has more than twenty years later been confirmed by the International Court of Justice at The Hague in its judgment in the *North Sea Continental Shelf Cases* (20 February 1969). In this judgment, the Court held that the rights of the coastal State in respect of the area of continental shelf constituting a natural prolongation of its land territory under the sea existed *ipso facto* and *ab initio*, by virtue of its sovereignty over the land.

The jurisdiction claimed by the Truman Proclamation became Federal Law on the occasion of the enactment of the Act of 7 August 1953 (amended), known as the Outer Continental Shelf Lands Act. In section 3 of the Act the national policy for the outer continental shelf has been clarified by stating the following principles:

(i) the subsoil and seabed of the outer continental shelf appertain to the US and are subject to its jurisdiction, control, and power of disposition as provided in the Act;

(ii) this Act shall be construed in such a manner that the character of the waters above the outer continental shelf as high seas and the right to navigation and fishing therein shall not be affected;

(iii) the outer continental shelf is a vital national resource reserve held by the Federal Government for the public, which should be made available for expeditious and orderly development, subject to environmental safeguards, in a manner which is consistent with the maintenance of competition and other national needs;

(iv) about rights and entitlements of coastal States;

(v) about the responsibilities of all States to preserve and protect marine, human and coastal environment; and

(vi) operations in the outer continental shelf should be conducted in a
safe manner by well-trained personnel using technology, precautions, and techniques sufficient to prevent or minimize the likelihood of blow-outs, loss of well control, fires, spillages, physical
obstruction to other users of the waters or subsoil and seabed, or
other occurrences which may cause damage to the environment or
to property, or endanger life or health.

Note. The 1958 Convention on the Continental Shelf became effective as law in
the United States in 1964.

9.3   PREPARATORY WORK ON CONVENTIONS

As could be expected, the Truman Proclamation triggered a series of
similar unilateral statements, proclamations and legislative actions of other
coastal States.

The first coastal States to do so were Mexico (29 October 1945),
Argentina (11 October 1946), Chile and Peru (1947). In these Latin-
American proclamations jurisdiction was claimed over both epicontinental
sea and continental shelf albeit the freedom of navigation was explicitly
declared to remain unaffected. Whereas Mexico and Argentina, the latter in
particular, were in possession of an extensive continental shelf, Peru and
Chile were both not so fortunate. In fact, the continental shelf adjacent to
the coast of the two countries (and the shelf adjacent to the coast of
Ecuador for that matter) is quite small and narrow. Since the coastal States
were primarily interested in protecting their fisheries, i.e., the living natural
resources of the superjacent waters as opposed to the non-living natural
resources of the seabed and subsoil, they needed a larger area of
jurisdiction, in which to create a protected fishing zone. This persuaded
those countries, joined for the occasion by Ecuador, to claim in 1952
sovereignty and jurisdiction over the contiguous sea up to a distance of 200
nautical miles as measured from their respective coasts. Incidentally, thirty
years later, this distance of 200 nautical miles would be adopted as the
outer limit of the Exclusive Economic Zone (EEZ), a Zone whose
establishment would be one of the main features of the 1982 Convention on
the Law of the Sea.

The Latin-American example was soon followed by the coastal States
in the Middle East Gulf area. On 28 May 1949 Saudi Arabia issued a
similar proclamation and soon thereafter, all in June of that year, Bahrain,
Qatar, Kuwait and the Trucial Coast sheikhdoms, among which Abu Dhabi

and Dubai, did the same. The Saudi proclamation claimed jurisdiction over the subsoil and seabed of those areas of the Gulf seaward from the coastal sea of Saudi Arabia, but contiguous to its coasts. A Saudi royal decree of the same date fixed the breadth of the coastal sea at 6 miles, 3 miles more than the international standard supported and recognized by the seafaring nations at that time. Interestingly, the stated jurisdiction was not restricted to the natural resources of the seabed and subsoil. This left open the possibility that the Saudi government could claim jurisdiction over cables and pipelines crossing its seabed. No statement was made with respect to the living resources of the superjacent waters as had been the case in Latin America. Overlapping claims would be settled in agreement with the State concerned in accordance with equitable principles. Iran enacted legislation concerning its continental shelf on 19 June 1955. The areas as well as the natural riches of the seabed and subsoil up to the limits of the continental shelf, which extends from the coasts of Iran and the Iranian islands in the Persian Gulf and the sea of Oman, were declared to belong to the Iranian government and to fall under its sovereignty. On 27 November 1957 the government of Iraq issued a statement claiming seabed and subsoil jurisdiction in respect of waters contiguous to Iraqi territorial waters along the pattern established by the earlier declarations of Saudi Arabia and the other Gulf countries.

After all these unilateral statements, proclamations and declarations, the international community realized that the matter of sovereignty over the natural resources of the continental shelf urgently needed regulation by an international convention.

By around 1948 the UN International Law Commission had already started work on a codification of the law of the sea. By 1957 the Commission had made such progress with its work that the UN General Assembly could decide (21 February 1957) to convene an international conference of plenipotentiaries in order to prepare and establish the text of one or more conventions on matters regarding the law of the sea. The intended conference convened in Geneva between 24 February and 27 April 1958. The Conference succeeded in adopting (in the Final Act) the text of four separate conventions, namely the Convention on the Continental Shelf; the Convention on the Territorial Sea and the Contiguous Zone; the Convention on the High Seas; and the Convention on Fishing and Conservation of the Living Resources. As had happened before in 1930, the Conference failed to reach agreement on the breadth of the territorial sea. However, agreement was reached on a seaward limit of 12 nautical miles in respect of the contiguous zone (i.e., a zone in the high seas contiguous to the territorial waters, in which zone the coastal State may exercise certain rights for protection of its interests). By limiting the contiguous zone to 12 nautical miles it is implied that no coastal State should claim a seaward limit of its territorial waters exceeding this distance. In order to bring the matter to a conclusion the UN General Assembly called for a second conference on the law of the sea. The Second UN Conference on the Law of the Sea took place again in Geneva from 17 March 1960 to 27 April 1960. At the Conference it proved impossible to get the required majority of votes for any proposed limit. The matter had to await the Third UN Conference on the Law of the Sea, which opened in December 1973 and closed in April 1982. At this Conference the seaward limit of the territorial sea was finally settled at 12 nautical miles (equals 22.224 km), the same distance earlier agreed as the seaward limit of the contiguous zone, now no longer existing as a separate zone.

9.4   THE 1958 CONVENTION ON THE CONTINENTAL SHELF

The Convention on the Continental Shelf signed on 29 April 1958 in Geneva provided the legal basis for undertaking offshore petroleum operations beyond the territorial waters of a coastal State, but within the limits of its continental shelf. For decades this Convention provided the legal framework within which the governments of coastal States developed their own offshore petroleum legislation. And even after the successor Convention, the 1982 Convention on the Law of the Sea, became effective on 16 November 1994, its basic articles concerning the continental shelf survived with one important exception, however, which was the definition of the continental shelf itself.

   In Article 1 of the Convention the term 'continental shelf' is defined as:

   (i) the seabed and the subsoil of the submarine areas adjacent to the coast but outside the area of the territorial sea, to a depth of 200 metres or, beyond that limit, to where the depth of the superjacent waters admits of the exploitation of the natural resources of the said areas; and
   (ii) the seabed and subsoil of similar submarine areas adjacent to the coasts of islands.

This definition has turned out to be a legal and not a geomorphological or geological definition, although in many places 200 metres water depth turns out to be the geomorphological limit of the continental shelf. However it was not intended that the coastal State should be restricted to this water depth if it would prove technically possible to develop and produce natural resources beyond that depth. Whereas, it was equally not intended that under the Convention coastal States could ever claim jurisdiction over the natural resources of the deep seabed area. To whom such sovereignty should be accorded was regarded, in absence of any technical possibility to make use of such rights, as a problem that did not have to be addressed by the Conference and could be left for regulation in the future.

From the description of the continental shelf as an area adjacent to the coast (but outside the territorial waters) it follows that strictly speaking between the coast and the seaward boundary of the shelf there may not be areas in which the water depth exceeds the water depth designated as the seaward boundary i.e., 200 metres or more, as the technical case may be. However, it was generally considered, as appears from state practice, e.g., the UK/Norway North Sea Boundary Agreement of 10 March 1965, that such areas of greater water depth should not be allowed to limit the continental shelf but should be treated as local features of the continental shelf. Nonetheless, the status of local feature was not considered to mean that such local areas of greater water depths would fall under the jurisdiction of the coastal State concerned. The latter could not exercise any sovereign rights over deeper water area until it would have become technically feasible to undertake exploitation work in such areas. The whole problem was solved by the 1982 Convention in accordance to which the continental shelf extends at least to 200 nautical miles as measured from the shoreline, regardless of the geomorphological features of the sea bottom.

No indication of what constitutes an island is given. Perhaps it was thought at the time that this was not needed. But what would certainly have been helpful if a distinction was made as to the size of an island i.e., there should be a difference between say Greenland and an isolated atoll in the South Pacific. The continental shelf of the latter could be, but not necessarily so, disproportional large.

The basic rights and obligations assigned to the coastal State and, as said before, have later been adopted by the 1982 Convention, are the following (Articles 2–5 inclusive)

The coastal State exercises over the continental shelf sovereign rights for the purpose of exploring it and exploiting its natural resources. These rights are exclusive in the sense that if the coastal State does not explore the continental shelf or exploit its natural resources, no one may undertake these activities, or make a claim to the continental shelf, without the express consent of the coastal State. The rights of the coastal State do not depend on occupation, effective or notional, or any express proclamation. Aforesaid natural resources consist of the mineral and other non-living resources of the seabed and subsoil together with living organisms belonging to sedentary species, that is to say, organisms which at the harvestable stage, either are immobile on or under the seabed or are unable to move except in constant physical contact with the seabed or the subsoil (Article 2).

The rights of the coastal State over the continental shelf do not affect the legal status of the superjacent waters as high seas, or that of the airspace above those waters (Article 3).

Subject to its right to take reasonable measures for the exploration of the continental shelf and the exploitation of its natural resources, the coastal State may not impede the laying or maintenance of submarine cables or pipelines on the continental shelf (Article 4).

The exploration of the continental shelf and the exploitation of its natural resources must not result in any unjustifiable interference with navigation, fishing or the conservation of the living resources of the sea, nor result in any interference with fundamental oceanographic or other scientific research carried out with the intention of open publication (Article 5.1). Subject to the provisions of Articles 5.1 and 5.6 the coastal State is entitled to construct and maintain or operate on the continental shelf installations and other devices necessary for its exploration and the exploitation of its natural resources, and to establish safety zones around such installations and devices, and to take in those zones measures necessary for their protection (Article 5.2). The safety zones referred to in Article 5.2 may extend to a distance of 500 metres around the installations and other devices which have been erected, measured from each point of their outer edge. Ships of all nationalities must respect these safety zones (Article 5.3). Such installations and devices, though under the jurisdiction of the coastal State, do not possess the status of islands. They have no territorial sea of their own, and their presence does not affect the delimitation of the territorial sea of the coastal State (Article 5.4). Due notice must be given of the construction of any such installations, and permanent means for giving warning of their presence must be maintained. Any installations, which are abandoned or disused, must be entirely removed (Article 5.5). Neither the installations or devices nor the safety zones around them may be established where interference may be caused to the use of recognized sea lanes essential to international navigation (Article 5.6). The coastal State is obliged to undertake, in the safety zones, all appropriate measures for the protection of the living resources of the sea from harmful agents (Article 5.7).

Article 6 of the Convention contains guidelines for demarcation of the continental shelf between opposite or adjacent coastal States. Where opposite coasts are involved the boundary of the continental shelf appertaining to such coastal States shall be determined by agreement between them. In the absence of agreement and, unless another boundary line is justified by special circumstances, the boundary is the median line, every point of which is equidistant from the nearest points of the baselines from which the breadth of the territorial sea of each State is measured (Article 6.1). Where adjacent coasts are involved the boundary of the continental shelf appertaining to such coastal States shall be determined by agreement between them. In the absence of agreement and, unless another boundary line is justified by special circumstances, the boundary shall be determined by application of the principle of equidistance from the nearest points of the baselines from which the breadth of the territorial sea of each State is measured (Article 6.2).

The median line or another line drawn on the basis of the principle of equidistance has later not been adopted in the 1982 Convention, but even during the period that the Convention was effective, such line did not always function as the boundary line of the last resort. Apart from the possibility that special circumstances could exist which made the application of the principle of equidistance difficult or impossible, the Convention (Article 12) allowed any State at the time of signature, ratification or accession to make reservations with respect to this article (as well as for that matter to any other article of the Convention, except Articles 1–3 inclusive). At the time, a number of States, realizing that due to the configuration of their coast the application of the equidistance principle would leave them with only a small portion of the adjacent continental shelf, made use of the possibility offered by the aforesaid Article 12 and submitted a reservation with respect to Article 6. The demarcation of the continental shelf between opposite or adjacent coastal States has frequently given rise to disputes between the States concerned. In most cases coastal States involved in such a demarcation dispute agreed to submit their dispute to international arbitration or to the International Court of Justice at The Hague. Well-known examples of such a settlement are the respective boundary agreements reached between the Netherlands, Denmark and the German Federal Republic on the division of their part of the North Sea continental shelf. Said agreements were based on a landmark judgment of the International Court of Justice at The Hague to which the States involved had agreed to submit their dispute (the *North Sea Continental Shelf Cases*, 20 February 1969).

9.5   THE 1970 UN GENERAL ASSEMBLY
               RESOLUTION 2749 (XXV)

The 1958 Convention was meant to regulate natural resources operations carried out on the continental shelf. The subject of deep sea mining fell outside its scope. However, deep sea mining was not listed in the Convention on the High Seas under the rights and freedoms of the high seas (viz. the freedom of navigation, fisheries, the laying of submarine cables and pipelines, the freedom of scientific research and the use of the airspace above the waters). In fact deep sea mining was completely ignored by the 1958 Conventions. In the 1960s, further developments in drilling technology and bottom sampling made clear that in the near future deep sea mining could become technically feasible. To make this a reality it was felt that a mining regime had to be developed that was suitable to regulate the exploration for and exploitation of deep sea mineral resources. The absence of such specific regime, so it was rightly feared, would have an inhibiting effect on the preparedness of the mining industry to embark on deep sea mining.

     For creating the desired mining regime, consideration was given to:

   (i) an appropriate adaptation of the 1958 Convention ensuring that this
        Convention would also become applicable to natural resources
        beyond the continental shelf;
  (ii) treating deep sea mining as one of the freedoms of the high seas;
        and
 (iii) using the flag-state approach.

With reference to (i). Under such an approach the 200 metres water depth criterion would have to be left out, retaining the technological water depth (i.e., the water depth where exploitation of minerals is still possible), as the only yardstick for determining the limits of the jurisdiction of the coastal State. In other words the seaward boundary of the continental shelf would move gradually to greater water depth as more sophisticated technology would be developed and become available. However, application of this system yields different results for different coastal States depending on their technological capabilities and local circumstances. This was perceived as a practical obstacle for applying this solution because it was not clear if one coastal State would be able to exploit minerals at say a depth of 2,500 metres and was entitled in this way to extend its continental shelf to that depth whether all other coastal States would automatically be similarly entitled to extend their continental shelf to that depth or only if they would have actually proven the exploitability at that depth on their coast. Apart from this technicality, a more serious objection was that the presence of mid-oceanic ridges and plateaus, separated from the continental shelf by greater water depths, where no exploitation is possible, could not be accommodated within this system. The conclusion that was reached at the time was that the rules of the Convention could only be used if water depth as limiting factor for the jurisdiction of the coastal State would be completely discarded. However, it was also realized that, if water depth would not be the limiting factor, application of the Convention would have the result that the oceans and other sea areas of the world would be divided by and between oceanic coastal States, an equally unacceptable result considering that there does not exist a natural, geomorphological link between any coastal State and the seabed and subsoil of the oceans, which prevents the latter area to be seen as the natural prolongation of the land mass of the coastal State, hence removing thereby the basis for the latter's claim (under international law, since the 1969 Judgment of the International Court of Justice in the *North Sea Continental Shelf Cases*) to jurisdiction over any adjacent sea area. Moreover, dividing the natural resources of the deep sea area between the oceanic coastal States only was not considered appropriate or equitable with respect to the land-locked States and other coastal States, i.e., coastal States bordering on narrow dependent seas or gulfs.

With reference to (ii). To treat deep sea mining as one of the freedoms of the high seas would have as a consequence that any person would be entitled to explore the area and exploit its deep sea mineral resources. However without a mining regime being in place a prospector making a discovery would have no means to protect its discovery and mining site against other prospectors also looking for exploitation possibilities. A chaotic situation would certainly develop, proving that the undertaking of mining operations, being tied to specific areas of the ocean bed, is completely different from that of exercising any of the other freedoms of the high seas. By their nature, mining operations cannot be undertaken within the framework of exercising a freedom, but need a proper mining regime, be it of national or international origin, providing for administration and protection of rights. Without such regime there would be no incentive and even be too risky for the industry to start searching for the resources of the deep sea area.

With reference to (iii). The flag-state approach would give any State the right to use its vessels to explore and exploit a certain area of the deep sea and to acquire the jurisdiction over such an area by occupation. This solution was also considered not to be a very practical one. A flag-state mining regime would certainly require international registration of claims, rules for settling disputes and overlapping claims, and international supervision over the operations, if only to prevent that harm is done to the marine environment.

Meanwhile, fearing that the deep sea resources in one way or other would come under the control of the Western States, given the progress made by those States and their enterprises in deep seabed mining technology, developing countries supported in 1967 a proposal made by Malta, to the effect that the UN General Assembly should declare that the deep seabed and its mineral resources should be reserved for peaceful purposes in the interest of mankind. GA Resolution 2749 (XXV) of 17 December 1970 laid down the following principles with respect to the international area (the Area) as envisaged in Malta's proposal:

   (i) the Area and its natural resources are the common heritage of mankind;
  (ii) no occupation by States or other natural or legal persons is permitted;
 (iii) no rights may be granted or claims be made which contradict the future international mining regime and the principles enunciated in this declaration;
  (iv) all mining operations have to fall under the scope of the aforesaid international mining regime;
   (v) the Area must be open for peaceful use by all States without discrimination in accordance with the international mining regime;
  (vi) all mining operations must be carried out in the interests and to the benefit of mankind, taking into account the interests and needs of the developing countries;
 (vii) the international regime must be incorporated in an universal Law of the Sea Convention to which every State may accede;
(viii) the status of the waters of the Area and the air space above it may not be affected.

9.6   THE 1982 CONVENTION ON THE LAW OF
             THE SEA

9.6.1   BACKGROUND

The Law of the Sea Convention of 1982 was the outcome of the Third UN Conference on the Law of the Sea (UNCLOS III). This Conference had been convened for the purpose of giving effect to the principles contained in UNGA Resolution 2749 (XXV) of 17 December 1970. The Conference began in December 1973 and ended with the signing of a Convention on 10 December 1982 at Montego Bay. It became effective on 16 November 1994 and as of that date superseded the four Geneva Conventions, without impairing or changing any inter-state agreements that in the meantime had been made under the rules of these Conventions. In particular, bilateral agreements relating to the delimitation of the continental shelf are respected as well as all other international agreements or conventions regarding the use of the sea and the prevention of pollution of the marine environment.

The main objective of the UN Conference, at least initially, had been to conclude a convention that would lay down the internationalization of the deep seabed area which in the UNGA Resolution 2749 (XXV) of 17 December 1970 had been referred to as the Area, and to proclaim according to this Resolution that this Area and its mineral resources *in situ* (among which petroleum) are the common heritage of mankind and that all rights in these mineral resources are vested in mankind as a whole, on whose behalf the International Seabed Authority shall act.

As far as petroleum operations on the continental shelf were concerned the Convention followed in this the example of the 1958 Convention with this important exception that the definition or description of what area constitutes the continental shelf became completely different, mostly in favour of the coastal State and with far reaching consequences for offshore petroleum operations.

9.6.2   CONTENTS OF THE CONVENTION (PARTS I, II, V, VI, VIII, XI AND XII)

Part I Definitions

'dumping' means: (i) any deliberate disposal of wastes or other matter from vessels, aircraft, platforms or other man-made structures at sea; (ii) any deliberate disposal of vessels, aircraft, platforms or other man-made structures at sea.

'dumping' does not include: (i) the disposal of wastes or other matter incidental to, or derived from the normal operations of vessels, aircraft, platforms or other man-made structures at sea and their equipment, other than wastes or other matter transported by or to vessels, aircraft, platforms or other man-made structures at sea, operating for the purpose of disposal of such matter or derived from the treatment of such wastes or other matter on such vessels, aircraft, platforms or structures; (ii) placement of matter for a purpose other than the mere disposal thereof, provided that such placement is not contrary to the aims of this Convention.

'pollution of the marine environment' means: the introduction by man, directly or indirectly, of substances or energy into the marine environment, including estuaries, which result or is likely to result in such deleterious effects as harm to living resources and marine life, hazards to human health, hindrance to marine activities, including fishing and other legitimate uses of the sea, impairment of quality for use of sea water and reduction of amenities.

Part II Territorial Sea and Contiguous Zone

The sovereignty of a coastal State extends beyond its land territory and internal waters to an adjacent belt of sea, described as the territoral sea.Every State has the right to establish the breadth of its territorial sea up to a limit not exceeding 12 nautical miles (equals 22.224 kms), measured from baselines determined in accordance with this Convention.

In a zone contiguous to its territorial sea, described as the contiguous zone, the coastal State may exercise the control necessary to (a) prevent infringement of its customs, fiscal, immigration or sanitary laws and regulations within its territory or territorial sea; (b) punish infrigments of the above laws and regulations committed within its territory or territorial sea.

The contiguous zone may not extend beyond 24 nautical miles from the baselines from which the breadth of the territorial sea is measured.

Part V The Exclusive Economic Zone (EEZ)

Every coastal State is assigned an Exclusive Economic Zone (EEZ). The EEZ is described as an area beyond and adjacent to the territorial sea which shall not extend beyond 200 nautical miles (equals 370 kms) from the baselines from which the breadth of the territorial sea is measured (Articles 55 and 57).

Note: Depending on local geomorphological circumstances the EEZ of a particular coastal State may well extend beyond the outer edge of the continental margin (see hereinafter) and could therefore comprise part of the deep seabed area.

As described in Article 56.1(a), (b), (c), a coastal State has in its EEZ:

   (a) sovereign rights for the purpose of exploring and exploiting, conserving and managing the natural resources, whether living or non-living, of the waters superjacent to the seabed and of the seabed and its subsoil, and with regard to other activities for the economic exploitation and exploration of the zone, such as the production of energy from the water, currents and winds;

(b) jurisdiction with regard to: (i) the establishment and use of artificial islands, installations and structures; (ii) marine scientific research; and (iii) the protection and preservation of the marine environment; and

(c) other rights and duties provided for in this Convention.

In exercising its rights with respect to the EEZ a coastal State must have due regard to the rights and duties of other States and shall act in a manner compatible with the provisions of this Convention (Article 56.2).

In the EEZ all States, whether coastal or land-locked, enjoy the freedoms of navigation and overflight and of the laying of submarine cables and pipelines, and other internationally lawful uses of the sea related to these freedoms, such as those associated with the operation of ships, aircraft and submarine cables and pipelines, and compatible with the other provisions of this Convention. In exercising their rights and performing their duties under this Convention in the EEZ, States shall have due regard to the rights and duties of the coastal State and shall comply with the laws and regulations adopted by the coastal State in accordance with the provisions of this Convention and other rules of international law in so far as they are not incompatible with this Part V (Article 58).

In its EEZ the coastal State shall have the exclusive right to construct and to authorize and regulate the construction, operation and use of:

(i) artificial islands;

(ii) installations and structures for the purposes provided for in Article 56 and other economic purposes;

(iii) installations and structures which may interfere with the exercise of the rights of the coastal State in the zone.

The coastal State shall have exclusive jurisdiction over such artificial islands, installations and structures, including jurisdiction with regard to customs, fiscal, health, safety and immigration laws and regulations (Articles 60.1 and 60.2).

Note. Having been granted the exclusive jurisdiction over installations and operations within the EEZ (and the continental shelf as well) the coastal State is responsible for preparing and establishing rules and regulations with regard to these operations and installations. However, on account of inter-state agreements and conventions, to which the coastal State is or becomes a party, the coastal State is also responsible for implementation of the rules, standards, procedures agreed in the context of these inter-state agreements and conventions. This means that the coastal State must incorporate and include the rules, etc. in its national legislation, but is allowed to take more stringent measures. This issue is taken up by Article 208 (see hereinafter).

Due notice must be given of the construction of such artificial islands, installations or structures, and permanent means for giving warning of their presence must be maintained. Any installations or structures, which are abandoned or disused, must be removed to ensure safety of navigation, taking into account any generally accepted international standards established in this regard by the competent international organization (currently the International Maritime Organization [IMO]). Such removal must also have due regard to fishing, the protection of the marine environment and the rights and duties of other States. Appropriate publicity shall be given to the depth, position and dimensions of any installations or structures not entirley removed. (Article 60.3).

Note 1.In contrast with the 1958 Convention (Article 5), there exists no longer an absolute obligation to remove installations or structures in their entirety.

Note 2. In 1984 the IMO was asked by the Oslo Commission (the Commission at the time operating under the 1972 Oslo Dumping Convention) to prepare the 'generally accepted international standards' asked for in Article 60.3. In 1989, IMO published its 'Guidelines and Standards on Removal', which since then have been followed when formulating national rules and regulations for de-commissoning plans which licensees are required to submit before the use of a facility is permanently terminated.

The coastal State may, where necessary, establish reasonable safety zones around such artificial islands, installations and structures in which it may take appropriate measures to ensure the safety both of navigation and of the artificial islands, installations and structures (Article 60.4).

The breadth of the safety zones shall be determined by the coastal State, taking into account applicable international standards. Such zones shall be designed to ensure that they are reasonably related to the nature and function of the artificial islands, installations or structures, and shall not exceed a distance of 500 metres around them, measured from each point of the outer edge, except as authorized by generally accepted international standards or as recommended by the competent international organization. Due notice shall be given of the extent of safety zones (Article 60.5).

All ships must respect these safety zones and shall comply with generally accepted international standards regarding navigation in the vicinity of artificial islands, installations, structures and safety zones (Article 60.6).

Artificial islands, installations and structures and the safety zones around them may not be established where interference may be caused to the use of recognized sea lanes essential to international navigation (Article 60.7).

Artificial islands, installations and structures do not possess the status of islands. They have no territorial sea of their own, and their presence does not affect the delimitation of the territorial sea, the EEZ or the continental shelf (Article 60.8).

The delimitation of the EEZ between States with opposite or adjacent coasts must be effected by agreement on the basis of international law in order to achieve an equitable solution (Article 74.1). If no agreement can be reached within a reasonable period of time, the States concerned shall resort to the procedures provided for in Part XV (Settlement of Disputes) (Article 74.2).

Note. In contrast to the 1958 Convention (Article 6), no reference is made to the principle of equidistance (median line) as the method of delimitation of the last resort. However, the reference to international law brings the whole body of judgments which were delivered by the International Court of Justice in continental shelf demarcation cases into focus, albeit these judgments may be irrelevant since based on interpretation of the terms of the 1958 Convention.

Pending agreement on a delimitation the States concerned, in a spirit of understanding and cooperation, shall make every effort to enter into provisional arrangements of a practical nature and, during this transitional period, not to jeopardize or hamper the reaching of the final agreement. Such arrangement shall be without prejudice to the final delimitation (Article 74.3).

Note. An important example of such a provisional arrangement of a practical nature is the 1989 Australia/Republic of Indonesia Agreement creating the Timor Gap Zone of Cooperation, an area measuring 62,000 square km. This interstate agreement concerning joint development is described hereinafter in Chapter 10.

Part VI The Continental Shelf

Apart from the EEZ, the Convention (Part VI) accords every coastal State a continental shelf. The continental shelf of a coastal State comprises the seabed and subsoil of the submarine areas that extend beyond its territorial sea throughout the natural prolongation of its land territory to the outer edge of the continental margin, or to a distance of 200 nautical miles from the baselines from which the breadth of the territorial sea is measured where the outer edge of the continental margin does not extend up to that distance (Article 76.1). The continental margin (Article 76.3) comprises the submerged prolongation of the land mass of the coastal State and consists of the seabed and subsoil of the shelf, the slope and the rise. It does not include the deep ocean floor with its oceanic ridges or the subsoil thereof.

In terms of the Convention the continental shelf, irrespective of the geomorphological conditions of the submarine areas, at least coincides with the EEZ, but may extend beyond this Zone. In quite a few instances the outer edge of the continental margin lies beyond 200 nautical miles from the baselines. On the other hand, the outer edge of the continental margin may fall short of this distance. Where this situation occurs the 'continental shelf' as defined in Article 76 will include part of the deep seabed area.

The outer edge of the continental margin must be established by a coastal State, wherever the margin extends beyond the EEZ (Article 76.4). In delineating the outer edge a coastal State shall make use of fixed points to be defined by geographical coordinates and connect these points by straight lines not exceeding 60 nautical miles in length (Article 76.7). A coastal State may choose between two types of fixed points:

(i) fixed points, at each of which the thickness of sedimentary rocks is at least 1 per cent of the shortest distance from such point to the foot of the continental slope; or

(ii) fixed points, which are located no more than 60 nautical miles from the foot of the continental slope.

The fixed points selected by the coastal State must be located either within 350 nautical miles from the baselines from which the breadth of the territorial sea is measured, or within one 100 nautical miles from the 2,500 metres isobath (Article 76.5).

Information on the limits of the continental shelf beyond the 200 nautical miles limit shall be submitted by the coastal State to the Commission on Limits of the Continental Shelf set up under Annex II of the Convention (see *Note 1* below). The Commission shall make recommendations to coastal States on matters related to the establishment of the outer limits of their continental shelf. The limits of the continental shelf established by a coastal State on the basis of these recommendations shall be final and binding (Article 76.8). The delimitation of the continental shelf between States with opposite or adjacent coasts is provided for (Article 83) in the same manner and in accordance with the same procedures and principles as set out in Article 74 with respect to the EEZ.

Note 1. Annex II of the Convention establishes a 'Commision on the Limits of the Continental Shelf beyond 200 nautical miles'. The Commission shall consist of 21 members who shall be experts in the field of geology, geophysics or hydrography, elected by States Parties to this Convention from among their nationals, having due regard to the need to ensure equitable geographical representation, who shall serve in their personal capacities. The functions of the Commission shall be (a) to consider the data and other material submitted by coastal States concerning the outer limits of the continental shelf in areas where those limits extend beyond 200 nautical miles, and to make recommendations in accordance with article 76; (b) to provide scientific and technical advice, if requested by the coastal State concerned during the preparation of the data referred to in (a). Where a coastal State intends to establish, in accordance with article 76, the outer limits of its continental shelf beyond 200 nautical miles, it shall submit particulars of such limits to the Commission along with supporting scientific and technical data as soon as possible but in any case within 10 years of the entry into force of this Convention for that State. The recommendations of the Commission shall be submitted in writing to the coastal State which made the submission and to the Secretary-General of the United Nations. Coastal States shall establish the outer limits of the continntal shelf in conformity with the provisions of article 76.8 and in accordance with the appropriate national procedures. In the case of disagreement by the coastal State with the recommendations of the Commission, the coastal State shall, within a reasonable time, make a revised or new submission to the Commission.

Note 2. There are worldwide 44 coastal States which have an extended continental shelf, 6 of them are Arctic coastal States, namely Canada, the United States, the Russian Federation, Norway, Demark, representing Greenland and Faroe Islands, and Iceland. These 6 countries cooperate with 2 non-Arctic coastal States, namely Finland and Sweden within the context of the Arctic Council, a forum for discussion and decision-taking on Arctic matters, that was already functioning since 1996, when it was established in Ottawa, Canada. Norway and the Russian Federation have already submitted (tentative) claims to the Commission, but is expected that the submission to the Commission of the final claims of all 6 countries will be coordinated by the Arctic Council. Apart from observing the 10-year time limits for the submissions, there appears to be no urgency in this matter of establishing outer limits of the continental shelf. Petroleum resources are expected to be largely located within the outer limits of the EEZ or even in the territorial seas and on land. Hence, the demarcation of the EEZ between adjacent coastal States needs to be given more and urgent attention. A first step was already taken by Norway and the Russian Federation when the two States concluded a

Boundary Treaty concerning the division of the Barents Sea continental shelf (17 September 2010).

The sovereign rights of a coastal State over the continental shelf are identical to the rights granted under the 1958 Convention (Article 77) and more restricted than the rights granted pursuant article 56 in the EEZ.

All States are entitled to lay submarine cables and pipelines on the continental shelf and subject to its right to take reasonable measures for the exploration of the continental shelf, the exploitation of its natural resources and the prevention, reduction and control of pollution from pipelines, the coastal State may not impede the laying or maintenance of such cables or pipelines (Article 79.2). Furthermore, the delineation of the course for the laying of other States' pipelines is subject to the consent of the coastal State (Article 79.3). The coastal State has the right to establish conditions for submarine cables or pipelines entering its territory or territorial sea and has jurisdiction over cables and pipelines constructed or used in connection with its natural resources operations (Article 79.4). States laying submarine cables or pipelines must respect cables or pipelines already in position and must not thereby jeopardize the possibilities of repairing these cables or pipelines (Article 79.5).

With respect to artificial islands, installations and structures on the continental shelf Article 60 (EEZ) is declared to apply *mutatis mutandis* to these constructions.

Note. Jurisdiction over marine scientific research and the protection and preservation of the marine environment is apparently exclusively reserved for the EEZ (Article 56 1 (b) (ii) and (iii)). As far as the extended continental shelf is concerned, Article 208 should cover the discrepancy, in as much that Article imposes on any coastal State the duty to prevent, reduce and control pollution of the marine environment arising from seabed activities under their jurisdiction (which by definition would include any mining activity on the extended continental shelf).

On the continental shelf the coastal State has been given the exclusive right to authorize and regulate drilling for all purposes (Article 81).

Article 82 stipulates that a coastal State should make payments or contributions in cash or kind in respect of the exploitation of the non-living resources of the extended continental shelf. The payments or contributions consist in the payment of an annual royalty commencing after the first five years of production. The payments or contributions shall be made through the Authority, which shall distribute them to the States Parties tot his

Convention, on the basis of equitable sharing criteria, taking into account the interests and needs of developing States, particularly the least developed and the land-locked among them.

The delimitation of the continental shelf between States with opposite or adjacent coasts must be effected by agreement on the basis of international law in order to achieve an equitable solution (Article 83.1). If no agreement can be reached within a reasonable period of time, the States concerned shall resort to the procedures provided for in Part XV (Settlement of Disputes) (Article 83.2).

Pending agreement on a delimitation the States concerned, in a spirit of understanding and cooperation, shall make every effort to enter into provisional arrangements of a practical nature and, during this transitional period, not to jeopardize or hamper the reaching of the final agreement. Such arrangement shall be without prejudice to the final delimitation (Article 83.3).

Note. Obviously, Article 83 should be identical to Article 74. It becomes only important if the continental shelf extends beyond 200 nautical miles and should be divided between coastal States.

Part VIII The Regime of Islands

In view of the rights granted to islands (EEZ, continental shelf), the Convention sought to come to a definition of what constitutes an island. Under the given definition not every piece of dry land qualifies for the application of the Convention in the matter of islands.

According to Article 121:

1. An island is a naturally formed area of land, surrounded by water, which is above water at high tide.
2. Except as provided for in paragraph 3, the territorial sea, the contiguous zone, the exclusive economic zone and the continental shelf of an island are determined in accordance with the provisions of this Convention applicable to other land territory.
3. Rocks which cannot sustain human habitation or economic life of their own shall have no exclusive economic zone or continental shelf.

If politically independent, islands are coastal States in their own right (e.g., United Kingdom, Ireland, Iceland, Madagascar, Cuba, etc.), otherwise islands fall under the jurisdiction of a coastal State (e.g., Andaman Islands, Corsica, Gotland, etc.) or constitute an archipelagic State (i.e., a State consisting of an agglomeration of islands (e.g., Indonesia, the Philippines). If not being rocks as described in Article 121.3 islands can claim an EEZ and a continental shelf. This claim may make the territorial jurisdiction over an island (if not being a coastal State in its own right) very valuable and important, if the area surrounding the island is thought to be a prospective area. If so, jurisdictional disputes about an island will be difficult to settle because much more is at stake than the territorial jurisdiction over the island itself. On the other hand jurisdictional disputes about reefs and rocks which do not qualify as islands in terms of Article 121 will be easier to settle.

Note. An isolated island of only 1 km^2 would be entitled to an EEZ comprising 430,000 km^2.

Part XI The Area

The deep seabed and its subsoil in so far not forming part of the EEZ or the continental shelf beyond 200 nautical miles constitute the Area. Petroleum belongs to the mineral resources of the Area, but from a geological point of view it is not expected that petroleum reservoirs will actually be found in the deep seabed, since their presence is bound to the continental shelf as defined in Article 76. All in all, it can safely be assumed that petroleum operations will exclusively take place in areas which are placed by the Convention under national jurisdiction.

Part XII: The Protection and Preservation of the Marine Environment

The main provisions of Part XII (Articles 192 to 212) are the following:

- States (whether coastal States or not) have the obligation to protect and preserve the marine environment (Article 192).
- States have the sovereign right to exploit their natural resources pursuant to their environmental policies and in accordance with their duty to protect and preserve the marine environment (Article 193).

States shall take, individually or jointly as appropriate, all measures consistent with the Convention that are necessary to prevent, reduce and control pollution of the marine environment from any source, using for this purpose the best practicable means at their disposal and in accordance with their capabilities, and they shall endeavour to harmonize their policies in this connection. The measures to be taken shall deal with all sources of pollution of the marine environment. These measures shall include, inter alia, those designed to minimize to the fullest possible extent:

(i) the release of toxic, harmful or noxious substances from land-based sources, from or through the atmosphere or by dumping;

(ii) pollution from vessels, in particular measures for preventing accidents and dealing with emergencies, ensuring the safety of operations at sea, preventing intentional and unintentional discharges, and regulating the design, construction, equipment, operation and manning of vessels;

(iii) pollution from installations and devices used in exploration or exploitation of the natural resources of the sea-bed and subsoil or from other installations and devices operating in the marine environment, in particular measures for preventing accidents and dealing with emergencies, ensuring the safety of operations at sea, and regulating the design, construction, equipment, operation and manning of such installations or devices (Article 194).

States shall cooperate on a global basis and, as appropriate, on a regional basis, directly or through competent international organizations (IMO) in formulating and elaborating international rules, standards and recommended practices and procedures consistent with this Convention, for the protection and preservation of the marine environment, taking into account characteristic regional features (Article 197).

Coastal States shall adopt laws and regulations to prevent, reduce and control pollution of the marine environment arising from or in connection with seabed activities subject to their jurisdiction and from artificial islands, installations and structures under their jurisdiction pursuant to Articles 60 and 80. Such laws, regulations and measures shall be no less effective than international rules, standards and recommended practices and procedures. States shall endeavour to harmonize their policies in this connection at the appropriate regional level. States, acting especially through competent international organizations or diplomatic conference, shall establish global and regional rules, standards and recommended practices and procedures to prevent, reduce and control pollution of the marine environment referred to above (Article 208).

Note. Submarine pipelines are not specifically mentioned in Part XII as a source of pollution, despite the fact that they are widely used in submarine long distance transport of oil or natural gas as well as in offshore petroleum operations for submarine transport of oil/gas production, oil products and chemicals to and from offshore installations. Submarine pipelines may become a source of pollution of the marine environment, if their condition deteriorates. It must be concluded that the matter of prevention, etc. of pollution arising from the presence and use of submarine pipelines can only been dealt with in the context of Article 208 referred to above, i.e., considering the use and operation of submarine pipelines as a seabed activity. As mentioned before, the sole specific reference to submarine pipelines appear in Article 79.4 giving the coastal State jurisdiction (and therefore responsibility) over cables and pipelines constructed or used in connection with the exploration of its continental shelf or exploitation of its resources or the operations of artificial islands, installations and structures under its jurisdiction. Less clear is the position of other submarine constructions such as submarine production installations which are fixed to the seabed. If these submarine constructions cannot be counted to belong to the category of artificial islands, installations and structures referred to in Articles 60 and 80, the coastal State should take responsibilty for pollution from this source under the coastal State's general obligations under the provisions of Part XII.

States shall adopt laws and regulations to prevent, reduce and control pollution of the marine environment by dumping. Such laws, regulations and measures shall ensure that dumping is not carried out without the permission of the competent authorities of States. States, acting especially through competent international organizations or diplomatic conference, shall endeavour to establish global and regional rules, standards and recommended practices and procedures to prevent, reduce and control such pollution. Dumping within the territorial sea and the EEZ or on the continental shelf shall not be carried out without the express prior approval of the coastal State, which has the right to permit, regulate and control such dumping after due consideration of the matter with other States which by reason of their geographical situation may be adversely affected thereby. National laws, regulations and measures shall be no less effective in preventing, reducing and controlling such pollution than the global rules and standards (Article 210).

In ice-covered areas coastal States have the right to adopt and enforce non-discriminatory laws and regulations for the prevention, reduction and control of marine pollution from vessels in ice-covered areas within the limits of the exclusive economic zone, where particular severe climatic conditions and the presence of ice covering such areas for most of the year create obstructions or exceptional hazards to navigation, and pollution of the marine environment could cause major harm to or irreversible disturbance of the ecological balance. Such laws and regulations shall have due regard to navigation and the protection and preservation of the marine environment based on the best available scientific evidence (Article 234).

Note. At the time of the Conference, apparently no thought was given to the possibilty that at some time in the future not only vessels but also installations and structures for petroleum operations would be used and operated in the Arctic.

Summarizing, the Convention recognizes several sources of pollution of the marine environment and imposes on all States, whether having a coastline or not, the obligation to protect and preserve this environment. The Convention does not contain any specific rules, procedures or standards by which States should guided or which States should adopt, when trying to implement their aforesaid duties. The Convention is only concerned in assigning and allocating responsibilities between States (States generally or coastal States exclusively) for designing and promulgating such rules and standards, while stipulating in this respect that States should especially act through competent international organisations or diplomatic conference.

Meanwhile, States have made great efforts in negotiating and agreeing global and regional rules and standards and procedures to prevent, reduce and control pollution of the marine environment.

9.6.3   THE 1992 CONVENTION FOR THE PROTECTION OF THE MARINE ENVIRONMENT OF THE NORTH-EAST ATLANTIC (OSPARCON)

This convention is an important and outstanding example of a regional convention in the matter of protecting the marine environment. The convention was signed in Paris on 22 September 1992 and represents a further development of both the Oslo Dumping Convention of 1972 and the Paris Convention of 1974. The 'maritime area' in respect of which OSPARCON is applicable is the North-East Atlantic. The Convention describes the sources of pollution, establishes a Commission and imposes on the Contracting Parties the obligation, individually and jointly to adopt programmes and measures and to harmonize their policies and strategies in order to prevent and eliminate pollution and to protect the maritime area against the adverse effects of human activities so as to safeguard human health and to conserve marine ecosystems and, when practicable, restore marine areas which have been adversely affected. The Contracting Parties are further obliged to apply the precautionary principle, by virtue of which preventive measures are to be taken; and the polluter pays principle, by virtue of which the costs of pollution prevention, control and reduction measures are to be borne by the polluter. The Contracting Parties shall define the application of 'best available techniques' and 'best environmental practice', including, where appropriate, 'clean technology' and ensure the application thereof in carrying out such programmes and measures, but they are not prevented to take, individually or jointly, more stringent measures. As sources of pollution are listed pollution from land-based sources (Annex I); pollution by dumping or incineration (Annex II, except where offshore installations and offshore pipelines are involved); pollution from offshore sources (Annex III).

As far as offshore sources are concerned, the Convention does not make a distinction between operational discharges and discharges connected with the offshore petroleum operations. Instead, all pollution matters concerning the use on, or the discharge from offshore installations or offshore pipelines of substances, which may reach and affect the maritime area, are covered by Annex III.

It is the duty of the Commission *inter alia* to supervise the implementation of the Convention; to review the condition of the maritime area and the effectiveness of the measures being adopted; to draw up (in accordance with the general obligations of the Convention) programmes and measures for the prevention and elimination of pollution and for the control of activities which may, directly or indirectly, adversely affect the maritime area; and to consider and, where appropriate, adopt proposals for the amendment of the Convention, including its Annexes and Appendices.

Annex III (re. Pollution from Offshore Sources) obliges the Contracting Parties, either individually or jointly, to require the use of best available techniques, best environmental practice and, where appropriate, clean technology. The terms 'best available techniques' and 'best environmental practice' are described and explained in Appendix 1 of the Convention. The relative value and significance of these concepts is recognized. It is stressed that what constitutes 'best available techniques' and 'best environmental practice in a particular case will change with time in the light of technological advances, economic and social factors, as well as changes in scientific knowledge and understanding'. (Note. The expression 'Clean Technology' is not described. However in Annex II of the 1992 Baltic Sea Convention (a very similar Convention) the concept is described as 'production systems which minimize, avoid or eliminate the generation of hazardous waste and hazardous products').

Annex III further requires that no disused offshore installation or disused offshore pipeline shall be dumped and no disused offshore installation shall be left wholly or partly in place in the maritime area without a permit issued by the competent authority of the relevant contracting state on a case-by-case basis.

Note. OSPARCON does not prescribe any specific rules or standards on how to conduct offshore petroleum operations; it only contains procedures leading to the establishment of such rules and standards. The latter have to be developed by the Commission and to be implemented by the Contracting Party under whose jurisdiction the offshore installations and pipelines are used. The Contracting Parties are bound to fulfil the general obligations imposed by the Convention, to use best available techniques and best environmental practice, including, where appropriate, clean technology, as these terms are defined in Appendix 1, and to apply or take into account the criteria and substances listed in Appendix 2 in assessing the nature and extent of their programmes and measures, and also bound to the rules and provisions of MARPOL with regard to operational discharges from (specialized) vessels and offshore installations. Within this framework and always subject to its obligations under the 1982 Convention, any Contracting Party (coastal State) retains its freedom to regulate the offshore petroleum operations under its jurisdiction with regard to the subject matter of the Convention as it sees fit. It is only bound to the decisions of the Commission, if it voted for it or notifies in writing that it agrees with them.

9.6.4   UNEP CONVENTIONS ON THE PREVENTION OF POLLUTION

OSPARCON and HELCON, the Baltic Sea Area Convention (a very similar Convention for the Baltic Sea area) are not the only regional conventions concerning the prevention of pollution which *inter alia* covers the matter of pollution resulting or likely to result from offshore petroleum operations. Several of other conventions have been developed under the Regional Sea programmes of the UN Environment programme (UNEP). Any UNEP programme is aimed at the adoption of an Action Plan and a convention containing the legal framework. Any convention is accompanied and complemented by Annexes and Protocols covering specific types of pollution.

    Examples of such UNEP inspired regional conventions are:

(i) the 1976 Barcelona Convention and its Protocols (Convention for the Protection of the Mediterranean Sea against Pollution, accompanied by three Protocols, viz. a Dumping Protocol (Protocol for the Prevention of Pollution of the Mediterranean Sea by Dumping from Ships and Aircraft) with three Annexes, Protocol concerning cooperation in combating Pollution of the Mediterranean Sea by Oil and other Harmful Substances in Cases of Emergency and a Protocol concerning Mediterranean Specially Protected Areas;

(ii) the 1978 Kuwait Convention (Kuwait Regional Convention for Cooperation on the Protection of the Marine Environment from Pollution) with an Action Plan and a single Protocol (Protocol

concerning Regional Cooperation in Combating Pollution by Oil
and other Harmful Substances in Cases of Emergency);
(iii) the 1982 Red Sea Convention (Regional Convention for the
Conservation of the Red Sea and the Gulf of Aden Environment)
with an Action Plan and a single Protocol (Protocol concerning
Regional Cooperation in combating Pollution by Oil and other
Harmful Substances in Cases of Emergency);
(iv) the 1983 Caribbean Convention currently accompanied by a single
Protocol concerning cooperation in combating oil spills in the
wider Caribbean region, no Action Plan is referred to in the
Convention.

The aforementioned Kuwait Convention, its Protocol and Action Plan were
signed on 24 April 1978 by the governments of the Gulf States. Offshore
petroleum operations take place in the area of the Convention, but only on
a modest scale. The real importance of the Convention rests on the fact that
it concerns a sea area through which a huge tonnage of crude oil is being
shipped. Therefore shipping and accidents with ships were seen as the main
possible sources of pollution for the prevention and abatement of which the
Convention had to make provisions. As customary in these cases, the
Convention is only providing a framework within which procedures and
standards can be developed for the purpose of preventing, abating and
combating pollution of the marine environment in the Convention Area.
The so-developed procedures and standards are to be used by the
Contracting Parties in taking measures and establishing national standards,
laws and regulations for this purpose. The Contracting Parties are obliged
to endeavour to harmonize their national policies and to cooperate with the
competent international, regional and sub-regional organizations to establish and adopt regional standards, recommended practices and procedures.
In the case of pollution caused by intentional or accidental discharges from
ships the Contracting Parties are obliged to ensure effective compliance in
the Convention Area with applicable international rules (e.g., MARPOL).

Chapter 10

Interstate Agreements on Joint Development of Petroleum Resources

10.1   INTRODUCTION

If with respect to a prospective area, onshore or offshore, State jurisdiction over the area in question is claimed by two or more States, the States involved will be frustrated in their attempts to issue petroleum authorizations for exploration and possible exploitation of petroleum resources within the disputed area. Obviously, in the light of such a territorial dispute, no commercial oil enterprise will risk to apply for an authorization when put on offer, fearing that the granting of the authorization and the authorization itself will be challenged by the other State.

In order not to hold up exploration activities, States may be persuaded to apply a practical solution which consists in demarcating and setting apart the disputed area (onshore or offshore), and enter into an agreement between them providing for a joint development of the petroleum resources (possibly) present in the subsoil of that area.

But when looking for putting an end to a dispute over territory on a permanent basis, distinction should be made between disputes involving onshore (land) territory and those involving offshore territory (continental shelf).

Disputes between States over land territory including (small) islands have to be settled on the basis of historic rights and claims. Bi-lateral negotiations, self-organized international arbitration, or submission of the claims to the International Court of Justice at the Hague, either for guidance of for final judgment, should bring the dispute to an end.

Offshore jurisdiction and disputes arising in connection with the same became only an issue after the 1958 Convention on the Continental Shelf became effective and coastal States were assigned sovereign rights over the continental shelf. Coastal States had to share these rights with other coastal States and, as could be expected, such sharing led to conflicting claims and ensuing disputes. However, offshore jurisdiction as granted by the Convention is built on and derives from onshore jurisdiction. If there would be any conflict concerning underlying onshore jurisdiction, such conflict should first be resolved before problems concerning offshore jurisdiction can be addressed.

The 1958 Convention left the delimination of the continental shelf between States with opposite or adjacent coasts to agreement between them, but stipulated that in the absence of agreement and, unless another boundary line is justified by special circumstance, the boundary line is the median line (opposite coasts) or a line construed on the basis of the equidistance principle (adjacent coasts).

Since 16 November 1994, the date upon which the 1982 Convention on the Law of the Sea became effective, the latter provided for more elaborate and flexible guidelines for delimination of the continental shelf, but the starting point has remained the same: coastal States should first try to reach agreement between themselves.

Said guidelines are the following:

(1) the delimitation of the continental shelf between States with opposite or adjacent coasts must be effected by agreement on the basis of international law in order to achieve an equitable solution.
(2) If no agreement can be reached within a reasonable period of time, the States concerned shall resort to the procedures provided for in Part XV (Settlement of Disputes) of the Convention.
(3) Pending agreement on a delimitation, the States concerned, in a spirit of understanding and cooperation, shall make every effort to enter into provisional arrangements of a practical nature and, during this transitional period, not to jeopardize or hamper the reaching of the final agreement. Such arrangement shall be without prejudice to the final delimitation.

Besides providing for guidelines to settle delimitation issues, the 1982 Convention has made it in two ways easier for States to reach an agreement between themselves on such matters.

First, the Convention assigned to coastal States and islands a 'minimum' continental shelf, i.e., a continental shelf that extends to 200 nautical miles from shore, and coincides with the exclusive economic zone, regardless the geomorphology of the seabed of this zone. Deep troughs situated within this 200 nautical miles distance could not be considered to be the outer limit of the continental shelf. Examples are the Okinawa trough in the Southern East China Sea and the Timor trough situated between East Timor (formerly part of Indonesia) and Northern Australia.

Second, the Convention included a definition of what constitutes an island, to the effect that rocks which cannot sustain human habitation or economic life of their own, cannot be considered to be islands for the purposes of the Convention, i.e., are not assigned an EEZ nor a continental shelf.

However, islands, that are very small, but still satisfies the qualification of being an island and not a unhabitated rock, are in a position to claim an exclusive economic zone and continental shelf, which are disproportionally large compared with the size of the island itself, provided always that the island in question is situated in an isolated position, i.e., far removed from a coastal state or from another island or islands. In this position an island having only a land surface of 1 km^2 may claim a continental shelf of (at least) 430,000 km^2. Under these circumstances, the matter of jurisdiction over such island becomes a very important issue, but only of course if the area around the island is thought or has proven to be a prospective area (not only for petroleum resources but also for fishing).

Meanwhile, quite a few of disputes over offshore jurisdiction have been settled in interstate joint development agreements and/or boundary agreements between involved States.

In this connection, it should be pointed out that there are also interstate joint development agreements focused on the joint development of specific petroleum reservoirs which happen to be split by the in a separate interstate boundary agreement established boundary line between the two States in question. Usually this special type of joint development agreement is referred to as a 'untization' agreement.

A good example of such an interstate boundary agreement containing a commitment regarding joint development of straddling petroleum reservoirs is the Boundary Agreement of 10 March 1965 concluded between the United Kingdom and Norway. This Agreement (Article 4) contains the following stipulations:

If any single petroleum reservoir extends across the dividing line and the part of such reservoir, which is situated on one side of the dividing line, is exploitable, wholly or in part, from the other side of the dividing line, the two States are obliged, in consultation with the licensees, if any, to seek to reach agreement as to the manner in which the petroleum reservoir shall be most effectively exploited and the manner in which the proceeds deriving therefrom shall be apportioned.

The desired joint exploitation of such an 'interstate' straddling petroleum reservoir requires an agreement between the States concerned.

An example of such interstate 'unitization' agreement is the agreement between the UK and Norway 'relating to the exploitation of the Statfjord Field Reservoirs and the Offtake of Petroleum therefrom' (see hereinafter), which is based on the abovementioned Agreement of 10 March 1965.

10.2   THE 1962 AGREEMENT BETWEEN THE
                  NETHERLANDS AND GERMANY

10.2.1   BACKGROUND

The contested area is formed by the estuary of the River Ems. In order to promote the development of the oil and natural gas reservoirs which were assumed to be present in the subsoil of the contested area, without awaiting a final determination of the boundary between the two States, the Netherlands and the Federal Republic of Germany signed on 14 May 1962 an Agreement for that purpose. In accordance with this Agreement, a so-called 'Common Area' (the Area) was created. This Area was bounded by the borders as respectively claimed by the two States. A line (referred to as 'the Line') was drawn more or less along the centre line (*thalweg*) of the river dividing the Area in two more or less equal parts. The significance of the Line is not explained, apparently because both State Parties did not want to prejudice the final fixing of a boundary.

Main Provisions (declared to be applicable to the oil and natural gas deposits present in the subsoil of the Area prior to the start of the production).

With respect to exploration and exploitation activities and installations used for these activities, German law is applicable on the German side of the Line and Netherlands' law on the Netherlands' side of the Line. Contracting Parties may in accordance with their own petroleum legislation grant petroleum rights which are valid for the whole Area, but the rights so granted and the rights already existing upon this Agreement entering into force may only be exercised in accordance with the provisions of this Agreement (Article 4).

Note. On the Netherlands' side a concession was granted on 30 May 1963, one year after the Agreement was signed. As agreed, this concession included the whole Area. On the German side two separate, independent concessions were granted, the first one on 20 June 1958, hence its existence was preceding the Agreement, and the second one on 17 September 1963. Taken together they were also covering the whole Area.

The German concession holders on the one hand and the Netherlands' concession holder on the other are entitled to receive one half of the quantity of oil and gas that is produced (from the deposits present in the subsoil of the Area prior to the start of production). Costs that can reasonably be attributed to the exploration and production of the aforesaid quantity are also equally divided (Article 5).

The concession holders on the one side of the Line shall for the purpose exploration and production closely cooperate with the concession holders on the other side. To this end they shall exchange work pro-grammes for the Area and their results. For the purpose of their cooperation the concession holders shall conclude as soon as possible agreements of cooperation which will provide for the following matters: (i) the manner in which the oil and gas reserves are calculated and the outcome of such calculations; (ii) particulars about the sharing of production and costs; (iii) a procedure for the settlement of disputes. The agreements of cooperation must to be submitted to the Contracting Parties for information (Article 7).

10.2.2   AGREEMENTS OF COOPERATION

In accordance with the Agreement, two agreements of cooperation, which are virtually identical, were concluded: each having on the one side the Netherlands' concession holder and on the other the two German conces-sion holders. Under both agreements the Netherlands' concession holder was appointed as the operator. In accordance with the Article 7.2 of the Agreement the agreements of cooperation contain rules and procedures concerning the calculation of the quantity of natural gas originally present in the subsoil of the Area and of the quantity that actually can be recovered therefrom, the latter always being a fraction of the former.

Since no wells were drilled in the Area itself and the gas that was actually being produced in the wells located on the land territory of the Netherlands' concession could never be identified as being gas that originated from the reservoirs in the subsoil of the Area, the quantity of natural gas that could be recovered from said reservoirs and that had be shared in equal proportions between the concession holders had to be calculated. The method according to which the calculations had to be performed was set out in the agreements.

Note. The natural gas deliveries from the operator to the two German concession holders have long since stopped. It was agreed between the parties and the two governments that a volume of 20 billion cubic metres had been over-delivered, for which the Netherlands' concession holder would have to be compensated. The matter of the amount of compensation to be paid had in the meantime been resolved by arbitration.

10.3   THE 1974 AGREEMENT BETWEEN JAPAN
              AND THE REPUBLIC OF KOREA
              CONCERNING JOINT DEVELOPMENT OF
              THE SOUTHERN PART OF THE
              CONTINENTAL SHELF ADJACENT TO THE
              TWO COUNTRIES

10.3.1   BACKGROUND

The division of continental shelf adjacent to Japan and the Republic of
Korea was an issue about Japan and the Republic of Korea disagreed, Japan
wishing to apply the median line principle as described in Article 6 of the
1958 Convention on the Continental Shelf, whereas the Republic of Korea
wanted to apply the natural prolongation principle as this was introduced
and formulated by the International Court of Justice at The Hague in its
Judgment of 20 February 1969 in the *North Sea Continental Shelf Cases*
(see Note hereinafter). The matter came to the foreground in 1970 when
Korea for the purpose of developing offshore mineral resources laid claim
on parts of the continental shelf which in the view of the government of
Japan, applying the median line principle, belonged to Japan. After
protracted negotiations on the matter the two countries concluded two
Agreements: the one Agreement establishing a boundary in the northern
part of the continental shelf adjacent to the two countries (Agreement of 5
February 1974) and the other establishing a Joint Development Zone (JDZ)
in the southern part of that area (Agreement of 30 January 1974).
    In the Agreement of 5 February 1974 it was agreed to delimitate the
northern part of continental shelf concerned by constructing a median line
up to the intersection with latitude 32 degrees 57 minutes north. In the
Agreement of 30 January 1974 which created the JDZ the latter was
described as an area bounded by straight lines connecting the points
defined in the Agreement (Article II). The north-westerly boundary of the
JDZ, starting at the end point of the boundary established under the
Agreement of 5 February 1974 (the northern boundary) and ending at the
intersection with latitude 30 degrees 46 minutes north, is constructed in
accordance with the median line principle and in fact a continuation in
southern direction of the northern boundary.

10.3.2   MAIN PROVISIONS (ARTICLES II TO XXXI INCLUSIVE)

An area of 82,665 km² in the southern part of the continental shelf adjacent
to both countries, is designated as a Joint Development Zone (JDZ) for the

purpose of the joint exploration and exploitation of petroleum resources in that area (Article II).

Concessionaires of both Parties shall enter into an operating agreement to carry out jointly exploration and exploitation of petroleum resources in the JDZ. Such operating agreement shall provide *inter alia* for the following: (i) details relating to the sharing of petroleum resources and expenses in accordance with Article IX; (ii) designation of operator; (iii) treatment of sole risk operations; (iv) adjustment of fisheries interests; (v) settlement of disputes. The operating agreement and modifications thereof shall enter into force upon approval by the Parties.

The operator shall be designated by agreement between concessionaires of both Parties.

The concessionaires shall have the right of exploration and of exploitation. The duration of the exploration right shall be eight years from the date of entry into force of the operating agreement. The duration of the exploitation right shall be thirty years from the date of establishment of such right. Concessionaires of both Parties may apply to the respective Parties for an extension of an additional period of five years. When commercial discovery of petroleum resources is made during the period of exploration right, concessionaires of both Parties may apply to the respective Parties for the establishment of exploitation right. When the Parties recognize that commercial discovery is made, each Party may request its concessionaire concerned to present an application for the establishment of exploitation right.

Either Party may, subject to its own laws and regulations concerning the protection of concessionaires, cancel exploration right or exploitation right of its concessionaire after consultations with the other Party, if such concessionaire fails to discharge any of its obligations under this Agreement or the operating agreement.

In the application of the laws and regulations of each Party to petroleum resources extracted in the JDZ, the share of such petroleum resources to which concessionaires of one Party are entitled under Article IX shall be regarded as petroleum resources extracted in the continental shelf over which that Party has sovereign rights.

Except where otherwise provided in this Agreement, the laws and regulations of one Party shall apply with respect to matters relating to exploration or exploitation of petroleum resources in the sub-zone with respect that Party has authorized concessionaires designated and acting as operators.

The Parties shall agree on measures to be taken to prevent collisions at sea and to prevent and remove pollution of the sea resulting from activities relating to exploration or exploitation of petroleum resources in the JDZ.

If any single geological structure or field of petroleum resources extends across any of the lines specified in paragraph 1 of Article II (Note. Meant here are the straight lines bounding the JDZ) and the part of such structure or field which is situated on one side of such lines is exploitable, wholly or in part, from the other side of such lines, concessionaires and other persons authorized by either Party to exploit such structure or field (hereinafter referred to as 'concessionaires and other persons') shall through consultations seek to reach agreement as to the most effective method of exploitation of such structure or field. When agreement concerning such method is reached the agreement (including modifications thereof) shall enter into force upon approval by the Parties. In cases of exploitation under the aforesaid agreement, petroleum resources extracted from such structure or field and expenses reasonably attributable to exploitation of such petroleum resources shall be shared among concessionaires and other persons in proportion to the quantities of producible reserves in the respective parts of such structure or field which are situated in the area with respect to which they have been authorized by either Party. The above provisions shall apply mutatis mutandis with respect to exploitation of a single geological structure or field of petroleum resources extending across lines bounding the sub-zones of the JDZ.

The Parties shall establish and maintain the Japan – Republic of Korea Joint Commission (hereinafter referred to as 'the Commission') as a means for consultation on matters concerning the implementation of this Agreement.

Any dispute between the Parties concerning the interpretation and implementation of this Agreement shall be settled, first of all, through diplomatic channels. Any dispute which fails to be so settled shall be referred for decision to an arbitration board composed of three arbitrators, with each party appointing one arbitrator and the third arbitrator to be agreed upon by the two arbitrators so chosen or the third arbitrator to be appointed by the government of a third country agreed upon by the two arbitrators, provided that the third arbitrator shall not be a national of either Party.

Nothing in this Agreement shall be regarded as determining the question of sovereign rights over all or any portion of the JDZ or as prejudicing the positions of the respective Parties with respect to the delimitation of the continental shelf.

This Agreement shall be ratified. (Note. Both Parties have done so.) This Agreement shall remain in force for a period of fifty years and shall continue in force thereafter until terminated by either Party by giving three years written notice to the other Party. Notwithstanding the foregoing provisions when either Party recognizes that petroleum resources are no longer economically exploitable in the JDZ, the Parties shall consult with each other whether to revise or terminate this Agreement.

Note. The two Agreements of 1974 were made in the period that the 1958 Convention on the Continental Shelf was still in force. Also known to the Parties was the Judgment of 20 February 1969 of the International Court of Justice at The Hague in the *North Sea Continental Shelf Cases*. In its Judgment the Court held that any coastal State has an original right to those areas of the continental shelf which constituted the natural prolongation of its land territory into and under the sea. The Republic of Korea based its position on that Judgment maintaining that the continental shelf adjacent to the two countries should be divided taking into account the natural prolongation of its land mass. When in 1994 the 1958 Convention was replaced by the 1982 Convention on the Law of the Sea the extent of the continental shelf was described in Article 76 of the Convention in accordance with the Court's Judgment of 1969, albeit coupled to a minimum distance of 200 nautical miles from the shoreline (thus coinciding with the Exclusive Economic Zone). Since both Parties reserved their position on the delimitation of the continental shelf, the final determination of the boundaries, if it would ever come to that, would have to be guided by said Article 76. From the outset it can be said that the outcome of such final determination is far from clear since both countries may at least claim the EEZ and whether there is room for an extended continental shelf which have to be demarcated remains to be seen.

10.4   THE 1989 AGREEMENT BETWEEN AUSTRALIA AND INDONESIA

The Agreement of 11 December 1989 ('the Agreement') made between Australia and the Republic of Indonesia created the Timor Gap Zone of Cooperation (the Zone) in an area of the continental shelf situated between the (then) Indonesian Province of East Timor and northern Australia, an area measuring 62,000 square km.

The Zone is divided in three parts, designated respectively as Area A, which is the middle and largest part, Area B and Area C. Areas B and C fall under the jurisdiction of Indonesia and Australia respectively, but each State has accepted to keep the other informed about the administration of its petroleum legislation with respect to its Area and, more importantly, to surrender to the other ten per cent of the relevant tax revenues collected by it from the producers in its Area.

In Area A, the area in the middle, there shall be joint control by the Contracting States of the exploration for and exploitation of petroleum resources, aimed at achieving optimum commercial utilization thereof and 50/50 sharing between the Contracting States of the benefits of the exploitation of petroleum resources as provided for in this Agreement (see Note 2 hereinbelow).

Operational activities in Area A are governed by the Petroleum Mining Code which is annexed to the Agreement as Annex B. Petroleum operations in Area A shall be carried out through production sharing contracts, a model of which is annexed to the Agreement as Annex C. The law applicable to a production sharing contract shall be specified in the contract.

Note 1. The model contract has to a large extent been modelled on the at the time latest Indonesian type of production sharing contract with the Joint Authority being substituted for Pertamina.

The joint administration shall be exercised by the Ministerial Council consisting of an equal number of Ministers designated by each Contracting State, and by the Joint Authority who shall be responsible to the Ministerial Council.

The Ministerial Council shall *inter alia*: give directions to the Joint Authority on the discharge of its functions; amend the Petroleum Mining Code and modify the Model Production Sharing Contract to facilitate petroleum operations in Area A; shall have to approve: (1) the terms of the production sharing contracts which the Joint Authority may propose to enter in with corporations; (2) the variation, with the agreement of the contractor, of the production sharing terms, the duration and area relinquishment rules; and (3) the distribution to Australia and the Republic of Indonesia of revenues derived from production sharing contracts in Area A.

The Joint Authority is required to divide Area A into contract areas, issuing prospecting approvals and commissioning environmental investigations prior to contract areas being advertised, advertising of contract areas, assessing applications and making recommendations to the Ministerial Council on applications for production sharing contracts. For the purpose of awarding contracts, Area A has been subdivided into fourteen contract areas. Each contract area is subdivided in geometric blocks measuring five minutes by five minutes.

The Joint Authority shall to enter into production sharing contracts with corporations subject to Ministerial Council approval, to supervise the activities of the contractor pursuant to the requirements of the Petroleum Mining Code and the terms and conditions set out in the contract; to recommend to the Ministerial Council the termination of production sharing contracts where contractors do not meet the terms and conditions of those contracts; etc.

The Joint Authority is required to issue regulations and giving directions under the Petroleum Mining Code on all matters related to the supervision of and control of petroleum operations including on health, safety, environmental protection and assessments and work practices, pursuant to the Petroleum Mining Code and to make recommendations to the Ministerial Council to amend the Code and to modify the Model Production Sharing Contract consistent with the objectives of this Treaty.

The Contracting States shall cooperate to prevent and minimize pollution of the marine environment arising from the exploration for and exploitation of petroleum in Area A. The Joint Authority shall issue regulations to protect the marine environment in Area A and shall establish a contingency plan for combating pollution from petroleum operations in that Area.

Contractors shall be liable for damage or expenses incurred as a result of pollution of the marine environment arising out of petroleum operations in Area A in accordance with contractual arrangements with the Joint Authority and the law of the Contracting State in which a claim in respect of such damage or expenses is brought.

If any single accumulation of petroleum extends across any of the boundary lines of Area A and the part of such accumulation that is situated on one side of a line, is exploitable, wholly or in part, from the other side of the line, the Contracting States shall seek to reach agreement on the manner in which the accumulation shall be most effectively exploited and on the equitable sharing of the benefits arising from such exploitation.

For the purposes of the taxation law related directly or indirectly to: (a) the exploration for or the exploitation of petroleum in Area A; or (b) acts, matters, circumstances and things touching, concerning, arising out or connected with any such exploration or exploitation, Area A shall be deemed to be and be treated by each Contracting State as part of that Contracting State. In the application of the taxation law in Area A Contracting State shall grant relief from double taxation in accordance with the Taxation Code contained in Annex D. In accordance with said Code, the business profits or losses of a person other than an individual (e.g., a contractor) derived from or incurred in Area A in a year shall be reduced by fifty per cent.

Note. 'Taxation law' means the federal law of Australia or the law of the Republic of Indonesia, from time to time in force, in respect of taxes to which this Agreement applies (excepting tax agreements between States).

Any dispute arising between the Contracting States concerning the inter-pretation or application of this Agreement shall be resolved by consultation or negotiation between the Contracting States.

Each production sharing contract entered into by the Joint Authority shall contain provisions to the effect that any dispute concerning the interpretation or application of such contract shall be submitted to a specified form of binding commercial arbitration. The Contracting States shall facilitate the enforcement in their respective courts of arbitral awards made pursuant to such arbitration.

The Agreement contains the assurance that, in case the Agreement ceases to exist following the conclusion of a further agreement between the Contracting States regarding the permanent delimitation of the continental shelf in the area of the Zone, any production sharing contract then existing shall continue to apply to each State, or its competent authority nominated in place of the Joint Authority in so far as the contract is to be performed within the area of its newly established jurisdiction.

Note 1. The Agreement was made against the background of the rules and provisions of the 1982 Convention on the Law of the Sea, including the new definition of 'continental shelf' contained in paragraph 1 of Article 76. This worked in favour of the Republic of Indonesia, which was faced with the geographical disadvantage of having the deep Timor trough close by, at least within 200 nautical miles from the coast.

Note 2. On 20 May 2002, the Indonesian Province of East Timor became an independent State named *Timor Lorosae* (East Timor). The new State shall have assumed all the rights and obligations of the Republic of Indonesia as Contracting State under this Agreement. Consequently any reference made in this Agreement to the Republic of Indonesia must be taken *mutatis mutandis* to be a reference to East Timor. Nonetheless, the Contracting States (Australia and East Timor) agreed in July 2002 to modify the terms of the Agreement to the effect that all revenues accruing to the Joint Authority under production sharing contracts in Area A would be shared between the Contracting States in a 90/10 (formerly 50/50) proportion in favour of East Timor.

10.5   THE 1979 STATFJORD AGREEMENT

The Statfjord Agreement (formally known as: 'Agreement between the Government of the United Kingdom of Great Britain and Northern Ireland and the Government of the Kingdom of Norway relating to the Exploitation of the Statfjord Field Reservoirs and the Offtake of Petroleum therefrom'), was signed on 16 October 1979.

The Statfjord Agreement (hereinafter 'the Agreement') implemented Article 4 of the Boundary Agreement of 10 March 1965 in making provision for the exploitation of the Statfjord Fields Reservoirs as a single unit and for the regulation of the offtake of production from the Statfjord Field Reservoirs.

The Agreement states as a basic principle that the Statfjord Field Reservoirs shall be exploited as a single unit. The respective licensees were required to enter into agreements between themselves for the purpose of regulating the exploitation in accordance with the provisions of the Agreement. Such agreements of cooperation (in fact the unitization agreement in the proper sense of the word) and any proposed amendment thereto need the prior approval of the two Governments.

The two Governments shall jointly demarcate the dividing line defined in the Agreement of 10 March 1965.

The two Governments shall consult each other with a view to agreeing determinations of the limits of the Statfjord Field Reservoirs, of estimated total reserves and of the apportionment of the Reserves as between the Norwegian and the UK parts of the continental shelf. The two Governments shall endeavour to agree the apportonment of the Reserves before production commencement date (which date is defined as the date of loading of the first tankship). The licensees are required to submit to the governments a proposal for such determinations.

'Reserves' are defined as the volume of oil present in the Statfjord Field Reservoirs before the start of production, measured and determined as 'stock tank oil originally in place', in accordance with the procedures to be described in the agreements of cooperation between the licensees.

The two Governments shall require there respective licensees at all times to share the production of Statfjord petroleum such that the cumulative volume of Statfjord petroleum received by the licensees of the UK Government and the cumulative volume of Statfjord petroleum received by the licensees of the Norwegian Government shall each correspond to the apportionment of the Reserves pursuant to the apportionment agreed between the two Governments before the production commencement date.

Either government may request a review of the limits of the Statfjord Field Reservoirs, of the total amount of the Reserves and of the apportionment of the Reserves or any of them in order to arrive at a re-determination according to a time schedule set out in the Agreement. The first date for a re-determination is set on the second 1st January following the production commencement date. The next date is on fourth 1st January and so on.

All re-determinations shall have effect from the first day of the month following the month when the re-determination has been agreed by both governments, the intention being that such agreement will be reached on or soon after the scheduled date of the relevant re-determination.

Each Government shall require its licensees to conduct all operations necessary for each revision and to secure that at the time the production from the Statfjord Field Reservoirs ceases the share of the total volume of Statfjord petroleum received by the licensees of the UK Government, and the share of the total volume of Statfjord petroleum received by the licensees of the Norwegian Government shall each correspond to the final apportionment of the Reserves.

Whenever the apportionment of the Reserves is revised the licensees shall adjust deliveries between themselves to ensure that imbalances deriving from the superseded apportionment are made good.

The Governments shall ensure that for the purposes of the exploitation of the Statfjord Field Reservoirs a unit operator is appointed by agreement between the licensees. The appointment shall be subject to the approval of the two Governments.

Licensees are required to exploit the Statfjord Field Reservoirs in accordance with a programme which has been approved by the two Governments. The Governments may jointly agree to its amendment at any time. The approval, amendment and implementation of the programme shall take account of the objective that the Statfjord Field Reservoirs be exploited in such manner as to prevent the waste of petroleum and minimize losses of reservoir energy.

In the event of the expiry, surrender or revocation of any production license or any part of such a license relating to any part of the Statfjord Field Reservoirs, the Government, which issued the license, shall ensure that the exploitation of the Statfjord Field Reservoirs is continued in accordance with the terms of the Agreement and the agreements between the licensees. In particular the Government concerned must take one of the following steps:

(i) issue a new license in replacement of the license which has expired or been surrendered or revoked; or

(ii) itself conduct such exploitation as if it were a licensee; or

(iii) take such other action to continue the exploitation of the Statfjord Field Reservoirs as the two Governments may agree.

Each Government affirms that it has the sole responsibilty for all inspections of installations situated its part of the continental shelf and of all operations carried out on such installations. Each Government undertakes to procure access to them and their equipment for, and the production of relevant information to inspectors appointed by the other Government to anable those inspectors to satisfy themselves that the fundamental interests of their Government with regard to safety, petroleum production and measurement are met.

Each Government recognizes the right of the other Government and of the licensees of the other Government to take directly from the Statfjord Area to the territory of the other Government that share of Statfjord petroleum to which the licensees of the other Government are entitled under the provisions of this Agreement, notwithstanding the location of the installatons from which the Statfjord petroleum is produced, and accordingly each Government shall in accordance with and subject to applicable laws grant any necessary licenses and grant any necessary consents concerning the construction and operation of any system of offtake to transport or transmit Statfjord petroleum in exercise of that right.

Note. The offloading into tankship has been chosen as the final solution of the oil transportation problem. For the transmission of associated gas a pipeline has been built bringing the gas to Karstö on the Norwegian mainland.

Profits, gains and capital in respect of the exploitation of the Statfjord Field Reservoirs shall be taxed in accordance with the laws of the United Kingdom and Norway respectively. This principle is worked out in separate protocols.

Nothing in this Agreement shall be interpreted as affecting the jurisdiction which each State has under international law over its part of the continental shelf. In particular, installations located on the UK part of the continental shelf shall be under UK jurisdiction and installations located on the Norwegian part of the continental shelf shall be under Norwegian jurisdiction.

Chapter 11

Cooperative Exploration and Production Agreements

11.1 THE EARLY PERIOD

In the wake of the boring of the first oil well by Drake in 1859, many landowners or their leaseholders in Pennsylvania and Ontario tried their luck and became oil producers. They worked on small-sized plots of land, on which they tried to install as many drilling derricks as space allowed in order to be able to produce oil at the highest rates possible. Although not having a clear idea about subsoil oil reservoirs and the flowing behaviour of oil therein, they were anyway convinced that any oil not produced by their wells would be produced by the wells drilled by their neighbours. Nonetheless, these pioneer producers worked their wells independently from one another, without any form of cooperation being considered necessary or desirable. This non-cooperative attitude was completely in line with the way gold prospectors in those days were accustomed to operate. The gold miner worked its staked-out plots inside the gold field (riverbank, etc.), independent from anyone else and was prepared to defend his claim territory against any newcomer. In contrast with the gold miner, however, the pioneer oil producer considered and treated his neighbours as competitors being under the impression that he and his neighbours were draining one and the same oil pool and that the oil contained in the pool would flow into and be caught in the neighbour's wells, if not timely caught in his own wells. Remarkably, among the producers and in the courts of law there was never any doubt regarding the producer's right to take possession and become the owner of any oil that entered any well drilled (vertically) by the producer within the confines of his land property or lease area. This right was referred to as 'the rule of capture' or *profit a prendre*. However, intentional deviation of a bore hole into the neighbour's domain and draining oil by means of such deviated hole was considered stealing and non-permissible. The question of who owns the oil in the subsoil reservoir (oil *in situ*) received generally little attention, the producers being only interested in producing their wells at maximum rates and selling a maximum quantity at the wellhead to the buyers from the numerous refineries that meanwhile had been installed for refining the oil into kerosene. In the course of time a market for oil developed in which many small volume producers traded with many small volume kerosene refiners. On the side of the producers, situations of over-supply alternated with periods of shortage due to the wasteful way in which the oil was being produced. This instability on the supply side caused hefty price fluctuations. In contrast with the producers the refinery owners (known as oil companies) aimed at organization and concentration of commercial power whereby Rockefeller's Standard Oil Company, established in 1870, restructured as the Standard Oil Trust in 1882, took the lead. When around 1885 oil was discovered outside Pennsylvania and oil production had started to spread over the US continent Standard Oil, later followed by the other oil companies, changed its policy of restricting itself to monopolizing the refinery sector. Instead, the oil companies started to intervene in the business of the producers by acquiring production leases for their own risk and account. The pattern that now established itself on the US continent was that of an oil company following the oil prospector and waiting for him to make a discovery. As soon as this would happen, the oil company would try and buy or lease any land on which the discovery was made, together with any land in the surrounding area. In this manner the oil companies sought to forestall that any prospective acreage would fall into the hands of speculators. In the process the oil companies were collecting large-sized leases thereby reducing the chance that an oil field would be developed and produced by a multitude of persons, resulting in a waste of capital, over-production and reservoir damage.

Note. In reaction to the inroads that the oil companies were making into the production sector, independent producers in the oldest producing areas were looking for protection and tried to find such protection in cooperating with independent refiners, forming a joint venture rather than an integrated venture.

Although the number of independent, small-sized lease holdings gradually diminished as a result of bundling and integration processes, on numerous occasions the new larger-sized lease areas still proved to be small compared with the size of the underground reservoir or proved to have the wrong orientation in respect thereof. In either case the new leaseholders were confronted with a situation in which a reservoir was shared between two or more of them. Over time, as more became known about petroleum reservoirs in general, and about the forces (known as the drive mechanisms) that were responsible for driving the oil or gas to the borehole, the new leaseholders, sharing a common reservoir, started to realize that to produce a common reservoir in an efficient manner, with the objective of maximizing the ultimate recovery, mutual cooperation in matters of production would be necessary. In particular, when it became clear that injection of water at the margins of a common oil accumulation would improve the ultimate recovery, the new leaseholders showed a willingness to consider and agree among themselves the joint, integral development and exploitation of such a reservoir. In this way, the ground was prepared for cooperation between producers, a new attitude that hitherto had never found favour among them.

11.2   THE MIDDLE EAST JOINT VENTURES

When moving into the Middle East, the major US and European oil companies established joint ventures for the purpose of acquiring concessions and producing oil from their areas except for the venture in Persia. In that country the search for oil followed the old pattern known from the early days in the US whereby the lonely prospector is being followed by an oil company waiting for the right moment (i.e., after a discovery was made) to take-over the lease in question and some more leases next to it. In this case, the prospector was William Knox D'Arcy, who was granted on 28 May 1901 a concession covering the whole country with (deliberate) deletion of the five northern provinces, the ones bordering on Tsarist Russia, and the oil company, that one year after oil was struck in 1908 at Masjid-I-Suleiman and after having raised the necessary finance, took over his concession was the Anglo-Persian Oil Company. Nonetheless, an incorporated joint venture was created when for strategic reasons the UK government acquired in August 1914, a few days after the outbreak of the First World War, a controlling interest of 51.7 per cent in the company.

On 20 March 1951 Anglo-Persian's 1933 concession agreement was taken over by the newly established National Iranian Oil Company (NIOC). After three and a half years of negotiations a contract of work, covering the area of the former concession, was made between NIOC and Iranian Oil Participants Ltd., a UK company, better known as the Consortium. The Iranian Oil Participants Ltd. constituted an incorporated joint venture replacing Anglo-Iranian the former sole concessionaire. Shareholders and shareholding in the new joint company were fixed as follows: 40 per cent for Anglo-Iranian Oil Company, the former concessionaire and on this occasion renamed British Petroleum Company (BP); 14 per cent for Royal Dutch/Shell; 6 per cent for CFP; 40 per cent for a group of US oil companies, this 40 per cent distributed among them as follows: 7 per cent for each of Standard of New Jersey, Standard of California, Socony Mobil, Texaco and Gulf Oil, and 5 per cent for Iricon

Agency, Ltd., the latter owned by 9 US oil companies, among them Standard of Ohio, Atlantic Refining and Getty Oil, the latter each having 0.417 per cent.

For the ventures in Iraq and the various countries of the Arabian Peninsula incorporated joint ventures were created from the outset because the participating companies were aware of the fact that they were dealing with large and largely unexplored areas that might require huge investments.

In the end, the concessions made in the 1930s in the Middle East Gulf area including the successor contract of work agreed with NIOC were all held by joint venture companies, the shares in which were held by affiliates of the participating major groups.

These joint venture companies were:

(i) Iraq Petroleum Company (IPC) and its sister-companies (companies in which the shares were held by the same companies holding shares in IPC, also known as IPC-group companies), representing a joint venture of BP, Royal Dutch/Shell, CFP, Exxon, Mobil and Partex (the IPC-group). IPC-group companies held concessions in respectively Iraq (three separate concessions), Qatar, Abu Dhabi and Oman.

(ii) The Iranian Oil Participants (the Consortium), a joint venture of BP, Royal Dutch/Shell, CFP, Gulf; and, as of 1954, holding a contract of work in respect of the area of Anglo-Iranian's former concession.

(iii) Kuwait Oil Company, a joint venture of BP and Gulf, covering the land territory of Kuwait.

(iv) Aramco, a joint venture of Texaco, Exxon, Chevron and Mobil (the Aramco partners).

Each joint venture company represented an incorporated joint venture. The joint venture company held, maintained and operated the concession concerned. It sold the realized production to its shareholders or rather to the trading companies established by the shareholders for this purpose. The trading companies bought their respective shareholders' production entitlements at cost and, in their turn, sold the production to their own shareholders at the applicable posted price. The trading companies were responsible for paying income taxes with respect to their profits calculated on the basis of the posted price. In its turn, the joint venture company, as concessionaire, was responsible for paying the royalties and fulfilling the other obligations imposed by the concession. The shareholders decided on policy matters and were responsible for making capital contributions, mostly in the forms of loans to the joint venture company. These loans were paid back by the company out of the sales proceeds. The shareholders' main responsibility was to decide on the development of production capacity determining future production levels, and to approve the capital and operating costs budgets. In view of the almost unlimited reserves contained in the respective concessions the production capacity had no natural constraints and could be developed solely and entirely in accordance with the long-term marketing requirements of the individual shareholders. In accordance with nomination procedures each shareholder made known (nominated) the quantity of oil that it required over three year cycles, the first year of the cycle divided in quarters. Each shareholder was entitled to nominate its shareholding percentage interest of the estimated production capacity as announced by the company in advance of the nomination procedure, but was free to nominate a lesser quantity, if temporarily it needed less oil for its markets. If due to under-nominations the installed production capacity was not fully utilized, a second round of nominations might follow in order to give participants that nominated their full entitlement the opportunity to become over-nominators within the limits of any surplus capacity. Nominations for the quarters of the first year of the cycle had to be firm with an offtake obligation attached to it; nominations for second and third year of the cycle were allowed to be tentative, subject to a further narrowing down as the year moved forwards in the cycle. On the basis of the nominations the operator would prepare the production schedule, aiming to produce sufficient oil to satisfy the total shareholders' demand, meaning the sum of the individual nominations. Capital contributions were not fixed in accordance with shareholding interests, but based on the shareholders' individual final nominations over the nomination cycle. The flexibility in making nominations, coupled with the flexibility in capital contributions, worked quite well against the background of an unlimited production potential, for participants, whose shareholding interest in the produced volumes often did not correspond with their marketing requirements, and for governments continuously pressing to increase production. Because of these flexible arrangements production capacity could be expanded and financed and production levels could be increased (in accordance with the wishes of the government), even if some of the participants might not need any such additional capacity and would, if operating the concession on their own and not being a participant in a joint venture, find it difficult to make additional capital available for that purpose.

Around 1975, the governments in the Middle East Gulf area completed their take-over of the concessions and concessionaires' other assets falling under their respective jurisdictions. The Middle East joint ventures were dissolved or completely restructured, but the experience gained with operating oil fields within the framework of a joint venture was not lost. On balance, this experience had been favourable, at least for the majors. Working together within the framework of the Middle East joint ventures had enabled the majors to control the supply to the market and to avoid price-cutting competition among them. In fact, market sharing between and among the majors actually took place when implementing the production nomination and allocation procedures envisaged by the joint venture agreement. The Middle East joint ventures were unique in the sense that production capacity could be developed in accordance with the marketing requirements of the participants, without being constrained by the size of the available reserves, and perhaps more importantly the abundant reserves could be developed in an inexpensive manner, making Middle East oil very competitive in the global oil market.

11.3   THE CONTEMPORARY JOINT VENTURE

11.3.1   PRINCIPLES AND OBJECTIVES

The example set by the Middle East joint ventures was followed by explorers and producers elsewhere in the world, even before the demise of said joint ventures. First of all, the major oil companies themselves showed their preference for extending their cooperation in exploration and production activities to areas outside the Middle East. Well-known examples are the joint venture formed by Royal Dutch/Shell and BP for operating the licenses and leases granted to them in Nigeria, and the joint ventures between Royal Dutch/Shell and Exxon in respect of respectively the Netherlands (onshore and offshore, including Western Europe's largest onshore gas field), and the UK part of the North Sea continental shelf, where subsequently many important oil and gas fields were discovered. Soon thereafter most commercial oil enterprises including state-owned enterprises embraced the joint venture approach when contemplating to start an exploration/production venture, so much so that setting up a joint venture for the purpose of jointly applying for or acquiring petroleum rights and for jointly conducting the authorized exploration and production operations has become standard practice.

The main reasons for this practice are the wish, not to say the absolute necessity to spread and minimize the various risks attached to the intended petroleum venture and to share among the participants the generally huge investments that will be required.

These risks can be summed up as follows:

(i) Geological risk. This is the risk that no commercial petroleum will be discovered.

(ii) Technical risk. This is the risk inherent in having to operate under difficult and hazardous conditions, such as difficult or extreme weather and sea conditions, floating icebergs and/or having to work under extreme circumstances like operating in very deep water or in the Arctic region.

(iii) Development risk. This is the risk that the petroleum encountered in the reservoir proves difficult to produce due the negative characteristics of the reservoir and/or of the petroleum itself.

(iv) Environmental risk. This is the risk that the operations undertaken are causing damage to the environment, when having to work in a from an environmental point of view, sensitive area: the Arctic is an example of a very sensitive area. The ultimate environmental risk is the risk that the operations have to be abandoned when it appears that they would have to be carried out under conditions so restricted that these cannot be met at reasonable cost.

(v) Political risk. This risk is nowadays perhaps the most powerful argument for setting up a joint exploration and production venture. In particular Western private sector oil enterprises when considering an exploration and production venture in a politically risky State are keenly interested in seeking the cooperation of a commercial oil enterprise owned by the State in question.

Apart from the wish to spread and minimize the aforementioned risks and to share large-scale investments, commercial oil enterprises may have other, secondary reasons for willingly seeking to cooperate with other similar enterprises. These reasons are:

(i) to improve the chance to be successful in a bidding procedure. This is a powerful reason for a Western private sector oil enterprise to seek cooperation with a state-owned oil enterprise generally, but by preference with an enterprise that is owned by the (prospective) host State;

(ii) to obtain a participating interest in a license or contract of work already awarded to another commercial oil enterprise; or

(iii) to benefit from the superior technology and/or geological knowledge or experience of another commercial oil enterprise. This is a powerful argument for a state-owned oil enterprise to seek cooperation with a Western private sector oil enterprise.

Commercial oil enterprises, wishing for any one of the aforementioned reasons to set up and participate in a joint exploration and production venture, must start by agreeing between and amongst themselves what type of joint venture, i.e., an incorporated joint venture or a non-incorporated one, they want to have.

Note. In case the interested parties opt for the incorporation of their joint venture, a joint venture company will have to be established, in which the participants become shareholders with individual shareholdings in proportion to their respective participating interests. This was the practice followed for the former Middle East joint ventures. But after the demise of these joint ventures, interested parties have shown to prefer the non-incorporated form of cooperation whereby each participant holds an undivided participating interest in the still to be applied for petroleum rights and in the venture that will be based thereon.

After having settled this, the interested parties now becoming committed participants, must take decisions regarding the following basic subjects:

   (i) the selection of the area for the intended venture;
  (ii) the distribution of the individual participating interests;
 (iii) the appointment of an operator.

With reference to (iii). The participant with the largest participating interest, and/or who possesses the right type of technology, and/or technical capability for undertaking the intended joint venture will usually be appointed as the operator. Otherwise, if there is little to choose between the participants, it will be the participant which took the initiative with regard to the venture. Once appointed, the operator will coordinate the bidding for the required petroleum rights in accordance with the terms and conditions of a bidding agreement made by the prospective participants.

If the committed participants wish and are legally not restrained from doing so to opt for the non-incorporated joint venture and after having made the decisions regarding the basic subjects listed above further agreement on the more detailed but still rather basic features of such type of joint venture should be reached at an early stage in order to forestall difficulties when a full-fledged joint operating agreement (JOA) has to be made. Said features to be agreed upon can be summed up as follows:

   (i) to apply for, acquire and hold in an undivided participating interest the necessary petroleum right with respect to the area that has been selected for the joint venture operations;

  (ii) to form a management committee for formulating policies and for approving the work programmes, development plans and corresponding budgets as prepared by the operator and in which committee all participants are represented with voting rights in accordance with their participating interests;

 (iii) to oblige the operator to conduct the joint operations in accordance with work programmes, development plans and corresponding budgets as approved by the said management committee; and

 (iv) to share in proportion to their participating interests any expenditure and expenses, any liabilities and risks associated with the joint operations, any production, that may be forthcoming from these operations and to which the participants are entitled under the rules of the license or contract, and similarly share any other assets acquired in the course of the joint operations.

11.3.2   COMMON CONDITIONS OF THE JOA

11.3.2.1   Introduction and Recitals

Identification of the participants and a description of the authorization (be it an exclusive license or a contract of work), on which the joint venture is based.

11.3.2.2   Definitions

It is customary to precede the main body of the agreement with an article containing definitions of important terms and expressions. It allows the text of the remainder of the agreement to be concise and easy to read. As required or desired this article may be confined to a limited number of typical expressions or include any expression that has a particular meaning in the context of the operations or procedures described in the agreement.

11.3.2.3   Duration

The main body of the JOA endures for as long as the underlying authorization remains valid and is held by two or more participants. Some articles are declared to remain in effect until certain events have been properly dealt with, such as the settlement of disputes or the abandonment of wells, field installations and other facilities.

11.3.2.4   Purpose and Scope

Basically, the cooperation takes place within the framework of a jointly owned authorization, be it an exclusive license or a production sharing contract, and is aimed at the production of oil and natural gas to the mutual commercial benefit of the participants. Mutual cooperation starts with the search for petroleum accumulations and ends at the point where the operator delivers to each participant its share of the oil and natural gas production to which the participants collectively are entitled under the rules of the authorization granted. Not all operations falling under the authorization are carried out as joint operations for the joint account of all participants. To a certain extent, departures from the joint venture principle are allowed. For this purpose a JOA will provide for a non-consent option, permitting participants to stay out of operations adopted and approved by the other participants possessing the majority required to take binding decisions, and for a sole risk option, permitting part of the authorized operations to be carried out for the sole risk and account of one or more but less than all participants.

In contrast, the scope of the joint venture and the extent of the joint operations may be extended to include the joint disposal of natural gas production. Such joint disposal and marketing of the natural gas production may be necessary in view of the requirements and peculiarities involved in the handling and transportation of natural gas and of its marketing. When the marketing is done on a joint basis, each participant dedicates its share of the natural gas production to the same long-term gas sales agreement (alternatively selling its share of the production on identical terms to the same buyer).

11.3.2.5   Participating Interests

The distribution of the participating interests among the participants belongs to the basic conditions of the joint venture agreement. In principle, the distribution does not have to be even, but an uneven distribution gives some participants a greater weight than others. The right balance between uneven interests has to be found in appropriate voting rules accompanied by procedures to protect the economic interests of frustrated participants, i.e., by providing for the aforementioned non-consent and sole risk options.

11.3.2.6 Basic Rights, Obligations and Liabilities

Participants own undivided interests in the underlying authorization, in the oil and gas production made available by the operator and to which the participants as licensee or contractor collectively are entitled under the terms of the said authorization, and in any other assets acquired by operator for or in the course of the operations (unless the ownership of those assets have to be or are automatically transferred to the state party in accordance with the terms of the underlying production sharing contract).

All obligations imposed under the authorization and all liabilities arising in connection with the conduct of the authorized operations and any and all expenditures incurred by the operator, and charged by the latter to the joint account or to any particular sole risk account, as the case may be, are shared and borne by the participants in proportion to their respective (relevant) participating interests in such account, except to the extent that the operator is solely liable (see below). Each participant is obliged to indemnify the operator or any other participant having to make a payment with respect to any such obligation or liability, if not charged to a joint or sole risk account, in proportion to its respective participating interest. Each participant has the basic duty to pay its proportional financial contributions in advance, in cash and in the currency as requested by the operator. Any JOA will contain a cash call procedure providing for cash calls to be made well in advance of the moment the operator is required to make payments in order to avoid the occurrence of cash shortages and to forestall that the operator should have to use its own funds.

11.3.2.7 The Operator

The JOA records the appointment of the operator of the joint venture and the fact that the participant so appointed agrees to act as operator. As said before, the appointment of the operator will already have taken place in the initial stage of setting up the joint venture. In rare cases, not the selected participant itself but one of its affiliated companies may become the operator. Such operator has no participating interest in the joint venture. Then there is, of course, always the possibility that the participants decide to appoint an independent third party as operator. This could be necessary if the participants have little experience with oil exploration or production matters. If any of the participants (or any of its affiliated companies) act as operator, it is recorded that such participant will make no profits nor has to suffer losses as a consequence of acting as operator.

The operator's rights comprise the following:

(i) the exclusive right to conduct and carry out the authorized operations;

(ii) to demand cash contributions in advance from the participants;

(iii) to represent the participants vis-à-vis the government and/or state party and vis-à-vis other third parties; in the latter context the operator shall represent the participants in disputes and the settlement thereof with third parties;

(iv) to employ and make use of sub-contractors and agents, provided the rules for awarding contracts as incorporated in the agreement (e.g., international tendering, specifications and final award subject to management committee's approval, etc.) are being observed;

(v) to employ expatriate and national personnel on the operator's conditions (level of salaries, currency of payment, special benefits, numbers, description of required qualifications, etc.);

(vi) to make use of the technical and personnel services of its parent company or of its specialized affiliated companies and to pay for such internal services at the rates provided for in the JOA.

The operator's main duties are:

(i) within the framework of and subject to the terms, conditions and instructions contained the underlying license or contract relating to approval of work programmes and development plans, to prepare and submit for the review and approval of the management committee annual work programmes and corresponding budgets; the development plan for any discovery declared to be commercial; special work programmes (i.e., work programmes meant for the evaluation and appraisal of any discovery made and work programmes made for the abandonment of wells, fields and installations) and corresponding budgets; and after approval having been given to carry out all such work programmes and development plans in accordance with the terms and conditions of the underlying license or contract;

(ii) to procure and maintain all insurance required under applicable law and/or petroleum right and such further insurance as the management committee may decide, provided always that each participant may refuse to participate in such additional insurance, obtaining instead its own insurance (e.g., a participant belonging to a large oil group may obtain insurance from one of its affiliated companies and opt for self-insurance), if considered adequate and acceptable by the management committee;

(iii) to carry a special liability for damages and losses arising in connection with its conduct of the operations, in case such damage or loss has been caused by the wilful misconduct or gross negligence of senior supervisory personnel of operator or any of its affiliates (if such affiliates have been engaged by operator for the purpose of the operations). In such case the operator or its affiliated companies carry the sole liability and the other participants do not have to indemnify the operator to the extent of their participating interest as they otherwise would have been obliged to do. Excluded from operator's special liability are any consequential damages, environmental damage, damage caused to a producing reservoir, loss of production and the cost of pollution control and that of environmental rehabilitation. These damages and costs, when occurring and irrespective of how caused, have to be borne by all participants in proportion to their respective (relevant) participating interests.

With reference to (i). In carrying out the said annual, special work programmes and development plans in the form as finally approved (and possibly amended) by the management committee in accordance with the relevant terms and conditions of the underlying license or contract, the operator has the right to incur over-expenditures within certain narrow limits expressed as a percentage of total budget and as a percentage of the individual budget item being overspent. Some JOAs provide for an Authority for Expenditure (AFE) procedure. This procedure requires the operator, before entering into any commitment or incurring any expenditure under an approved work programme and budget, to submit an AFE in respect thereof. The information to be included in an AFE is set out in the accounting procedure. AFEs have to be approved by the management committee. Voting requirements with respect to decisions regarding an AFE will be as prescribed with respect to routine operational matters, because the AFE concerns expenditure and commitments under an already approved budget. To the extent that the management committee approves an AFE the operator will be authorized and obligated to proceed with such commitment or expenditure;

The provisions regarding the operator are completed with a procedure dealing with the resignation, removal and succession of the operator.

11.3.2.8   The Management Committee

The JOA stipulates the establishment of a management committee, in which all participants are represented with voting rights in proportion to their respective participating interests. The task and mandate of the management is (i) to ensure that all work programmes, development plans, production schedules, etc. as prepared and submitted by the operator are in conformity with the terms and conditions of the underlying license or contract related to the approval of such programmes, plans and schedules, to provide guidelines for the operator for this purpose, and generally to prevent at all times that the license or contract will be revoked because of non-compliance with its terms; (ii) to formulate policy and to make binding decisions in joint venture matters, provided any such decision is supported by the voting majority required therefore as specified and stipulated in the JOA.

The required voting majorities may range from unanimity to any kind of qualified majority to a simple majority, depending on the subject matter to be decided upon, on the number of participants and the distribution of participating interests among the latter, and on whether the JOA contains a non-consent option and/or a sole risk option.

Meetings of the management committee are called by the operator. The main business at the meetings of the management committee consists of ensuring compliance with the terms and conditions of the underlying license or contract, and within this context and for this purpose reviewing, discussing, amending, if necessary, and finally approving in accordance with the voting rules of the JOA:

   (i) the annual work programmes and corresponding budgets as pre-
         pared and submitted by the operator;
  (ii) a notification of a (commercial) discovery and any subsequent plan
         of appraisal or development, as the case may be;
 (iii) production schedules;
 (iv) programmes and budgets concerning the abandonment of produc-
         tion facilities; and
  (v) conditions and specifications of the international tendering of
         major contracts and the award thereof.

11.3.2.9   The Non-consent Option

The non-consent option is an option available to any participant permitting the latter to opt out of participating in an operation that was adopted and approved by the management committee in accordance with the voting rules of the JOA, provided the participant in question had voted against the operation, when it was proposed in a meeting of the management committee, and provided the operation proposed was not an operation aimed at (i) fulfilling any obligatory exploration work programme, (ii) implementing a development plan approved by the competent authority under the relevant terms of the license or contract; or (iii) the abandonment of a production facility (abandonment operation). After use is made of the non-consent option, the remaining, consenting participants are not obliged to proceed with the proposed operation. In turn each of them has the right to withdraw its given consent and withdraw from the proposed operation. If all remaining participants decide to withdraw their consent, the operation will be cancelled.

11.3.2.10   The Sole Risk Option

The sole risk option aims to protect the economic interests of any participant, whose proposal of making investments or further investments in the venture is rejected in a meeting of the management committee, or who opposes a proposal to abandon a production facility, being itself in favour of continuing production.

In principle the sole risk option is available for any operation that can (also) be carried out as a joint operation but cannot be exercised with respect to (a) any operation with forms part of (i) a development plan that has been prepared and submitted to and received approval of the competent authority under the terms of the underlying license or contract; (ii) an enhanced recovery scheme; or (b) any operation aimed at the abandonment of a production facility.

The sole risk option permits the participant, who wishes to make use of this option, to request the operator to carry out the rejected operation or to operate the production facility, which was earmarked for abandonment, for said participant's sole risk and account.

If the sole risk option is exercised in respect of a discovery not declared to be commercial by the other participants, the sole risk party shall request the operator to give to the competent authorities a notice of commercial discovery in conformity with the relevant terms and conditions of the underlying license or contract, and shall subsequently request the operator to prepare a plan of development and to submit the same to the compentent authority for approval.

The operator has the exclusive right and duty to carry out any sole risk operation but must give precedence to joint operations.

Non-sole risk participants have to be kept fully informed about the operation, its progress and the results obtained. Upon the completion of any particular sole risk operation, other than a sole risk development operation; a sole risk continuation of exploitation or a sole risk enhanced recovery scheme, the operator must prepare and submit a complete report;

Upon receiving the operator's aforesaid report, non-sole risk participants have the right to re-enter and join in any follow-up operation against the payment of a reimbursement in cash of their share of the costs incurred plus a premium in cash (as far as sole risk seismic work is concerned) or in kind (i.e., in oil and gas production generated by the field discovered as a result of a sole risk drilling operation). The said premium, which is expressed as a multiple of the amount of the reimbursement, is meant to compensate the sole risk participant(s) for the risk taken with their operation. A higher risk is compensated by a higher premium

11.3.2.11   Disposition of Production

Any participant is entitled to receive at the point of delivery described in the JOA its participating interest share as modified with respect to sole risk production, if any, of the oil and gas production made available to the participants at said point by the operator in accordance with the terms of the underlying license or production sharing contract. Delivery of oil production to which any participant is entitled takes place within the framework of an offtake agreement, allowing oil liftings deviating from the proportional shares but only for limited periods. Natural gas production will usually be disposed of on a joint and integrated basis and sold to a single buyer in accordance with the terms of a single long-term gas sales agreement (or a number of identical gas sales agreement, each of the latter covering the share of an individual participant).

11.3.2.12   Default

Any participant has the basic obligation to make its proportional cash contribution in response to monthly cash calls issued in advance by the operator. Any participant failing to do so is in default. The obligation to transfer cash to the operator in response to a cash call is an absolute obligation from which no participant is excused, even not so if a valid claim can be made to have been affected by force majeure. Notice of a default is given by operator to the defaulting participant and any other participant. The other, non-defaulting participants are obliged to make up the cash shortage caused by the non-contribution of the defaulting participant. A default is only allowed to exist for a specified period, usually sixty days, unless special circumstances exist which allow an extension of this period. If before the expiry of the period or any extension thereof the defaulting participant has not remedied its default, the participant has to withdraw from the venture and surrender its participating interest to the remaining participants. During the period of the default the operator may sell the oil and gas entitlement, if any, of the defaulting participant and recover the cash contribution due from the realized proceeds.

11.3.2.13   Assignment of Interest

Any participant may freely assign its interest to anyone of its affiliates, subject to giving proper notice to the other participants. If a participant wishes to assign its interest to a third party, not being an affiliate, or to another participant, it must notify the non-involved participants offering the latter the opportunity to acquire the interest on the same or equivalent terms and conditions as have been agreed in a final form with the intended assignee (subject only to the preferential rights of the other participants). If none of the non-involved participants are interested to take the whole interest the participant may complete the transaction with the intended assignee, provided the terms and conditions as notified to the non-involved participants, and on which they based their decision not to make use of their preferential right remain the same. If the intended assignee is one of the participants and if anyone of the non-involved participant expresses an interest in an acquisition on the terms offered, then the offered interest will be shared among them in proportion to their respective participating interests. If controlling shares in a participant or controlling shares in an affiliate holding the participating interest are on offer, or a third party or another participant makes an offer for a controlling interest in a participant or in an affiliate holding the participating interest, the participant or affiliate must offer its participating interest to the non-involved participants on reasonable and fair terms. Any direct assignment of a participating interest involves the assignment of a corresponding share in the underlying authorization. Since the latter assignment requires the approval of government or state entity, as the case may be, assignments of a participating interest are usually made subject to the condition that such approval is obtained.

11.3.2.14 Withdrawal

In principle, any participant may withdraw from the joint venture at any time subject only to giving a few months' written notice. After expiry of the notice period the withdrawal becomes effective. However, no participant is permitted to withdraw from the joint venture where the minimum exploration work programme and the minimum exploration expenditure commitments have not been fulfilled or the signature bonus has not been paid, unless the participant wishing to withdraw guarantees to contribute its (former) participating interest of the commitments after and irrespective of its withdrawal. After the effective date of its withdrawal, a withdrawing party remains liable for its participating interest share of all costs of joint operations or sole risk operations, that had been approved by a decision taken by respectively the management committee or the sole risk participants prior to the notice of withdrawal, unless the withdrawing participant had been a non-consenting participant. Similarly, a withdrawing party remains liable for all obligations and liabilities arising from events or acts that took place or were committed prior to the effective date of withdrawal. A withdrawing participant remains liable for future costs, resulting from joint commitments made prior to the notice of withdrawal, the most important of which are the costs of abandonment involving production facilities. A withdrawing participant may be required to provide security in the form of a bank guarantee for these future liabilities. The share to be contributed or to be guaranteed by a withdrawing participant in respect of abandonment liabilities is not necessarily the withdrawing participant's original participating interest share but in principle a share that takes into account the length of time that the withdrawing participant had enjoyed the use of or has benefited from the asset (well, field or installation) about to be abandoned. The withdrawing participant's participating interest to be surrendered will be distributed over the remaining participants in proportion to their respective participating interests, unless another distribution is agreed among them. The withdrawing participant's participating interest to be surrendered will be distributed over the remaining participants in proportion to their respective participating interests, unless another distribution is agreed among them. If the remaining participants refuse to accept the withdrawing participant's interest the joint venture will be terminated. As far as the jointly owned authorization is concerned, a withdrawing party must assign its participating interest therein to the remaining participants in accordance with the applicable rules of the authorization. Similarly as for external assignments, an internal assignment requires the approval of the government or the state entity as the case may be. If such approval is not forthcoming, a formal internal assignment cannot take place. The withdrawing participant remains formally, i.e., from the point of view of the government or the state entity, one of the participants. The withdrawing participant is compelled then to stay in the joint venture but its participating interest is held for the risk, account and benefit of the remaining participants. The latter are solely responsible and have to keep the withdrawing participant secured and indemnified against any claims or demands brought against the latter by government, state entity or any other third party.

11.3.2.15   Confidentiality

Each participant is obliged to keep all information concerning the joint venture including information about the underlying authorization or information about or generated by the operations undertaken by the operator strictly confidential and may only disclose said information to its parent company and affiliated companies. Any participant wishing to disclose such information to independent third parties needs the consent in writing of the other participants. No such consent will be needed in certain special circumstances, such as when a participant wishes to disclose information to financial institutions in order to obtain a loan or guarantee; to a stock exchange, where its shares or the shares of its parent company are listed, as required in accordance with the latter's rules; to a consultant to the extent needed by the latter in order to be able to render his services; to arbitrators in the context of the settlement of a dispute; or to an independent third party being a bona fide prospective buyer for the whole or part of the disclosing participant's interest. Usually, a disclosing participant is obliged to obtain from the person, to whom information is disclosed under the aforementioned circumstances, the undertaking to keep confidential the information disclosed to it and not to use such information for any purpose other than the purpose for which the disclosure was made. Furthermore any participant is free to disclose information if disclosure is required under applicable legislation.

The operator shall be authorized to disclose any information which must be disclosed to the competent authorities in accordance with the relevant provisions of the license or contract.

Each participant, in particular the operator, may put its proprietary technology at the disposal of the participants for use and application in the conduct of the joint or of any sole risk operations on such conditions as the participant intending to make its technology available may formulate. If the other participants do not agree to the conditions proposed by the disposing participant they have the right to reject and prohibit the use and application by the operator of the proprietary technology offered. The usual condition proposed is that the proprietary technology is applied on a 'black box basis', meaning that participants will be informed about the results obtained by the application of the technology without being informed about the technology itself. This approach leaves the receiving participants in the dark about the technology and makes it not possible for them to verify the results.

11.3.2.16   Force Majeure

If as a result of force majeure circumstances any one participant is not able to fulfil its obligations under the JOA, other than the obligation to pay any amounts of cash required to be paid, then the participant must immediately give notice to the operator and all other participants.

Force majeure circumstances are circumstances which are beyond the reasonable control of the participant concerned, including in particular strikes, lockouts and other labour disputes. A participant will not be compelled to settle any such dispute except on terms acceptable to it.

The participant's obligations affected by force majeure shall be suspended for as long as necessary for the participant to put an end to the force majeure situation. If the operator is affected by force majeure it must resign as operator and transfer the operatorship to another participant. If the force majeure situation endures for an unreasonably long period the affected participant should leave the joint venture and sell its participating interest to the remaining participants or an independent third party in accordance with the rules of the agreement. As noted before, a participant is never excused by force majeure when failing to make its cash contributions in response of a cash call from the operator. Any such failure makes the participant into a defaulting party with all the consequences thereof as set out in the JOA.

Note. Preferably, force majeure shall be defined in the same terms as are used in the underlying authorization.

11.3.2.17   Settlement of Disputes

Generally, participants, if of different nationalities, prefer to settle disputes arising between them in connection with their joint venture through international commercial arbitration. International arbitration is preferred over a procedure before the courts of law of the host country for three reasons: first, because the JOA is an international agreement binding parties of different nationalities; second, because the arbitration procedure as opposed to a procedure before a court of law allows participants to choose the individuals who will act as arbitrators, which offers the possibility to select persons who are familiar with petroleum operations and with the problems that may arise between commercial enterprises engaged in that activity, and third, because, if the host country is a non-Western country, the law chosen by the participants to govern their JOA will almost certainly not be the law of the host country, a law with which the national courts of law will not be familiar and will find difficult to apply if it comes to a procedure before them.

Participants generally choose the arbitration procedures and rules of the International Chamber of Commerce (ICC), but those of the UN Commission on International Trade Law (UNCITRAL) are also frequently referred to in a JOA. If the choice has fallen on ICC-arbitration the JOA will stipulate that any dispute shall be finally settled by three arbitrators appointed in accordance with the ICC Rules. As a rule, it is further stipulated that the nationality of the third arbitrator or referee shall be different from the nationality of any one of the participants. Furthermore the language of the arbitration procedure and the place of arbitration are specified. Additionally it is stated that the arbitral award is binding on the participants and may be entered into any court of law having jurisdiction.

11.3.2.18   Governing Law

Participants have to make a choice regarding the law system that will govern their JOA. The choice to be made depends to a large extent on the nationalities of the participants. If the law of the home country of one of the participants is chosen it would give this particular participant an advantage because the participant has or at least is assumed to have a superior knowledge about the law of its home country and the way this law is applied in practice. It should not be overlooked that the governing law is also the law that shall have to be applied in case of arbitration, in particular that part of the law that deals with contractual arbitration procedures. Generally, participants prefer to select a well-developed and sophisticated system of law that happens not to be the national law of any of them.

11.3.2.19   Accounting Procedure

The accounting procedure is an integral part of the JOA. This part provides for the rules in accordance with which the operator should keep and maintain the books of the joint account. The same rules apply and will be applied by the operator with respect to any particular sole risk account. The accounting procedure contains the cash call procedures, the classification of costs (whereby the classification used in the contract or applicable fiscal legislation is adhered to), rules about the acquisition and disposal of materials, payment for services rendered or materials supplied by operator's parent company or affiliated companies, audit rights to be exercised by the non-operating participants, the taking of inventories, etc. By preference, the rules of keeping books of accounts, that are customary within the group of companies, to which the participant/operator belongs, are adopted. This is one of the privileges of being selected and appointed as the operator.

11.4   THE UNITIZATION AGREEMENT

11.4.1   PRINCIPLES AND OBJECTIVES

A unitization agreement embodies and provides for cooperation between two or more persons holding separate exploitation rights, be it licenses or contracts, in respect of a 'straddling' reservoir. In this context a 'straddling' petroleum reservoir means a single, continuous petroleum reservoir that extends across the boundary of the one exploitation right into the adjacent area of another exploitation right.

The agreement's objective is to develop and produce such a straddling reservoir (hereinafter referred to as the 'unit') in an integrated manner for the common benefit of all the holders of the exploitation rights involved. Its basic principle is that costs, liabilities, petroleum production and other benefits of the intended joint exploitation, are shared among and between the said holders on the basis of their respective shares in the unit.

A unitization agreement may be described as a simplified form of a joint operating agreement to which some special features are added. These special features then concern the identification and demarcation of the straddling petroleum reservoir and the allocation of the percentage shares therein to each individual participating exploitation right. These percentage shares are referred to as tract participations.

For simplicity's sake, it is assumed here that there are only two exploitation rights involved and that those exploitation rights are licenses covering the adjacent areas. In this case, The unit is divided between the two participating licenses and tract participation then become unit participation. It is further assumed that each of the two participating licenses is held by one person.

Note. Where the exploitation rights involved are production sharing contracts instead of licenses the state entity concerned will supervise, control and effectuate the unitization of the straddling petroleum reservoir in question on the basis of the same principles and rules *mutatis mutandis* as set out hereinafter for licenses.

11.4.2   THE PRE-CONTRACTUAL PERIOD

The pre-contractual period is the period preceding the date of signing the unitization agreement during which the two participating licensees have to reach agreement (to be laid down in the aforesaid unitization agreement) on the following subjects:

  (i) the limits, extent, and configuration of the common petroleum reservoir to be unitized;
 (ii) the mineral characteristics and mechanical condition of the reservoir rock and the characteristics of the petroleum contained therein;
(iii) a definition of 'petroleum reserves' which will have to be divided between the licensees;
 (iv) the manner in which the aforesaid petroleum reserves should be so divided (the calculation of the initial unit participations);
  (v) the time schedule for any re-determinations of the limits of the unit, total petroleum reserves and unit participations;
 (vi) the appointment of a unit operator;
(vii) the outline of the development plan; and
(viii) sharing or non-sharing of pre-unitization costs.

With reference to (i) and (ii). The main activity during the pre-contractual period consists in collecting information regarding the straddling reservoir, including carrying out seismic work and possibly the drilling of wells. In principle, any such work has to be paid for by the licensee, on whose side of the common boundary the work has to be carried out. Sharing of costs in proportion to unit participation interests starts not before the unitization agreement has become effective, unless and to the extent the licensees agree otherwise. Collection of information is stopped as soon as both licensees feel that there is a reasonable basis on which to conclude a unitization agreement with confidence. The matter becomes more compli-cated, if at the start of this period more information about the one part of the reservoir is available than about the other, simply because the licensee on the one side of the common boundary had started its exploration operations earlier than the licensee on the other side. In many cases, drilling has taken place on the one side, while perhaps only seismic work has been done on the other. Collecting more information is then the responsibility of the licensee that is lacking in this respect and any make-up work has to be carried out before the negotiations on the formation of the unit can be continued.

With reference to (ii) and (iv). Having agreed that sufficient informa-tion is available with respect to both parts of the reservoir, the licensees have to reach agreement on the methods, formulae and information to be used to assess and establish the initial allocation of the petroleum reserves to the participating licensees (such methods and formulae also to be used for any subsequent re-determination).

In principle, each licensee should be entitled to receive the quantity of petroleum that can be extracted or recovered from its part of the unit. However implementing this principle is not simple. Information is needed on the limits of both parts of the unit, the quantity of petroleum contained therein and the applicable recovery factor, i.e., the fraction of said quantity that actually can be recovered. The quantity *in situ* is found by calculating the quantity of petroleum occurring per cubic metre of reservoir rock and the volume of the reservoir rock saturated with oil or natural gas. Using this method, the Stock Tank Oil Initially in Place (STOIIP) or the Gas Initially in Place (GIIP) is found. As far as oil is concerned, samples have to be taken and analysed in order to determine the quantity of gas dissolved in the oil and the shrinkage factor to arrive at the stock tank oil volume. When the allocation of the reserves is based on the aforesaid recovery principle, the calculated quantity of STOIIP or GIIP has to be multiplied by the recovery factor. The latter however is difficult to determine because its value depends on the following factors:

(i) the mineral characteristics of the reservoir rock (grain size distri-bution, clay distribution, cementation, porosity, permeability, etc.);
(ii) the mechanical condition of the reservoir rock, such as the presence of sealing or non-sealing faults;
(iii) the flow properties of the petroleum to be extracted from the reservoir rock, such as viscosity; and
(iv) on the methods of extraction that will be applied within the framework of a development plan still to be agreed, such as the tightness of the drilling pattern, the use of horizontal drilling and

the application of enhanced recovery methods, e.g., the injection of either water, natural gas, steam or CO_2.

All the above listed factors and the methods of extraction cannot be finally decided upon before the development plan has been agreed and a few development wells have been drilled. Moreover, the mineral characteristics of the reservoir rock may change over time as a result of the compaction of the reservoir rock caused by the extraction of the petroleum. Any such change will certainly affect the numerical value of the aforesaid recovery factor.

If the unit is composed of reservoir rock which is not homogeneous, such that the one part of the unit has excellent reservoir characteristics and the other part not, then a proper and fair implementation of the division of the unit on the basis of quantities of petroleum recoverable from each part of the unit becomes too complicated. A practical solution can be found in an adjustment of the STOIP/GIIP calculation method and to adopt a formula in accordance with which the unit participation (UP) is calculated partly, say ten per cent, on the basis of STOIIP or GIIP and partly, say (1-X) per cent, on the basis of a property (P) of the reservoir rock, i.e., the property, which is mainly responsible for the excellent recovery (meaning a high value of the recovery factor). This approach yields a formula of the general form of: UP =[X per cent STOIIP]+[(1-X) per cent P]. In this manner, the well-developed part of the unit benefiting from a high recovery factor is assigned a greater unit participation. Obviously, after having decided to make use of such a weighted formula, the licensees have still to agree on which reservoir rock property should be used as 'P', on the value of the factor X and, not to forget, on the limits of the unit itself.

With reference to (v). During the pre-contractual period the licensees have also to reach agreement on the timing of the re-determinations. Re-determinations work retroactively up to the moment the unit was formed and the initial tract participations were determined. A re-determination re-establishes with respect to that particular moment the mineral characteristics and mechanical properties of the reservoir rock, the limits of the unit, and the volume and characteristics of the petroleum contained therein and recalculates, on the basis of this new data, the apportionment of the (possibly on the same occasion re-determined) unit. The so re-calculated apportionment is assumed and considered to have been in effect from the date the initial apportionment had been in effect and applied. Re-determinations are necessary because, due to information obtained from the drilling of the development wells and from additional seismic work, more and more details about the extent and configuration of the unit become known. Chances are that the initial determinations will prove not to be correct. Furthermore, as far as the unit itself is concerned, it may appear that contrary to earlier expectations the unit proves to be in communication with other petroleum reservoirs in the vicinity causing an in-flow of petroleum from these other reservoirs. However, it may also possible that the unit proves to be smaller than originally thought due to the presence of sealing faults, causing a compartmentalization of the unit. Under these circumstances, the licensees have to re-establish the limits of the unit which may result in the inclusion of the nearby reservoirs in the unit (unless the petroleum extracted from the other reservoirs can easily be accounted for and in one way or another can be kept separate from unit production), or may lead to the exclusion of certain compartments from the unit. If the licensees were not given the assurance that the initial unit participations would regularly be re-examined and, if need be, re-determined in the light of the latest information about the rock strata, much more appraisal work on either side of the dividing line and for the sole account of the licensee concerned would have to be done during the pre-contractual period, causing unnecessary drilling and unnecessary costs.

Re-determinations have important consequences. The licensees will acquire with retroactive effect new unit participations. This means that the licensee's rights and obligations, which are expressed in terms of its unit participation interest, such as the obligation to contribute cash and the entitlement to a percentage share of unit production, have to be revised and the appropriate adjustments have to be made. If, in practice, it appears that only a small part of the reservoir is extending across the common boundary, and that this part can easily be exploited by wells drilled on the other side, then the licensee in possession of the smallest part may simply agree to forego any re-determination.

With reference to (vi). In complex and time consuming cases, negotiating licensees may decide, before starting the negotiations, to appoint an operator, whose first task will be to organize the whole process of making the intended unitization agreement. Usually special negotiating committees are set up over which the various subjects are distributed.

11.4.3   THE CONTENTS OF A UNITIZATION AGREEMENT

Preliminary Note. For simplicity's sake it is again assumed here that only two licensees holding adjacent licenses which cover a straddling petroleum reservoir.

11.4.3.1   Participating Licensees

The agreement identifies and describes the participating licensees and the licenses held by them.

11.4.3.2   Definitions

With respect to definitions there is no difference with a customary joint operating agreement, except for the addition of some specific expressions related to the unitization process, such as 'the unit', 'unit participation', 're-determinations', 'petroleum reserves', 'STOIIP', 'GIIP', 'recovery factor', etc.

11.4.3.3   Purpose and Scope

The scope and purpose of a unitization agreement is the exploitation of the unit for the joint account of the participating licensees on the basis of sharing costs, liabilities, oil and gas production and other benefits in proportion to their unit participation interests, and in accordance with the provisions of the agreement and the respective licenses.

11.4.3.4   Description and Demarcation of the Unit

The unit is described in geological terms, accompanied by a demarcation thereof. The demarcation is on the one hand depicted on a map, which also contains the boundaries of the participating licenses, and on the other defined in terms of coordinates. The area so demarcated and defined is the unit area. Generally, it is stipulated that the unit as defined is subject to re-determination from time to time in accordance with the rules provided for by the agreement.

11.4.3.5   Duration

The unitization agreement will endure as long as the participating licenses endure, including any extensions thereof.

11.4.3.6   Unit Participations

The agreement establishes the initial unit participations of the participating licenses. These unit participations are subject to re-determinations from time to time in accordance with the provisions of the agreement.

11.4.3.7   Re-determinations

The limits of the unit, the petroleum reserves contained therein and the allocation of the reserves to the licenses (i.e., unit participations), are subject to re-determination from time to time. The methods, formulae and information to be used for the division of the unit on the basis of the reserves will be described in an annex to the agreement. It will be made clear therein whether the division of the unit (and its own possible re-determination) will be based on reserves *in situ* (STOIP or GIIP calculation), on recoverable reserves (applying a recovery factor) or on a mixture of both types of reserves.

11.4.3.8   Adjustments after Re-determination

Any re-determination of the unit participations resulting in a change in percentage figures has retroactive effect. Any change requires adjustments of the past cash contributions and offtake of unit production. The over-contributing licensee is paid back with interest. The under-lifting licensee receives a make-up right at the expense of the over-lifting licensee, to be exercised within a specified period and restricted to a certain percentage of the unit participation interest of the over-lifter. Any remaining imbalance is to be settled in cash.

11.4.3.9   The Unit Operator

One of the licensees is appointed as operator of the unit. Authorities and duties of the unit operator are similar to those described in a customary joint operating agreement. The unit operator is authorized to make cash calls on each licensee in proportion to the latter's unit participating interest. Any appointment of a unit operator should be made in consultation with the competent authorities and after having received their approval.

11.4.3.10   The Unit Management Committee

The operations are supervised and controlled by a unit management committee in which each licensee is represented with the right to cast a vote in proportion to its unit participating interest.
   The main task of the unit management committee is:

  (i) to supervise the implementation of the unit development plan in accordance with the principles and outline thereof as laid down in an annex to the agreement;
 (ii) the award of major contracts; and
(iii) the supervision of the re-determinations in accordance with the rules and procedures annexed to the agreement, which may include the supervision of the work of independent experts, if the re-determinations have been entrusted to such persons.

Decisions of the management committee are binding on the participants if taken with the required majority of votes. When there only two licensees participating, as has been assumed here, it may be decided that for some matters or subjects, such as the unit development plan, unanimity is required.

11.4.3.11   The Unit Development Plan

Development of the unit has to take place within the framework of the development plan agreed and set out in an annex to the agreement. A different plan may be adopted by the management committee, if so warranted by new information or other circumstances. Any significant change can only be adopted by unanimous vote.

11.4.3.12   Sole Risk Operations

In the context of a re-determination, each licensee has the right to execute for its own account and risk seismic work and/or a drilling operation within the boundaries of its license for the purpose of obtaining information expected to have a significant bearing on the outcome of a forthcoming re-determination. The sole risk work will be carried out by the unit operator. If the unit management committee so agrees, any well drilled in this context may, if suitably located and fitting into the unit development plan, be taken over by the unit and used as a production well. In such event, the costs incurred by the sole risking licensee will be reimbursed to it. If a sole risk well has yielded data which appears to be of significant influence on the outcome of a re-determination, the unit is obliged to take-over the well and the sole risking licensee shall be compensated for the costs incurred by it. The question of whether data obtained from a sole risk well have made such a significant contribution that the well must be taken over by the unit, may be submitted to an independent expert for a binding decision.

11.4.3.13   Non-unit Operations

Any unitization agreement may provide depending on the circumstances of the case that the unit drilling and unit production installations and unit field pipelines may be used for the development and production of reservoirs located outside the unit. For such use, a tariff has to be paid to the unit owners. This is a very useful provision in cases where the unit is surrounded by small, independent, non-straddling reservoirs which cannot be exploited on a stand alone basis.

11.4.3.14   Default

Each licensee is obliged to make proportional cash contributions in response to cash calls from the unit operator, if and when made in accordance with the procedures of the agreement. A lack of response for whatever reasons to such cash calls constitutes default. The customary joint venture rules about the consequences of default will be applicable.

11.4.3.15   Withdrawal

Each licensee has the right at any time to withdraw from the unit but will in such case be obliged to assign its unit participating interest to the other, remaining licensee, unless both licensees agree to terminate the unitization agreement. If the unitization agreement is not terminated as aforesaid, the withdrawing licensee remains liable for paying its unit participation percentage share of the costs of settling liabilities that arose before the effective date of withdrawal, and an appropriate share of abandonment expenditure arising in the future with respect to unit facilities installed prior to the effective date of withdrawal.

11.4.3.16 Assignment of Unit Interests

Assignments of unit interests may be voluntary or compulsory. Assignment to affiliated companies is free but the other licensee has got a matching right in case a transfer to an independent third party is intended. Compulsory assignment is the assignments to be made to the other licensee in case of default or withdrawal. In all cases the approval of the competent authorities will be required.

11.4.3.17 Other Conditions

Other conditions, such as conditions concerning confidentiality of information, giving and receiving notices, settlement of disputes, and governing law, are similar as those contained in a customary joint operating agreement.

11.4.3.18 Approval

The unitization agreement and its annexes will have to be approved by the authority which has granted the licenses. Usually, any re-determination of the limits of the unit, the total reserves and the unit participation interests, are subject to the competent authority's approval.

Note. How the unit is divided between the two adjacent licenses may be of interest to the competent authority if the licenses had been granted under different rounds of licensing and as a result thereof could contain different terms as to government take, etc.

11.4.3.19 Accounting Procedure

The unit operator must keep the books of the unit accounts in accordance with the rules of a customary joint venture accounting procedure.

11.4.3.20 Annexes

The unitization agreement is accompanied by the appropriate number of annexes covering the following subjects:

   (i) the geological and topographical description of the unit;
  (ii) the definition and calculation of the petroleum reserves contained
       in the unit;
 (iii) the allocation of the reserves to the participating licenses;
  (iv) the methods and information to be used in the successive re-
       determinations of the reserves, unit participations and the extent of
       the unit; and
   (v) the procedures to be followed in appointing an independent expert
       and a description of the task to be performed by such expert.

Bibliography

Aghazadeh, G. 'The Imperative Need for Oil Producer-Consumer Cooperation in the 1990s'. *Middle East Economic Survey,* 3 June 1991.

Ait-Laoussine, N. 'OPEC Could Slash Output, Still Meet Own Needs'. *Petroleum Intelligence Weekly,* 22 September 1980.

Ait-Laoussine, N. 'The 1986 OU Price War: an Economic Fiasco'. *Middle East Economic Survey,* 6 October 1986.

Ait-Laoussine, N. 'Recent Developments in the Oil Market, 1986 Revisited?'. *Middle East Economic Survey,* 22 February 1988.

Ait-Laoussine, N. & J. Wood-Collins. 'Energy and the Environment'. *Middle East Economic Survey,* 19 March 1990.

Al-Chalabi, I. 'The Oil Market: The Shape of Things to Come'. *Middle East Economic Survey,* 23 October 1989.

Al-Farsy, F. *Modernity and Tradition, The Saudi* Equation. Kegan Paul International Ltd: London, 1990.

Anderson, R.N. 'Oil Production in the 21th Century'. *Scientific American,* March 1998.

Baker, A. 'Oudook for the Coal Industry'. In Proceedings of the Mining Students Society's Symposium on Potential Resources for the Coming Century (Delft University of Technology, Delft, November 1992).

Ballou, G.T. 'Oil Industry and Government Relations, A Study of Emerging Patterns'. *The Exploration and Economics of the Petroleum Industry,* vol. 4 (The Southwestern Legal Foundation, Gulf Publishing Company, Houston, Texas, 1966).

Bambridge, M. 'Unitisation Agreements'. In Proceedings of the Conference on Oil and Gas Agreements (Langham Oil Conferences Ltd, London, November 1996).

Banks, F.E. 'Some Economic Aspects of the World Coal Market'. *Resources Policy,* December 1989.

Barbier, E.B. 'The Global Greenhouse Effect'. *Natural Resources Forum,* February 1989.

Barents, R. 'Legal Aspects of Dutch Energy Policy'. *Journal of Energy and Natural Resources Law,* 1982.

Baum, V. 'World Bank-Aid for Third World Energy Projects'. *Petroleum Economist,* March 1986.

Beal, A. 'North Sea Joint Bidding and Joint Operating Agreements'. In Proceedings of the Conference on Oil and Gas Agreements (Langham Oil Conferences Ltd, London, November 1996).

Bley, L. 'Environment-Greenhouse Gas Emission Divisions'. *Petroleum Economist,* October 1990.

Boehmer-Christiansen, S. 'Marine Pollution Control: UNCLOS III as the Partial Codification of International Practice'. 7 *Environmental Policy and Law,* 1981.

Bohm, J.T.C. 'Waste Products Generated by Petroleum Operations: Dumping, Discharging, Prevention or Re-use?'. In Proceedings of the Mining Students Society's Symposium on Dealing with the Environmental Problem in the Mining and Petroleum Industry (Delft University of Technology, Delft, April 1990).

Bourne, L. 'United States – The Importance of Imported Oil'. *Petroleum Economist,* August 1990.

Bourne, L. 'Whither OPEC Production Now?'. *Petroleum Economist,* September 1990.

Breij, A.C.M. *The Coal Mines Went Open, the Coal Mines Closed Down* (ICOB cv, Alphen aan de Rijn, the Netherlands, 1991).

Broches, A. 'The Convention on the Settlement of Investment Disputes: Some Observations on Jurisdiction'. 5 *Columbia Journal of Transnational Law,* 1966.

Broecker, W.S. & G.H. Denton. 'What Drives Glacial Cycles?'. *Scientific American,* January 1990.

Brondel, G. 'Co-operation Between the European Community and the Developing Countries in the Energy Field'. In Proceedings of the United Nations Symposium on Financing of Petroleum Exploration and Development in Developing Countries (Athens, 22–27 April 1985).

Brothwood, M. 'Legal Aspects of Gas Carriage'. *4 Journal of Energy and Natural Resources Law,* vol. 6, 1988.

Brown, E.D. 'The UN Convention on the Law of the Sea 1982'. *Journal of Energy and Natural Resources Law,* 1984.

Brown, R. 'Choice of Law Provisions in Concession and Related Contracts'. 39 *The Modern Law Review,* November 1976.

Brown, R. 'The Relationship between the State and the Multinational Corporation in the Exploitation of Resources'. *International and Comparative Law Quarterly,* January 1984.

Brown, R. 'Contract Stability in International Petroleum Operations'. 29 *The UNCTC Reporter,* 1990.

Brtjmfield, J.B. 'State and Federal Laws and Regulations on Offshore Leases, Drilling and Production'. *Ralph Slovenko's Oil and Gas Operations: Legal Considerations in the Tidelands and on Land* (Tulane University School of Law, Claitor's Law Books, Claitor's Book Store, 1963).

Bums, N. 'The Oil Industry in Transition'. *Oil & Gas Journal,* 8 November 1982.

Cameron, P. The Regulation of Energy Supply: The Netherlands'. *Journal of Energy & Natural Resources Law,* Supplement, December 1989.

Campbell, C.J. & J.H. Laherrere. 'The End of Cheap Oil'. *Scientific American,* March 1998.

Campbell Jr, N.J. 'International Law Developments concerning National Claims to and in Offshore Areas'. *Ralph Slovenko's Oil and Gas Operations: Legal Considerations in the Tidelands and on Land* (Tulane University School of Law, Claitor's Law Books, Claitor's Book Store, 1963).

Carpio, D.T. 'The World Bank's Approach to Financing Petroleum Projects'. In Proceedings of the United Nations Symposium on Financing of Petroleum Exploration and Development in Developing Countries (Athens, 22-27 April 1985).

Champion, D., C. Girard, & T. Daubignard. 'Oil and Gas Reserves of the Middle East and North Africa'. *Natural Resources Forum,* August 1991.

Clark, W.C. 'Managing Planet Earth'. *Scientific American,* September 1989.

Daintith, T. (ed.). *The Legal Character of Petroleum Licences: A Comparative Study* (University of Dundee, Centre for Petroleum and Mineral Law Studies, 1981).

Dalgaard-Knudsen, E. 'Exploitation Concessions: Contracts or Permits? Contributions from the Norwegian Phillips/Ekofisk Case'. *3 Journal of Energy and Natural Resources Law, vol. 5, 1987.*

Date-Bah, S.K. 'The Contract as a Mechanism for Taxation'. *Journal of Energy & Natural Resources Law* 1988.

Davidson, A.G.H. 'Tax Issues'. In Proceedings of the Conference on Unitisation of Oil and Gas Fields (Langham Oil Conferences Ltd, London, May 1991).

Davis, G.R. 'Energy for Planet Earth'. *Scientific American,* September 1990.

Davis, M.J. 'The Challenge of a Changing World'. *Ralph Slovenko's Oil and Gas Operations: Legal Considerations in the Tidelands and on Land* (Tulane University School of Law, Claitor's Law Books, Claitor's Book Store, 1963).

Davis, W. 'Global Energy Issues from the Standpoint of the Private Corporation'. *Houston Law Review,* vol. 17:1005, 1980.

De Sitter, L.U. 'Petroleum Geology', *Servire's Encyclopaedic, Servire* (The Hague, 1950).

Decker, H. 'Oil's Future - Its Challenges and Opportunities'. *The Economics of the Petroleum Industry,* vol. 2 (The Southwestern Legal Foundation, Gulf Publishing Company, Houston, Texas, 1964).

Delaume, G.R. 'Convention on the Settlement of Investment Disputes between States and Nationals of Other States'. 1 *International Lawyer,* vol. I, 1966.

Denekamp, E.J. 'The European Energy Charter'. In Proceedings of the Mining Students Society's Symposium on Potential Resources for the Coming Century (Delft University of Technology, Delft, November 1992).

Despraires, P. 'Oil Demand Prospects'. 19 *Middle East Economic Survey,* May 1986.

Desprairies, P. 'The World Energy Situation'. *Natural Resources Forum,* February 1989.

Driessen, C.F. 'Oil Concessions: Governments and Oil Companies & Oil Laws in Malta and Elsewhere'. Paper given at the Malta Oil Seminar (October 1971).

Driver, J.M. *The Templars, Holy Warrior Monks of the Ancient Lands.* London: Kandour Limited, 2007.

Dryland, N.H.H. 'Government View on Promoting Investments'. In Proceedings of the Mining Students Society's Symposium on the Current Political and Economic Outlook for the Mining and Petroleum Industry (Delft University of Technology, Delft, November 1987).

Ely, N. 'Summary of the Mining and Petroleum Legislation of the United States of America'. In Proceedings of the ECAFE Seminar on Mining Legislation and Administration (Manila, October 1969).

Ely, N. 'Changing Concepts of the World's Mineral Development Laws'. In Proceedings of the IBA Seminar on World Energy Laws (Stavanger, Norway, May 1975).

English, W. 'Unitisation Agreements'. In Proceedings of the Conference on Oil and Gas Agreements (Langham Oil Conferences Ltd, London, December 1994).

European Commission. 'Energy for a New Century: The European Perspective'. *Energy in Europe,* Special Issue, July 1990.

Fee, D. *Petroleum Exploitation Strategy.* Belhaven Press: London, 1988.
Fouda, S.A. 'Liquid Fuels from Natural Gas'. *Scientific American,* March 1998.
Frihagen, A. 'The Legal Protection of a Production Licence Holder against New Regulations and Other Government Interference'. In Proceedings of the 10th annual Bergen Oil and Gas Conference (Solstrand, Norway, December 1987).
Fulkerson, W., R.R. Judkins, & M.K. Sanghvi. 'Energy from Fossil Fuels'. *Scientific American,* September 1990.

Gallins, G. 'Bilateral Investment Protection Treaties'. *Journal of Energy and Natural Resources Law* 1983.
Gault, I.T. 'Joint Development of Offshore Mineral Resources – Progress and Prospects for the Future'. 3 *Natural Resources Forum,* vol. 12, 1988.
George, R.L. 'Mining for Oil'. *Scientific American,* March 1998.
Glraud, P.N. 'International Coal Prices'. *Natural Resources Forum,* November 1989.
Graedel, T.E. & P.J. Crutzen. 'The Changing Atmosphere'. *Scientific American,* September 1989.
Greenwald, G.B. 'Natural Gas Contracts Under Stress: Price, Quantity and Take or Pay'. *Journal of Energy and Natural Resources Law* 1987.
Greenwald, G.B. 'Encouraging Natural Gas Exploration in Developing Countries'. 3 *Natural Resources Forum,* vol. 12, 1988.
Gribben, R. 'Kuwait's Treasure Chest'. *Petroleum Economist,* September 1990.
Grotens, A.H.P. 'The Dutch Gas Supply System in the 1990s'. In Proceedings of the Workshop 'The Eve of the 7th Round' (organized by the Firms Loyens & Volkmaars and Nauta Van Haersolte. The Hague, November 1989).

Hammer, A. *Hammer: Witness to History.* Simon & Schuster Limited: 1987.
Hangher, L. & T. Daintith. 'The Regulation of Energy Supply: The United Kingdom' . *Journal of Energy and Natural Resources Law,* Supplement, December 1989.

Hancher, L. 'A Single European Market for Oil and Gas – The Legal Obstacles'. 2 *Journal of Energy and Natural Resources Law,* vol. 8, 1990.

Harders, J.E. 'The EEC's Continental Shelf: A "Terra Incognita"'. 4 *Journal of Energy and Natural Resources Law,* vol. 8, 1990. HEARD, Wilbur W. 'Pending Legislation to Amend the Natural Gas Act'. *Ralph Slovenko's Oil and Gas Operations: Legal Considerations in the Tidelands and on Land* (Tulane University School of Law, Claitor's Law Books, Claitor's Book Store, 1963).

Heren, P. 'Natural Gas – Green and Growing Markets'. *Petroleum Economist,* August 1990.

Hlgginson, A.J. 'Comparison of Terms to Attract Petroleum Development in Four Countries: The Arab Republic of Egypt'. In Proceedings of the IBA Energy Law Seminar, vol. 2, 1979.

Hlllyer Jr, H.H. 'A Primer on Producer Price Regulation'. *Ralph Slovenko's Oil and Gas Operations: Legal Considerations in the Tidelands and on Land* (Tulane University School of Law, Claitor's Law Books, Claitor's Book Store, 1963).

Hodgshon, S. & B. Popescu. 'Survey of World Petroleum Activity'. *Petroleum Economist,* October 1989.

Horgan, J. 'Fusion's Future: Will fusion-energy reactors be too complex and cosdy?'. *Scientific American,* February 1989.

Horn, N., et al. 'Legal Problems of Codes of Conduct for Multinational Enterprises'. In *Studies in Transnational Economic Law,* vol. 1 (Kluwer: Deventer, 1980).

Houghton, R.A. & G.M. Woodwell. 'Global Climatic Change'. *Scientific American,* April 1989.

Htun, N. 'Environmental Perspectives and Response Options'. In Proceedings of the Mining Students Society's Symposium on Dealing with the Environmental Problem in the Mining and Petroleum Industry (Delft University of Technology, Delft, April 1990).

Hughes, I.W.G. 'The UK Department of Energy's View on Unitisation'. In Proceedings of the Conference on Unitisation of Oil and Gas Fields (Langham Oil Conferences Ltd, London, May 1991).

Hurst, C. *The Continental Shelf.* Transactions of the Grotius Society, vol. 34, reproduced in the Proceedings of the 1950 ILA Copenhagen Conference on the Rights to the Seabed and its Subsoil (1950).

Huxtable, A. 'Joint Bidding Agreements'. In Proceedings of the Conference on Oil and Gas Agreements (Langham Oil Conferences Ltd, London, December 1994).

ILA. 'The Exploration and Exploitation of Minerals on the Ocean Bed and
    its Subsoil'. In Proceedings of the ILA Conference (Buenos Aires,
    1968).
ILA. *Removal of Installations in the Exclusive Economic %one.* Report of
    the Netherlands Branch (October 1983).
ILO. *Social and Economic Effects of Petroleum Development Programmes.*
    Consultant's Report (International Labour Office, Geneva, September
    1984).

Jaidah, A.M. 'OPEC, Non-OPEC and Cooperation in Pursuit of Price and
    Market Stability'. *Middle East Economic Survey,* 11 March 1985.
Jaworek, W.G. 'Forecasting the Future of the International Petroleum
    Industry'. *The Exploration and Economics of the Petroleum Industry,*
    vol. 5 (The Southwestern Legal Foundation, Gulf Publishing Com-
    pany, Houston, TX, 1967).
Johnson, C.J. 'Establishing an Effective Production Sharing Type Regime
    for Petroleum'. *Resources Policy* 1981.
Johnson, C.J. 'Ranking Countries for Minerals Exploration'. *Natural
    Resources Forum,* August 1990.
Johnston, F.M. 'Political Risk Market Expansion Broadens OPIC's Role'.
    Risk Management, February 1984.
Jones, A. 'Russia'. *Petroleum Economist,* Special Supplement 1992.
Jonk, G.J. *The Search for, the Demand, the Supply and the Price of Oil in
    the Future.* (Delft University of Technology, January 1990).
Jonker, J., J.L. van Zanden, S. Howarth & K. Sluyterman. *A History of
    Royal Dutch Shell,* Vols 1, 2 & 3. Oxford University Press, 2007.
Jonkman, R.M. *Modern Production Sharing Contracts.* Shell Internation-
    ale Petroleum Maatschappij B.V: The Hague, October 1990.

Kapteyn, P.J.G. 'The United Nations and the International Economic
    Order'. *Studies of International Economic Law, Part LI.* T.M.C Asser
    Institute: The Hague, 1977.
Karl, T.R., N. Nicholls, & J. Gregory. 'The Coming Climate'. *Scientific
    American,* May 1997.
Kellogg, W.W. 'Modelling Future Climate'. *Ambio, a Journal of the
    Human Environment.* The Royal Swedisch Academy of Sciences:
    Stockhom, 1981.
Kemp, A.G. 'Petroleum Exploitation and Contract Terms in Developing
    Countries after the Oil Price Collapse'. *Natural Resources Forum,* May
    1989.

Kemp, A.G. & D. Rose. 'Investment in Oil Exploration and Development: A Comparative Study of the Effects of Taxation'. In Proceedings of the International Conference on Risks and Returns in Large-Scale Natural Resources Projects (Bellagio, Italy, 17–19 November 1982).

Klnna, J.C. 'Investing in Developing Countries: Minimisation of Political Risk'. *Journal of Energy and Natural Resources Law* 1982.

Konoplyanik, A. 'Time to Harmonise Russian Oil Law'. *Petroleum Economist,* April 1992.

Krapels, E.N. 'Evolution and Reform: The Art of Transition in Energy Pricing Policy'. 3 *Natural Resources Forum,* vol. 12, 1988.

Kuehne, G. 'Oil and Gas Licensing: Some Comparative United Kingdom-German Aspects'. 3 *Journal of Energy and Natural Resources Law,* vol. 4, 1986.

Kuehne, G. 'The Regulation of Energy Supply: Federal Republic of Germany'. *Journal of Energy and Natural Resources Law,* Supplement, December 1989.

Lauterpacht, E. 'Issues of Compensation and Nationality in the Taking of Energy Investments'. 4 *Journal of Energy and Natural Resources Law,* vol. 8, 1990.

Lavenant, R.P. 'Changing Concepts of the World's Mineral Development Laws with Special Reference to West Africa'. In Proceedings of the IBA Seminar on World Energy Laws (Stavanger: Norway, May 1975).

Leckow, R.B. & L. A. Mallory. 'The Relaxation of Foreign Investment Restrictions in Canada'. *ICSID Review-Foreign Investment Law Journal* 1991.

Lenczowski, G. *Oil and State in the Middle East.* Cornell University Press: New York, 1960.

Lichtblau, J.H. 'OPEC's Challenge: Surviving Until the Mid-1990s'. *Petroleum Intelligence Weekly,* 13 May 1985.

Lukman, R. 'OPEC's Efforts to Stabilise the Oil Price Structure'. In Proceedings of the Mining Students Society's Symposium on the Current Political and Economic Outlook for the Mining and Petroleum Industry (Delft University of Technology, Delft, November 1987).

Mabro, R. 'Oil Prices in the 1990s: It all Depends on Capacity'. *Middle East Economic Survey.* 6 November 1989.

MacDonald, D.S. 'Current Developments in Oil and Gas Law, Canada'. In Proceedings of the IBA Energy Law Seminar, 1981.

Mahaffie, C.D. 'The International Energy Agency in Operation'. *Houston Law Review,* vol. 17:961, 1980.

Manly Horton, Jr, C. 'Effect of Conservation Laws and Regulations on Contracts and Mineral Leases'. *Ralph Slovenko's Oil and Gas Operations: Legal Considerations in the Tidelands and on Land* (Tulane University School of Law, Claitor's Law Books, Claitor's Book Store, 1963).

Martin, J.M. 'From the Erosion of Crude Oil Prices to the Re-organisation of the Oil Industry'. *Natural Resources Forum,* May 1989.

Mcclendonj, S. 'Alternate Methods of Dispute Settlement'. *Houston Law Review,* vol. 17:979, 1980.

McHugh,J. 'Farmout Agreements'. In Proceedings of the Conference on Oil and Gas Agreements (Langham Oil Conferences Ltd, London, December 1994).

Mestad, O. *The Ekojisk Royalty Case: Construction of Regulations to Avoid Retro-activity.* (Arbeidsdokument til Solstrandseminaret, 2/3 December 1987).

Mikdashi, Z. 'Global Oil: Some Key Issues and Challenges'. *Natural Resources Forum,* August 1989.

Miller, P.P. 'The Statfjord and Murchison Oilfield Units'. In Proceedings of the IBA Energy Law Seminar. vol. I, 1979.

Miller, P.P. 'Comparison of Terms to Attract Petroleum Development in Four Countries: Indonesia'. In Proceedings of the IBA Energy Law Seminar, vol. II, 1979.

Mitchell, J.G. 'Oil on Ice'. (1997) 4 *National Geographic,* vol. 191, April 1997.

Morrison, M.R. 'Current Developments in Petroleum Exploration Offshore Malaysia'. In Proceedings of the IBA Energy Law Seminar, vol. I, 1979.

Mouton, H.W. & others. 'Deep-Sea Mining', A Report of the Deep-Sea Mining Committee of the International Law Association. Proceedings of the ILA Buenos Aires Conference, 1968.

Nazer, H.M. 'Market Stability and Energy Security'. *Middle East Economic Survey,* 6 November 1989.

Nazer, H.M. 'The Interdependence of Oil Producers and Consumers in the Oil Market'. *Middle East Economic Survey,* 3 June 1991.

New Scientist. 'Greenhouse Wars'. *New Scientist,* 19 July 1997.

Oddie. 'The Technical Basis of Unitisation'. In Proceedings of the Conference on Unitisation of Oil and Gas Fields (Langham Oil Conferences Ltd, London, May 1991).

OECD. Committee on Fiscal Affairs. *Transfer Pricing and Multinational Enterprises.* OECD (Paris, 1979).
Omorogbe, Y. 'The Legal Framework for the Production of Petroleum in Nigeria'. 4 *Journal of Energy and Natural Resources Law,* vol. 5, 1987.
Outhit, P.A. 'The Frigg Gas Field Unit'. In Proceedings of the IBA Energy Law Seminar, vol. I, 1979.

Parra, A.A. 'OPEC and Market Share: A Change of Direction'. *Middle East Economic Survey,* 26 May 1986.
Patterson, W. 'Fifty Years of Hopes and Fears' .*Nature,* vol. 449. 11 October 2007.
Pletrowski, R.E. 'International Law Applicable to Deep Sea Mining'. In Proceedings of the IBA Energy Law Seminar, vol. I, 1979.
Plnot, L. & J-M. Le. 'Petroleum Exploration and Production in France'. *Petroleum Economist,* Special Supplement, September 1991.
Prahalad, C. & Y. Doz. *Responding to Host Government Policies, The Multinational Mission* (The Free Press: New York, 1987).

Raschke, M.G. 'World Coal Outlook: 1990s'. *Natural Resources Forum,* August 1989.
Read, A.D. *Protection of the Marine Environment - An Industry View* (E & P Forum: London, September 1989).
Record, R.H. 'Current Developments in Oil and Gas Law in the United States of America'. In Proceedings of the IBA Energy Law Seminar, 1981.
Reddy, A.K.N. & J. Goldenberg. 'Energy for the Developing World'. *Scientific American,* September 1990.
Robinson, M.S. 'Anatomy of Downstream Integration by Oil-Producing Countries'. *Natural Resources Forum,* February 1989.
Roggenkamp, M.M. *The Legal Framework of Pipelines in the Oil and Gas Industry.* Doctorate dissertation (Leyden University, Intersentia Law Publishers: Leyden, 3 February 1999).
Roland, A. 'Secrecy, Technology, and War: Greek Fire and the Defense of Byzantium, 678-1204'. *Society for the History of Technology,* 1992.
Ronne, A. 'The Regulation of Energy Supply: Denmark'. *Journal of Energy and Natural Resources Law,* Supplement, December 1989.
Rugman, A.M. et al. *International Business, Firm and Environment* (McGraw Hill International Editions: Singapore, 1986).

Salden, K. *Legal Aspects of State Jurisdiction over Offshore Oil and Gas Pipelines with Particular Reference to the ^eepipe Project* (Leyden University: December 1988).

Schneider, S.H. 'The Changing Climate'. *Scientific American,* September 1989.

Shatalov, A.T. 'The Gas Industry of Russia-Modern Conditions and Perspectives'. In Proceedings of the Mining Students Society's Symposium on Potential Resources for the Coming Century (Delft University of Technology: Delft, November 1992).

Schenck, PA. *The Past, the Present, the Future; Fossil & Contemporary.* (Delft University of Technology: Delft, 1993).

Scherer, H.J. 'Strict Liability for Environmental Damage in Germany'. *International Business Lawyer,* June 1991.

Schierbeek, P. *Mining Law and Policy* (Uitgeverij Waltman: Delft, February 1965).

Schierbeek, P. *Mine and Tours* (Delft University Press: Delft, May 1980).

Schneider, D. 'The Rising Seas'. *Scientific American,* March 1997.

Schneider, D. 'Burying the Problem'. *Scientific American,* January 1998.

Seymour, A. & N. Antill. 'OPEC Revenues and Foreign Investments'. *Middle East Economic Survey,* 14 December 1998.

Seymour, I. 'OPEC Extends Economic Olive Branch to Western World'. *Middle East Economic Survey,* 31 January 1975.

Shaw, S. Joint Operating Agreements'. In Proceedings of the Conference on Oil and Gas Agreements (Langham Oil Conferences Ltd, London, December 1994).

Shihata, I.F.I. 'The Multilateral Investment Guarantee Agency (MIGA)'. In Proceedings of the Mining Students Society's Symposium on the Current Political and Economic Outlook for the Mining and Petroleum Industry (Delft University of Technology, Delft, November 1987).

Sle, S.T. *Black Gold, White Gold and the Philosophers' Stone* (Delft University of Technology: Delft, February 1992).

Sle, S.T. *Catalysis and Reactor Design* (Delft University of Technology: Delft, 1997).

Slater, J. 'Recent Developments in United Kingdom North Sea Law'. vol. 4 (iii) *International Business Lawyer,* 1976.

Sliepcevich, C.M. 'Marine Transportation of Natural Gas'. *The Exploration and Economics of the Petroleum Industry,* vol. 5 (The Southwestern Legal Foundation, Gulf Publishing Company, Houston, TX, 1967).

Stone, R. 'The Long Shadow of Chernobyl'. *National Geographic,* April 2006.

Strongman, J.E. 'The Evolving Role of the World Bank Strategies to Attract Private Mining Investments'. In Proceedings of the Mining Students Society's Symposium on Potential Resources for the Coming Century (Delft University of Technology: Delft, November 1992). Suplee, C. 'Unlocking the Climate Puzzle'. 5 *National Geographic,* vol. 193, May 1998.

Symonds, E. 'Investment without Risk?'. *Petroleum Economist,* May 1990.

Taverne, B.G. 'Methods of Participation of Host Countries in Crude Oil Exploration and Production Ventures in the Middle East and Northern Africa'. In Proceedings of the IBA Seminar on World Energy Laws, 1975.

Taverne, B.G. 'Concessions and New Types of Exploration/Production Contracts'. In Proceedings of the IBA Energy Law Seminar, vol. I, 1979.

Taverne, B.G. *Government, Public Enterprise and EC Law* (Leyden University, August 1987).

Taverne, B.G. 'Mineral Resources in Contested Boundary Areas'. In Proceedings of the Conference on International Boundaries (The Royal Institute of International Affairs, London, January 1992).

Taverne, B.G. *Principles of Petroleum Regulation and Government Policy* (Delft University Press: Delft, 1993).

Taverne, B.G. *An Introduction to the Regulation of the Petroleum Industry (Laws, Contracts and Conventions)* (Kluwer Law International: London/The Hague/ Boston, December 1994).

Taverne, B.G. 'Production Sharing Agreements'. In Proceedings of the Conference on Oil and Gas Agreements (Langham Oil Conferences Ltd, London, December 1994/November 1996).

Taverne, B.G. *Co-operative Agreements in the Extractive Petroleum Industry* (Kluwer Law International: London/The Hague/Boston, December 1996).

Taverne, B.G. 'Production Sharing Agreements in Principle and in Practice'. Chapter 4 of *Upstream Oil and Gas Agreements* (Sweet & Maxwell: London, 1996).

Tayler, M.P.G. 'The Legal Background and Structure of Unitisation Agreements'. In Proceedings of the Conference on Unitisation of Oil and Gas Fields (Langham Oil Conferences Ltd, London, May 1991).

Thornley, N. 'Gas Transportation Agreements'. In Proceedings of the Conference on Oil and Gas Agreements (Langham Oil Conferences Ltd, London, November 1996).

Trimble, N. 'Gas Sales Agreements'. In Proceedings of the Conference on
    Oil and Gas Agreements (Langham Oil Conferences Ltd, London,
    November 1996).
Tucker, E.S. 'Bright Future for Coal'. *Petroleum Economist,* October 1989.

United Nations, Department of Technical Co-operation for Development.
    'Petroleum Exploration Strategies in Developing Countries'. In Pro-
    ceedings of a United Nations Meeting held in The Hague, March 1981
    (Graham & Trotman Ltd, London, 1982).

Van De Vljver, J.J. et al. *Abandonment Obligations (Removal of Offshore
    Structures).* Sub-committee D of the E & P Forum, London, August
    1985.
Van Der Llnde, C. *Dynamic International Oil Markets* (Kluwer Academic
    Publishers: Dordrecht, 1991.
Vareberg, T.V.A. 'Current Prospects for the European Oil and Gas Market'.
    In Proceedings of the Mining Students Society's Symposium on
    Potential Resources for the Coming Century (Delft University of
    Technology, Delft, November 1992).
Verloren Van Themaat, P. *The Legal Fundament of the New International
    Economic Order,* Studies of International Economic Law, Part II
    (T.M.C. Asser Institute: The Hague, 1979).
Vintner, G. 'EC Aspects'. *Petroleum Economist,* Special Supplement,
    September 1991.
Vock, R.D. 'Petroleum Development Agreements: Form and Drafting'. 4
    Journal of Energy and Natural Resources Law, vol. 8 1990.

Walde, T. 'Third World Mineral Development: Recent Issues and Litera-
    ture'. *Journal of Energy and Natural Resources Law,* 1984.
Walde, T. 'Mineral Development Legislation: Result and Instrument of
    Mineral Development Planning'. 2 *Natural Resources Forum,* vol. 12,
    1988.
Waldock, C.H.M. 'The Legal Basis of Claims to the Continental Shelf'.
    Transactions of the Grotius Society, vol. 36, reproduced in the
    Proceedings of the ILA Copenhagen Conference on the Rights to the
    Seabed and its Subsoil (1950).
Walser, C.H. 'Multilateral Development Assistance for Petroleum Explo-
    ration and Production'. In Proceedings of the IBA Energy Law
    Seminar, vol. I, 1979.
Weisenborn, C.M.M. *The Obligatory Guarantee Agreement* (Law Faculty,
    Leyden University, December 1992).

Willheim, E. 'Australia-Indonesia Sea-Bed Boundary Negotiations – Proposals for a Joint Development Zone in the "Timor Gap"'. In Proceedings of the Seminar on Australia and the Law of the Sea (Sydney February 1987).

Wocol. *Coal – Bridge to the Future* (Ballinger Publishing Company: Cambridge, MA, 1980).

Wood, W. A. 'Legal Aspects of Foreign Investment in Oil and Gas Exploration and Development in Brazil'. *Journal of Energy and Natural Resources Law* 1989.

Woodliffej. C. 'International Unitisation of an Offshore Gas Field'. 2 *International and Comparative Law Quarterly,* April 1977.

Wright, C.J. The Role of the Industry in the IEA'. In Proceedings of the IBA Energy Law Seminar, vol. I, 1979.

Wright, M. 'Recent Decisions on the Law of Oil and Gas'. *Ralph Slovenko's Oil and Gas Operations: Legal Considerations in the Tidelands and on Land* (Tulane University School of Law, Claitor's Law Books, Claitor's Book Store, 1963).

Wyatt, D. & A. Dashwood. *The Substantive Law of the EEC* (Sweet & Maxwell: London, 1980).

Yamani, A.Z. 'The Influence of Political Decisions on Oil Economics'. *Middle East Economic Survey,* 4 July 1988.

Yamani, A.Z. 'American Dependence on Arab Oil in the Years to Come'. *Middle East Economic Survey,* 27 November 1989.

Yergin, D. *The Prize; the Epic Quest for Oil, Money and Power.* Simon & Schuster: New York, 1991.

Zakariya, H.S. 'Political Risks of Transnational Petroleum Investment: The Mitigating Role of National and International Insurance Programmes'. 2 *Natural Resources Forum,* vol. II, 1987.

Zillman, D.N. & W. Fox. 'The Regulation of Energy Supply: The United States'. *Journal of Energy and Natural Resources Law,* Supplement, December 1989.

Zillman, D.N., A.R. Lucas & G. Pring. *Human Rights in Natural Resource Development, Public Participation in the Sustainable Development of Mining and Energy Resources* (Oxford University Press, 2002).

Index

ENERGY AND ENVIRONMENTAL LAW & POLICY SERIES

1. Stephen J. Turner, *A Substantive Environmental Right: An Examination of the Legal Obligations of Decision-makers towards the Environment*, 2009 (ISBN 978-90-411-2815-7).
2. Helle Tegner Anker, Birgitte Egelund Olsen & Anita Rønne (eds), *Legal Systems and Wind Energy: A Comparative Perspective*, 2009 (ISBN 978-90-411-2831-7).
3. David Langlet, *Prior Informed Consent and Hazardous Trade: Regulating Trade in Hazardous Goods at the Intersection of Sovereignty, Free Trade and Environmental Protection*, 2009 (ISBN 978-90-411-2821-8).
4. Louis J. Kotzé and Alexander R. Paterson (eds), *The Role of the Judiciary in Environmental Governance: Comparative Perspectives*, 2009 (ISBN 978-90-411-2708-2).
5. Tuula Honkonen, *The Common but Differentiated Responsibility Principle in Multilateral Environmental Agreement's: Regulatory and Policy Aspects*, 2009 (ISBN 978-90-411-3153-9).
6. Barbara Pozzo (ed.), *The Implementation of the Seveso Directives in an Enlarged Europe: A Look into the Past and a challenge for the Future*, 2009 (ISBN 978-90-411-2854-6).
7. Henrik M. Inadomi, *Independent Power Projects in Developing Countries: Legal Investment Protection and Consequences for Development*, 2010 (ISBN 978-90-411-3178-2).
8. Nahid Islam, *The Law of Non-Navigational Uses of International Watercourses: Options for Regional Regime-Building in Asia*, 2010 (ISBN 978-90-411-3196-6).
9. Yasuhiro Shigeta, *International Judicial Control of Environmental Protection: Standard Setting, Compliance Control and the Development of International Environmental Law by the International Judiciary*, 2010 (ISBN 978-90-411-3151-5).
10. Katleen Janssen, *The Availability of Spatial and Environmental Data in the European Union: At the Crossroads between Public and Economic Interests*, 2010 (ISBN 978-90-411-3287-1).
11. Henrik Bjørnebye, *Investing in EU Energy Security: Exploring the Regulatory Approach to Tomorrow's Electricity Production*, 2010 (ISBN 978-90-411-3118-8).
12. Véronique Bruggeman, *Compensating catastrophe victims: A Comparative Law and Economics Approach*, 2010 (ISBN 978-90-411-3263-5).
13. Michael G. Faure, Han Lixin & Shan Hongjun, *Maritime Pollution Liability and Policy: China, Europe and the US*, 2010 (ISBN 978-90-411-2869-0).

14. Anton Ming-Zhi Gao, *Regulating Gas Liberalization: A Comparative Study on Unbundling and Open Access Regimes in the US, Europe, Japan, South Korea and Taiwan*, 2010 (ISBN 978-90-411-3347-2).
15. Mustafa Erkan, *International Energy Investment Law: Stability through Contractual Clauses*, 2011 (ISBN 978-90-411-3411-0).
16. Levente Borzsa´k, *The Impact of Environmental Concerns on the Public Enforcement Mechanism under EU law: Environmental protection in the 25th hour*, 2011 (ISBN 978-90-411-3408-0).
17. Tarcísio Hardman Reis, *Compensation for Environmental Damages under International Law: The Role of the International Judge*, 2011 (ISBN 978-90-411-3437-0).
18. Kim Talus, *Vertical Natural Gas Transportation Capacity, Upstream Commodity Contracts and EU Competition Law*, 2011 (ISBN 978-90-411-3407-3).
19. WangHui, *Civil Liability for Marine Oil Pollution Damage: A Comparative and Economic Study of the International, US and Chinese Compensation Regime*, 2011 (ISBN 978-90-411-3672-5).
20. Chowdhury Ishrak Ahmed Siddiky, *Cross-Border Pipeline Arrangements: What Would a Single Regulatory Framework Look Like?*, 2012 (ISBN 978-90-411-3844-6).
21. Rozeta Karova, *Liberalization of Electricity Markets and Public Service Obligations in the Energy Community*, 2012 (ISBN 978-90-411-3849-1).
22. Sandra Cassotta, *Environmental Damage and Liability Problems in a Multilevel Context: The Case of the Environmental Liability Directive*, 2012 (ISBN 978-90-411-3830-9).
23. Mark Wilde, *Civil Liability for Environmental Damage: Comparative Analysis of Law and Policy in Europe and US*, 2013 (ISBN 978-90-411-3233-8).
24. Bernard Taverne, *Petroleum, Industry and Governments: A Study of the Involvement of Industry and Governments in Exploring for and Producing Petroleum*, 2013 (978-90-411-4563-5).

Lightning Source UK Ltd.
Milton Keynes UK
UKOW03n1141111213

222807UK00001B/24/P

9 789041 145635